TOYOTA COROLLA
1990-93 REPAIR MANUAL

President, Chilton Enterprises	David S. Loewith
Senior Vice President	Ronald A. Hoxter
Publisher & Editor-In-Chief	Kerry A. Freeman, S.A.E.
Managing Editors	Peter M. Conti, Jr., W. Calvin Settle, Jr., S.A.E.
Assistant Managing Editor	Nick D'Andrea
Senior Editors	Debra Gaffney, Ken Grabowski, A.S.E., S.A.E.
	Michael L. Grady, Richard J. Rivele, S.A.E.
	Richard T. Smith, Jim Taylor
	Ron Webb
Project Managers	Martin J. Gunther, Jeffrey M. Hoffman
Director of Manufacturing	Mike D'Imperio

CHILTON BOOK COMPANY

ONE OF THE DIVERSIFIED PUBLISHING COMPANIES,
A PART OF CAPITAL CITIES/ABC,INC.

CONTENTS

GENERAL INFORMATION AND MAINTENANCE

7 SERIAL NUMBER IDENTIFICATION
7 ROUTINE MAINTENANCE
21 FLUIDS AND LUBRICANTS
33 PUSHING AND TOWING
34 JACKING

ENGINE PERFORMANCE AND TUNE-UP

38 TUNE-UP PROCEDURES
42 FIRING ORDERS
42 ELECTRONIC IGNITION
48 IGNITION TIMING
50 VALVE LASH

ENGINE AND ENGINE OVERHAUL

57 ENGINE ELECTRICAL
66 ENGINE MECHANICAL
130 EXHAUST SYSTEM

EMISSION CONTROLS

135 EMISSION CONTROLS
143 VACUUM DIAGRAMS

FUEL SYSTEM

148 ELECTRONIC FUEL INJECTION SYSTEM
164 FUEL TANK

CHASSIS ELECTRICAL

168 SUPPLEMENTAL RESTRAINT SYSTEM (SRS)
177 WINDSHIELD WIPERS
182 LIGHTING
187 TRAILER WIRING
188 CIRCUIT PROTECTION

DRIVE TRAIN

192 MANUAL TRANSAXLE
206 AUTOMATIC TRANSAXLE
209 TRANSFER CASE
209 DRIVELINE

SUSPENSION AND STEERING

217 FRONT SUSPENSION
228 REAR SUSPENSION
237 DISARMING THE AIR BAG
237 STEERING

BRAKES

256 FRONT DISC BRAKES
263 REAR DISC BRAKES
268 PARKING BRAKE

BODY

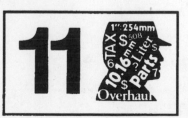

269 EXTERIOR
279 INTERIOR

MECHANIC'S DATA

293
295 GLOSSARY
302 INDEX

156 CHILTON'S FUEL ECONOMY AND TUNE-UPS TIPS

268 CHILTON'S BODY REPAIR TIPS

SAFETY NOTICE

Proper service and repair procedures are vital to the safe, reliable operation of all motor vehicles, as well as the personal safety of those performing repairs. This manual outlines procedures for servicing and repairing vehicles using safe, effective methods. The procedures contain many NOTES, CAUTIONS, and WARNINGS which should be followed along with standard procedures to eliminate the possibility of personal injury or improper service which could damage the vehicle or compromise its safety.

It is important to note that the repair procedures and techniques, tools and parts for servicing motor vehicles, as well as the skill and experience of the individual performing the work vary widely. It is not possible to anticipate all of the conceivable ways or conditions under which vehicles may be serviced, or to provide cautions as to all of the possible hazards that may result. Standard and accepted safety precautions and equipment should be used when handling toxic or flammable fluids, and safety goggles or other protection should be used during cutting, grinding, chiseling, prying,or any other process that can cause material removal or projectiles.

Some procedures require the use of tools specially designed for a specific purpose. Before substituting another tool or procedure, you must be completely satisfied that neither your personal safety, nor the performance of the vehicle will be endangered.

Although information in this manual is based on industry sources and is complete as possible at the time of publication, the possibility exists that some car manufacturers made later changes which could not be included here. While striving for total accuracy, Chilton Book Company cannot assume responsibility for any errors, changes or omissions that may occur in the compilation of this data.

PART NUMBERS

Part numbers listed in this reference are not recommendation by Chilton for any product by brand name. They are references that can be used with interchange manuals and aftermarket supplier catalogs to locate each brand supplier's discrete part number.

SPECIAL TOOLS

Special tools are recommended by the vehicle manufacturer to perform their specific job. Use has been kept to a minimum, but where absolutely necessary, they are referred to in the text by the part number of the tool manufacturer. These tools can be purchased, under the appropriate part number, from your dealer or regional distributor, or an equivalent tool can be purchased locally from a tool supplier or parts outlet. Before substituting any tool for the one recommended, read the SAFETY NOTICE at the top of this page.

ACKNOWLEDGMENTS

The Chilton Book Company expresses appreciation to the Toyota Motor Co. for their generous cooperation.

No part of this publication may be reproduced, transmitted or stored in any form or by any means, electronic or mechanical, including photocopy, recording, or by information storage or retrieval system without prior written permission from the publisher.

Copyright © 1994 by Chilton Book Company
All Rights Reserved
Published in Radnor, Pennsylvania 19089, by Chilton Book Company

Manufactured in the United States of America
   1234567890 3210987654

Chilton's Repair Manual: TOYOTA COROLLA
ISBN 0-8019-8434-3 pbk.
Library of Congress Catalog Card No. 92-054886

HOW TO USE THIS BOOK

Chilton's Repair Manual for the Toyota Corolla is intended to teach you more about the inner workings of your automobile and save you money on its upkeep. Chapters 1 and 2 will probably be the most frequently used in the book. The first Chapter contains all the information that may be required at a moment's notice. Aside from giving the location of various serial numbers and the proper towing instructions, it also contains all the information on basic day-to-day maintenance that you will need to ensure good performance and long vehicle component life. Chapter 2 contains the necessary tune-up procedures to assist you not only in keeping the engine running properly and at peak performance levels, but also in restoring some of the more delicate vehicle components to operating condition in the event of a failure. Chapters 3 through 10 cover repairs (rather than maintenance) for various portions of your vehicle.

When using the Table of Contents, refer to the bold listings for the subject of the Chapter and the smaller listings (or the index) for information on a particular component.

In general, there are some things a proficient mechanic has which must be allowed for when a non-professional does work on his/her car. These are:

1. A sound knowledge of the construction of the parts he is working with; their order of assembly, etc.

2. A knowledge of potentially hazardous situations; particularly how to prevent them.

3. Manual dexterity and common sense.

This book provides step-by-step instructions and illustrations whenever possible. Use them carefully and wisely — don't just jump headlong into disassembly (review the complete service procedure first!). When there is doubt about being able to readily reassemble something, make a careful drawing (mark vacuum hoses etc. or matchmark components such as a driveshaft to rear flange) of the component before taking it apart. Assembly always looks simple when everything is still assembled.

Always replace cotter pins, gaskets, O-rings and oil seals etc. with new ones. Non-reusable parts are indicated in most component illustrations by a diamond symbol.

CAUTIONS WARNINGS, AND NOTES will be provided where appropriate to help prevent you from injuring yourself or damaging your car. Consequently, you should always read through the entire procedure before beginning the work so as to familiarize yourself with any special problems which may occur during the given procedure. Since any amount of warnings could not cover every possible situation, you should work slowly and try to envision what is going to happen in each operation ahead of time.

When it comes to tightening things, there is generally a slim area between too loose to properly seal or resist vibration and so tight as to risk damage or warping. When dealing with major engine parts, or with any aluminum component, it pays to buy a torque wrench and go by the recommended figures.

When reference is made in this book to the right side or the left side of the car, it should be understood that the positions are always to be viewed from the front seat. This means that the LEFT SIDE of the car is the DRIVER'S SIDE and RIGHT SIDE is the PASSENGER'S SIDE. This will hold true throughout the book, regardless of how you might be looking at the car at the time.

Always be conscious of the need for safety in your work. Never get under a car unless it is firmly supported by jackstands or ramps. Never smoke near, or allow flame to get near the battery or the fuel system. Keep your clothing, hands and hair clear of the fan and pulleys when working near the engine if it is running. Most importantly, try to be patient; even in the midst of an argument with a stubborn bolt, reaching for the largest hammer in the garage is usually a cause for later regret and more extensive repair. As you gain confidence and experience, working on your car will become a source of pride and satisfaction.

TOOLS AND EQUIPMENT

NOTE: *Special tools are occasionally necessary to perform a specific job or are recommended to make a job easier. Their use has been kept to a minimum. When a special tool is indicated, it will be referred to by the manufacturer's designation. Toyota designates these as SST (Special Shop Tools), followed by the part number. Where possible, an illustration will be provided. Some special tools are unique to the vehicle, others are the manufacturer's version of common repair tools. These tools can usually be purchased from your local Toyota dealer or from an automotive parts store.*

The service procedures in this book pre–suppose a familiarity with hand tools and their proper use. However, it is possible that you may have a limited amount of experience with the sort of equipment needed to work on an automobile. This section is designed to help you assemble a basic set of tools that will handle most of the jobs you may undertake.

In addition to the normal assortment of screwdrivers and pliers, automotive service work requires an investment in wrenches, sockets (and the handles needed to drive them), and various measuring tools such as a torque wrench and feeler gauges.

You will find that virtually every nut and bolt on your Toyota is metric. Therefore, despite a few close size similarities, standard inch size tools will not fit and MUST NOT be used. You will need a set of metric wrenches as your most basic tool kit, ranging from about 6mm to 17mm in size. High quality forged wrenches are available in three styles: open end, box end, and combination open/box end. The combination tools are generally the most desirable as a starter set; the wrenches shown in the accompanying illustration are of the combination type. If you plan to do any work on the hydraulic system, a set of line wrenches (sometimes called flare nut wrenches) is highly recommended.

The other set of tools inevitably required is a ratchet handle and socket set. This set should have the same size range as your wrench set. The ratchet, extension, and flex drives for the sockets are available in many sizes; it is advisable to choose a $3/8$ in. drive set initially. One break in the inch/metric sizing war is that metric sized sockets sold in the U.S. have inch sized drive ($1/4$ in., $3/8$ in., $1/2$ in., etc.). Thus, if you already have an inch sized socket set, you need only buy new metric sockets in the sizes needed. Sockets are available in 6- and 12-point versions; 6-point types are stronger and are a good choice for a first set. The choice of a drive handle for the sockets should be made with some care.

If this is your first set, take the plunge and invest in a flex–head ratchet; it will get into many places otherwise accessible only through a long chain of universal joints, extensions, and adapters. An alternative is a flex handle, which lacks the ratcheting feature but has a head which pivots 180°; such a tool is shown below the ratchet handle in the illustration. In addition to the range of sockets mentioned, a rubber lined spark plug socket should be purchased with the set. Since spark plug size varies, know (or ask) which size is appropriate for your car.

The most important thing to consider when purchasing hand tools is quality. Don't be misled by the low cost of "bargain tools". Forged wrenches, tempered screwdriver blades, and fine tooth ratchets are much better investments than their less expensive counterparts. The skinned knuckles and frustration inflicted by poor quality tools make any job an unhappy chore. Another consideration is that quality hand tools come with an unbeatable replacement guarantee: if the tool breaks, you get a new one, no questions asked.

Most jobs can be accomplished using the tools on the accompanying lists. There will be an occasional need for a special tool, such as snapring pliers; that need will be mentioned in the text. It would not be wise to buy a large assortment of tools on the theory that someday they will be needed. Instead, the tools should be acquired one or two at a time, each for a specific job. This will avoid unnecessary expense and help insure that you have the right tool for the job at hand.

The tools needed for basic maintenance jobs, in addition to the wrenches and sockets mentioned, include:

1. A floor jack, with a lifting capacity at least equal to the weight of the car. Capacity of 1½ times the weight is better.
2. Jackstands, for support
3. Oil filter wrench
4. Oil filler spout or funnel
5. Grease gun
6. Battery post and clamp cleaner
7. Container for draining oil
8. Many rags for the inevitable spills
9. Oil absorbent gravel or cat box filler gravel, for absorbing spilled fluids. Keep a broom handy.

In addition to these items there are several others which are not absolutely necessary, but handy to have around. These include a transmission funnel and filler tube, a drop (trouble) light on a long cord, an adjustable (crescent) wrench, and slip joint pliers. After performing a few projects on the car, you'll be amazed at the other tools and non-tools on your workbench. Some useful household items to have around are: a large turkey baster or siphon, empty coffee cans and ice trays (storing parts), ball of twine, assorted tape, markers and pens, whisk broom, tweezers, golf tees (for plugging vacuum lines), metal coat hangers or a roll of mechanics's wire (holding things out of the way), dental pick or similar long, pointed probe, a strong magnet, a small mirror (for seeing into recesses and under

manifolds) and various small pieces of lumber.

A hydraulic floor jack is one of the best investments you can make if you are serious about repairing and maintaining your own car. The small jack that comes with the car is simply NOT SAFE enough to use when doing anything more than changing a flat. The hydraulic floor jack (1½ ton is fine for the Toyota) will pay for itself quickly in convenience, utility and much greater safety. Watch the ads for your local department or automotive store. A good jack is always on special sale somewhere.

A more advanced list of tools, suitable for tune-up work, can be drawn up easily. While the tools are slightly more sophisticated, they need not be outrageously expensive. The key to these purchases is to make them with an eye towards adaptability and wide range. A basic list of tune-up tools could include:

10. Tachometer/dwell meter
11. Spark plug gauge and gapping tool
12. Feeler gauges for valve adjustment
13. Timing light.

You will need both wire type and flat type feeler gauges, the former for the spark plugs and the latter for the valves. The choice of a timing light should be made carefully. A light which works on the DC current supplied by the car battery is the best choice; it should have a xenon tube for brightness. Since most newer cars have electronic ignition, the light should have an inductive pickup which clamps around the number one spark plug cable (the timing light illustrated has one of these pickups).

In addition to these basic tools, there are several other tools and gauges which you may find useful. These include:

14. A compression gauge. The screw-in type is slower to use, but eliminates the possibility of a faulty reading due to escaping pressure.
15. A manifold vacuum gauge.
16. A test light.
17. A combination volt/ohmmeter.

Finally, you will find a torque wrench necessary for all but the most basic work. The beam-type models are perfectly adequate. The click-type (breakaway) torque wrenches are easier to use, but are much more expensive.

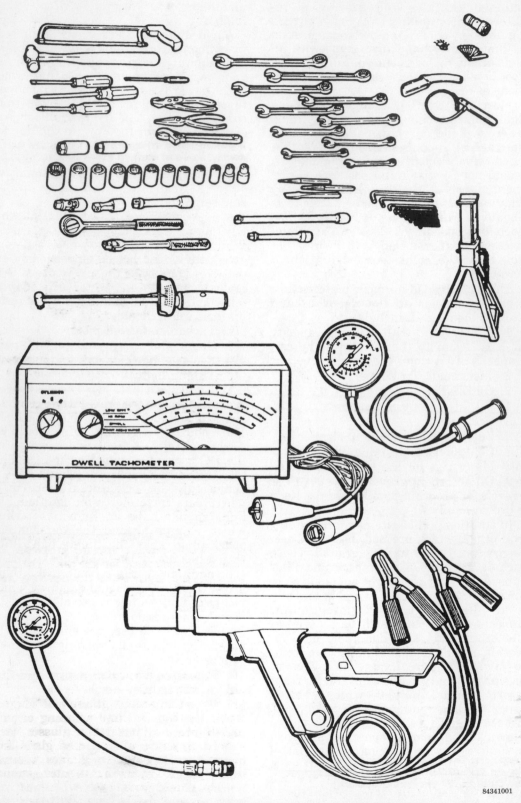

You need only a basic assortment of hand tools for most maintenance and repair jobs

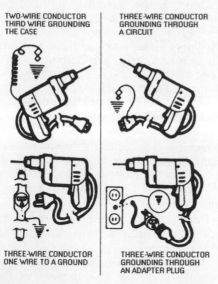

TWO-WIRE CONDUCTOR
THIRD WIRE GROUNDING
THE CASE

THREE-WIRE CONDUCTOR
GROUNDING THROUGH
A CIRCUIT

THREE-WIRE CONDUCTOR
ONE WIRE TO A GROUND

THREE-WIRE CONDUCTOR
GROUNDING THROUGH
AN ADAPTER PLUG

84341002

When using electric tools make sure they are properly grounded

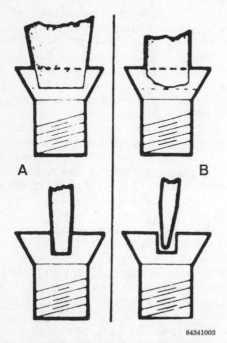

A   B

84341003

Keep screwdriver tips in good shape. They should fit in slot as shown in "A". If they look like those in "B" they need replacing

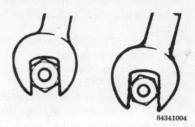

84341004

If you are using an open end wrench, use the correct size and position it properly on the nut or bolt

84341005

Always support the car securely with jackstands; never use cinder blocks, tire changing jacks or the like

SERVICING YOUR VEHICLE SAFELY

It is virtually impossible to anticipate all of the hazards involved with automotive maintenance and service, but care and common sense will prevent most accidents.

The rules of safety for mechanics range from "don't smoke around gasoline", to "use the proper tool for the job". The trick to avoiding injuries is to develop safe work habits and take every possible precaution.

Dos

• Do keep a fire extinguisher and first aid kit within easy reach.

• Do wear safety glasses or goggles when cutting, drilling, grinding or prying. If you wear corrective glasses, they should be made of hardened glass that can serve also as safety glasses, or wear safety goggles over your regular glasses.

• Do shield your eyes whenever you work around the battery. Batteries contain sulfuric acid. In case of contact with the eyes or skin, flush the area with water or a mixture of water and baking soda and get medical attention immediately.

• Do use safety stands for any under-car service. Jacks are for raising vehicles; safety stands are for making sure the vehicle stays raised until you want it to come down. Whenever the car is raised, block the wheels remaining on the ground and set the parking brake.

• Do use adequate ventilation when working with any chemicals or hazardous materials. Like carbon monoxide, the asbestos dust resulting from brake lining wear can be poisonous in sufficient quantities.

• Do disconnect the negative battery cable when working on the electrical system. The secondary ignition system can contain up to 40,000 volts.

• Do follow manufacturer's directions whenever working with potentially hazardous materials. Both brake fluid and antifreeze are poisonous if taken internally.

• Do properly maintain your tools. Loose hammerheads, mushroomed punches and chisels, frayed or poorly grounded electrical cords, excessively worn screwdrivers, spread wrenches (open end), cracked sockets, slipping ratchets, or faulty droplight sockets can cause accidents.

• Do use the proper size and type of tool for the job being done.

• Do when possible, pull on a wrench handle rather than push on it, and adjust your stance to prevent a fall.

• Do be sure that adjustable wrenches are tightly closed on the nut or bolt and pulled so that the face is on the side of the fixed jaw.

• Do select a wrench or socket that fits the nut or bolt. The wrench or socket should be straight, not cocked.

• Do set the parking brake and block the drive wheels if the work requires the engine running.

Don'ts

• Don't run an engine in a garage or anywhere else without proper ventilation — EVER! Carbon monoxide is poisonous; it takes a long time to leave the human body and you can build up a deadly supply of it in your system by simply breathing in a little every day. You may not realize you are slowly poisoning yourself. Always use power vents, windows, fans or open the garage doors.

• Don't work around moving parts while wearing a necktie or other loose clothing. Short sleeves are much safer than long, loose sleeves; hard-toed shoes with neoprene soles protect your toes and give a better grip on slippery surfaces. Jewelry such as watches, fancy belt buckles, beads or body adornment of any kind is not safe working around a car. Long hair should be hidden under a hat or cap.

• Don't use pockets for toolboxes. A fall or bump can drive a screwdriver deep into your body. Even a wiping cloth hanging from the back pocket can wrap around a spinning shaft or fan.

• Don't smoke when working around gasoline, cleaning solvent or other flammable material.

• Don't smoke when working around the battery. When the battery is being charged, it gives off explosive hydrogen gas.

• Don't use gasoline to wash your hands; there are excellent soaps available. Gasoline may contain lead, and lead can enter the body through a cut, accumulating in the body until you are very ill. Gasoline also removes all the natural oils from the skin so that bone dry hands will suck up oil and grease.

• Don't service the air conditioning system unless you are equipped with the necessary tools and training. The refrigerant is extremely cold when compressed, and when released into the air will instantly freeze any surface it contacts, including your eyes. Although the refrigerant is normally non-toxic; it becomes a deadly poisonous gas in the presence of an open flame. One good whiff of the vapors from burning refrigerant can be fatal.

• Don't use screwdrivers for anything other than driving screws! A screwdriver used as a prying tool or chisel can snap when least expected, causing bodily harm. Besides, you ruin a good tool when it is used for purposes other than those intended.

• Don't use the jack that comes with the car for anything other than changing a flat tire! If you are serious about repairing and maintaining your own car, then one of the best investments you can make is in a hydraulic floor jack of at least 1½ ton capacity.

SERIAL NUMBER IDENTIFICATION

Vehicle

The serial number on all models consists of a 17 digit format. All models have the Vehicle Identification Number (VIN) stamped on a plate which is attached to the left side of the instrument panel or dashboard (this 17 digit VIN is displayed in three separate locations-see illustration). This plate is visible through the windshield.

This number has also been stamped on the Vehicle Identification Number Plate and Certification Regulation label. Refer to the necessary illustration.

Engine

The engine serial number is stamped on the engine block as shown. Refer to the necessary illustration.

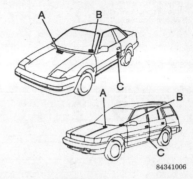

84341006

Serial number identification

ENGINE IDENTIFICATION

Year	Model	Engine Displacement Liters (cc)	Engine Series (ID/VIN)	Fuel System	No. of Cylinders	Engine Type
1990	Corolla	1.6 (1587)	4A-FE	EFI	4	DOHC
	Corolla	1.6 (1587)	4A-GE	EFI	4	DOHC
1991	Corolla	1.6 (1587)	4A-FE	EFI	4	DOHC
	Corolla	1.6 (1587)	4A-GE	EFI	4	DOHC
1992	Corolla	1.6 (1587)	4A-FE	EFI	4	DOHC
1993	Corolla	1.6 (1587)	4A-FE	EFI	4	DOHC
	Corolla	1.8 (1762)	7A-FE	EFI	4	DOHC

DOHC—Double Overhead Camshaft
EFI—Electronic Fuel Injection

84341009

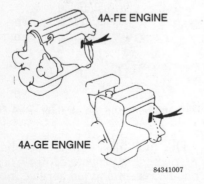

4A-FE ENGINE

4A-GE ENGINE

84341007

Engine number identification

Transaxle

The manual and automatic transaxle identification number is stamped on the assembly housing.

ROUTINE MAINTENANCE

Air Cleaner

All of the dirt and dust present in the air is kept out of the engine by means of the air cleaner filter element. Proper maintenance is vital, as a clogged element not only restricts the air flow and thus the power, but can also cause premature engine wear.

The filter element should be cleaned/inspected every 6 months or 7,500–10,000 miles or more often if the car is driven under dry, dusty conditions. Remove the filter element and using low pressure compressed air, blow the dirt out.

NOTE: *The filter element used on Toyota vehicles is of the dry, disposable type. It should never be washed, soaked or oiled.*

The filter element must be replaced at 36 months or 30,000 mile intervals or more often under dry, dusty conditions.

Check the model code to see what type of model your vehicle is.

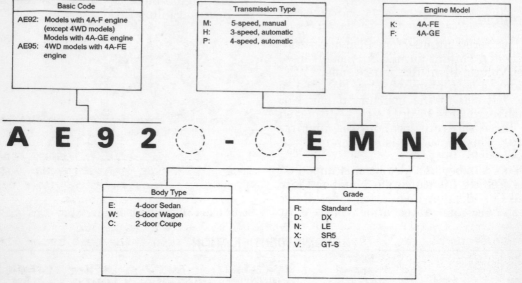

Basic Code	
AE92:	Models with 4A-F engine (except 4WD models) Models with 4A-GE engine
AE95:	4WD models with 4A-FE engine

Transmission Type	
M:	5-speed, manual
H:	3-speed, automatic
P:	4-speed, automatic

Engine Model	
K:	4A-FE
F:	4A-GE

A E 9 2 ○ - ○ E M N K ○

Body Type	
E:	4-door Sedan
W:	5-door Wagon
C:	2-door Coupe

Grade	
R:	Standard
D:	DX
N:	LE
X:	SR5
V:	GT-S

The model code appears on the Certification Regulation Label.

84341008

Model code

Be sure to use the correct air filter element for your engine.

REMOVAL & INSTALLATION

1. Release the clips and remove the cover and air filter element.
2. Clean out the filter case (air cleaner) with a shop towel or rag. Fit the filter element into the air cleaner. Make certain (filter usually marked for correct installation) it is not upside down. Double check that the element is properly seated; if it is crooked, the cover won't seat and air leaks will admit unfiltered air into the engine.
3. Installation is the reverse of the removal procedures.

NOTE: *Do not drive the vehicle with the air cleaner cover removed as damage to the engine or vehicle could occur.*

Fuel Filter

The replaceable fuel filter is in the fuel line mounted on the firewall under the hood.

The filter should be inspected for external damage and/or leakage at least once a

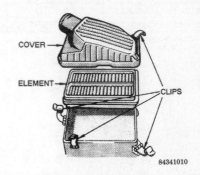

84341010

Checking and replacing the air filter — 4A-FE engine

year. The fuel filter should be changed only as necessary. Toyota Motor Corporation has no recommended service interval for replacing the fuel filter on these vehicles.

NOTE: *Fuel lines and connections, fuel tank vapor vent system hoses and fuel tank bands should be inspected every 60,000 miles or every 36 months. The fuel tank cap gasket should be replaced 60,000 miles or every 72 months.*

REMOVAL & INSTALLATION

CAUTION: *Safety is very important when preforming fuel system maintenance. Always perform this service operation on a COLD engine. The fuel system is under pressure — fuel pressure must be released before removing the fuel filter. Failure to conduct fuel system maintenance and repairs in a safe manner may result in serious personal injury.*

1. Disconnect the negative battery cable. Unbolt the retaining screws and remove the protective shield for the fuel filter (if so equipped).

2. Place a large pan under the delivery pipe (large connection) to catch the dripping fuel and SLOWLY loosen the union bolt to bleed off the fuel pressure.

3. Remove the union bolt and drain the remaining fuel.

4. Disconnect and plug the inlet line.

5. Unbolt and remove the fuel filter.

NOTE: *When tightening the fuel line bolts to the fuel filter, use a torque wrench. The tightening torque is very important, as under or over tightening*

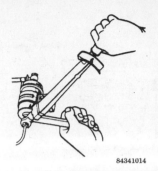

A torque wrench is essential when tightening the fuel lines to the fuel filter

may cause fuel leakage. Insure that there is no fuel line interference and that there is sufficient clearance between it and any other parts.

6. Coat the flare nut, union nut and bolt threads with engine oil.

7. Hand tighten the inlet line to the fuel filter.

8. Install the fuel filter and then tighten the inlet bolt to 22 ft. lbs.

9. Reconnect the delivery pipe using new gaskets and then tighten the union bolt to 22 ft. lbs.

10. Run the engine for a few minutes and check for any fuel leaks.

11. Install the protective shield (if so equipped).

PCV Valve

SERVICING, REMOVAL & INSTALLATION

The PCV valve regulates crankcase ventilation during various engine operating conditions. Inspect the PCV valve system every 60,000 miles or every 36 months. Toyota Motor Corporation has no recommended service interval for replacing the PCV valve on these vehicles.

1. Check the ventilation hoses for leaks or clogging. Clean or replace as necessary.

2. Locate the PCV valve in the cylinder head cover and remove it.

3. Blow into the crankcase end of the valve. There should be a free passage of air through the valve.

4. Blow into the intake manifold end of the valve. There should be little or no passage of air through the valve.

5. If the PCV valve failed either of the preceding two checks, it will require replacement.

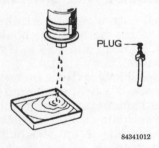

When removing the fuel lines it is always a good idea to place a pan underneath to catch the dripping fuel

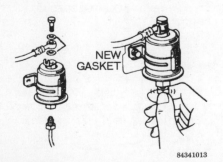

Hand tighten the fuel inlet first

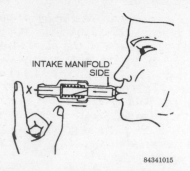

84341015

Air should not pass through the PCV valve when blowing through the intake manifold side

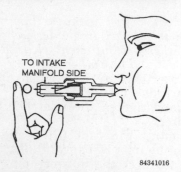

84341016

Air should pass through the PCV valve when blowing into the crankcase side

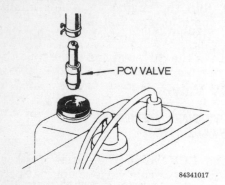

84341017

Removing the PCV valve

6. Installation is in the reverse order of removal procedure. Replace ventilation hose and clamp if necessary.

NOTE: *On some engine applications there is no PCV valve. The vapor passage in the ventilation lines is controlled by two orifices. To check the PCV system on these models, inspect the hoses for cracks, leaks or other damage. Blow through the hose and orifices to make sure they are not blocked. Replace components as necessary.*

Evaporative Canister and System

SERVICING, REMOVAL & INSTALLATION

Inspect the charcoal canister assembly every 60,000 miles or 72 months. Replace the charcoal canister assembly only as needed. Check the fuel and vapor lines and the vacuum hoses for proper connections and correct routing, as well as condition. Replace clogged, damaged or deteriorated parts as necessary.

If the charcoal canister is clogged, (check for clogged filter or stuck check valve) it may be cleaned using low pressure compressed air. When cleaning, air should flow through (out the bottom) freely and no charcoal should come out.

The canister is removed by unfastening the various hoses from the canister (mark all hoses for correct installation), and removing the mounting bolts from the mounting bracket or loosening the mounting clamp and removing the canister. Installation is the reverse order of removal.

Battery

SPECIFIC GRAVITY TEST (EXCEPT MAINTENANCE FREE BATTERIES)

At least once a year, check the specific gravity of the battery. It should be between 1.20 in.Hg and 1.26 in.Hg at room temperature.

The specific gravity can be checked with the use of a hydrometer, an inexpensive instrument available from many sources, including auto parts stores. The hydrometer has a squeeze bulb at one end and a nozzle at the other. Battery electrolyte is sucked into the hydrometer until the float is lifted from its seat. The

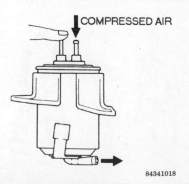

84341018

Charcoal canister servicing

specific gravity is then read by noting the position of the float. Generally, if after charging, the specific gravity between any two cells varies more than 50 points (0.050), the battery is bad and should be replaced.

It is not possible to check the specific gravity in this manner on sealed (maintenance free) batteries. Instead, the indicator built into the top of the case must be relied on to display any signs of battery deterioration. If the indicator is dark, the battery can be assumed to be OK. If the indicator is light, the specific gravity is low, and the battery should be charged or replaced.

SERVICING CABLES AND CLAMPS

Once a year (or as necessary), the battery terminals and the cable clamps should be cleaned. Loosen the clamps and remove the cables, negative cable first. On batteries with posts on top, the use of a puller specially made for the purpose is recommended. These are inexpensive, and available in auto parts stores. Side terminal battery cables are secured with a bolt.

Clean the cable clamps and the battery terminal with a wire brush, until all cor-

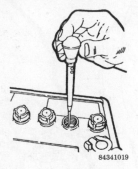

84341019

The specific gravity of the battery can be checked with a simple float-type hydrometer

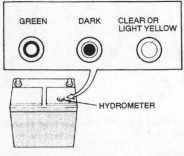

84341020

Maintenance free battery

rosion, grease, etc., is removed and the metal is shiny. It is especially important to clean the inside of the clamp (use old knife or equivalent) thoroughly, since a small deposit of foreign material or oxidation there will prevent a sound electrical connection and inhibit either starting or charging. Special tools are available for cleaning these parts, one type for conventional batteries and another type for side terminal batteries.

Before installing the cables, loosen the battery hold-down clamp or strap, remove the battery and check the battery tray. Clear it of any debris, and check it for soundness (the battery tray can be cleaned with baking soda and water solution). Rust should be wire brushed away, and the metal given a couple of coats of anti-rust paint. Replace the battery and tighten the hold-down clamp or strap securely, but be careful not to overtighten, which will crack the battery case.

After the clamps and terminals are clean, reinstall the cables, negative cable last; DO NOT hammer on the clamps to install. Tighten the clamps securely, but do not distort them. Give the clamps and terminals a thin external coat of grease or equivalent after installation, to retard corrosion.

Check the cables at the same time that the terminals are cleaned. If the cable insulation is cracked or broken, or if the ends are frayed, the cable should be replaced with a new cable of the same length and gauge.

NOTE: *Keep flame or sparks away from the battery; it gives off explosive hydrogen gas. Battery electrolyte contains sulfuric acid. If you should splash any on your skin or in your eyes, flush the affected area with plenty of clear water; if it lands in your eyes, get medical help immediately.*

CHECKING FLUID LEVEL

Check the battery electrolyte level (if possible) at least once a month, or more often in hot weather or during periods of extended car operation. The level can be checked through the case on translucent batteries; the cell caps must be removed on other models. The electrolyte level in each cell should be kept filled to the split ring inside, or the line marked on the outside of the case.

If the level is low, add only distilled water, or colorless, odorless drinking

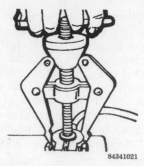

Special pullers are available to remove cable clamps

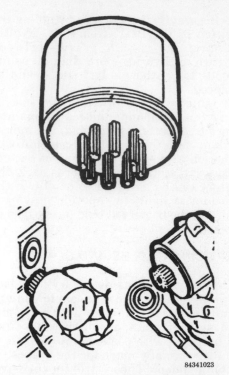

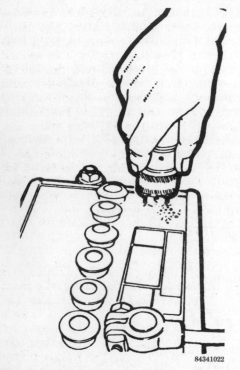

Clean the battery posts with a wire brush, or the special tool shown

Special tools are also available for cleaning the posts and clamps on side terminal batteries

water, through the opening until the level is correct. Each cell is completely separate from the others, so each must be checked and filled individually.

If water is added in freezing weather, the car should be driven several miles to allow the water to mix with the electrolyte. Otherwise, the battery could freeze.

REPLACEMENT

When it becomes necessary to replace the battery, select a battery with a rating equal to or greater than the battery originally installed. Deterioration and just plain aging of the battery cables, starter

Clean the inside of the clamps with a wire brush or special tool

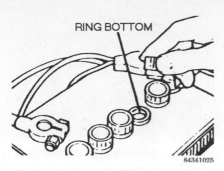

Fill each battery cell to the bottom of the split ring with water

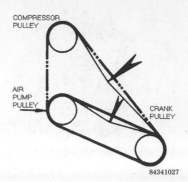

Typical drive belt tension checking locations

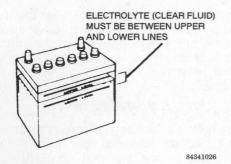

Some batteries have level indicator lines on the side

motor, and associated wires makes the battery's job harder in successive years. The slow increase in electrical resistance over time makes it prudent to install a new battery with a greater capacity than the old. Details on battery removal and installation are covered in Chapter 3.

Belts

INSPECTION

Check the condition of the drive belts and check and adjust the belt tension every 10,000–15,000 miles or 1 year. Toyota Motor Corporation recommended service interval for checking drive belts is first period, 60,000 miles or 72 months and after first period inspect every 7,500 miles or 12 months. Replace as necessary.
1. Inspect the belts for signs of glazing or cracking. A glazed belt will be perfectly smooth from slippage, while a good belt will have a slight texture of fabric visible. Cracks will usually start at the inner edge of the belt and run outward. Replace the belt at the first sign of cracking or if the glazing is severe.

2. By placing your thumb midway between the two pulleys, it should be possible to depress the belt about ¼–½ inch (6–13mm). It is best to use a drive belt tension gauge to check belt tension. If any of the belts can be depressed more than this, or cannot be depressed this much, adjust the tension. Inadequate tension will result in slippage and wear, while excessive tension will damage bearings and cause belts to fray and crack.
3. Drive belts should be replaced for preventive maintenance. It is always best to replace all drive belts at one time during this service operation.

ADJUSTING

Alternator

To adjust the tension of the alternator drive belt on all models, loosen the pivot and mounting bolts on the alternator. Using a wooden hammer handle, a broomstick or your hand, move the alternator one way or the other until the proper tension is achieved. Do not use a screwdriver or any other metal device such as a pry bar, as a lever. Tighten the mounting bolts securely, run the engine about minute, stop the engine then recheck the belt tension.

Air Conditioning Compressor

A/C compressor (always use caution when working near the A/C compressor) belt tension can be adjusted by turning the tension adjusting bolt which is located on the compressor tensioner bracket. Turn the bolt clockwise to tighten the belt and counterclockwise to loosen it.

Power Steering Pump

Tension on the power steering belt is adjusted by means of an idler pulley (some models may use just a lower ad-

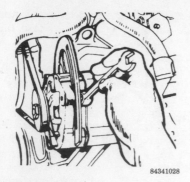

Loosen the pivot bolt

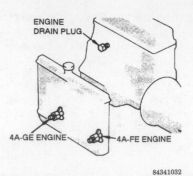

Locations of draincocks of the cooling system

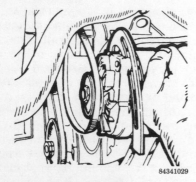

Push the component inwards

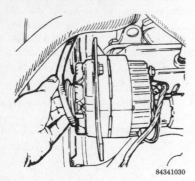

Slip the old belt off and the new one on

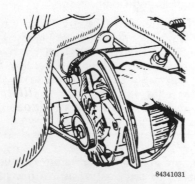

Pull outwards to tension the belt

justing bracket setup — similar to alternator adjustment service procedure). Loosen the lock bolt and turn the adjusting bolt on the idler pulley until the desired tension is felt and then tighten the lock bolt.

REMOVAL & INSTALLATION

If a belt must be replaced, the driven unit must be loosened and moved to its extreme loosest position, generally by moving it toward the center of the motor. After removing the old belt, check the pulleys for dirt or built-up material which could affect belt contact. Carefully install the new belt, remembering that it is new and unused — it may appear to be just a little too small to fit over the pulley flanges. Fit the belt over the largest pulley (usually the crankshaft pulley at the bottom center of the motor) first, then work on the smaller one(s). Gentle pressure in the direction of rotation is helpful. Some belts run around a third or idler pulley, which acts as an additional pivot in the belt's path. It may be possible to loosen the idler pulley as well as the main component, making your job much easier. Depending on which belt(s) you are changing, it may be necessary to loosen or remove other interfering belts to get at the one(s) you want.

When buying replacement belts, remember that the fit is critical according to the length of the belt, the width of the belt, the depth of the belt and the angle or profile of the V shape (always match up old belt with new belt if possible). The belt shape should exactly match the shape of the pulley; belts that are not an exact match can cause noise, slippage and premature failure.

After the new belt is installed, draw tension on it by moving the driven unit away from the motor and tighten its mounting bolts. This is sometimes a three- or four-handed job; you may find an assistant helpful. Make sure that all the bolts you loosened get retightened and that any other loosened belts also have the correct tension. A new belt can be expected to stretch a bit after installation so be prepared to re-adjust your new belt.

NOTE: *After installing a new belt, run the engine for about 5 minutes and then recheck the belt tension.*

Hoses

The upper and lower radiator hoses and all heater hoses should be checked for deterioration, leaks (hoses sometime swell up before breaking) and loose hose clamps every 15,000 miles or 1 year. Replace the hose clamps when replacing the radiator hose or heater hose.

REMOVAL & INSTALLATION

1. Drain the cooling system. This is always done with the engine COLD. Follow this service procedure:

a. Remove the radiator cap.

b. Position the drain pan under the draincock on the bottom of the radiator. Additionally, some engines have a draincock on the side of the engine block, near the oil filter. This may be opened to aid in draining the cooling system. If for some reason the radiator draincock can't be used, you can loosen and remove the lower radiator hose at its joint to the radiator.

c. If the lower hose is to be used as the drain, loosen the clamp on the hose and slide it back so it's out of the way. Gently break the grip of the hose on its fitting by twisting or prying with a suitable tool. Do not exert too much force or you will damage the radiator fitting. As the hose loosens, you can expect a gush of fluid to come out — be ready!

d. Remove the hose end from the radiator and direct the hose into the drain pan. You now have fluid running from both the hose and the radiator.

e. When the system stops draining, proceed with replacement of the damaged hose.

2. Loosen the hose clamps at each end of the hose to be removed.

3. Working the hose back and forth, slide it off its connection and remove the old hose. Install the new hose as needed. A small amount of light grease on the inside of the hose end will ease installation.

NOTE: *Radiator and heater hoses should be routed with no kinks and, when installed, should be in the same position as the original. If other than specified hose is used, make sure it does not rub against either the engine or the frame while the engine is running, as this may wear a hole in the hose. Contact points may be insulated with a piece of sponge or foam; plastic wire ties are particularly handy for this job.*

4. Position the new hose clamps at least 6mm (¼ in.) or more from the end of the hose and tighten them. Make sure that the hose clamps are beyond the bead and placed in the center of the clamping surface before tightening them.

5. Fill the system with coolant. Toyota strongly recommends the coolant mixture be a 50/50 mix of antifreeze and water. This mixture gives best combination of antifreeze and anti-boil characteristics for year-round driving.

6. Install and tighten the radiator cap. Start the engine and check visually for leaks. Allow the engine to warm up fully and continue to check your work for signs of leakage. Leaks at hose ends are generally clamp related and can be cured by snugging the clamp. Larger leaks may require removing the hose again — to do this you MUST WAIT UNTIL THE ENGINE HAS COOLED DOWN. NEVER UNCAP A HOT RADIATOR. After all leaks are cured, check the coolant level in the radiator (with the engine cold) and fill with coolant as necessary.

Air Conditioning System

NOTE: *R-12 refrigerant is a chlorofluorocarbon which, when released into the atmosphere, contributes to the depletion of the ozone layer in the upper atmosphere. Ozone filters out harmful radiation from the sun. Consult the laws in your area before servicing the air conditioning system. In some states it is illegal to perform repairs involving refrigerant unless the work is done by a certified technician.*

SAFETY PRECAUTIONS

There are two particular hazards associated with air conditioning systems and they both relate to refrigerant gas.

The refrigerant (generic designation: R-12, trade name: Freon, a registered trademark of the DuPont Co.) is an extremely cold substance. When exposed to air, it will instantly freeze any surface it comes in contact with, including your eyes.

The other hazard relates to fire. Although normally non-toxic, refrigerant gas becomes highly poisonous in the presence of an open flame. One good whiff of the vapor formed by refrigerant can be fatal. Keep all flame sources (including cigarettes) well clear of the air conditioning system.

Most repair work on the A/C system, should be left to a professional mechanic (ASE certified) with the proper equipment and related training.

SYSTEM CHECKS

A lot of A/C problems can be avoided by simply running the air conditioner at least once a week, regardless of the season. simply let the system run for at least 5 minutes a week (even in the winter), and you'll keep the internal parts lubricated as well as preventing the hoses from hardening.

Checking For A/C Oil Leaks

Refrigerant leaks show up only as oily areas on the various components because the compressor oil is transported around the entire system along with the refrigerant. Look for oily spots on all the hoses and lines, and especially on the hose and tube connections. If there are oily deposits, the system may have a leak, and you should have it checked by a qualified mechanic.

Check the A/C Compressor Belt

The compressor drive belt should be checked frequently for tension and condition.

Keep the A/C Condenser Clear

The condenser is mounted in front of the radiator. It serves to remove heat from the air conditioning system and cool the refrigerant. Proper air flow through the condenser is critical to the operation of the system.

Periodically inspect the front of the condenser for bent fins or foreign material (dirt, bugs, leaves, etc.). If any cooling fins are bent, straighten them carefully with needle nose pliers. You can remove any debris with a stiff bristle brush or hose.

A/C Refrigerant Level Check

Factory installed Toyota air conditioning systems have a sight glass for checking the refrigerant charge. The sight glass is on top of the receiver/drier which is located in the front of the engine compartment.

NOTE: *If your car is equipped with an aftermarket air conditioner, the following system check may not apply. Contact the manufacturer of the unit for instructions on system checks.*

1. With the engine and the air conditioning system running, look for the flow of refrigerant through the sight glass. If the air conditioner is working properly, you'll be able to see a continuous flow of clear refrigerant through the sight glass, with perhaps an occasional bubble at very high temperatures.

2. Cycle the air conditioner ON and OFF to make sure what you are seeing is refrigerant. Since the refrigerant is clear, it is possible to mistake a completely discharged system for one that is fully charged. Turn the system off and watch the sight glass. If there is refrigerant in the system, you'll see bubbles during the off cycle. If you observe no bubbles when the system is running and the air flow from the unit in the car is delivering cold air, everything is OK.

3. If you observe bubbles in the sight glass while the system is operating, the system is low on refrigerant.

4. Oil streaks in the sight glass are an indication of trouble. Most of the time, if

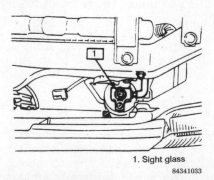

1. Sight glass

84341033

Location of the receiver-drier and sight glass

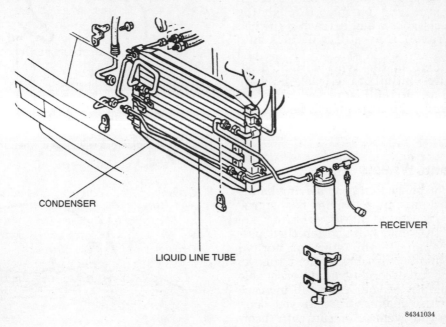

CONDENSER

RECEIVER

LIQUID LINE TUBE

84341034

Sight glass for checking refrigerant level

you see oil in the sight glass, it will appear as a series of streaks, although occasionally it may be a solid stream of oil. In either case, it means that part of the charge has been lost. This is almost always accompanied by a reduction in cold air output within the car.

Windshield Wipers

For maximum effectiveness and longest element life, the windshield and wiper blades should be kept clean. Dirt, tree sap, road tar and so on will cause streaking, smearing and blade deterioration if left on the glass. It is advisable to wash the windshield carefully with a commercial glass cleaner at least once a month. Wipe off the rubber blades with the wet rag afterwards. Do not attempt to move the wipers back and forth by hand; damage to the motor and drive mechanism will result.

If the blades are found to be cracked, broken or torn, they should be replaced immediately. Replacement intervals will vary with usage, although deterioration usually limits blade life to about one year. If the wiper pattern is smeared or streaked, or if the blade chatters across

the glass, the blades should be replaced. It is easiest and most sensible to replace them in pairs.

There are basically three different types of wiper blade refills, which differ in their method of replacement. One type has two release buttons, approximately 1/3 of the way up from the ends of the blade frame. Pushing the buttons down releases a lock and allows the rubber blade to be removed from the frame. The new blade slides back into the frame and locks into place.

The second type of refill has two metal tabs which are unlocked by squeezing them together. The rubber blade can then be withdrawn from the frame jaws. A new one is installed by inserting it into the front frame jaws and sliding it rearward to engage the remaining frame jaws. There are usually four jaws; when installing, be certain that the refill is engaged in all of them. At the end of its travel, the tabs will lock into place on the front jaws of the wiper blade frame.

The third type is a refill made from polycarbonate. The refill has a simple locking device at one end which flexes downward out of the groove into which the jaws of the holder fit, allowing easy release. By sliding the new refill through all the jaws and pushing through the slight resistance when it reaches the end of its travel, the refill will lock into position.

Regardless of the type of refill used, make sure that all of the frame jaws are engaged as the refill is pushed into place and locked. The metal blade holder and frame will scratch the glass if allowed to touch it.

Tires and Wheels

Common sense and good driving habits will afford maximum tire life. Fast starts, sudden stops and hard cornering are hard on tires and will shorten their useful life span. If you start at normal speeds, allow yourself sufficient time to stop, and take corners at a reasonable speed, the life of your tires will increase greatly. Also make sure that you don't overload your vehicle or run with incorrect pressure in the tires. Both of these practices increase tread wear.

Inspect your tires frequently. Be especially careful to watch for bubbles in the tread or side wall, deep cuts, or underin-

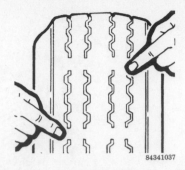

Tread wear indicators will appear when the tire is worn out

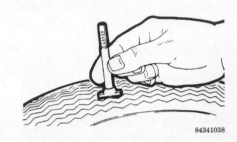

Tread depth can also be checked with a gauge

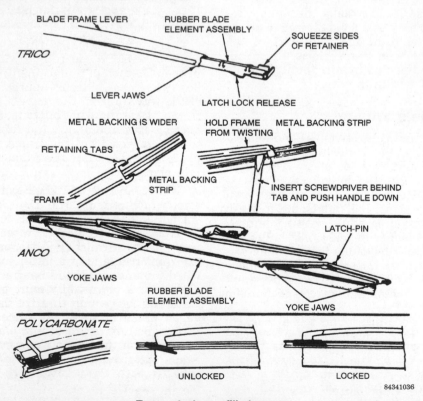

Types of wiper refill elements

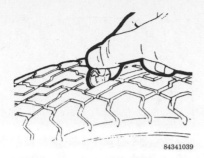

84341039

A penny works well for checking tread depth; when the top of Lincoln's head is visible, it is time for new tires

flation. Remove any tires with bubbles. If the cuts are so deep that they penetrate to the cords, discard the tire. Any cut in the sidewall of a radial tire renders it unsafe. Also look for uneven tread wear patterns that indicate that the front end is out of alignment or that the tires are out of balance.

Store the tires at the proper inflation pressure if they are mounted on wheels. Keep them is a cool dry place, laid on their sides. If the tires are stored in the garage or basement, do not let them stand on a concrete floor; set them on strips of wood.

TIRE ROTATION

So that the tires wear more uniformly, it is recommended that the tires be rotated every 7,500 miles (12,000km) — NEVER USE COMPACT SPARE TIRE OTHER THAN FOR TEMPORARY USE! This can only be done when all four tires are of the same size and load rating capacity. Any abnormal wear should be investigated and the cause corrected.

Radial tires may be cross-switched; newer production methods have eliminated the need to keep them on one side of the car. Studded snow tires will lose their studs if their direction of rotation is reversed.

Mark the wheel position or direction of rotation on radial studded snow tires before removal.

NOTE: *Avoid overtightening the lug nuts or the brake disc or drum may become permanently distorted. Alloy wheels can be cracked by overtightening. The specified lug nut torque is 76 ft. lbs. Always tighten the lug nuts in a criss-cross pattern.*

TIRE DESIGN

When buying new tires, you should keep the following points in mind, especially if you are switching to larger tires or a different profile series (50, 60, 70, 78):

1. All four tires should be of the same construction type. Radial, bias, or bias-belted tires should NOT BE MIXED. Radial tires are highly recommended for their excellent handling and fuel mileage characteristics.

2. The wheels must be the correct width for the tire. Tire dealers have charts of tire and wheel compatibility. A mismatch can cause sloppy handling and rapid tread wear. The tread width should match the rim width (inside bead to inside bead) within 25mm (1 in.). For radial tires the rim width should be 80% or more of the tire (not tread) width. The illustration gives an example of a tire size designation number.

3. The height (mounted diameter) of the new tires can change speedometer accuracy, engine speed per given road speed, fuel mileage, acceleration, and ground clearance.

4. Most models use a space-saving spare tire mounted on a special wheel. This wheel and tire is for EMERGENCY USE ONLY. Never try to mount a regular tire on a special spare wheel.

5. There shouldn't't be any body interference when the car is loaded, on bumps or in turning through maximum range.

TIRE INFLATION

The importance of proper tire inflation cannot be overemphasized. A tire employs air under pressure as part of its structure. It is designed around the supporting strength of air at a specified pressure. For this reason, improper inflation drastically reduces the tire's ability to perform as it was intended. A tire will lose some air in day-to-day use; having to add a few pounds of air periodically is not necessarily a sign of a leaking tire.

Tire pressures should be checked regularly with a reliable pressure gauge. Too often the gauge on the end of the air hose at your corner garage or service station is not accurate enough because it suffers too much abuse. Always check tire pressure when the tires are cold, as pressure increases with temperature. If you must move the vehicle to check the tire inflation, do not drive more than 1 mile

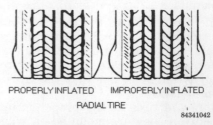

Tire rotation pattern A is recommended, B is acceptable. Note the spare tire is not used in the rotation

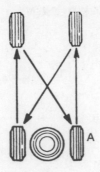

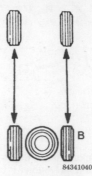

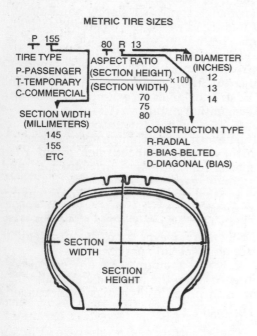

Common tire coding

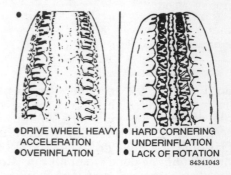

Radial tires have a sidewall bulge — don't try to estimate the air pressure by looking at the tire. Always use a quality air pressure gauge

- DRIVE WHEEL HEAVY ACCELERATION
- OVERINFLATION

- HARD CORNERING
- UNDERINFLATION
- LACK OF ROTATION

Examples of inflation related tire wear patterns

(1.6km) before checking. A cold tire is one that has not been driven for a period of a couple of hours.

Never exceed the maximum tire pressure embossed on the tire! This maximum pressure is rarely the correct pressure for everyday driving. Consult your owners' manual for the proper tire pressures for your vehicle.

CARE OF SPECIAL WHEELS

If you have invested money in magnesium, aluminum alloy or sport wheels, special precautions should be taken to make sure your investment is not wasted

and that your special wheels look good for the lifetime of the car.

Special wheels are easily scratched and/or damaged. Occasionally check the rims for cracking, impact damage or air leaks. If any of these are found, replace the wheel. In order to prevent this type of damage, and the costly replacement of a special wheel, observe the following precautions:

• Use extra care not to damage the wheels during removal, installation, balancing, etc. After removal of the wheels from the car, place them on a mat or other protective surface. If they are to be stored for any length of time, support them on strips of wood.

• While driving, watch for sharp obstacles.

• When washing, use a mild detergent and water. Avoid cleansers with abrasives or the use of hard brushes. There are many cleaners and polishes available for special wheels.

• If possible, remove your special wheels from the car during the winter months. Salt and sand used for snow removal can severely damage the finish.

• Make sure that the recommended lug nut torque is never exceeded or the wheel may crack. Never use snow chains on special wheels; severe scratching will occur.

FLUIDS AND LUBRICANTS

Fluid Disposal

Used fluids such as engine oil, transmission fluid, antifreeze and brake fluid are hazardous wastes and must be disposed of properly. Before draining any fluids consult with the local authorities; in many areas, waste oil etc. is being accepted as a part of recycling programs. A number of service stations and auto parts stores are also accepting waste fluids for recycling.

Be sure of the recycling center's policies before draining any fluids, as many will not accept different fluids that have been mixed together, such as oil and antifreeze.

Oil and Fuel Recommendations

OIL

The SAE (Society of Automotive Engineers) grade number indicates the viscosity of the engine oil and thus its ability to lubricate at a given temperature. The lower the SAE grade number, the lighter the oil; the lower the viscosity, the easier it is to crank the engine in cold weather.

Oil viscosities should be chosen from those oils recommended for the lowest anticipated temperatures during the oil change interval.

Multi-viscosity oils (10W–30, 20W–50, etc.) offer the important advantage of being adaptable to temperature extremes. They allow easy starting at low tempera-

tures, yet they give good protection at high speeds and engine temperatures. This is a decided advantage in changeable climates or in long distance touring.

The API (American Petroleum Institute) designation indicates the classification of engine oil used under certain given operating conditions. Only oils designated for use "Service SG" should be used. Oils of the SG type perform a variety of functions inside the engine in addition to their basic function as a lubricant. Through a balanced system of metallic detergents and polymeric dispersions, the oil prevents the formation of high and low temperature deposits and also keeps sludge and particles of dirt in suspension. Acids, particularly sulfuric acid, as well as other by-products of combustion, are neutralized. Both the SAE grade number and the API designation can be found on top of the oil can.

SYNTHETIC OIL

There are many excellent synthetic and fuel-efficient oils currently available that can provide better gas mileage, longer service life, and in some cases better engine protection. These benefits do not come without a few hitches, however, the main one being the price of synthetic oils, which is three or four times the price per quart of conventional oil.

Synthetic oil is not for every car and every type of driving, so you should consider your engine's condition and your type of driving. Also, check your car's warranty conditions regarding the use of synthetic oils.

Both brand new engines and older, high mileage engines are the wrong candidates for synthetic oil. The synthetic oils are so slippery that they can prevent the proper break-in of new engines; most manufacturer's recommend that you wait

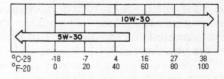

RECOMMENDED OIL VISCOSITY (SAE):

Temperature range anticipated before next oil change.

84341044

Oil viscosity chart

until the engine is properly broken in — 5,000 miles (8,046km) — before using synthetic oil. Older engines with wear have a different problem with synthetics: they use (consume during operation) more oil as they age. Slippery synthetic oils get past these worn parts easily. If your engine is using conventional oil, it will use synthetics much faster. If your car is leaking oil past old seals you'll have a much greater leak problem with synthetics.

Consider your type of driving. If most of your accumulated mileage is high speed, highway type driving, the more expensive synthetic oils may be of benefit. Extended highway driving gives the engine a chance to warm up, accumulating less acids in the oil and putting less stress on the engine over the long run. Under these conditions, the oil change interval can be extended (as long as your oil filter can last the extended life of the oil) up to the advertised mileage claims of the synthetics. Cars with synthetic oils may show increased fuel economy in highway driving, due to less internal friction. However, many automotive experts agree that 50,000 miles (80,465km) is too long to keep any oil in your engine.

Cars used under harder circumstances, such as stop-and-go, city type driving, short trips, or extended idling, should be serviced more frequently. For the engines in these cars, the much greater cost of synthetic or fuel-efficient oils may not be worth the investment. Internal wear increases much quicker on these cars, causing greater oil consumption and leakage.

NOTE: *The mixing of conventional and synthetic oils is NOT recommended. If you are using synthetic oil, it might be wise to carry 2 or 3 quarts with you no matter where you drive, as not all service stations carry this type of lubricant.*

FUEL

All vehicles are designed to run on unleaded fuel. The use of leaded fuel in a car requiring unleaded fuel will plug the catalytic converter (NEVER USE LEADED FUEL IN AN UNLEADED FUEL VEHICLE), rendering it inoperative and will increase exhaust back-pressure to the point where engine output will be severely reduced. In all cases, the minimum octane rating of the fuel used must be at least Research Octane No. 91 (octane rating 87) or higher. All unleaded fuels sold

in the U.S. are required to meet this minimum octane rating.

The use of a fuel too low in octane (a measurement of anti-knock quality) will result in spark knock. Since many factors affect operating efficiency, such as altitude, terrain, air temperature and humidity, knocking may result even though the recommended fuel is being used. If persistent knocking occurs, it may be necessary to switch to a higher grade of fuel. Continuous or heavy knocking may result in engine damage.

NOTE: *Your engine's fuel requirement can change with time, mainly due to carbon buildup, which changes the compression ratio. If your engine pings, knocks or runs on, switch to a higher grade of fuel. Sometimes just changing brands will cure the problem.*

OPERATION IN FOREIGN COUNTRIES

If you plan to drive your car outside the United States or Canada, there is a possibility that fuels will be too low in anti-knock quality and could produce engine damage. It is wise to consult with local authorities upon arrival in a foreign country to determine the best fuels available.

Engine
OIL LEVEL CHECK

CAUTION: *Prolonged and repeated skin contact with used engine oil, with no effort to remove the oil, may be harmful. Always follow these simple precautions when handling used motor oil.*
- Avoid prolonged skin contact with used motor oil.
- Remove oil from skin by washing thoroughly with soap and water or waterless hand cleaner. Do not use gasoline, thinners or other solvents.
- Avoid prolonged skin contact with oil-soaked clothing.Every time you stop for fuel, check the engine oil as follows:
  1. Park the car on level ground.
  2. When checking the oil level it is best for the engine to be at operating temperature, although checking the oil immediately after stopping will lead to a false reading. Wait a few minutes after turning off the engine to allow the oil to drain back into the crankcase.
  3. Open the hood and locate the dipstick. Pull the dipstick from its tube, wipe it clean and reinsert it.

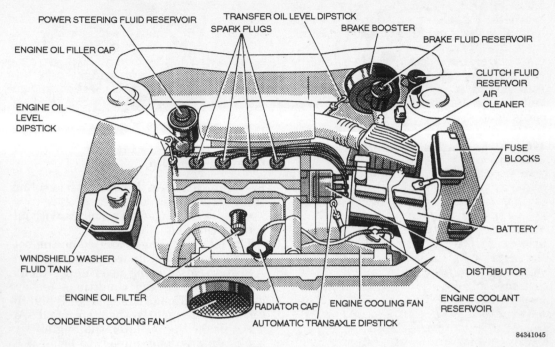

POWER STEERING FLUID RESERVOIR

TRANSFER OIL LEVEL DIPSTICK
SPARK PLUGS

BRAKE BOOSTER

BRAKE FLUID RESERVOIR

ENGINE OIL FILLER CAP

CLUTCH FLUID
RESERVOIR
AIR
CLEANER

ENGINE OIL
LEVEL
DIPSTICK

FUSE
BLOCKS

BATTERY

WINDSHIELD WASHER
FLUID TANK

DISTRIBUTOR

ENGINE OIL FILTER

ENGINE COOLANT
RESERVOIR

CONDENSER COOLING FAN

RADIATOR CAP   ENGINE COOLING FAN

AUTOMATIC TRANSAXLE DIPSTICK

84341045

Engine compartment service locations-1992 Corolla

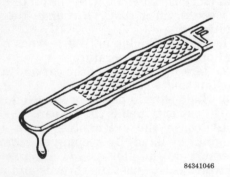

84341046

Oil dipstick

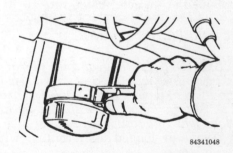

84341048

Remove the oil filter with a strap wrench

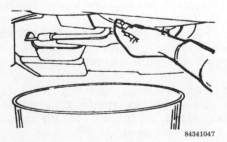

84341047

By keeping an inward pressure on the drain plug as you unscrew it, the oil won't escape past the threads

4. Pull the dipstick out again and, holding it horizontally, read the oil level. The oil should be between the **F** and **L** or high and low marks on the dipstick. If the oil is below the **L** or low mark, add oil of the proper viscosity through the capped opening on the top of the cylinder head cover.

5. Replace the dipstick and check the oil level again after adding any oil. Be careful not to overfill the crankcase. Approximately 1 quart (0.9L) of oil will raise the level from the **L** or low mark to the **F**

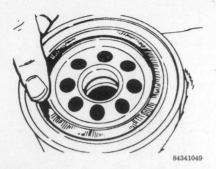

Lubricate the gasket on the new oil filter with clean engine oil

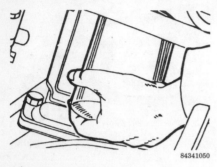

Install the new oil filter by hand

or high mark. Excess oil will generally be consumed at an accelerated rate.

OIL AND FILTER CHANGE

CAUTION: *Prolonged and repeated skin contact with used engine oil, with no effort to remove the oil, may be harmful. Always follow these simple precautions when handling used motor oil:*

• Avoid prolonged skin contact with used motor oil.

• Remove oil from skin by washing thoroughly with soap and water or water-

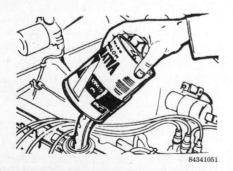

Add oil through the cylinder head cover only

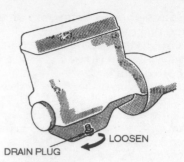

Oil drain plug location

less hand cleaner. Do not use gasoline, thinners or other solvents.

• Avoid prolonged skin contact with oil-soaked clothing.

The oil drain plug is located on the bottom of the engine, underneath the car.

If your car is being used under dusty, polluted or off-road conditions (severe driving conditions), change the oil and filter more frequently than specified. Always drain the oil after the engine has been running long enough to bring it to normal operating temperature. Hot oil will flow easier and more contaminants will be removed along with the oil than if it were drained cold. To change the oil and filter:

1. Run the engine until it reaches normal operating temperature.

2. Jack up the front of the car and support on safety stands.

3. Slide a drain pan of at least 6 quart (5.7L) capacity under the oil pan.

4. Loosen the drain plug. Turn the plug out by hand. By keeping an inward pressure on the plug as you unscrew it, oil won't escape past the threads and you can remove it without being burned by hot oil. The engine oil will be hot. Keep your arms, face and hands away from the oil as it drains out.

5. Allow the oil to drain completely and then install the drain plug. Don't over-tighten the plug, or you'll be buying a new pan or a replacement plug for stripped threads.

6. Using a strap wrench, remove the oil filter. Keep in mind that it's holding about 1 quart (0.9L) of dirty, hot oil.

7. Empty the old filter into the drain pan and dispose of the filter.

NOTE: *Please dispose of used motor oil properly. Do not throw it in the trash or pour it on the ground. Take it to your dealer or local service station for recycling.*

8. Using a clean rag, wipe off the filter adapter on the engine block. Be sure that the rag doesn't't leave any lint which could clog an oil passage.

9. Coat the rubber gasket on the filter with fresh oil. Spin it onto the engine by hand; when the gasket touches the adaptor surface give it another ½–¾ turn. No more, or you'll squash the gasket and it will leak (some oil filters have installation directions about how tight to make the oil filter — follow the directions as necessary).

10. Refill the engine with the correct amount of fresh oil. See the Capacities Chart.

11. Check the oil level on the dipstick. It is normal for the level to be a bit above the full mark. Start the engine and allow it to idle for a few minutes.

NOTE: *Do not run the engine above idle speed until it has built up oil pressure, indicated when the oil light goes out.*

12. Shut off the engine, allow the oil to drain for a minute, and check the oil level. Check around the filter and drain plug for any leaks, and correct as necessary.

Manual Transaxle

FLUID RECOMMENDATIONS

All manual transaxles use API GL–4 or GL–5 (oil grade) SAE 75W-90 or SAE 80W-90 (viscosity).

LEVEL CHECK

The oil in the manual transaxle should be checked at least every 15,000 miles or 24 months. If vehicle is operated under severe conditions change the manual transaxle oil at this service interval.

1. With the car parked on a level surface, remove the filler plug from the side of the transaxle housing.

2. If the lubricant begins to trickle out of the hole, there is enough. Otherwise, carefully insert your finger (watch out for sharp threads) and check to see if the oil is up to the edge of the hole.

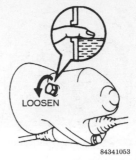

Checking the oil level with your finger-manual transaxle

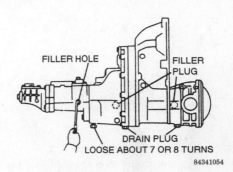

Drain plug and filler plug locations

3. If not, add oil through the hole until the level is at the edge of the hole. Most gear lubricants come in a plastic squeeze bottle with a nozzle, making additions simple. You can also use a common everyday kitchen baster.

4. Replace the filler plug.

DRAIN AND REFILL

1. Raise and safely support the vehicle as necessary. The oil must be hot before it is drained. If the car is driven until the engine is at normal operating temperature, the oil should be hot enough.

2. Remove the filler plug to provide a vent.

3. The drain plug is on the bottom of the transaxle. Place a large container underneath the transaxle and remove the plug.

4. Allow the oil to drain completely. Clean off the plug and replace it. Tighten it until it is just snug.

5. Fill the transaxle with the proper oil. This usually comes in a plastic squeeze bottle or use a kitchen baster to squirt the oil in. Refer to the Capacities Chart for the proper amount of oil to add.

6. The oil level should come up to the top of the filler hole.

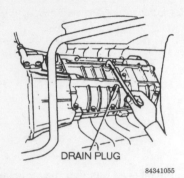

DRAIN PLUG

84341055

Manual transaxle drain plug

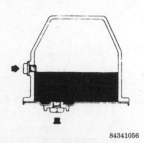

84341056

The manual transaxle oil level should be up to the bottom of the filler (upper plug)

7. Replace the filler plug, drive the car for a few minutes, stop, and check for any leaks.

Automatic Transaxle

FLUID RECOMMENDATIONS

All vehicles equipped with automatic transaxles use Dexron®II automatic transaxle fluid except All-Trac/4WD models which use Toyota automatic transaxle fluid type T or equivalent.

LEVEL CHECK

The oil in the automatic transaxle should be checked at least every 15,000 miles or 24 months. If vehicle is operated under severe conditions change the automatic transaxle oil at this service interval.

The fluid level should be checked only when the transaxle is HOT (normal operating temperature). The transaxle is considered hot after about 20 miles of highway driving.

1. Park the car on a level surface with the engine idling. Shift the transaxle into **N** or **P** and set the parking brake.

2. Remove the dipstick, wipe it clean and reinsert it firmly. Be sure that it has been pushed all the way in. Remove the dipstick and check the fluid level while holding it horizontally. With the engine running, the fluid level should be between the second and third notches on the dipstick.

3. If the fluid level is below the second notch, add the required type of transaxle fluid until the proper level is reached. This is easily done with the aid of a funnel. Check the level often as you are filling the transaxle. Be extremely careful not to overfill it. Overfilling will cause slippage, seal damage and overheating. Approximately one pint (0.47L) of transaxle fluid will raise the level from one notch to the other.

The fluid on the dipstick should always be a bright red color. If it is discolored (brown or black), or smells burnt, serious transaxle troubles, probably due to overheating, should be suspected. The transaxle should be inspected by a qualified service (ASE certified) technician to locate the cause of the burnt fluid.

DRAIN AND REFILL

The automatic transaxle has a drain plug so you can remove the plug, drain the fluid, replace the plug and then refill the transaxle.

1. Raise and safely support the vehicle as necessary. Remove the plug and drain the fluid into a large pan.

2. Install the drain plug.

3. It is a good idea to measure the amount of fluid drained from the transaxle to determine the correct amount of fresh fluid to add. This is because some parts of the transaxle may not drain completely and using the dry refill amount specified in the Capacities Chart could lead to overfilling. Fluid is added only

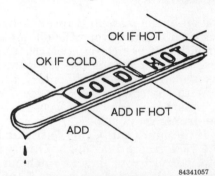

OK IF HOT

OK IF COLD

ADD IF HOT

ADD

84341057

Typical automatic transaxle dipstick

through the dipstick tube. Always use the proper type automatic transaxle fluid.

4. Add automatic transaxle fluid (vehicle must be on a level surface when refilling) to the correct level.

5. Replace the dipstick after filling. Start the engine and allow it to idle. DO NOT race the engine.

6. After the engine has idled for a few minutes, shift the transaxle slowly through the gears (always hold your foot on the brake pedal) and then return it to **P**. With the engine still idling, check the fluid level on the dipstick. If necessary, add more fluid to raise the level to where it is supposed to be.

7. Check the drain plug for transaxle fluid leakage. Dispose of used oil properly. Do not throw it in the trash or pour it on the ground.

PAN AND FILTER SERVICE

The automatic transaxle filter should be changed every time the transaxle fluid is change. Always replace the transaxle pan gasket when oil pan is removed. Note location of all transaxle oil filter (strainer) retaining bolts. Always torque

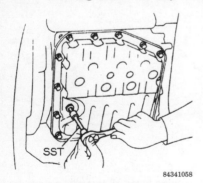

84341058

Drain plug location-automatic transaxle

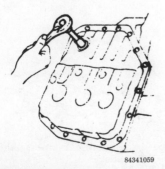

84341059

Drain plug location-automatic transaxle

all transaxle oil pan retaining bolts in progressive steps.

NOTE: *This service operation should be performed with the engine and transaxle COLD.*

1. Raise and safely support the vehicle as necessary. Remove the plug and drain the fluid. When the fluid stops coming out of the drain hole, loosen the pan retaining screws until the pan can be pulled down at one corner. If the pan is stuck, tap the edges lightly with a plastic mallet to loosen it; DON't pry it or wedge a screwdriver into the seam. Lower the corner of the pan and allow the remaining fluid to drain out.

2. After the pan has drained completely, remove the pan retaining screws and then remove the pan and gasket.

3. Clean the pan thoroughly and allow it to air dry. If you wipe it out with a rag you run the risk of leaving bits of lint in the pan which will clog the tiny hydraulic passages in the transaxle.

4. With the pan removed, the transaxle filter (strainer) is visible. The filter should be changed any time the transaxle oil is drained. Remove the bolts holding the filter and remove the filter and gasket if so equipped.

NOTE: *Some filter retaining bolts are different lengths and MUST BE reinstalled in their correct locations. Take great care not to interchange them.*

5. Clean the mating surfaces for the oil pan and the filter; make sure all traces of the old gasket material is removed.

6. Install the new filter assembly (some models use a gasket under the oil filter). Install the retaining bolts in their correct locations and tighten evenly.

7. Install the pan (magnets in the correct location in oil pan if so equipped) using a new gasket and torque retaining bolts in progressive steps to about 60 inch lbs.

8. Install the drain plug.

9. It is a good idea to measure the amount of fluid drained from the transaxle to determine the correct amount of fresh fluid to be added. This is because some parts of the transaxle may not drain completely. Do not overfill the transaxle assembly.

10. With the engine off, add new automatic transaxle fluid through the dipstick tube to the correct level. Refer to the Capacities Chart at the end of Chapter 1 as necessary.

11. Start the engine (always hold your foot on the brake) and shift the gear selector into all positions, allowing each gear to engage momentarily. Shift into **P**. DO NOT race the engine!

12. With the engine idling, check the fluid level. Add fluid up to correct level on the dipstick.

13. Check the transaxle oil pan and drain plug for oil leakage. Dispose of used oil properly. Do not throw it in the trash or pour it on the ground.

Rear Drive Axle

FLUID RECOMMENDATIONS

All 4WD vehicles use API GL–5 hypoid type gear oil (oil grade) SAE 80W–90 (viscosity).

LEVEL CHECK

The oil in the rear differential should be checked at least every 15,000 miles or 24 months. If vehicle is operated under severe conditions change the automatic transaxle oil at this service interval.

1. With the car parked on a level surface, remove the filler plug from the back of the differential assembly. The plug on the bottom of the differential assembly is the drain plug.

2. If the oil begins to trickle out of the hole, there is enough. Otherwise, carefully insert your finger (watch for sharp threads) into the hole and check to see if the oil is up to the bottom edge of the filler hole.

3. If not, add oil through the hole until the level is at the edge of the hole. Most gear oils come in a plastic squeeze bottle with a nozzle, making additions simple. You can also use a common everyday kitchen baster.

4. Replace the filler plug.

DRAIN AND REFILL

To drain and fill the rear differential, proceed as follows:

1. Park the vehicle on a level surface. Set the parking brake.

2. Remove the filler (upper) plug. Place a container which is large enough to catch all of the differential oil, under the drain plug.

3. Remove the drain (lower) plug and gasket, if so equipped. Allow all of the oil to drain into the container.

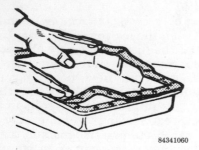

84341060

Always replace the gasket when installing the oil pan

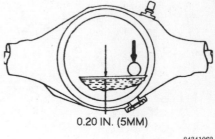

0.20 IN. (5MM)

84341062

The fluid level in the differential should be up to the edge of the filler hole (large arrow)

OIL STRAINER

84341061

Removing oil filter-automatic transaxle

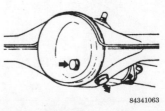

84341063

Filler (upper) plug and drain (lower) plug locations-4WD models

4. Install the drain plug. Tighten it so that it will not leak, but do not overtighten.

5. Refill with the proper grade and viscosity of axle lubricant. Be sure that the level reaches the bottom of the filler plug.

6. Install the filler plug and check for leakage.

Cooling System

FLUID RECOMMENDATIONS

The correct coolant is any permanent, high quality ethylene glycol antifreeze mixed in a 50/50 concentration with water. This mixture gives the best combination of antifreeze and anti-boil characteristics within the engine.

LEVEL CHECK

CAUTION: *Always allow the car to sit and cool for an hour or so (longer is better) before removing the radiator cap. To avoid injury when working on a warm engine, cover the radiator cap with a thick cloth and turn it slowly counterclockwise until the pressure begins to escape. After the pressure is completely removed, remove the cap. Never remove the cap until the pressure is gone.*

It's best to check the coolant level when the engine is COLD. The radiator coolant level should be between the LOW and the FULL lines on the expansion tank when the engine is cold. If low, check for leakage and add coolant up to the FULL line but do not overfill.

NOTE: *Check the freeze protection rating of the antifreeze at least once a year or as necessary with a suitable antifreeze tester.*

DRAIN AND REFILL

The engine coolant should be changed every 30,000 miles or 2 years, whichever comes first. Replacing the coolant is necessary to remove the scale, rust and chemical by-products which build up in the system.

1. Draining the cooling system is always done with the engine **COLD**.

2. Remove the radiator cap.

3. Position the drain pan under the draincock on the bottom of the radiator. Additionally, some engines have a draincock on the side of the engine block, near the oil filter. This should be opened

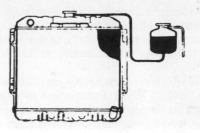

Always check the level in the expansion tank; do not remove the cap if there is any heat in the system

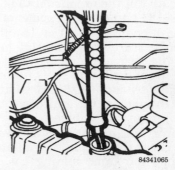

The freezing protection rating can be checked with an antifreeze tester

to aid in draining the cooling system completely. If for some reason the radiator draincock can't be used, you can loosen and remove the lower radiator hose at its joint to the radiator.

CAUTION: *When draining the coolant, keep in mind that cats and dogs are attracted by the ethylene glycol antifreeze, and are quite likely to drink any that is left in an uncovered container or in puddles on the ground. This will prove fatal in sufficient quantity. Always drain the coolant into a sealable container. Coolant should be reused unless it is contaminated or several years old.*

4. If the lower hose is to be used as the drain, loosen the clamp on the hose and slide it back so it's out of the way. Gently break the grip of the hose on its fitting by twisting or prying with a suitable tool. Do not exert too much force or you will damage the radiator fitting. Remove the hose end from the radiator and direct the hose into the drain pan. You now have fluid running from both the hose and the radiator.

5. When the system stops draining, close both draincocks as necessary.

6. Using a funnel if necessary, fill the radiator with a 50/50 solution of anti-freeze and water. Allow time for the fluid to run through the hoses and into the engine.

7. Fill the radiator to just below the filler neck. With the radiator cap off, start the engine and let it idle; this will circulate the coolant and begin to eliminate air in the system. Top up the radiator as the level drops.

8. When the level is reasonably stable, shut the engine OFF, and replace the radiator cap. Fill the expansion tank to the correct level and cap the expansion tank.

9. Drive the car for 10 or 15 minutes; the temperature gauge should be fully within the normal operating range. It is helpful to set the heater to its hottest setting while driving — this circulates the coolant throughout the entire system and helps eliminate air bubbles.

10. After the engine has cooled (2–3 hours), check the level in the radiator and the expansion tank, adding coolant as necessary.

Clean the radiator fins of any debris which impedes air flow

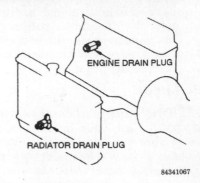

Drain plug locations

CLEANING AND FLUSHING THE COOLING SYSTEM

Proceed with draining the system as outlined above. When the system has drained, reconnect any hoses close to the radiator draincock. Move the temperature control for the heater to its hottest position; this allows the heater core to be flushed as well. Using a garden hose or bucket, fill the radiator and allow the water to run out the engine drain cock. Continue until the water runs clear. Be sure to clean the expansion tank as well.

If the system is badly contaminated with rust or scale, you can use a commercial flushing solution to clean it out. Follow the manufacturer's instructions. Some causes of rust are air in the system, failure to change the coolant regularly, use of excessively hard or soft water, and/or failure to use the correct mix of antifreeze and water.

After the system has been flushed, continue with the refill procedures outlined above. Check the condition of the radiator cap and its gasket, replacing the radiator cap as necessary.

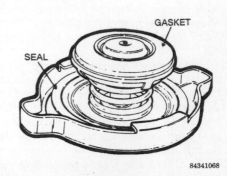

Check the radiator cap seal and gasket condition

Brake and Clutch Master Cylinders

FLUID RECOMMENDATIONS

All vehicles use DOT 3 or SAE J1703 brake fluid. The brake and clutch master cylinders use the same type brake fluid.

LEVEL CHECK

The brake and clutch master cylinders are located under the hood, in the left rear section of the engine compartment. They are made of translucent plastic so that the levels may be checked without removing the tops. The fluid level in both reservoirs should be checked at least every 15,000 miles or 1 year. The fluid level should be maintained at the uppermost mark on the side of the reservoir. Any sudden decrease in the level indicates a possible leak in the system and should be checked out immediately.

When adding fluid, use only fresh, uncontaminated brake fluid meeting or exceeding DOT 3 standards. Be careful not to spill any brake fluid on painted surfaces, as it eats the paint. Do not allow the brake fluid container or the master cylinder reservoir to remain open any longer than necessary; brake fluid absorbs moisture from the air, reducing its effectiveness and causing corrosion in the lines.

Power Steering Pump

FLUID RECOMMENDATIONS

All vehicles use Dexron®II automatic transmission fluid.

LEVEL CHECK

The fluid level in the power steering reservoir should be checked at least every 15,000 miles or 1 year. The vehicle should be parked on level ground, with the engine warm and running at normal idle. If the level is low, add Dexron®II type ATF until the proper level is achieved.

Chassis Greasing

Chassis lubrication is limited to greasing the lower ball joint every 12,000 miles or 1 year. At this service interval inspect lower ball joint boots for damage.

1. Remove the screw plug from the ball joint. Install a grease nipple.

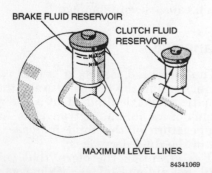

Checking brake and clutch fluid

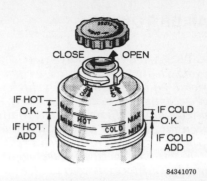

Checking power steering fluid

2. Using a hand-operated grease gun, lubricate the ball joint with NLGI #1 or NLGI #2 molybdenum-disulphide lithium-based grease.

3. Remove the nipple and reinstall the screw plug.

4. Repeat for the other ball joint.

Body Lubrication

There is no set period recommended by Toyota for body lubrication. However, it is a good idea to lubricate the following body points at least once a year, especially in the fall before cold weather.**Lubricate with engine oil:**

• Door lock latches
• Door lock rollers
• Door, hood and hinge pivots **Lubricate with Lubriplate:**
• Trunk lid latch and hinge
• Glove box door latch
• Front seat slides **Lubricate with silicone spray:**
• All rubber weather stripping
• Hood stops

When finished lubricating a body part, be sure that all the excess lubricant has been wiped off, especially in the areas of the car which may come in contact with clothing.

Wheel Bearings

REMOVAL & INSTALLATION

No maintenance (repacking wheel bearings with grease) service is necessary for the rear wheel bearings on these vehicles. The rear wheel bearings are a complete assembly that require no maintenance.

TRAILER TOWING

NOTE: *Always consult with your Toyota Dealer about trailer weight and special equipment. Some vehicles are not recommend to tow a trailer; some vehicles have different weight limits between manual and automatic transaxle types. Toyota All-Trac vehicles require a hitch with a special protector. Please consult your local Toyota dealer for specific advice regarding this hitch assembly. Towing a trailer qualifies as severe duty for the tow vehicle. Maintenance must be performed more frequently.*

The gross vehicle weight must not exceed the Gross Vehicle Weight Rating (GVWR) indicated on the Certification Regulation Plate. The gross vehicle weight is the sum of the weights of the unloaded vehicle, driver, passengers, luggage, hitch and trailer tongue load. It also includes the weight of any special equipment installed on your vehicle.

General Recommendations

Your vehicle was primarily designed to carry passengers and cargo. It is impor-

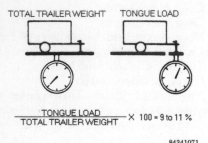

$$\frac{\text{TONGUE LOAD}}{\text{TOTAL TRAILER WEIGHT}} \times 100 = 9 \text{ to } 11 \%$$

84341071

The trailer cargo load should be distributed so that the tongue load is 9–11% of the total trailer weight, not exceeding the maximum of 150 lbs.

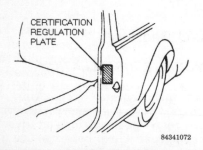

84341072

Vehicle certification/regulation plate location

tant to remember that towing a trailer will place additional loads on your vehicle's engine, drive train, steering, braking and other systems. However, if you find it necessary to tow a trailer, using the proper equipment is a must.

Local laws may require specific equipment such as trailer brakes or fender mounted mirrors. Check your local laws.

The trailer hitch assembly should conform to all applicable laws and be sufficient for the maximum trailer load.

Almost all trailers now come equipped with rear and side lighting. A wiring harness must be installed to connect the automotive lighting and brake light systems to the trailer. Any reputable hitch installer can perform this installation. You can also install the harnesses, but great care must be paid to matching the correct wires during the installation. Each circuit must be wired individually for tail lights, brake lights, right and left turn signals and in many cases, reverse lights. If the trailer is equipped with electric brakes, the wiring for this circuit should be installed at the same time as the lighting harness. Remember that the additional lighting may exceed the present fuse rating in the car's fusebox; upgrading the fuse may be necessary.

Cooling System

One of the most common, if not the most common, problem associated with trailer towing is engine overheating.

The cooling system should be checked frequently and maintained in top notch condition. If the engine temperature gauge indicates overheating, particularly on long grades, immediately turn off the air conditioner (if in use), pull off the road and stop in a safe location. Do not attempt to "limp in" with a hot engine — you'll cause severe damage.

Transaxle

The increased load of a trailer causes an increase in the temperature of the automatic transaxle fluid. Heat is the worst enemy of an automatic transaxle. As the temperature of the fluid increases, the life of the fluid decreases.

It is essential, therefore, that you install an automatic transaxle cooler or supplement the one already present.

The cooler, which consists of a multi-tube, finned heat exchanger, is usually installed in front of the radiator or air conditioning compressor, and hooked in-line with the transaxle cooler tank inlet line. Follow the cooler manufacturer's installation instructions.

Select a cooler of at least adequate capacity, based upon the combined gross weights of the car and trailer.

Cooler manufacturers recommend that you use an aftermarket cooler in addition to the present cooling tank in your radiator.

NOTE: *A transaxle cooler can sometimes cause slow or harsh shifting in the transaxle during cold weather, until the fluid has a chance to come up to normal operating temperature. Some coolers can be purchased with or retrofitted with a temperature bypass valve which will allow fluid flow through the cooler only when the fluid has reached operating temperature or above.*

Handling A Trailer

Towing a trailer with ease and safety requires a certain amount of skill that can only be gained through experience. Many trailer accidents occur because the driver, however skilled, forgot some of the basics.

• When loading the trailer, keep about 60% of the weight forward of the axle. This will prevent the trailer from trying to pass the car during cornering.

• Always perform a walk-around check of all the lighting before pulling out.

• Check the tire pressure and condition on both the car and trailer frequently. Underinflated tires are a hazard.

• After connecting the trailer, observe the car for any extreme nose-up or nose-down attitudes. If the car is not approximately level with the trailer connected, rebalance the load in the trailer.

• Stopping distances are increased dramatically. Allow plenty of room and anticipate stops. Sudden braking may jack-knife the trailer or throw the car into a skid.

• Accelerate slowly and smoothly. Jerky driving will cause increased wear on the drive line.

• Avoid sharp turns. The trailer will always turn "inside" the car; allow plenty of room.

• Crosswinds and rough roads increase instability. Know when you're about to be passed by a large vehicle and prepare for it.

• If swaying begins, grip the steering wheel firmly and hold the vehicle straight ahead. Reduce speed gradually without using the brake. If you make NO extreme corrections in brakes, throttle or steering, the car and trailer will stabilize quickly.

• Passing requires much greater distances for acceleration. Plan ahead. Remember to allow for the length of the trailer when pulling back in.

• Use a lower gear to descend long grades. Slow down before downshifting.

• Avoid riding the brake. This will overheat the brakes and reduce their efficiency.

• When parking the combination, always apply the parking brake and place blocks under the trailer wheels. A heavy trailer may literally drag the car down a grade. Don't forget to remove the chocks before leaving.

• Backing up with a trailer is a skill to be practiced before it is needed. Find a large open area (get permission if necessary) and spend at least an hour learning how to do it.

PUSHING AND TOWING

Pushing Starting the Vehicle

Push starting these vehicles is not recommended. However, it is possible to push start a manual transaxle vehicle as an emergency, no-alternative measure. To push start the car; turn the ignition switch to the **ON** position, push in the clutch pedal, put the gear shift lever in second or third gear and depress the gas pedal just a bit. As the car begins to pick up momentum while being pushed, release the clutch pedal. Immediately as the engine catches, push the clutch pedal in and apply sufficient throttle to keep the engine running. NEVER attempt to push start the car while it is in REVERSE.

Vehicles equipped with an automatic transaxle can NOT be push started.

Towing the Vehicle

The absolute best way to have the car towed or transported is on a flat-bed or rollback transporter. These units are becoming more common and are very useful for moving disabled vehicles quickly. Most vehicles have lower bodywork and undertrays which can be easily damaged by the sling of a conventional tow truck; an operator unfamiliar with your particular model can cause severe damage to the suspension or drive line by hooking up chains and J-hooks incorrectly.

If a flatbed is not available (you should specifically request one), the car may be towed by a hoist or conventional tow vehicle. Front wheel drive cars with automatic transaxle must be towed with the drive wheels off the ground. FWD cars with a manual transaxle can be towed with either end up in the air or with all four wheels on the ground. You need only remember that the transaxle must be in neutral, the parking brake must be off and the ignition switch must be in the **ACC** position. The steering column lock is not strong enough to hold the front wheels straight under towing.

The Corolla All-Trac vehicle presents its own towing problems. Since the front and rear wheels are connected through the drive system, all four wheels must be considered in the towing arrangement. If a flatbed is not available, the All-Trac should be towed with the front end elevated. As the rear wheels roll on the ground, the front wheels will turn. They must be clear of the hoist and sling equipment. If the vehicle cannot be towed front-end-up, both ends must be elevated, using a set of dolly wheels.

Most vehicles have conveniently located tie-down hooks at the front of the vehicle. These make ideal locations to secure a rope or chain for towing the car or extracting it from an off-road excursion. The vehicle may only be towed on hard surfaced roads and only in a normal or forward direction.

A driver must be in the towed vehicle to control it. Before towing, the parking brake must be released and the transaxle put in neutral. Do NOT flat tow the vehicle if the brakes, steering, axles, suspension or drive line is damaged. If the engine is not running, the power assists for the steering and brakes will not be operating. Steering and braking will require more time and much more effort without the assist.

JACKING

There are certain safety precautions which should be observed when jacking the vehicle. They are as follows:

1. Always jack the car on a level surface.

2. Set the parking brake, and block the rear wheels, if the front wheels are to be raised. This will keep the car from rolling backward off the jack.

3. If the rear wheels are to be raised, block off the front wheels to keep the car from rolling forward.

4. Block the wheel diagonally opposite the one which is being raised.

NOTE: *The tool kit which is supplied with most Toyota passenger cars includes a wheel block.*

5. If the vehicle is being raised in order to work underneath it, support it with jackstands. Do not place the jackstands against the sheet metal panels beneath the car or they will become distorted.

CAUTION: *Do not work beneath a vehicle supported only by a tire changing jack.*

6. Do not use a bumper jack to raise the vehicle; the bumpers are not designed for this purpose.

TIE-DOWN TABS
84341073

Tie down locations

PRECAUTIONS WHEN TOWING FULL-TIME 4WD VEHICLES

1. Use one of the methods shown below to tow the vehicle.
2. When there is trouble with the chassis and drivetrain, use method ① (flat bed truck) or method ② (sling type toe truck with dollies)
3. Recommended Methods: No. ① , ② or ③
   Emergency Method: No. ④

Type of Transaxle / Towing Method	Manual Transaxle			Automatic Transaxle			
	Parking Brake	T/M Shift Lever Position	Center Diff.	Parking Brake	T/M Shift Lever Position	Center Diff. Control Switch	Mode Select Lever on Transaxle
① Flat Bed Truck ② Sling-Type Tow Truck with Dollies	Applied	1st Gear	Free or Lock (Center Differential Control Switch "ON" or "OFF")	Applied	"P" range	"AUTO" or "OFF"	Free (Normal Driving) No Special Operation Necessary
③ Sling-Type Two Truck (Front wheels must be able to rotate freely)	Released	Neutral	Free (Center Differential Control Switch "OFF")	Release	"N" range	"OFF"	↑
④ Towing with a Rope	Released	Neutral	Free (Center Differential Control Switch "OFF")	Released	"N" range	"OFF"	↑
				NOTE: Do not tow the vehicle at a speed faster than 18 mph (30 km/h) or a distance greater than 50 miles (80 km).			

NOTE: Do not use any towing methods other than those shown above.
For example, the towing method shown below is dangerous, so do not use it.

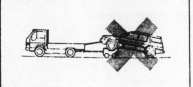

During towing with this towing method, there is a danger of the drivetrain heating up and causing breakdown, or of the front wheels flying off the dolly.

84341074

Towing procedures

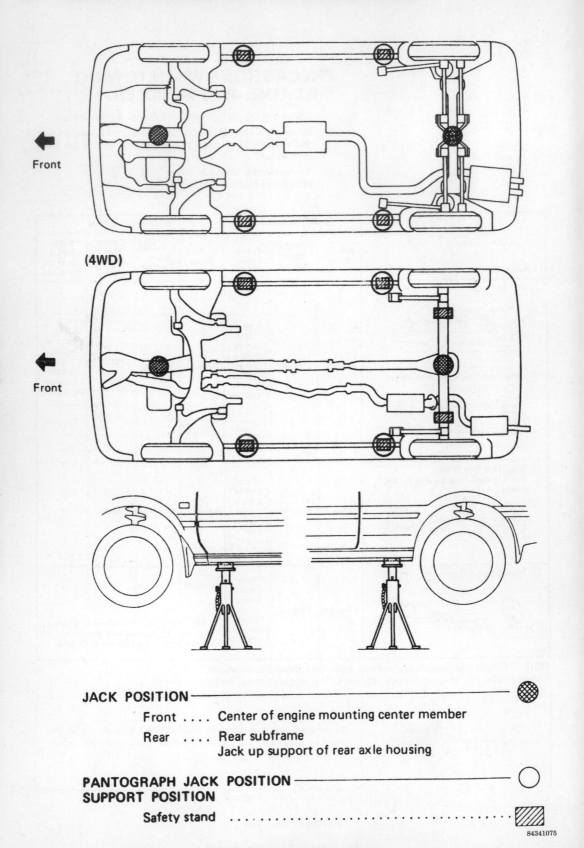

Front

(4WD)

Front

JACK POSITION——————————————————————————— ⬤

      Front . . . . Center of engine mounting center member

      Rear   . . . . Rear subframe
                   Jack up support of rear axle housing

PANTOGRAPH JACK POSITION———————————————— ◯
SUPPORT POSITION

     Safety stand . . . . ▨

84341075

Vehicle lift and support locations

CAPACITIES

Year	Model	Engine ID/VIN	Engine Displacement Liters (cc)	Engine Crankcase with Filter	Transmission (pts.)			Transfer Case (pts.)	Drive Axle		Fuel Tank (gal.)	Cooling System (qts.)
					4-Spd	5-Spd	Auto.		Front (pts.)	Rear (pts.)		
1990	Corolla	4A-FE	1.6 (1587)	3.4	—	5.4	7.2	—	—	2.4	13.2	6.6
	Corolla	4A-GE	1.6 (1587)	3.9	—	5.4	7.2	—	—	2.4	13.2	6.3
1991	Corolla	4A-FE	1.6 (1587)	3.4	—	5.4	7.2	—	—	2.4	13.2	6.6
	Corolla	4A-GE	1.6 (1587)	3.9	—	5.4	7.2	—	—	2.4	13.2	6.3
1992	Corolla	4A-FE	1.6 (1587)	3.4	—	5.4	7.2	—	—	2.4	13.2	6.6
1993	Corolla	4A-FE	1.6 (1587)	3.4	—	5.4	7.2	—	—	2.4	13.2	6.6
	Corolla	7A-FE	1.8 (1762)	3.9	—	5.4	7.2	—	—	2.4	13.2	6.6

84341077

Maintenance Intervals Chart

Miles × 1000 or months of age	10 / 12	20 / 24	30 / 36	40 / 48	50 / 60	60 / 72
Engine oil and filter	R	R	R	R	R	R
Body lubrication	•	I	•	I	•	I
Engine idle speed	I	•	I	•	•	I
Engine coolant	•	•	I	•	•	R
Spark plugs	•	•	I	•	•	R
Air filter	I	•	R	•	•	R
Valve clearance	•	•	•	•	•	A
Engine drive belts	•	I	•	I	•	I
Charcoal canister	•	•	•	•	•	I
Fuel lines and connections	•	•	I	•	•	I
Fuel filter cap gasket	•	•	I	•	•	R
Exhaust system	•	I	•	I	•	I
Engine timing belt	•	•	I	•	•	R
Wheels and tires	I	I	I	I	I	I
Brakes	•	I	•	I	•	I
Fluid levels check	I	I	I	I	I	I
Transmission fluid	I	I	I	I	I	I

R: Replace
I: Inspect and clean, adjust, repair, service or replace as necessary
REMINDER: These are maximum intervals, not to be exceeded. More frequent maintenance and inspection may be required depending on usage of the vehicle. See service maintenance interval chart in your owner's manual.
NOTE: This chart is to be used as a maintenance service guide only.
    Consult your owner's manual as necessary.

84341076

Maintenance intervals

Engine Performance and Tune-Up

2

TUNE-UP PROCEDURES

In order to extract the full measure of performance and economy from your engine it is essential that it be properly tuned at regular intervals. A regular tune-up will keep your Toyota's engine running smoothly and will prevent the annoying minor breakdowns and poor performance associated with an untuned engine.

A complete tune-up (replace spark plugs, air filter, make necessary adjustments etc.) should be performed every 30,000 miles or 36 months, whichever comes first. This interval time or mileage should be halved or adjusted as necessary if the car is operated under severe conditions, such as trailer towing, prolonged idling, continual stop and start driving, or if starting or running problems are noticed. It is assumed that the routine maintenance (described in Chapter 1) has been kept up, as this will have a decided effect on the results of a tune-up.

If the specifications on the tune-up sticker in the engine compartment of your Toyota disagree with the Tune-Up Specifications chart in this Chapter, the figures on the sticker MUST BE USED. The sticker often reflects changes made during the production run.

NOTE: *On some vehicles platinum-tipped spark plugs may be used, in which case the recommended change interval is 60,000 miles or every 72 months. The platinum-tipped spark plugs are identified by blue rings on the ceramic. Do not reuse platinum-tipped spark plugs by cleaning or regapping.*

Spark Plugs

Spark plugs ignite the air and fuel mixture in the cylinder as the piston reaches the top of the compression stroke. The controlled explosion that results forces the piston down, turning the crankshaft and the rest of the drive train.

The average life of a normal, spark plug (platinum plugs 60,000 mile change interval) is about 15,000–20,000 miles, although manufacturers are now claiming spark plug lives of up to 30,000 miles or more. This is, however, dependent on a number of factors: the mechanical condition of the engine, the type of fuel, the driving conditions and the driver.

Manufacturers are now required to certify that the spark plugs in their engines will meet emission specifications for 30,000 miles if all maintenance is performed properly. Certain types of plugs can be certified even beyond this point.

When you remove the spark plugs, check their condition. They are a good indicator of the condition of the engine.

When a regular spark plug is functioning normally or, more accurately, when the plug is installed in an engine that is functioning properly, the plugs can be taken out, cleaned, gapped, and reinstalled without doing the engine any harm.

NOTE: *On platinum spark plug applications DO NOT use a wire brush for cleaning spark plugs. NEVER attempt to adjust gap/clean used platinum spark plugs. Platinum spark plugs should be replaced every 60,000 miles.*

When, and if, a spark plug fouls and begins to misfire, you will have to investigate, correct the cause of the fouling, and either clean or replace the plug.

Spark plugs suitable for use in your Toyota's engine are offered in a number of different heat ranges. The amount of heat which the plug absorbs is determined by the length of the lower insulator. The longer the insulator, the hotter the plug will operate; the shorter the insulator, the cooler it will operate. A spark plug that absorbs (or retains) little heat and remains too cool will accumulate deposits of lead, oil, and carbon, because it is not hot enough to burn them off. This leads to fouling and consequent misfiring. A spark plug that absorbs too much heat will have no deposits, but the electrodes will burn away quickly and, in some cases, pre-ignition may result. Pre-ignition occurs when the spark plug tips get so hot that they ignite the fuel/air mixture before the actual spark fires. This premature ignition will usually cause a pinging sound under conditions of low speed and heavy load. In severe cases, the heat may become high enough to start the fuel/air mixture burning throughout the combustion chamber rather than just to the front of the plug. In this case, the resultant explosion will be strong enough to damage pistons, rings, and valves.

In most cases the factory recommended heat range is correct; it is chosen to perform well under a wide range of operating conditions. However, if most of your driving is long distance, high speed travel, you may want to install a spark plug one step colder than standard. If most of your driving is of the short trip variety, when the engine may not always reach operating temperature, a hotter plug may help burn off the deposits normally accumulated under those conditions.

REMOVAL

1. Number the spark plug wires (mark at the end of plug wire or boot) so that you won't cross them when you replace them.

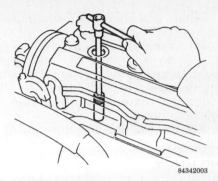

Remove the spark plug using the proper tools

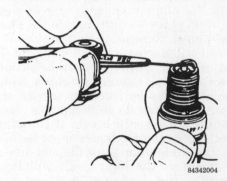

Always use a wire gauge to check the plug gap

2. Remove the wire from the end of the spark plug by grasping the wire by the rubber boot. If the boot sticks to the plug, remove it by twisting and pulling at the same time. Do not pull the wire itself or you will damage the core.

3. Use the correct size spark plug socket (spark plug sockets come in two sizes ⅝ and 1/6 in. — use the correct size socket for the spark plug) to loosen all of the plugs about two turns.

4. If removal of the plugs is difficult, apply a few drops of penetrating oil or silicone spray to the area around the base

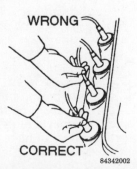

When removing the spark plug wire, always remove it by the rubber boot

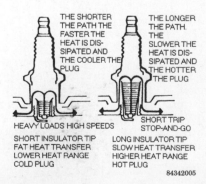

Spark plug heat range

of the plug, and allow it a few minutes to work.

5. If compressed air is available, apply it to the area around the spark plug holes. Otherwise, use a rag or a brush to clean the area. Be careful not to allow any foreign material to drop into the spark plug holes.

6. Remove the plugs by unscrewing by hand the rest of the way from the engine.

INSPECTION

Check the spark plugs for deposits and wear. If they are not going to be replaced, clean the plugs thoroughly (never clean platinum plugs — just replace the platinum plugs). Remember that any kind of deposit will decrease the efficiency of the plug. Regular spark plugs can be cleaned on a spark plug cleaning machine, which can sometimes be found in service stations, or you can do an acceptable job of cleaning with a stiff brush. If the plugs are cleaned, the electrodes must be filed flat. Use an ignition point file, not an emery board or the like, which will leave deposits. The electrodes must be filed perfectly flat with sharp edges; rounded edges reduce the spark plug voltage by as much as 50%.

84342006

Adjust the spark plug gap by bending the side electrode

Check spark plug gap before installation. The ground electrode (the L-shaped one connected to the body of the plug) must be parallel to the center electrode and the specified size wire gauge (see Tune-Up Specifications) should pass through the gap with a slight drag.

NOTE: *Never adjust the gap or try to clean a used platinum tipped spark plug.*

Always check the gap on new regular spark plugs, too; they are not always set correctly at the factory. Do not use a flat feeler gauge when measuring the gap, because the reading will be inaccurate. Wire gapping tools usually have a bending tool attached, use that to adjust the side electrode until the proper distance is obtained. Absolutely never bend the center electrode. Also, be careful not to bend the side electrode too far or too often; it may weaken and break off within the engine, causing serious damage.

INSTALLATION

1. Lubricate the threads of the spark plugs with a drop of oil. Install the plugs and tighten them hand tight (a long piece of vacuum hose attached to the top of the spark plug will help you start the spark plug by hand). Take care not to cross-thread them.

2. Tighten the spark plugs with the correct size spark plug socket. Do not apply the same amount of force you would use for a bolt; just snug them in. If a torque wrench is available, tighten to 13–15 ft. lbs.

3. Install the spark plug wires on their respective spark plugs. Make sure the spark plug wires are firmly connected. You will be able to feel them click into place.

GASOLINE ENGINE TUNE-UP SPECIFICATIONS

Year	Engine ID/VIN	Engine Displacement Liters (cc)	Spark Plugs Gap (in.)	Ignition Timing (deg.) MT	AT	Fuel Pump (psi)	Idle Speed (rpm) MT	AT	Valve Clearance In.	Ex.
1990	4A-FE	1.6 (1587)	0.031	10B	10B	38–44	750	750	0.006–0.010	0.008–0.012
	4A-GE	1.6 (1587)	0.031	10B	10B	38–44	800	800	0.006–0.010	0.008–0.012
1991	4A-FE	1.6 (1587)	0.031	10B	10B	38–44	750	750	0.006–0.010	0.008–0.012
	4A-GE	1.6 (1587)	0.031	10B	10B	38–44	800	800	0.006–0.010	0.008–0.012
1992	4A-FE	1.6 (1587)	0.031	10B	10B	38–44	750	750	0.006–0.010	0.008–0.012
1993	4A-FE	1.6 (1587)	0.031	10B	10B	38–44	750	750	0.006–0.010	0.008–0.012
	7A-FE	1.8 (1762)	0.031	10B	10B	38–44	800	800	0.006–0.010	0.008–0.012

NOTE: The underhood specifications sticker often reflects tune-up specification changes in production. Sticker figures must be used if they disagree with those in this chart.

B—Before Top Dead Center

84342001

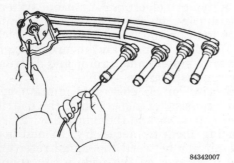

84342007

Checking the spark plug wires for correct resistance

Spark Plug Wires

CHECKING AND REPLACING

At every tune-up, visually inspect the spark plug cables for burns, cuts, or breaks in the insulation. Check the boots and the nipples on the distributor cap and coil. Replace any damaged wiring.

Every 30,000 miles or so, the resistance of the wires may be checked with an ohmmeter. Wires with excessive resistance will cause misfiring, and may make the engine difficult to start in damp weather. Generally the useful life of the cables is 30,000–50,000 miles.

To check resistance, remove the distributor cap, leaving the wires attached. Connect one lead of an ohmmeter to an electrode within the cap; connect the other lead to the corresponding spark plug terminal (remove it from the plug for this test). Replace any wire which shows a resistance over 25,000 ohms per wire.

It should be remembered that resistance is also a function of length; the longer the cable, the greater the resistance. Thus, if the cables on your car are longer than the factory originals, resistance will be higher, quite possibly outside these limits.

When installing new spark plug wires (cables), replace them ONE AT A TIME to avoid mix-ups. Start by replacing the longest one first. Install the boot firmly over the spark plug. Route the wire over the same path as the original. Insert the nipple firmly into the tower on the cap or the coil.

FIRING ORDERS

NOTE: *To avoid confusion, spark plug wires should be replaced one at a time.*
84342001

4A-FE and 7A-FE Engines
Engine Firing Order: 1-3-4-2
Distributor Rotation: Counterclockwise

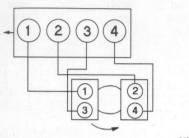

84342009

4A-GE Engine
Engine Firing Order: 1-3-4-2
Distributor Rotation: Counterclockwise

ELECTRONIC IGNITION

Service Precautions

• Do not leave the ignition switch on for more than 10 minutes if the engine will not start.
• With a tachometer connected to the the system, connect the test probe of the tachometer to terminal IG- of the check connector.
• As some tachometers are not compatible with this ignition system, confirm the compatibility of your unit before using.
• Never allow the tachometer terminal to touch ground as this could damage the igniter and/or the ignition coil.
• Do not disconnect the battery when the engine is running.
• Check that the igniter is properly grounded to the body.

Description and Operation

Electronic ignition systems offer many advances over the conventional breaker point ignition system. By eliminating the points, maintenance requirements are greatly reduced. An electronic ignition system is capable of producing much higher voltage, which in turn aids in starting, reduces spark fouling and provides better emission control.

The electronic ignition system consists of a distributor with a signal generator, an ignition coil and an electronic igniter. The signal generator is used to activate the electronic components of the ignition. It is located in the distributor and consists of three main components; the signal rotor, the pick-up coil and the permanent magnet. The signal rotor (not to be confused with the normal rotor) revolves with the distributor shaft, while the pickup coil and the permanent magnet are stationary. As the signal rotor spins, the teeth on it pass a projection leading from the pickup coil. As they pass, voltage is allowed to flow through the system, firing the spark plugs. There is no physical contact and no electrical arcing, hence no need to replace burnt or worn parts.

The electronic control unit is programmed with data for optimum ignition timing under any and all operating conditions. Using data provided by the sensors which monitor various engine functions (rpm, intake air volume, engine temperature, etc.) the electronic control unit microcomputer triggers the spark at precisely the right instant.

The Integrated Ignition Assembly (IIA) is a typical electronic ignition system. The major components consist of an integral ignition coil, signal generator (pickup), igniter, vacuum and governor weight advance system and a rotor and distributor cap distribution system.

Service on all electronic ignition systems consists of inspection of the distributor cap, rotor and the ignition wires, replacing them as necessary. In addition, the air gap between the signal rotor and the projection on the pickup coil should be checked periodically.

Diagnosis and Testing

If ignition problems or a no start condition are encountered, first preform an "On Vehicle Inspection Spark Test". Check that spark occurs--if no spark occurs follow the correct diagnostic flow chart (engine and year) and necessary service procedures.

ON VEHICLE INSPECTION SPARK TEST

1. On 4A-FE and 7A-FE engines, tag and disconnect the spark plug wires from the spark plugs. Remove the spark plugs and install the spark plug wires to each

spark plug. Ground (do not hold spark plug) the spark plug--check if spark occurs while engine is being cranked.

2. On 4A-GE engine disconnect the coil wire from distributor. Hold the coil wire end about ½ inch from a good body ground--check if spark occurs while engine is being cranked.

NOTE: *Crank the engine for no more than 2 seconds at a time to prevent flooding the engine with gasoline.*

3. If good spark does not occur, follow the correct diagnostic flow chart (engine and year) and necessary service procedures.

PRIMARY COIL RESISTANCE TEST

4A-FE and 7A-FE Engines

1. Using a suitable ohmmeter, measure the resistance between the positive and negative terminals.

2. The primary coil resistance (cold) should be 1.28–1.56 ohms on 1990–91 models or 1.1–1.7 ohms on 1992–93 models.

3. If the resistance is not within specifications, replace the ignition coil.

4A-GE Engine

1. Using a suitable ohmmeter, measure the resistance between the positive and negative terminals.

2. The primary coil resistance (cold) should be 0.4–0.5 ohms.

3. If the resistance is not within specifications, replace the ignition coil.

SECONDARY COIL RESISTANCE TEST

4A-FE and 7A-FE Engines

1. Using a suitable ohmmeter, measure the resistance between the positive terminal and the high tension terminal.

2. The secondary coil resistance (cold) should be 10.4–14.0 kilo-ohms on 1990–91 models or 9–15 kilo-ohms on 1992–93 models.

3. If not within specifications, replace the ignition coil.

4A-GE Engine

1. Using a suitable ohmmeter, measure the resistance between the positive terminal and the high tension terminal.

2. The secondary coil resistance (cold) should be 10.2–13.8 kilo-ohms.

3. If not within specifications, replace the ignition coil.

SIGNAL GENERATOR (PICK-UP) RESISTANCE TEST

4A-FE and 7A-FE Engines

1. Using a suitable ohmmeter, check the resistance between terminals G1 and G- and NE and G- of the signal generator.

2. The signal generator (pick-up coil) resistance cold should be 205–255 ohms on 1990–91 models or 185–265 ohms on 1992–93 models.

3. If the resistance is not correct, replace the distributor housing.

4A-GE Engine

1. Using a suitable ohmmeter, check the resistance of the two signal generators between terminals G+ and G- and NE+ and NE- of the signal generator.

2. The two signal generators resistance should be 205–255 ohms.

3. If the resistance is not correct, replace the distributor housing.

SIGNAL GENERATOR AIR-GAP INSPECTION

1. Remove the distributor cap.

2. Measure the gap between the signal rotor and the pick-up coil projection, by using a non-ferrous feeler gauge (use paper, brass or plastic gauge).

3. The air gap should be 0.008–0.0016 in. (0.2–0.4mm).

4. If the air gap is not correct, replace the distributor housing.

IGNITER TEST

To test the igniter preform the"On Vehicle Inspection Spark Test". Check that spark occurs. If no spark occurs follow the correct diagnostic flow chart and necessary service procedures.

Adjustments

The air gap is non-adjustable. Should it be out of specification, the entire distributor must be replaced.

Parts Replacement

On the 1990–91 vehicles with a 4A-GE engine the distributor that is used is not serviceable aside from distributor cap and distributor rotor. Any failed item in the distributor requires replacement of the complete unit.

On the 1990–93 vehicles with the 4A-FE and 7A-FE engines an Integrated Ignition Assembly (IIA) type distributor is

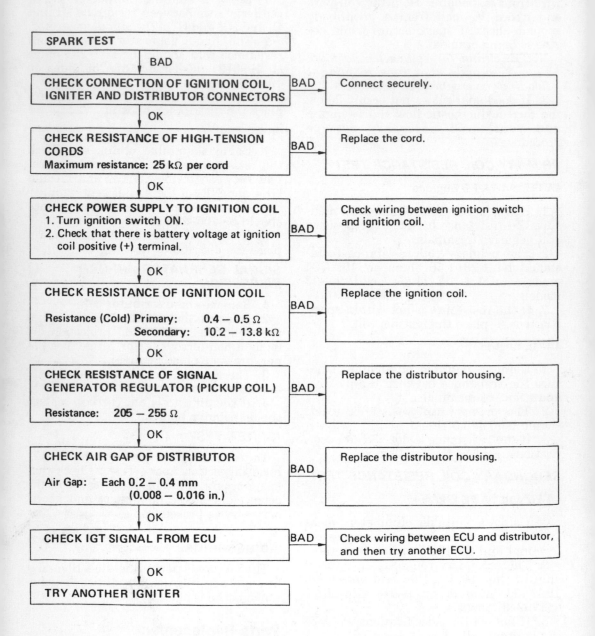

SPARK TEST		
↓ BAD		
CHECK CONNECTION OF IGNITION COIL, IGNITER AND DISTRIBUTOR CONNECTORS	BAD →	Connect securely.
↓ OK		
CHECK RESISTANCE OF HIGH-TENSION CORDS Maximum resistance: 25 kΩ per cord	BAD →	Replace the cord.
↓ OK		
CHECK POWER SUPPLY TO IGNITION COIL 1. Turn ignition switch ON. 2. Check that there is battery voltage at ignition coil positive (+) terminal.	BAD →	Check wiring between ignition switch and ignition coil.
↓ OK		
CHECK RESISTANCE OF IGNITION COIL Resistance (Cold) Primary: 0.4 − 0.5 Ω Secondary: 10.2 − 13.8 kΩ	BAD →	Replace the ignition coil.
↓ OK		
CHECK RESISTANCE OF SIGNAL GENERATOR REGULATOR (PICKUP COIL) Resistance: 205 − 255 Ω	BAD →	Replace the distributor housing.
↓ OK		
CHECK AIR GAP OF DISTRIBUTOR Air Gap: Each 0.2 − 0.4 mm (0.008 − 0.016 in.)	BAD →	Replace the distributor housing.
↓ OK		
CHECK IGT SIGNAL FROM ECU	BAD →	Check wiring between ECU and distributor, and then try another ECU.
↓ OK		
TRY ANOTHER IGNITER		

84342010

Spark Test — 1990–91 4A-GE engine

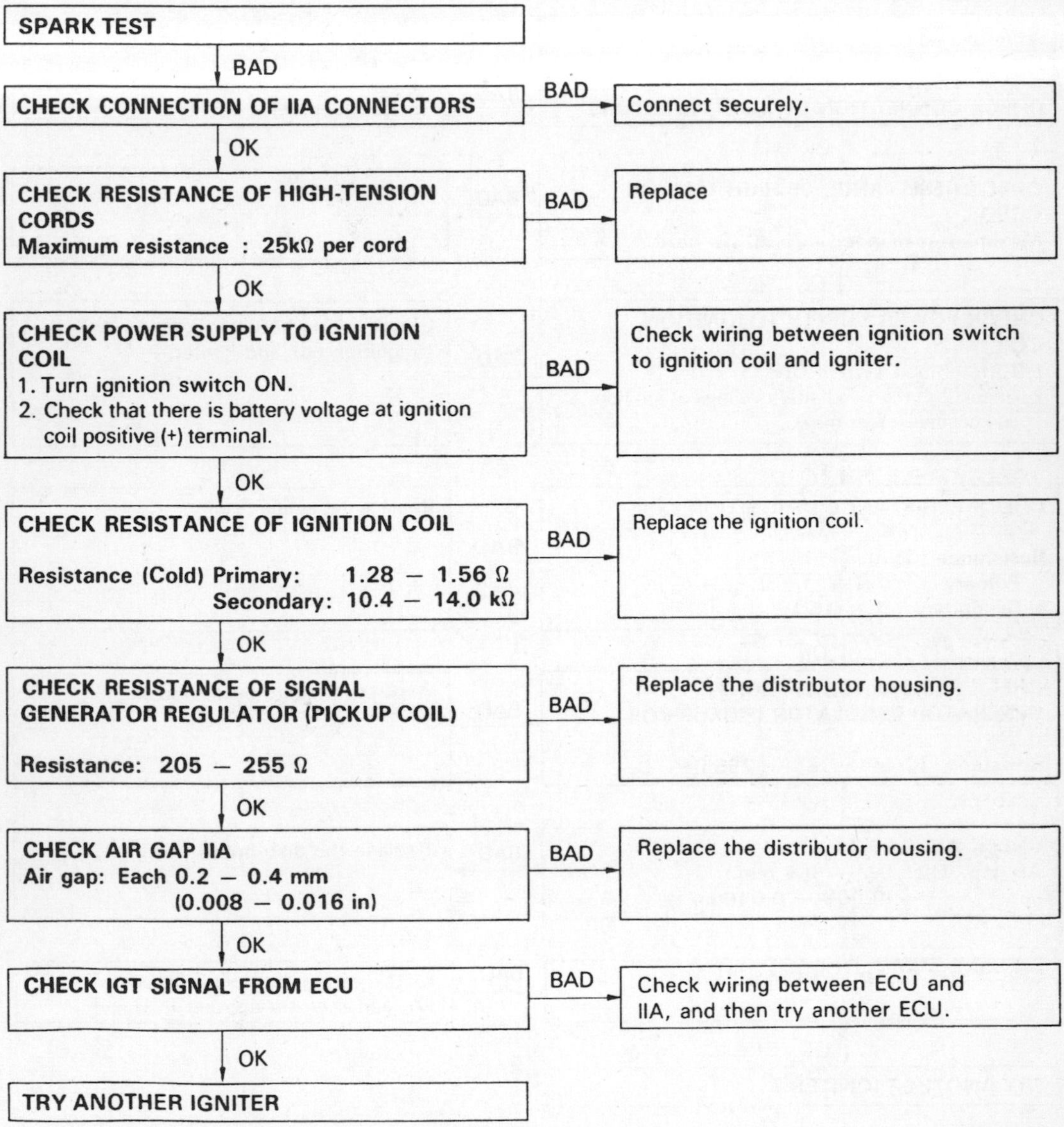

SPARK TEST		

↓ BAD

CHECK CONNECTION OF IIA CONNECTORS	BAD →	Connect securely.

↓ OK

CHECK RESISTANCE OF HIGH-TENSION CORDS **Maximum resistance : 25kΩ per cord**	BAD →	Replace

↓ OK

CHECK POWER SUPPLY TO IGNITION COIL 1. Turn ignition switch ON. 2. Check that there is battery voltage at ignition coil positive (+) terminal.	BAD →	Check wiring between ignition switch to ignition coil and igniter.

↓ OK

CHECK RESISTANCE OF IGNITION COIL **Resistance (Cold) Primary: 1.28 — 1.56 Ω** **Secondary: 10.4 — 14.0 kΩ**	BAD →	Replace the ignition coil.

↓ OK

CHECK RESISTANCE OF SIGNAL GENERATOR REGULATOR (PICKUP COIL) **Resistance: 205 — 255 Ω**	BAD →	Replace the distributor housing.

↓ OK

CHECK AIR GAP IIA **Air gap: Each 0.2 — 0.4 mm** ** (0.008 — 0.016 in)**	BAD →	Replace the distributor housing.

↓ OK

CHECK IGT SIGNAL FROM ECU	BAD →	Check wiring between ECU and IIA, and then try another ECU.

↓ OK

TRY ANOTHER IGNITER		

84342011

Spark Test — 1990–91 4A-FE engine

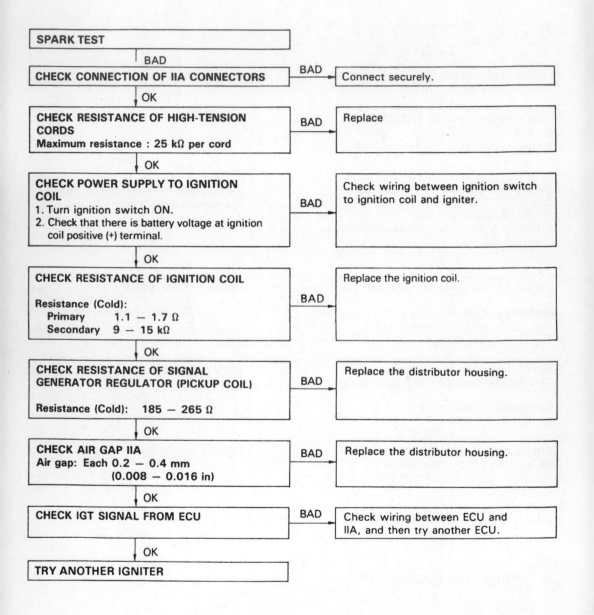

SPARK TEST	
↓ BAD	
CHECK CONNECTION OF IIA CONNECTORS	BAD → Connect securely.
↓ OK	
CHECK RESISTANCE OF HIGH-TENSION CORDS Maximum resistance : 25 kΩ per cord	BAD → Replace
↓ OK	
CHECK POWER SUPPLY TO IGNITION COIL 1. Turn ignition switch ON. 2. Check that there is battery voltage at ignition coil positive (+) terminal.	BAD → Check wiring between ignition switch to ignition coil and igniter.
↓ OK	

CHECK RESISTANCE OF IGNITION COIL
 	
Resistance (Cold):
  Primary   1.1 — 1.7 Ω
  Secondary   9 — 15 kΩ
	BAD → Replace the ignition coil.

↓ OK	
CHECK RESISTANCE OF SIGNAL GENERATOR REGULATOR (PICKUP COIL) Resistance (Cold): 185 — 265 Ω	BAD → Replace the distributor housing.
↓ OK	
CHECK AIR GAP IIA Air gap: Each 0.2 — 0.4 mm (0.008 — 0.016 in)	BAD → Replace the distributor housing.
↓ OK	
CHECK IGT SIGNAL FROM ECU	BAD → Check wiring between ECU and IIA, and then try another ECU.
↓ OK	
TRY ANOTHER IGNITER	

84342012

Spark Test — 1992–93 4A-FE and 7A-FE engines

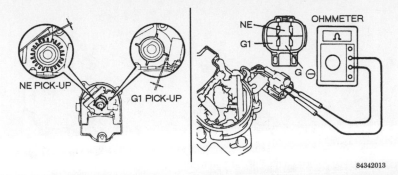

84342013

Inspection of air gap and pick-up coil resistance test — 4A-FE and 7A-FE engines

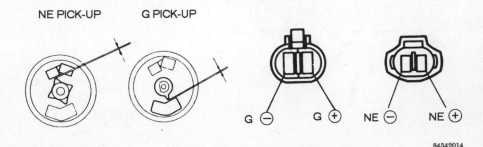

84342014

Inspection of air gap and pick-up coil resistance test — 4A-GE engine

used. On IIA type distributor assembly the distributor cap, distributor rotor, ignition coil and igniter assembly are serviceable. In most cases, removal of the IIA type distributor assembly from the engine is necessary.

INTEGRATED IGNITION ASSEMBLY

Disassembly and Assembly

1. Remove the distributor as outlined in Chapter 3. Make certain the negative battery cable is disconnected before beginning the work.

2. Remove the distributor rotor.

3. Remove the dust cover over the distributor components and remove the dust cover over the ignition coil.

4. Remove the nuts and disconnect the wiring from the ignition coil.

5. Remove the 4 screws and remove the ignition coil and gasket from the distributor.

6. At the igniter terminals, disconnect the wiring from the connecting points.

7. Loosen and remove the two screws holding the igniter and remove it from the distributor.

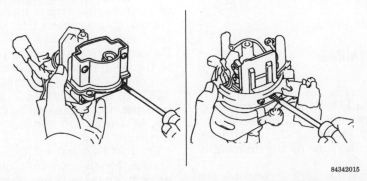

84342015

Removing the coil (top) and the igniter (bottom) — Integrated Ignition Assembly

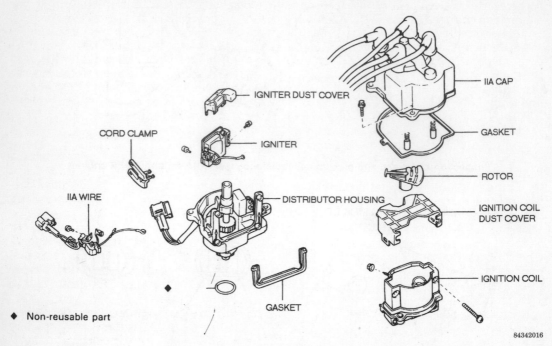

CORD CLAMP

IGNITER DUST COVER

IGNITER

IIA CAP

GASKET

ROTOR

IIA WIRE

DISTRIBUTOR HOUSING

IGNITION COIL
DUST COVER

IGNITION COIL

◆ Non-reusable part

GASKET

84342016

Exploded view — Integrated Ignition Assembly

To install:

8. Install the igniter and connect its wiring. Pay particular attention to the correct routing of the wiring within the housing. There is one correct position only; any other wiring placements risk damage.

9. Install the ignition coil and gasket and secure its wiring. Again, watch the wiring positions.

10. Reinstall the dust covers and distributor rotor.

11. Reinstall the distributor and set the engine timing.

IGNITION TIMING

Ignition timing is the measurement (in degrees) of crankshaft position at the instant the spark plug fires. Ignition timing is adjusted by loosening the distributor locking device and turning the distributor in the engine.

It takes a fraction of a second for the spark from the plug to completely ignite the mixture in the cylinder. Because of this, the spark plug must fire before the piston reaches TDC (top dead center, the highest point in its travel), if the mixture is to be completely ignited as the piston passes TDC. This measurement is given in degrees (of crankshaft rotation) before the piston reaches top dead center (BTDC). If the ignition timing setting for your engine is 7° BTDC, this means that the spark plug must fire at a time when the piston for that cylinder is 7° before top dead center of its compression stroke. However, this only holds true while your engine is at idle speed.

As you accelerate from idle, the speed of your engine (rpm) increases. The increase in rpm means that the pistons are now traveling up and down much faster. Because of this, the spark plugs will have to fire even sooner if the mixture is to be completely ignited as the piston passes TDC. To accomplish this, the distributor incorporates means to advance the timing of the spark as the engine speed increases.

On fuel injected vehicles (All 1990–93 Toyota Corolla's are fuel injected) there is no centrifugal advance or vacuum unit to advance the timing. All engine timing changes are controlled electronically by the ECU. This solid state "brain" ECU receives data from many sensors and commands changes in spark timing based on immediate driving conditions. This instant response allows the engine to be kept at peak performance and economy throughout the driving cycle. Basic timing and idle speed can still be checked and adjusted on these engines.

If the ignition timing is set too far advanced (BTDC), the ignition and expansion of the air/fuel mixture in the cylinder will try to force the piston down while it is still traveling upward. This causes engine ping, a sound which resembles marbles being dropped into an empty tin can. If the ignition timing is too far retarded (after, or ATDC), the piston will have already started down on the power stroke when the air/fuel mixture ignites and expands. This will cause the piston to be forced down only a portion of its travel. This results in poor engine performance and lack of power.

Ignition timing adjustment is checked with a timing light. This instrument is connected to the number one (No. 1) spark plug of the engine. The timing light flashes every time an electrical current is sent from the distributor through the No. 1 spark plug wire to the spark plug. The crankshaft pulley and the front cover of the engine are marked with a timing pointer and a timing scale.

When the timing pointer is aligned with the 0 mark on the timing scale, the piston in the No. 1 cylinder is at TDC of it compression stroke. With the engine running, and the timing light aimed at the timing pointer and timing scale, the stroboscopic (periodic) flashes from the timing light will allow you to check the ignition timing setting of the engine. The timing light flashes every time the spark plug in the No. 1 cylinder of the engine fires. Since the flash from the timing light makes the crankshaft pulley seem to stand still for a moment, you will be able to read the exact position of the piston in the No. 1 cylinder on the timing scale on the front of the engine.

If you're buying a timing light, make sure the unit you select is rated for electronic or solid-state ignitions. Generally, these lights have two wires which connect to the battery with alligator clips and a third wire which connects to the No. 1 plug wire. The best lights have an inductive pick-up on the third wire; this allows you to simply clip the small box over the wire. Older lights may require the removal of the plug wire and the installation of an in-line adapter. Since the spark plugs in the twin-cam engines (4A-GE and 4A-FE) are in deep wells, rigging the adapter can be difficult. Buy quality the first time and the tool will give lasting results and ease of use.

CHECKING AND ADJUSTMENT

This service procedure is for setting base ignition timing. Refer to underhood emission sticker for any additional service procedure steps and/or specifications.

These engines require a tachometer hook-up to the check connector — see illustrations. NEVER allow the tachometer terminal to become grounded; severe and expensive damage can occur to the coil and/or igniter.

Some tachometers are not compatible with this ignition system, confirm the compatibility of your unit before using.

1. Warm the engine to normal operating temperature. Turn off all electrical accessories. Do not attempt to check timing specification or idle speed on a cold engine.

2. Connect a tachometer (connect the tachometer (+) terminal to the terminal IG- of the check connector) and check the engine idle speed to be sure it is within the specification given in the Tune-Up Specifications chart or underhood emission sticker.

3. Remove the cap on the diagnostic check connector. Using a small jumper wire or Special Service Tool SST 09843-18020, short terminals TE1 (test terminal No. 1) and E1 (earth-ground) together.

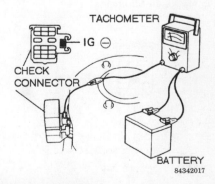

Tachometer installation

4. If the timing marks are difficult to see, shut the engine off and use a dab of paint or chalk to make them more visible.

5. Connect a timing light according to the manufacturer's instructions.

6. Start the engine and use the timing light to observe the timing marks. With the jumper wire in the check connector the timing should be to specifications (refer to underhood emission sticker as necessary) with the engine fully warmed up (at correct idle speed) and the transmission in correct position. If the timing is not correct, loosen the bolts at the distrib-

84342019

Ignition timing marks 4A-GE engine — note the small notch on the pulley, this is the mark to align with the degree scale

84342020

Timing marks 4A-FE engine

utor just enough so that the distributor can be turned. Turn the distributor to advance or retard the timing as required. Once the proper marks are seen to align with the timing light, timing is correct.

7. Without changing the position of the distributor, tighten the distributor bolts and double check the timing with the light (check idle speed as necessary).

8. Disconnect the jumper wire or Special Service Tool (SST) at the diagnostic check connector.

9. Refer to the underhood emission sticker for timing specification and any additional service procedure steps. If necessary, repeat the timing adjustment procedure.

10. Shut the engine off and disconnect all test equipment. Roadtest the vehicle for proper operation.

VALVE LASH

NOTE: *Check and adjust the valve clearance every 60,000 miles or 72 months.*

Valve clearance is one factor which determines how far the intake and exhaust valves will open into the cylinder. If the valve clearance is too large, part of the lift of the camshaft will be used up in removing the excessive clearance, thus the valves will not be opened far enough. This condition has two effects, the valve train components will emit a tapping noise as they take up the excessive clearance, and the engine will perform poorly, since the less the intake valve opens, the smaller the amount of air/fuel mixture that will be admitted to the cylinders. The less the exhaust valves open, the greater the back-pressure in the cylinder

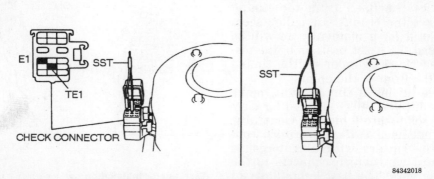

84342018

Check connector and SST tool for base timing adjustment

which prevents the proper air/fuel mixture from entering the cylinder.

If the valve clearance is too small, the intake and exhaust valves will not fully seat on the cylinder head when they close. When a valve seats on the cylinder head it does two things, it seals the combustion chamber so none of the gases in the cylinder can escape and it cools itself by transferring some of the heat it absorbed from the combustion process through the cylinder head and into the engine cooling system. Therefore, if the valve clearance is too small, the engine will run poorly due to gases escaping from the combustion chamber, and the valves will overheat and warp since they cannot transfer heat unless they are touching the seat in the cylinder head.

ADJUSTMENT

NOTE: *The use of the correct special tools or their equivalent is REQUIRED for this procedure. The valve adjustment requires removal of the adjusting shims (Tool kit J–37141 available from Kent-Moore Tool or a Toyota equivalent No. 09248–55010) and accurate measurement of the shims with a micrometer. A selection of replacement shims (refer to parts department of your Toyota dealer) is also required. Do not attempt this procedure if you are not equipped with the proper tools. Valves on these engines are adjusted with the engine cold. Do not attempt adjustment if the engine has been run within the previous 4 hours. An overnight cooling period is recommended.*

1. Remove the valve cover following procedures discussed in Chapter 3.

2. Turn the crankshaft to align the groove in the crankshaft pulley with the **0** mark on the timing belt cover. Removing the spark plugs makes this easier, but is not required.

3. Check that the lifters on No.1 cylinder are loose and those on No.4 are tight. If not, turn the crankshaft pulley one full revolution (360°).

4. Using the feeler gauge, measure the clearance on the valves in the positions shown in the diagram labeled First Pass. Make a written record of any measurements which are not within specification.

5. Rotate the crankshaft pulley one full turn (360°) and check the clearance on the other valves. The positions are

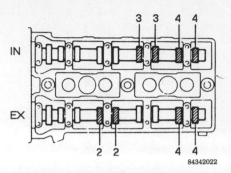

Second Pass-checking valve clearance

shown on the diagram labeled Second Pass. Any measurements not within specification should be added to your written record.

6. For ANY given valve needing adjustment:

a. Turn the crankshaft pulley until the camshaft lobe points upward over the valve. This takes the tension off the valve and spring.

b. Using the forked tool, press the valve lifter downward and hold it there. Some tool kits require a second tool for holding the lifter in place, allowing the first to be removed.

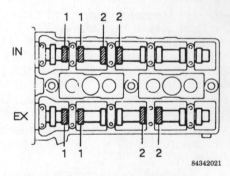

First Pass-checking valve clearance

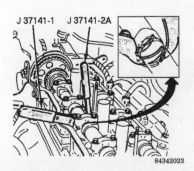

Use the correct tools to depress and hold down the valve lifter

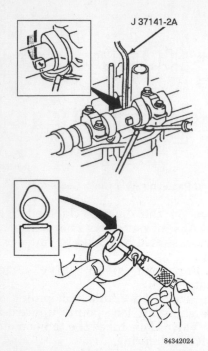

J 37141-2A

84342024

Remove the shim to be replaced (above) with a small screwdriver and magnetic tools-clean and dry the shim before measuring with a micrometer (below).

c. Using small magnetic tools, remove the adjusting shim from the top of the lifter.

d. Use the micrometer and measure the thickness of the shim removed. Determine the thickness of the new shim using the formula below or the selection charts. For the purposes of the following formula, T = Thickness of the old shim; A = Valve clearance measured; N = Thickness of the new shim

- Intake side (camshaft nearest intake manifold): N = T + (A - 0.20mm (0.008 in.))

- Exhaust side (camshaft nearest exhaust manifold): N = T + (A - 0.25mm (0.010 in.)

7. Select a shim closest to the calculated thickness. Use the lifter depressor tool to press down the lifter and install the shim. Shims are available in 17 sizes from 2.50mm to 3.30mm. The standard increment is 0.05mm.

8. Repeat steps a through e for each valve needing adjustment.

9. Reinstall the valve cover, following the procedures outlined in Section 3.

10. Check and adjust the timing and idle speed, following the procedures out-lined in this section. Road test the vehicle for proper operation.

IDLE SPEED AND MIXTURE ADJUSTMENT

HOT IDLE SPEED ADJUSTMENT

Follow the correct service adjustment procedure for your engine. Review the complete procedure before starting.

One of the merits of electronic fuel injection is that it requires so little adjustment. The computer (ECM) does most of the work in compensating for changes in climate, engine temperature, electrical load and driving conditions. The idle on the fuel injected engines should be checked periodically (15,000 miles or 24 months) but not adjusted unless out of specifications by more than 50 rpm.

The idle speed adjusting screw is located on the side of the throttle body. You can find the the throttle body by following the accelerator cable to its end. The adjusting screw may have a cap over it. If so, pop the cap off with a small screwdriver.

If for any reason the idle cannot be brought into specification by this adjustment procedure, return the screw to its original setting and follow other diagnostic procedures to find the real cause of the problem. Do not try to cure other problems with this adjustment.

4A-FE and 7A-FE Engines

This engine requires a tachometer hook-up to the check connector-see illustrations. NEVER allow the tachometer terminal to become grounded; severe and expensive damage can occur to the coil and/or igniter. Some tachometers are not compatible with this ignition system, confirm the compatibility of your unit before using.

1. Idle speed adjustment is performed under the following conditions:

Engine at normal operating temperature.

Air cleaner installed.

Air pipes and hoses of the air induction and EGR systems properly connected.

All vacuum lines and electrical wires connected and plugged in properly.

All electrical accessories in the **OFF** position.

Transaxle in the **N** position.

Intake

Shim selection chart — Installed Shim Thickness (mm)

Column headers (Installed Shim Thickness, mm): 2.500, 2.525, 2.550, 2.575, 2.600, 2.620, 2.640, 2.650, 2.680, 2.700, 2.720, 2.740, 2.760, 2.780, 2.800, 2.820, 2.840, 2.850, 2.860, 2.880, 2.900, 2.920, 2.940, 2.950, 2.960, 2.980, 3.000, 3.020, 3.040, 3.050, 3.060, 3.080, 3.100, 3.120, 3.140, 3.150, 3.160, 3.180, 3.200, 3.225, 3.250, 3.275, 3.300

Measured Clearance (mm) rows:

Measured Clearance (mm)
0.000 – 0.009
0.010 – 0.025
0.026 – 0.029
0.030 – 0.040
0.041 – 0.050
0.051 – 0.070
0.071 – 0.075
0.076 – 0.090
0.091 – 0.100
0.101 – 0.120
0.121 – 0.125
0.126 – 0.140
0.141 – 0.149
0.150 – 0.250
0.251 – 0.270
0.271 – 0.275
0.276 – 0.290
0.291 – 0.300
0.301 – 0.320
0.321 – 0.325
0.326 – 0.340
0.341 – 0.350
0.351 – 0.370
0.371 – 0.375
0.376 – 0.390
0.391 – 0.400
0.401 – 0.420
0.421 – 0.425
0.426 – 0.440
0.441 – 0.450
0.451 – 0.470
0.471 – 0.475
0.476 – 0.490
0.491 – 0.500
0.501 – 0.520
0.521 – 0.525
0.526 – 0.540
0.541 – 0.550
0.551 – 0.570
0.571 – 0.575
0.576 – 0.590
0.591 – 0.600
0.601 – 0.620
0.621 – 0.625
0.626 – 0.640
0.641 – 0.650
0.651 – 0.670
0.671 – 0.675
0.676 – 0.690
0.691 – 0.700
0.701 – 0.720
0.721 – 0.725
0.726 – 0.740
0.741 – 0.750
0.751 – 0.770
0.771 – 0.775
0.776 – 0.790
0.791 – 0.800
0.801 – 0.820
0.821 – 0.825
0.826 – 0.840
0.841 – 0.850
0.851 – 0.870
0.871 – 0.875
0.876 – 0.890
0.891 – 0.900
0.901 – 0.925
0.926 – 0.950
0.951 – 0.975
0.976 – 1.000
1.001 – 1.025

Shim thickness — mm (in.)

Shim No.	Thickness	Shim No.	Thickness
02	2.500 (0.0984)	20	2.950 (0.1161)
04	2.550 (0.1004)	22	3.000 (0.1181)
06	2.600 (0.1024)	24	3.050 (0.1201)
08	2.650 (0.1043)	26	3.100 (0.1220)
10	2.700 (0.1063)	28	3.150 (0.1240)
12	2.750 (0.1083)	30	3.200 (0.1260)
14	2.800 (0.1102)	32	3.250 (0.1280)
16	2.850 (0.1122)	34	3.300 (0.1299)
18	2.900 (0.1142)		

Intake valve clearance (cold):
0.15 – 0.25 mm (0.006 – 0.010 in.)

Example: A 2.800 mm shim is installed
and the measured clearance
is 0.450 mm.
Replace the 2.800 mm shim
with shim No. 24 (3.050 mm).

84342025

Shim selection chart

Exhaust

Shim selection chart — Installed Shim Thickness (mm)

Measured Clearance (mm)	Installed Shim Thickness (mm)
0 000 – 0 009	02 02 02 04 04 04 06 06 06 08 08 08 10 10 10 12 12 14 14 14 16 16 18 18 18 18 20 20 22 22 24 24
0 010 – 0 025	02 02 04 04 06 06 06 08 08 08 10 10 10 12 12 14 14 14 16 16 18 18 18 20 20 22 22 22 24 24 26
0 026 – 0 040	02 02 02 04 04 04 06 06 06 08 08 08 10 10 10 12 12 14 14 14 16 16 18 18 18 20 20 20 22 22 24 24 26
0 041 – 0 050	02 02 04 04 04 06 06 06 08 08 08 10 10 10 12 12 14 14 14 16 16 18 18 18 20 20 22 22 22 24 24 26 26
0 051 – 0 070	02 02 04 04 04 06 06 06 08 08 08 10 10 10 12 12 12 14 14 16 16 16 18 18 20 20 20 22 22 24 24 26 26
0 071 – 0 090	02 02 04 04 04 06 06 06 08 08 08 10 10 12 12 14 14 14 16 16 16 18 18 20 20 22 22 22 24 24 26 26
0 091 – 0 100	02 02 02 04 04 04 06 06 06 08 08 08 10 10 12 12 12 14 14 14 16 16 18 18 18 20 20 22 22 24 24 26 26
0 101 – 0 120	02 02 02 04 04 06 06 06 08 08 08 10 10 10 12 12 14 14 14 16 16 18 18 18 20 20 22 22 22 24 24 26 28 28
0 121 – 0 140	02 02 02 04 04 04 06 06 06 08 08 08 10 10 10 12 12 14 14 14 16 16 16 18 18 20 20 22 22 24 24 26 26 28 28
0 141 – 0 150	02 02 04 04 04 06 06 06 08 08 08 10 10 10 12 12 14 14 14 16 16 18 18 20 20 20 22 22 24 24 26 26 28 28 30
0 151 – 0 170	02 02 04 04 04 06 06 06 08 08 08 10 10 10 12 12 12 14 14 16 16 18 18 20 20 22 22 24 24 26 26 28 28 30 30
0 171 – 0 190	02 02 04 04 04 06 06 06 08 08 08 10 10 10 12 12 14 14 14 16 16 18 18 20 20 20 22 22 24 24 26 26 28 28 30 30 32
0 191 – 0 199	02 02 04 04 06 06 06 08 08 08 10 10 10 12 12 12 14 14 16 16 16 18 18 20 20 20 22 22 24 24 26 26 28 28 30 30 32
0 200 – 0 300	
0 301 – 0 320	04 06 06 08 08 10 10 10 12 12 14 14 14 16 16 16 18 18 18 20 20 22 22 22 24 24 26 26 26 28 28 30 30 30 32 32 34
0 321 – 0 325	04 06 06 08 08 08 10 10 12 12 12 14 14 16 16 16 18 18 18 20 20 22 22 22 24 24 26 26 28 28 28 30 30 30 32 32 34 34
0 326 – 0 340	06 06 08 08 10 10 10 12 12 12 14 14 16 16 16 18 18 20 20 22 22 22 24 24 24 26 26 28 28 30 30 30 32 32 34 34
0 341 – 0 350	06 06 08 08 10 10 12 12 12 14 14 14 16 16 18 18 18 20 20 20 22 22 24 24 24 26 26 28 28 28 30 30 32 32 32 34 34
0 351 – 0 370	06 08 08 10 10 12 12 12 14 14 14 16 16 16 18 18 18 20 20 22 22 24 24 24 26 26 28 28 28 30 30 32 32 32 34 34
0 371 – 0 375	06 08 08 10 10 12 12 12 14 14 14 16 16 16 18 18 20 20 20 22 22 24 24 24 26 26 26 28 28 30 30 30 32 32 32 34 34
0 376 – 0 390	08 08 10 10 12 12 12 14 14 14 16 16 18 18 18 20 20 22 22 22 24 24 26 26 26 28 28 28 30 30 30 32 32 34 34 34
0 391 – 0 400	08 08 10 10 12 12 14 14 14 16 16 16 18 18 20 20 22 22 22 24 24 26 26 26 28 28 30 30 30 32 32 32 34 34 34
0 401 – 0 420	08 10 10 12 12 14 14 14 16 16 18 18 18 20 20 22 22 24 24 24 26 26 28 28 28 30 30 30 32 32 34 34 34
0 421 – 0 425	08 10 10 12 12 14 14 14 16 16 16 18 18 20 20 20 22 22 24 24 24 26 26 28 28 28 30 30 32 32 32 34 34 34
0 426 – 0 440	10 10 12 12 14 14 14 16 16 18 18 18 20 20 20 22 22 24 24 24 26 26 28 28 28 30 30 30 32 32 34 34 34
0 441 – 0 450	10 10 12 12 14 14 16 16 16 18 18 20 20 20 22 22 24 24 24 26 26 28 28 28 30 30 30 32 32 32 34 34 34
0 451 – 0 470	10 12 12 14 14 16 16 16 18 18 20 20 20 22 22 24 24 26 26 28 28 28 30 30 30 32 32 32 34 34
0 471 – 0 475	10 12 12 14 14 16 16 18 18 18 20 20 22 22 22 24 24 26 26 28 28 28 30 30 30 32 32 34 34 34
0 476 – 0 490	12 12 14 14 16 16 16 18 18 20 20 22 22 22 24 24 26 26 28 28 28 30 30 30 32 32 34 34 34
0 491 – 0 500	12 12 14 14 16 16 18 18 18 20 20 22 22 22 24 24 26 26 26 28 28 30 30 30 32 32 32 34 34
0 501 – 0 520	12 14 14 16 16 18 18 18 20 20 22 22 22 24 24 26 26 28 28 30 30 30 32 32 34 34 34
0 521 – 0 525	12 14 14 16 16 18 18 18 20 20 22 22 22 24 24 26 26 28 28 30 30 30 32 32 34 34 34
0 526 – 0 540	14 14 16 16 18 18 18 20 20 22 22 24 24 24 26 26 28 28 30 30 30 32 32 34 34 34
0 541 – 0 550	14 14 16 16 18 18 20 20 20 22 22 24 24 24 26 26 28 28 28 30 30 32 32 32 34 34
0 551 – 0 570	14 16 16 18 18 20 20 20 22 22 24 24 24 26 26 28 28 28 30 30 30 32 32 34 34 34
0 571 – 0 575	14 16 16 18 18 20 20 20 22 22 24 24 24 26 26 28 28 30 30 30 32 32 34 34 34
0 576 – 0 590	16 16 18 18 20 20 20 22 22 24 24 24 26 26 28 28 30 30 30 32 32 34 34 34
0 591 – 0 600	16 16 18 18 20 20 22 22 22 24 24 26 26 26 28 28 30 30 30 32 32 34 34 34
0 601 – 0 620	16 18 18 20 20 22 22 22 24 24 26 26 26 28 28 30 30 30 32 32 34 34 34
0 621 – 0 625	16 18 18 20 20 22 22 22 24 24 26 26 28 28 30 30 30 32 32 34 34 34
0 626 – 0 640	18 18 20 20 22 22 22 24 24 26 26 28 28 30 30 30 32 32 32 34 34 34
0 641 – 0 650	18 18 20 20 22 22 24 24 24 26 26 28 28 30 30 32 32 32 34 34
0 651 – 0 670	18 20 20 22 22 24 24 24 26 26 28 28 30 30 30 32 32 32 34 34
0 671 – 0 675	18 20 20 22 22 22 24 24 26 26 28 28 30 30 30 32 32 34 34
0 676 – 0 690	20 20 22 22 24 24 24 26 26 28 28 30 30 30 32 32 34 34 34
0 691 – 0 700	20 20 22 22 24 24 26 26 26 28 28 30 30 30 32 32 34 34 34
0 701 – 0 720	20 22 22 24 24 26 26 26 28 28 30 30 32 32 32 34 34
0 721 – 0 725	20 22 22 24 24 26 26 28 28 28 30 30 32 32 32 34 34
0 726 – 0 740	22 22 24 24 26 26 26 28 28 30 30 32 32 32 34 34
0 741 – 0 750	22 22 24 24 26 26 28 28 28 30 30 32 32 32 34 34
0 751 – 0 770	22 22 24 24 26 26 28 28 28 30 30 32 32 32 34 34
0 771 – 0 775	22 24 24 26 26 28 28 28 30 30 32 32 32 34 34
0 776 – 0 790	24 24 26 26 28 28 30 30 30 32 32 32 34 34 34
0 791 – 0 800	24 24 26 26 28 28 30 30 30 32 32 34 34 34
0 801 – 0 820	24 26 26 28 28 30 30 30 32 32 34 34 34
0 821 – 0 825	24 26 26 28 28 30 30 30 32 32 32 34 34
0 826 – 0 840	26 26 28 28 30 30 30 32 32 32 34 34
0 841 – 0 850	26 26 28 28 30 30 32 32 32 34 34
0 851 – 0 870	26 28 28 30 30 32 32 32 34 34
0 871 – 0 875	26 28 28 30 30 32 32 32 34 34
0 876 – 0 890	28 28 30 30 32 32 32 34 34 34
0 891 – 0 900	28 28 30 30 32 32 34 34 34
0 901 – 0 925	28 30 30 32 32 34 34 34
0 926 – 0 950	30 30 32 32 34 34
0 951 – 0 975	30 32 32 34 34
0 976 – 1 000	32 32 34 34
1 001 – 1 025	32 34 34
1 026 – 1 050	34 34
1 051 – 1 075	34

Shim thickness mm (in.)

Shim No.	Thickness	Shim No.	Thickness
02	2.500 (0.0984)	20	2.950 (0.1161)
04	2.550 (0.1004)	22	3.000 (0.1181)
06	2.600 (0.1024)	24	3.050 (0.1201)
08	2.650 (0.1043)	26	3.100 (0.1220)
10	2.700 (0.1063)	28	3.150 (0.1240)
12	2.750 (0.1083)	30	3.200 (0.1260)
14	2.800 (0.1102)	32	3.250 (0.1280)
16	2.850 (0.1122)	34	3.300 (0.1299)
18	2.900 (0.1142)		

Exhaust valve clearance (cold):
0.20 – 0.30 mm (0.008 – 0.012 in.)

Example: A 2.800 mm shim is installed
and the measured clearance
is 0.450 mm.
Replace the 2.800 mm shim
with shim No. 22 (3.000 mm).

84342026

Shim selection chart

2. Connect a tachometer to the engine. Connect the probe of the tachometer to terminal IG- of the check connector.

3. Run the engine at 2500 rpm for 90 seconds.

4. Short the check connector at terminals **TE1** and **E1** using a suitable jumper wire or special service tool.

5. Adjust the idle speed by turning the idle speed adjusting screw to specification.

NOTE: *Refer to underhood emission sticker to confirm idle speed specification. Always follow the emission sticker specification.*

6. Remove the jumper wire or special service tool from the connector terminals.

7. Disconnect the tachometer. Road test the vehicle for proper operation.

4A-GE Engine

NOTE: *This engine requires a tachometer hook-up to the check connector-see illustrations. NEVER allow the tachometer terminal to become grounded; severe and expensive damage can occur to the coil and/or igniter. Some tachometers are not compatible with this ignition system, confirm the compatibility of your unit before using.*

1. Idle speed adjustment is performed under the following conditions:

Engine at normal operating temperature.

Air cleaner installed.

Air pipes and hoses of the air induction and EGR systems properly connected.

All vacuum lines and electrical wires connected and plugged in properly.

All electrical accessories in the **OFF** position.

Transaxle in the **N** position.

2. Connect a tachometer to the engine. Connect the probe of the tachometer to terminal IG- of the check connector.

3. Run the engine at 2500 rpm for 90 seconds.

4. Adjust the idle speed by turning the idle speed adjusting screw to specification.

NOTE: *Refer to underhood emission sticker to confirm idle speed specification. Always follow the emission sticker specification.*

5. Disconnect the tachometer. Road test the vehicle for proper operation.

MIXTURE ADJUSTMENT

The air/fuel ratio burned within the engine is controlled by the ECM, based on

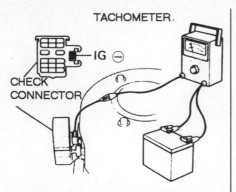
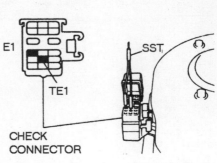
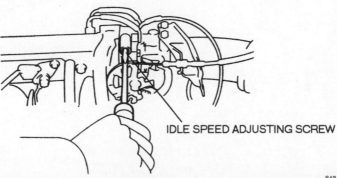

84342027

Tachometer installation and idle adjustment — 4A-FE and 7A-FE engines

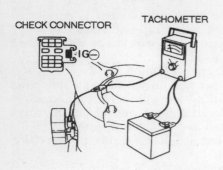

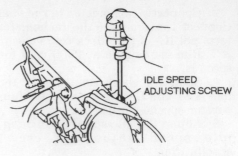

CHECK CONNECTOR

TACHOMETER

IDLE SPEED
ADJUSTING SCREW

84342028

Tachometer installation and idle adjustment — 4A-GE engine

information delivered by the various sensors on the engine. It is not adjustable as a routine maintenance item. The easiest way to check the air/fuel mixture is to put the car through a tailpipe emissions test. Whether or not this is required in your area, it's a good way of putting numbers on the combustion efficiency of the engine. The engine can only burn so much fuel; if too much is being delivered, it will show up on the test as unburned hydrocarbons (HC).

Putting the car through this test once a year from the time it is newly acquired can provide an excellent baseline for diagnosing future problems.

ENGINE ELECTRICAL

Ignition Coil

TESTING/PRIMARY RESISTANCE CHECK

NOTE: *This test requires the use of an ohmmeter. When using this tool, make sure the scale is set properly for the range of resistance you expect to encounter during the test. Always perform these tests with the ignition OFF.*

Using an ohmmeter, check the resistance between the positive (+) and the negative (-) terminals on the coil. The resistance COLD should be:

1990–91 4A-GE engine: 0.4–0.5 ohms
1990–92 4A-FE engine: 1.25–1.56 ohms
1992–93 4A-FE engine: 1.11–1.75 ohms
1993 7A-FE engine: 1.11–1.75 ohms

If the resistance is not within specification, the coil will require replacement.

TESTING/SECONDARY RESISTANCE CHECK

NOTE: *This test requires the use of an ohmmeter. When using this tool, make sure the scale is set properly for the range of resistance you expect to encounter during the test. Always perform these tests with the ignition OFF.*

Using an ohmmeter, check the resistance between the positive terminal (+) and the coil wire terminal. The resistance COLD should be:

1990–91 4A-GE engine: 10.2–13.8 kilohms
1990–92 4A-FE engine: 10.4–14.0 kilohms
1992–93 4A-FE engine: 9.0–15.7 kilohms
1993 7A-FE engine: 9.0–15.7 kilohms

If the resistance is not within specification, the coil will require replacement.

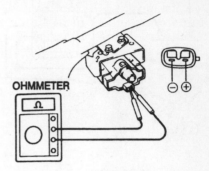

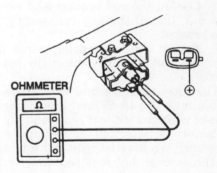

84343001

Testing coil — 4A-GE engine

REMOVAL & INSTALLATION

The external coil used on the 4A-GE engine (coil assembly which is not built into the distributor) is easily replaced by the following service procedure:

1. Make certain the ignition is OFF and the key is removed. Disconnect the negative battery cable.

2. Disconnect the high tension wire or coil wire (running between the coil and the distributor) from the coil.

3. Disconnect the low tension wires from the coil.

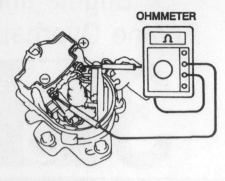

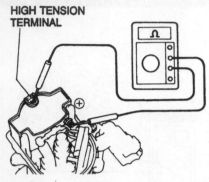

Testing coil — 4A-FE and 7A-FE engines

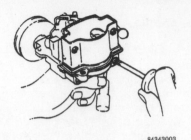

The internal coil is easily removed with the distributor out of the car

To install:

11. Install the ignition coil, gasket, screws and secure its wiring. Again, watch the wiring positions.

12. Reinstall the dust covers and distributor rotor.

13. Reinstall the distributor and set the engine timing. Refer to service procedures in Chapter 2.

Distributor

REMOVAL

NOTE: *Once the distributor is removed, the engine should NOT be turned or moved out of position. Should this occur, please refer to the engine rotated installation procedure.*

1. Disconnect the negative battery cable.

2. Disconnect the distributor wire(s) at its connector.

3. Remove the distributor cap (leave the spark plug wires connected) and swing it out of the way. If necessary, label and disconnect the coil and spark plug wiring at the distributor cap.

4. Carefully note the position of the distributor rotor relative to the distributor housing (also note position of distributor to the engine assembly); a mark made on the casing/housing will be necessary for reassembly. Use a marker or tape so the mark doesn't't rub off during handling of the case/housing.

5. Remove the distributor hold-down bolts.

6. Carefully pull the distributor from the engine assembly. Remove the O-ring from the distributor shaft.

4. Loosen the coil bracket and remove the coil. Install the new coil and tighten the bracket.

5. Attach the low tension wires first, then the coil wire. Reconnect the battery cable.

The internal coil found within the distributor on the 4A-FE and 7A-FE engines can be changed without removing the distributor (a selection of various short screwdrivers may be required for access to the screws) but it is recommended to remove the distributor and then replace the coil assembly.

6. Remove the distributor. Make certain the negative battery cable is disconnected before beginning the work.

7. Remove the distributor rotor.

8. Remove the dust cover over the distributor components and remove the dust cover over the ignition coil.

NOTE: *Note position and routing of all internal distributor assembly wiring.*

9. Remove the nuts and disconnect the wiring from the ignition coil.

10. Remove the 4 screws and remove the ignition coil and gasket from the distributor.

INSTALLATION

Engine Not Rotated

1. Install a new O-ring on the distributor shaft.
2. If the engine has not been moved out of position, align the rotor with the mark you made earlier and reinstall the distributor, aligning the mark made for distributor housing to engine assembly. Position it carefully and make sure the drive gear engages properly within the engine.
3. Install the hold-down bolts.
4. Install the distributor cap.
5. Install the wiring to the distributor, and connect the battery cable.
6. Check and adjust the timing as necessary.

Engine Rotated

If the engine has been cranked, dismantled or the timing otherwise lost while the distributor was out, proceed as follows:
1. Remove the No. 1 spark plug.
2. Place your finger over the spark plug hole and rotate the crankshaft clockwise to TDC (Top Dead Center). Watch the timing marks on the pulley; as they approach the ZERO point, you should feel pressure (compression) on your finger. If not, turn the crankshaft another full rotation and line up the timing marks.
NOTE: *The spark plugs are in deep wells; use a screwdriver or equivalent to fill the hole and feel the compression.*
3. Temporarily install the rotor in the distributor without the dust cover, if equipped. Turn the distributor shaft so that the rotor is pointing toward the No. 1 terminal in the distributor cap. On the 4A-GE engine, align the drilled mark on the driven gear with the groove of the housing. On the 4A-FE and 7A-FE engines, align the cutout of the coupling with the line of the housing.
4. Align the matchmarks on the distributor body and the engine block which were made during removal. Install the distributor in the block by rotating it slightly (no more than one gear tooth in either direction) until the driven gear (lubricate drive gear with clean engine oil) meshes with the drive.
5. Temporarily tighten the distributor hold-down bolts.

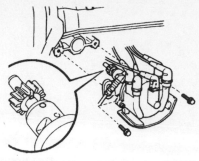

Distributor installation — 4A-GE engine

84343004

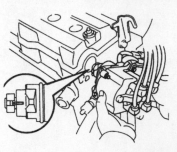

84343005

Distributor installation — 4A-FE and 7A-FE engines

6. Remove the rotor and install the dust cover, if equipped. Replace the rotor and the distributor cap.
7. Reconnect all electrical connections. Install the No. 1 spark plug and all plug wires if necessary.
8. Check ignition timing and tighten the distributor hold-down bolts.

Igniter (Ignition Module)

REMOVAL & INSTALLATION

NOTE: *Review the complete service procedure before this repair. Note position, color of wire and routing of all internal distributor assembly wiring.*
1. Remove the distributor as outlined. Make certain the negative battery cable is disconnected before beginning the work.
2. Remove the distributor rotor.
3. Remove the dust cover over the distributor components and remove the dust cover over the ignition coil.
4. Remove the nuts and disconnect the wiring from the ignition coil.
5. Remove the 4 screws and remove the ignition coil and gasket from the distributor.

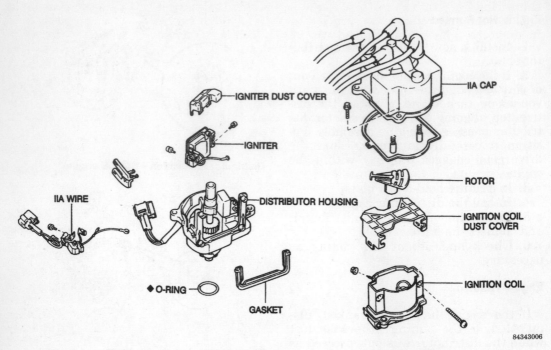

IGNITER DUST COVER

IGNITER

IIA CAP

IIA WIRE

DISTRIBUTOR HOUSING

ROTOR

IGNITION COIL DUST COVER

◆ O-RING

GASKET

IGNITION COIL

84343006

Exploded view of IIA type distributor — 4A-FE and 7A-FE engines

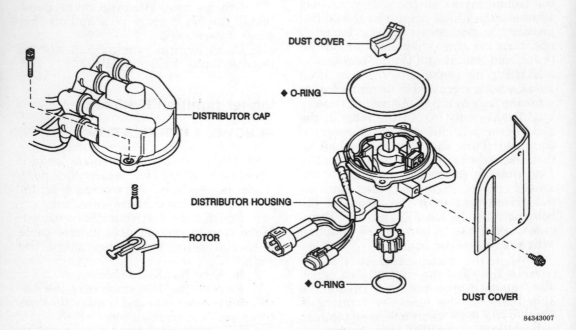

DUST COVER

◆ O-RING

DISTRIBUTOR CAP

DISTRIBUTOR HOUSING

ROTOR

◆ O-RING

DUST COVER

84343007

Exploded view of the distributor assembly — 4A-GE engine

6. At the igniter terminals, disconnect the wiring from the connecting points.

7. Loosen and remove the two screws holding the igniter and remove it from the distributor.

To install:

8. Install the igniter and connect its wiring. Pay particular attention to the correct routing of the wiring within the housing. There is one correct position only; any other wiring placements risk damage.

9. Install the ignition coil and gasket and secure its wiring. Again, watch the wiring positions.

10. Reinstall the dust covers and distributor rotor.

11. Reinstall the distributor and set the ignition timing.

Alternator

ALTERNATOR PRECAUTIONS

Several precautions must be observed with alternator equipped vehicles to avoid damaging the unit. They are as follows:

1. If the battery is removed or disconnected for any reason, make sure that it is reconnected with the correct polarity. Reversing the battery connections may result in damage to the one-way rectifiers.

2. When utilizing a booster battery as a starting aid, always connect it as follows: positive to positive, and negative (booster battery) to a good ground on the engine of the car being started.

3. Never use a fast charger as a booster to start a car with an alternator.

4. When servicing the battery with a fast charger, always disconnect the car battery cables.

5. Never attempt to polarize an alternator.

6. Never apply more than 12 volts when attempting to jump start the vehicle.

7. Do not short across or ground any of the terminals on the alternator.

8. Never disconnect the alternator or the battery with the engine running.

9. Always disconnect the battery terminals when performing any service on the electrical system.

10. Disconnect the battery ground cable if arc welding (such as body repair) is to be done on any part of the car.

Noise from an alternator may be caused by a loose drive pulley, a loose belt, loose mounting bolts, worn or dirty bearings or worn internal parts. A high frequency whine that is heard at high engine speed or full alternator output is acceptable and should not be considered a sign of alternator failure.

TESTING — ON VEHICLE INSPECTION

1. Inspect the battery specific gravity and electrolyte level. Check the specific gravity of each cell. The standard specific gravity of each cell is 1.25–1.27 when fully charged at 68°F. On a Delco battery with a "maintenance eye" look for a GREEN DOT which means the battery is fully charged. The DARK eye (GREEN DOT NOT VISIBLE) means the battery must be charged. The CLEAR or LIGHT YELLOW eye means the battery must be replaced.

2. Make sure the battery terminals are not loose or corroded. Check the fusible link for continuity.

3. Inspect the drive belt for excessive wear. Check the drive belt tension. If necessary adjust the drive belt.

4. Check the following fuses for continuity: ENGINE, CHARGE, IGN fuses.

5. Visually check alternator wiring and listen for abnormal noises.

6. Check that the discharge warning light comes ON when the ignition switch is turned ON. Start the engine. Check that the warning light goes out.

7. Check the charging circuit WITHOUT A LOAD. Connect a battery/alternator tester according to the manufacturer's instructions.

8. Check the charging circuit WITH A LOAD (turn on high beams and heater fan). Connect a battery/alternator tester according to the manufacturer's instructions.

9. Replace the necessary parts. Recheck the charging system. The standard amperage with a load on the system should be 30 amps. If a battery is fully charged, sometimes the indication will be less than 30 amps.

REMOVAL & INSTALLATION

1. Disconnect the negative battery cable.

NOTE: *Failure to disconnect the battery can cause personal injury and damage to the car. If a tool is accidentally shorted at the alternator, it can become hot enough to cause a serious burn. It may be necessary to remove the gravel shield and work from underneath the car in order to gain access to the alternator retaining bolts.*

2. Disconnect the electrical wiring from the alternator.

3. Loosen the adjusting lock bolt (lower bolt) and pivot (upper) bolt. Remove the drive belt. It may be necessary to remove other belts for access.

4. Remove the lower bolt first, support the alternator and remove the upper pivot bolt. Remove the alternator from the car.

5. Installation is the reverse of the removal procedure. When reinstalling, remember to leave the bolts finger tight so that the belt may be adjusted to the correct tension.

6. Make sure that the electrical plugs and connectors are properly seated and

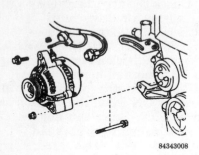

84343008

Alternator removal and installation — 4A-GE engine

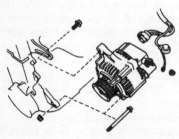

84343009

Alternator removal and installation — 4A-FE engine

secure in their mounts. Adjust belt tension and tighten all necessary hardware. Reconnect the negative battery cable.

Regulator

REMOVAL & INSTALLATION

The voltage regulator is contained within the alternator. It is an Integrated Circuit (IC) type. The alternator must be removed to replace the regulator.

1. Disconnect the negative battery cable.

2. Remove the alternator.

3. Support the alternator on a workbench, pulley end down but not resting on the pulley.

4. At the side of the alternator, remove the nut and the plastic terminal insulator.

5. Remove the three nuts and remove the end cover.

6. Remove the five screws and carefully remove the brush holder and then the IC regulator. Be careful to keep track of various small parts (washers, etc) — they will be needed during reassembly.

To install:

7. Place the cover over the brush holder. Install the regulator and the brush holder onto the alternator and secure them with the five screws. Make sure the brush holder's cover doesn't't slip to one side during installation.

8. Before reinstalling the rear cover, check that the gap between the brush holder and the connector is at least 1mm. After confirming this gap, install the rear alternator cover and its three nuts.

9. Install the terminal insulator and its nut. Hold the alternator horizontally and spin the pulley by hand. Make sure everything turns smoothly and there is no sign of noise or binding.

Battery

REMOVAL & INSTALLATION

1. Disconnect the negative battery cable (special pullers are available to remove the clamps).

CAUTION: *Spilled acid can be neutralized with a baking soda and water solution. If you somehow get acid into your eyes, flush it out with lots of clean water and get to a doctor as quickly as possible.*

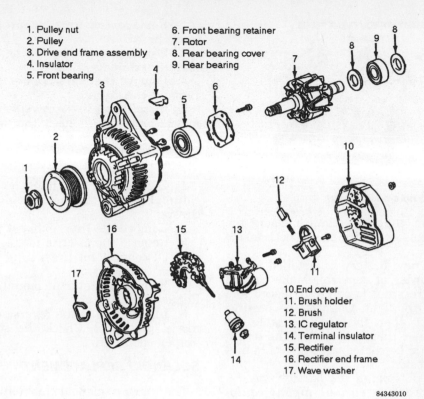

1. Pulley nut
2. Pulley
3. Drive end frame assembly
4. Insulator
5. Front bearing
6. Front bearing retainer
7. Rotor
8. Rear bearing cover
9. Rear bearing

10. End cover
11. Brush holder
12. Brush
13. IC regulator
14. Terminal insulator
15. Rectifier
16. Rectifier end frame
17. Wave washer

84343010

Exploded view of alternator assembly

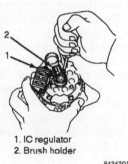

1. IC regulator
2. Brush holder

84343011

Removing the IC regulator from the alternator

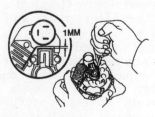

84343012

Maintain the minimum clearance between the brush holder and the connector when reassembling

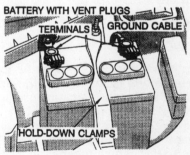

BATTERY WITH VENT PLUGS
TERMINALS
GROUND CABLE
HOLD-DOWN CLAMPS

84343013

Battery and hold-down clamp

2. Disconnect the positive battery cable.

3. Remove the front battery retainer (hold-down) bolt first, then the rear battery retainer (hold-down) bolt and the retainer.

4. Remove the battery. The battery is fairly heavy, so use care in lifting it out of the car.

5. Clean the battery posts thoroughly before reinstalling or when installing a new one.

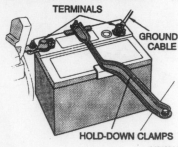

BATTERY WITHOUT VENT PLUGS
TERMINALS
GROUND CABLE
HOLD-DOWN CLAMPS
84343014

Battery and hold-down clamp

6. Clean the cable clamps, using the special tools or a wire brush, both inside and out.

7. The new battery is installed in the reverse order of removal. Make certain that the retainer is correctly placed and its bolts are tight. Connect the positive cable first, then the negative cable. Do not hammer them into place. The terminals should be coated with grease to prevent corrosion.

NOTE: *Removing the battery may require resetting various digital equipment such as radio memory and the clock.*

Starter

TESTING

1. Inspect the battery specific gravity and electrolyte level. Check the specific gravity of each cell. The standard specific gravity of each cell is 1.25–1.27 when fully charged at 68°F. On a Delco battery with a "maintenance eye" look for a GREEN DOT which means the battery is fully charged. The DARK eye (GREEN DOT NOT VISIBLE) means the battery must be charged. The CLEAR or LIGHT YELLOW eye means the battery must be replaced.

2. Make sure the battery terminals are not loose or corroded. Check the fusible link for continuity.

3. For further starting system troubleshooting, refer to the troubleshooting chart to find the problem and possible cause and remedy. Replace or repair the necessary items.

REMOVAL & INSTALLATION

4A-FE and 7A-FE Engines

1. Disconnect the negative battery cable.

2. Remove the air cleaner assembly (with hose).

3. Disconnect all the wiring from the starter terminals.

4. Remove the starter mounting bolts. Remove the starter.

5. Installation is the reverse of the removal procedure. Check the starter for proper operation.

4A-GE Engine

1. Disconnect the negative battery cable. Remove the both engine under covers.

2. Remove the front exhaust pipe.

3. Remove the electric cooling fan.

4. Disconnect all the wiring from the starter terminals.

5. Remove the starter mounting bolts. Remove the starter.

6. Installation is the reverse of the removal procedure. Check the starter for proper operation.

SOLENOID REPLACEMENT

The starter solenoid (magnetic switch) is an integral part of the starter assembly.

1. Remove the starter from the car. Remove the heat insulator from the starter assembly, if equipped.

2. Disconnect the wire lead from the magnetic switch terminal.

3. Remove the two long, through bolts holding the field frame to the magnetic switch. Pull out the field frame with the armature from the magnetic switch.

4. On 1.0kw starters, remove the felt seal. On 1.4kw starters, remove the O-ring.

5. To remove the starter housing from the magnetic switch assembly:

   a. On 1.0 kw starters, remove the two screws and remove the starter housing with the idler gear and clutch assembly.

   b. On 1.4kw units, remove the two screws and remove the starter housing with the pinion gear, idler and clutch assembly.

To install:

6. If necessary, install the gears and clutch assembly to the starter housing. Apply grease to the gear and clutch assemblies and:

   a. On 1.0kw starters, place the clutch assembly, idler gear and bearing in the starter housing.

Problem	Possible cause	Remedy
Engine will not crank	Battery charge low	Check battery specific gravity
		Charge or replace battery
	Battery cables loose, corroded or worn	Repair or replace cables
	Clutch start switch faulty (M/T)	Adjust or replace clutch start switch
	Clutch starter relay faulty (M/T)	Replace starter relay
	Neutral start switch faulty (A/T)	Replace switch
	Fusible link blown	Replace fusible link
	Starter faulty	Repair starter
	Ignition switch faulty	Replace ignition switch
Engine cranks slowly	Battery charge low	Check battery specific gravity
		Charge or replace battery
	Battery cables loose, corroded or worn	Repair or replace cables
	Starter faulty	Repair starter
Starter keeps running	Starter faulty	Repair starter
	Ignition switch faulty	Replace ignition switch
	Short in wiring	Repair wiring
Starter spins — engine will not crank	Pinion gear teeth broken or faulty starter	Repair starter
	Flywheel teeth broken	Replace flywheel

84343015

Starter troubleshooting chart

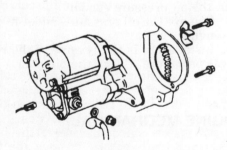

84343016

Starter assembly removal

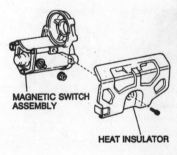

MAGNETIC SWITCH
ASSEMBLY

HEAT INSULATOR

84343018

Removing the heat insulator from the starter assembly

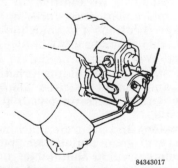

84343017

Separate the starter components by removing the 2 through bolts

b. On 1.4kw starters, place the clutch assembly, idler gear, bearing and pinion gear in the starter housing.

7. Insert the spring into the clutch shaft hole and place the starter housing onto the magnetic switch. Install the two screws.

8. On 1.0kw units, install the felt seal on the armature shaft. On 1.4kw units, install the O-ring on the field frame.

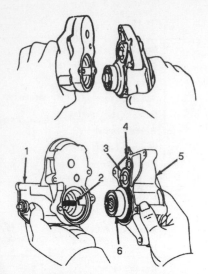

1. Starter solenoid assembly
2. Spring
3. Idler gear
4. Pinion gear
5. Drive housing
6. Clutch and drive assembly

84343019

Disassembly of the magnetic switch (solenoid) from the drive housing

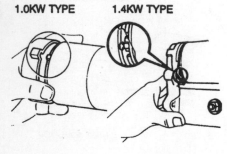

1.0KW TYPE   1.4KW TYPE

84343020

Match the field protrusion during reassembly

9. Install the field frame with the armature onto the magnetic switch assembly and install the two through bolts.
NOTE: *There is a protrusion or tab on each part; make sure you line them up correctly.*
10. Connect the wire to the terminal on the magnetic switch. Install the heat insulator, if equipped.
11. Reinstall the starter on the vehicle. Check starter system for proper operation.

Sending Units and Sensors
REMOVAL & INSTALLATION
Water Temperature Sender

1. Disconnect the negative battery cable.
2. Drain the cooling system.
3. Disconnect the electrical connector from the sensor.
4. Remove the sensor from the engine. On some applications, the water temperature sender threads into the thermostat housing.
5. Installation is the reverse of the removal procedure. Fill the cooling system.

Low Oil Pressure Warning Sensor

1. Disconnect the negative battery cable.
2. Disconnect the electrical connector from the sensor.
3. Remove the sensor from the engine.
4. Installation is the reverse of the removal procedure. Check the oil level.

Oil Pressure Sender

1. Disconnect the negative battery cable.
2. Disconnect the electrical connector from the oil pressure sender.
3. Remove the oil pressure sender from the engine.
4. Installation is the reverse of the removal procedure. Check the oil level.

ENGINE MECHANICAL

Engine Overhaul Tips

Most engine overhaul procedures are fairly standard. In addition to specific parts replacement procedures and complete specifications for your individual engine, this Chapter also is a guide to accepted rebuilding procedures. Examples of standard rebuilding practice are shown and should be used along with specific details concerning your particular engine.

Competent and accurate machine shop services will ensure maximum performance, reliability and engine life.

In most instances it is more profitable for the do-it-yourself mechanic to remove, clean and inspect the component, buy the necessary parts and deliver these to a shop for actual machine work.

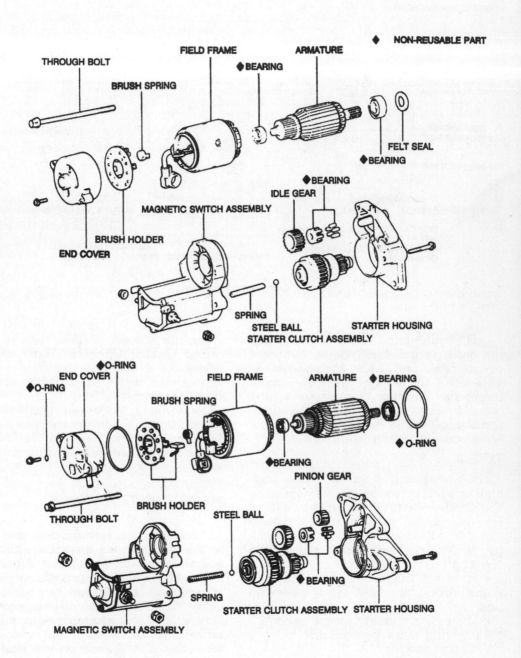

◆ NON-REUSABLE PART

THROUGH BOLT

BRUSH SPRING

FIELD FRAME

◆BEARING

ARMATURE

FELT SEAL

◆BEARING

◆BEARING

IDLE GEAR

MAGNETIC SWITCH ASSEMBLY

BRUSH HOLDER

END COVER

SPRING

STEEL BALL

STARTER CLUTCH ASSEMBLY

STARTER HOUSING

◆O-RING

END COVER

◆O-RING

BRUSH SPRING

FIELD FRAME

ARMATURE

◆BEARING

◆O-RING

◆BEARING

PINION GEAR

BRUSH HOLDER

STEEL BALL

THROUGH BOLT

◆BEARING

SPRING

STARTER CLUTCH ASSEMBLY   STARTER HOUSING

MAGNETIC SWITCH ASSEMBLY

84343021

Exploded view of starter motors — magnetic switch is integral part of the starter assembly

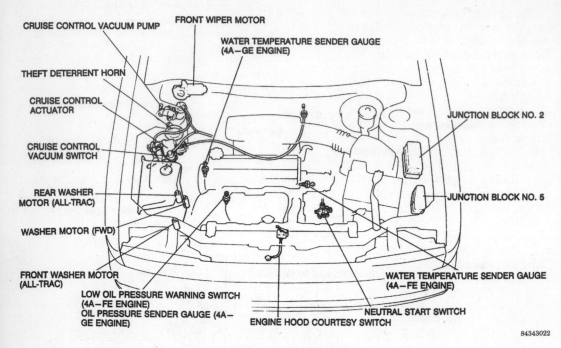

Component locations

On the other hand, much of the rebuilding work (crankshaft, block, bearings, piston rods, and other components) is well within the scope of the do-it-yourself mechanic. Patience, proper tools, and common sense coupled with a basic understanding of the engine can yield satisfying and economical results.

TOOLS

The tools required for an engine overhaul or parts replacement will depend on the depth of your involvement. With a few exceptions, they will be the tools found in a mechanic's tool kit (see Chapter 1). More in-depth work will require any or all of the following:

• A dial indicator (reading in thousandths) mounted on a universal base
• Micrometers and telescope gauges
• Jaw and screw-type pullers
• Gasket scrapers
• Valve spring compressor
• Ring groove cleaner
• Piston ring expander and compressor
• Ridge reamer
• Cylinder hone or glaze breaker
• Plastigage®
• Engine stand

The use of most of these tools is illustrated in this Chapter. Many can be rented for a one-time use from a local parts jobber or tool supply house specializing in automotive work.

Occasionally, the use of special tools is called for. See the information on Special Tools and Safety Notice in the front of this book before substituting another tool.

INSPECTION TECHNIQUES

Procedures and specifications are given in this Chapter for inspecting, cleaning and assessing the wear limits of most major components. Other procedures such as Magnaflux® and Zyglo® can be used to locate material flaws and stress cracks. Magnaflux® is a magnetic process applicable only to ferrous (iron and steel) materials. The Zyglo® process coats the material with a fluorescent dye penetrant and can be used on any material. Checks for suspected surface cracks can be more readily made using spot check dye. The dye is sprayed onto the suspected area, wiped off and the area sprayed with a developer. Cracks will show up brightly.

OVERHAUL TIPS

Aluminum has become extremely popular for use in engines, due to its low weight. Observe the following precautions when handling aluminum parts:

• Never hot tank aluminum parts (the caustic hot tank solution will eat the aluminum.)

• Remove all aluminum parts (identification tag, etc.) from engine parts prior to the tanking.

• Always coat threads lightly with engine oil or anti-seize compounds before installation to prevent seizure.

• Never overtighten bolts or spark plugs, especially in aluminum threads.

Stripped threads in any component can be repaired using any of several commercial repair kits (Heli-Coil®, Microdot®, Keenserts®, etc.).

When assembling the engine, any parts that will be in frictional contact must be prelubed to provide lubrication at initial start-up.

When semi-permanent (locked, but removable) installation of bolts or nuts is desired, threads should be cleaned and coated with Loctite® or other similar, commercial non-hardening sealant.

REPAIRING DAMAGED THREADS

Several methods of repairing damaged threads are available. Heli-Coil®, Keenserts® and Microdot® are among the most widely used. All involve basically the same principle — drilling out stripped threads, tapping the hole and installing a prewound insert — making welding, plugging and oversize fasteners unnecessary.

Two types of thread repair inserts are usually supplied: a standard type for most Inch Coarse, Inch Fine, Metric Course and Metric Fine thread sizes and a spark plug type to fit most spark plug port sizes. Consult the individual manufacturer's catalog to determine exact applications. Typical thread repair kits will contain a selection of prewound threaded inserts, a tap (corresponding to the outside diameter threads of the insert) and an installation tool. Spark plug inserts usually differ because they require a tap equipped with pilot threads and a combined reamer/tap section. Most manufacturers also supply blister-packed thread repair inserts separately in addition to a master kit containing a variety of taps and inserts plus installation tools.

Before effecting a repair to a threaded hole, remove any snapped, broken or damaged bolts or studs. Penetrating oil can be used to free frozen threads. The offending item can be removed with locking pliers or with a screw or stud extractor. After the hole is clear, the thread can be repaired, as shown in the series of accompanying illustrations.

CHECKING ENGINE COMPRESSION

A noticeable lack of engine power, excessive oil consumption and/or poor fuel mileage measured over an extended pe-

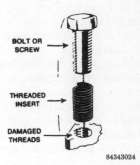

84343023

Standard thread repair insert (left) and spark plug thread insert (right)

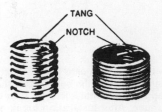

84343024

Damaged bolt holes can be repaired with thread repair inserts

84343025

Drill out the damaged threads with the specified drill. Drill completely through the hole or to the bottom of the blind hole

84343026

With the tap supplied, tap the hole to receive the thread insert. Keep the tap well oiled and back it out frequently to avoid clogging the threads

84343027

Screw the thread insert onto the installation tool until the tang engages the bolt. Screw the insert into the tapped hole until it is ¼–½ turn below the top surface. After installation break off the tang with a hammer and punch

riod are all indicators of internal engine wear. Worn piston rings, scored or worn cylinder bores, leaking head gaskets, sticking or burnt valves and worn valve seats are all possible causes. A check of each cylinder's compression will help you locate the problem.

As mentioned in the Tools and Equipment section of Chapter 1, a screw-in type compression gauge is more accurate than the type you simply hold against the spark plug hole, although it takes slightly longer to use. It's worth it to obtain a more accurate reading. Follow the procedures below.

1. Warm up the engine to normal operating temperature.

2. Disconnect the cold start injector connector, if so equipped.

3. Disconnect all distributor connector(s).

4. Remove all the spark plugs.

5. Screw the compression gauge into the No.1 spark plug hole until the fitting is snug. Fully open the throttle.

NOTE: *Be careful not to crossthread the plug hole. On aluminum cylinder heads use extra care, as the threads in these heads are easily ruined.*

6. While you read the compression gauge, ask an assistant to crank the engine two or three times in short bursts using the ignition switch.

NOTE: *Always use a fully charged battery for correct compression test results.*

7. Read the compression gauge at the end of each series of cranks, and record the highest of these readings. Repeat this procedure for each of the engine's cylinders.

As a general rule, new engines will have compression on the order of 190 pounds per square inch (psi). This number will decrease with age and wear. The number of pounds of pressure that your test shows is not as important as the evenness between all the cylinders.

Compare the highest reading of all the cylinders. Any variation of more than about 10% should be considered a sign of potential trouble. For example, if your compression readings for cylinders 1 through 4 were: 135 psi, 125 psi, 90 psi and 125 psi, it would be fair to say that cylinder number 3 is not working efficiently and is almost certainly the cause of your oil burning, rough idle or poor fuel mileage.

8. If a cylinder is unusually low, pour a tablespoon of clean engine oil into the cylinder through the spark plug hole and repeat the compression test. If the compression comes up after adding the oil, it appears that the cylinder's piston rings and/or bore are damaged or worn. If the pressure remains low, the valves may not be seating properly or the head gasket may be blown near that cylinder. If compression in any two adjacent cylinders is low, and if the addition of oil doesn't't help the compression, there is leakage past the head gasket. Oil and coolant in the combustion chamber can result from this problem. There may be evidence of water droplets on the engine dipstick when a head gasket has blown.

GENERAL ENGINE SPECIFICATIONS

Year	Engine ID/VIN	Engine Displacement Liters (cc)	Fuel System Type	Net Horsepower @ rpm	Net Torque @ rpm (ft. lbs.)	Bore × Stroke (in.)	Compression Ratio	Oil Pressure (psi)
1990	4A-FE	1.6 (1587)	EFI	102 @ 5800	101 @ 4800	3.19 × 3.03	9.5:1	36–71 ①
	4A-GE	1.6 (1587)	EFI	130 @ 6800	102 @ 5800	3.19 × 3.03	9.5:1	36–71 ①
1991	4A-FE	1.6 (1587)	EFI	102 @ 5800	101 @ 4800	3.19 × 3.03	9.5:1	36–71 ①
	4A-GE	1.6 (1587)	EFI	130 @ 6800	105 @ 6000	3.19 × 3.03	9.5:1	36–71 ①
1992	4A-FE	1.6 (1587)	EFI	102 @ 5800	101 @ 4800	3.19 × 3.03	9.5:1	36–71 ①
1993	4A-FE	1.6 (1587)	EFI	105 @ 5800	100 @ 4800	3.19 × 3.03	9.5:1	36–71 ①
	7A-FE	1.8 (1762)	EFI	115 @ 5600	115 @ 2800	3.19 × 3.37	9.5:1	36–71 ①

NOTE: Horsepower and torque are SAE net figures. They are measured at the rear of the transmission with all accessories installed and operating. Since the figures vary when a given engine is installed in different models, some are representative rather than exact.
EFI—Electronic Fuel Injection
① At 3000 rpm, with engine at normal operating temperature

84343029

CAMSHAFT SPECIFICATIONS

All measurements given in inches.

Year	Engine ID/VIN	Engine Displacement Liters (cc)	Journal Diameter 1	2	3	4	5	Elevation In.	Ex.	Bearing Clearance	Camshaft End Play
1990	4A-FE	1.6 (1587)	0.9035–0.9041 ①	0.9035–0.9041	0.9035–0.9041	0.9035–0.9041	—	1.3862–1.3902	1.3744–1.3783	0.0015–0.0028	②
	4A-GE	1.6 (1587)	1.0610–1.0616	1.0610–1.0616	1.0610–1.0616	1.0610–1.0616	—	1.3823–1.3980	1.3823–1.3980	0.0014–0.0028	0.0031–0.0075
1991	4A-FE	1.6 (1587)	0.9035–0.9041 ①	0.9035–0.9041	0.9035–0.9041	0.9035–0.9041	—	1.3862–1.3902	1.3744–1.3783	0.0015–0.0028	②
	4A-GE	1.6 (1587)	1.0610–1.0616	1.0610–1.0616	1.0610–1.0616	1.0610–1.0616	—	1.3823–1.3980	1.3823–1.3980	0.0014–0.0028	0.0031–0.0075
1992	4A-FE	1.6 (1587)	0.9035–0.9041 ①	0.9035–0.9041	0.9035–0.9041	0.9035–0.9041	—	1.3862–1.3902	1.3744–1.3783	0.0014–0.0028	②
1993	4A-FE	1.6 (1587)	0.9822–0.9829	0.9822–0.9829	0.9822–0.9829	0.9822–0.9829	—	1.6450–1.6539	1.6520–1.6560	0.0014–0.0028	②
	7A-FE	1.8 (1762)	0.9822–0.9829	0.9822–0.9829	0.9822–0.9829	0.9822–0.9829	—	1.6450–1.6539	1.6520–1.6560	0.0014–0.0028	②

① Exhaust No. 1: 0.9822–0.9829
② Intake Camshaft: 0.0012–0.0033
   Exhaust Camshaft: 0.0014–0.0035

84343030

CRANKSHAFT AND CONNECTING ROD SPECIFICATIONS
All measurements are given in inches.

Year	Engine ID/VIN	Engine Displacement Liters (cc)	Crankshaft				Connecting Rod		
			Main Brg. Journal Dia.	Main Brg. Oil Clearance	Shaft End-play	Thrust on No.	Journal Diameter	Oil Clearance	Side Clearance
1990	4A-FE	1.6 (1587)	1.8891–1.8898	0.0006–0.0013	0.0008–0.0087	3	1.5742–1.5748	0.0008–0.0020	0.0059–0.0098
	4A-GE	1.6 (1587)	1.8891–1.8898	0.0006–0.0013	0.0008–0.0087	3	1.6529–1.6535	0.0008–0.0020	0.0059–0.0098
1991	4A-FE	1.6 (1587)	1.8891–1.8898	0.0006–0.0013	0.0008–0.0087	3	1.5742–1.5748	0.0008–0.0020	0.0059–0.0098
	4A-GE	1.6 (1587)	1.8891–1.8898	0.0006–0.0013	0.0008–0.0087	3	1.6529–1.6535	0.0008–0.0020	0.0059–0.0098
1992	4A-FE	1.6 (1587)	1.8891–1.8898	0.0006–0.0013	0.0008–0.0087	3	1.5742–1.5748	0.0008–0.0020	0.0059–0.0098
1993	4A-FE	1.6 (1587)	1.8891–1.8898	0.0006–0.0013	0.0008–0.0087	3	1.5742–1.5748	0.0008–0.0020	0.0059–0.0098
	7A-FE	1.8 (1762)	1.8891–1.8898	0.0006–0.0013	0.0008–0.0087	3	1.8891–1.8898	0.0008–0.0017	0.0059–0.0098

84343031

VALVE SPECIFICATIONS

Year	Engine ID/VIN	Engine Displacement Liters (cc)	Seat Angle (deg.)	Face Angle (deg.)	Spring Test Pressure (lbs. @ in.)	Spring Installed Height (in.)	Stem-to-Guide Clearance (in.)		Stem Diameter (in.)	
							Intake	Exhaust	Intake	Exhaust
1990	4A-FE	1.6 (1587)	45	44.5	34.8①	1.366	0.0010–0.0024	0.0012–0.0026	0.2350–0.2356	0.2348–0.2354
	4A-GE	1.6 (1587)	45	44.5	35.9①	1.366	0.0010–0.0024	0.0012–0.0026	0.2350–0.2356	0.2348–0.2354
1991	4A-FE	1.6 (1587)	45	44.5	34.8①	1.366	0.0010–0.0024	0.0012–0.0026	0.2350–0.2356	0.2348–0.2354
	4A-GE	1.6 (1587)	45	44.5	35.9①	1.366	0.0010–0.0024	0.0012–0.0026	0.2350–0.2356	0.2348–0.2354
1992	4A-FE	1.6 (1587)	45	44.5	34.8①	1.366	0.0010–0.0024	0.0012–0.0026	0.2350–0.2356	0.2348–0.2354
1993	4A-FE	1.6 (1587)	45	44.5	37.3②	1.248	0.0010–0.0024	0.0012–0.0026	0.2350–0.2356	0.2348–0.2354
	7A-FE	1.8 (1762)	45	44.5	37.3②	1.248	0.0010–0.0024	0.0012–0.0026	0.2350–0.2356	0.2348–0.2354

① Spring test pressure at installed length
   1.366 inch
② Spring test pressure at installed length
   1.248 inch

84343032

PISTON AND RING SPECIFICATIONS

All measurements are given in inches.

Year	Engine ID/VIN	Engine Displacement Liters (cc)	Piston Clearance	Ring Gap			Ring Side Clearance		
				Top Compression	Bottom Compression	Oil Control	Top Compression	Bottom Compression	Oil Control
1990	4A-FE	1.6 (1587)	0.0024–0.0031	0.0098–0.0177	0.0059–0.0157	0.0039–0.0276	0.0016–0.0031	0.0012–0.0028	Snug
	4A-GE	1.6 (1587)	0.0039–0.0047	0.0098–0.0185	0.0079–0.0165	0.0059–0.0205	0.0012–0.0031	0.0012–0.0028	Snug
1991	4A-FE	1.6 (1587)	0.0024–0.0031	0.0098–0.0177	0.0059–0.0157	0.0039–0.0276	0.0016–0.0031	0.0012–0.0028	Snug
	4A-GE	1.6 (1587)	0.0039–0.0047	0.0098–0.0185	0.0079–0.0165	0.0059–0.0205	0.0012–0.0031	0.0012–0.0028	Snug
1992	4A-FE	1.6 (1587)	0.0024–0.0031	0.0098–0.0177	0.0059–0.0157	0.0039–0.0276	0.0016–0.0031	0.0012–0.0028	Snug
1993	4A-FE	1.6 (1587)	0.0033–0.0041	0.0098–0.0177	0.0138–0.0197	0.0059–0.0177	0.0018–0.0033	0.0012–0.0028	—
	7A-FE	1.8 (1762)	0.0033–0.0041	0.0098–0.0177	0.0138–0.0197	0.0059–0.0177	0.0018–0.0033	0.0012–0.0028	—

84343033

TORQUE SPECIFICATIONS

All readings in ft. lbs.

Year	Engine ID/VIN	Engine Displacement Liters (cc)	Cylinder Head Bolts	Main Bearing Bolts	Rod Bearing Bolts	Crankshaft Damper Bolts	Flywheel Bolts	Manifold		Spark Plugs	Lug Nut
								Intake	Exhaust		
1990	4A-FE	1.6 (1587)	44①	44	36	87	58⑤	14	18	13	76
	4A-GE	1.6 (1587)	②	44	③	101	54	16	29	13	76
1991	4A-FE	1.6 (1587)	44①	44	36	87	58⑤	14	18	13	76
	4A-GE	1.6 (1587)	②	44	③	101	54	.20	29	13	76
1992	4A-FE	1.6 (1587)	44①	44	36	87	58⑤	14	18	13	76
1993	4A-FE	1.6 (1587)	②	44	④	87	58⑤	14	29	13	76
	7A-FE	1.8 (1762)	②	44	④	87	58	14	29	13	76

① Torque in sequence, in 3 steps
② Step 1: 22 ft. lbs. in sequence
  Step 2: An additional 90° turn in sequence
  Step 3: An additional 90° turn in sequence
  All 3 steps must be completed for correct
  torque of cylinder head
③ 29 ft. lbs. plus an additional 90° turn
④ 22 ft. lbs. plus an additional 90° turn
⑤ A/T: 47 ft. lbs.

84343034

4A-FE

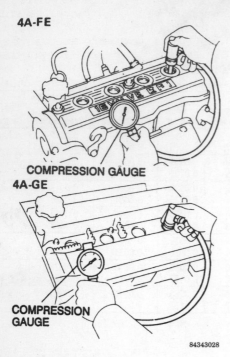

COMPRESSION GAUGE

4A-GE

COMPRESSION GAUGE

Compression test gauge

Location of water hose at the water inlet housing — 4A-GE engine

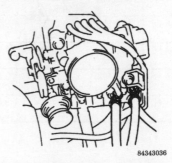

Disconnect the heater and air hoses from the air valve — 4A-GE engine

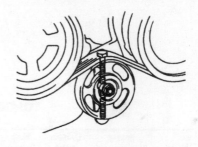

Idler pulley adjuster — 4A-GE engine

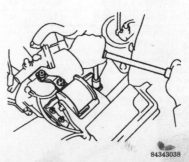

Removing the left side engine mount at the transaxle — 4A-GE engine

Engine

REMOVAL & INSTALLATION

4A-GE Engine

1. Relieve the fuel system pressure. Disconnect the negative battery cable.

2. With a helper remove the hood (mark hood hinges for correct installation) from the car. Use care not to damage the paint finish on the vehicle.

3. Drain the engine oil.

4. Drain the cooling system. Save the coolant for reuse.

5. Drain the transaxle oil.

6. Remove the air cleaner assembly.

7. Remove the coolant reservoir tank and remove the PCV hose.

8. Remove the heater hoses from the water inlet housing.

9. Disconnect the fuel inlet hose from the fuel filter.

NOTE: *The fuel system is under pressure. Release pressure slowly and contain spillage. Observe no smoking/no open flame precautions. Have a Class B-C (dry powder) fire extinguisher within arm's reach at all times.*

10. Disconnect the heater and air hoses from the air valve.

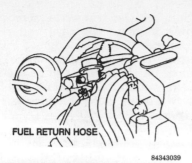

FUEL RETURN HOSE

84343039

Location of the fuel return hoses at the pressure regulator — 4A-GE engine

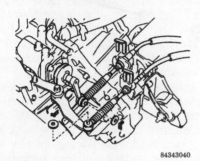

84343040

Removing the control cables at the transaxle — 4A-GE engine

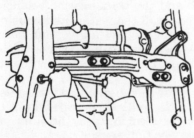

84343041

Removing the engine mounts from the crossmember — 4A-GE engine

11. Remove the fuel return hose from the pressure regulator.

12. If equipped with a manual transaxle, remove the slave cylinder from the housing. Loosen the mounting bolts and move the cylinder out of the way but do not loosen or remove the fluid hose running to the cylinder.

13. Disconnect the vacuum hose running to the charcoal canister.

14. Disconnect the shift control cable, the speedometer cable (at the transaxle) and the accelerator cable (at the throttle body).

15. If equipped with cruise control, disconnect the cables. Remove the cruise control actuator by:

   a. Disconnecting the vacuum hose.

   b. Removing the cover and the 3 bolts.

   c. Disconnecting the actuator connector and removing the actuator.

16. Remove the ignition coil.

17. Remove the main engine wiring harness in the following steps:

   a. From inside the car, remove the right side cowl (kick) panel.

   b. Disconnect the connectors at junction block 4.

   c. Remove the cover over the Electronic Control Module (ECM) and carefully disconnect the ECM plugs.

   d. Pull the main wiring harness into the engine compartment.

18. Disconnect the wiring at the number 2 junction block in the engine compartment.

19. Remove the engine and transaxle ground straps.

20. Disconnect the washer valve connector.

21. Remove the wiring at the cruise control vacuum pump connector and the vacuum switch connector.

22. Remove the hose from the brake vacuum booster.

23. Depending on equipment, remove the air conditioning compressor and/or the power steering pump. Note that the units are to be removed from their mounts and placed out of the way — hoses and lines DO NOT disconnect from the units.

   a. Remove the power steering pump pulley nut.

   b. Loosen the idler pulley adjusting bolt and pulley bolt.

   c. Remove the four compressor mounting bolts.

   d. Move the compressor aside and suspend it with stiff wire out of the way.

   e. Loosen the compressor bracket bolts.

   f. Disconnect the oil pressure connector.

   g. Loosen the power steering pump lock bolts and pivot bolts.

   h. Remove the pump and its bracket; suspend it out of the way with a piece of stiff wire.

24. Safely raise the vehicle and support on jackstands. Double check the stands

and make sure the vehicle is solidly supported.

25. Remove the splash shields under the car.

26. Disconnect the oil cooler hoses.

27. Disconnect the exhaust pipe from the exhaust manifold.

28. Carefully disconnect the wiring from the oxygen sensor.

29. Remove the cover under the flywheel.

30. Remove the front and rear motor mounts from the center crossmember.

31. Remove the center crossmember.

32. Disconnect the right side control arm at the steering knuckle.

33. Disconnect the halfshafts from the transaxle.

34. Lower the vehicle to the ground. Install the engine hoist to the lifting bracket on the engine. Hang the engine wires and hoses on the lift chain. Take tension on the hoist sufficient to support the engine; double check all hoist attaching points.

35. Disconnect the right side engine mount by removing the bolt.

36. Disconnect the left side motor mount from the transaxle bracket.

37. Lift the engine and transaxle from the vehicle. Be careful to avoid hitting the steering box and the throttle position sensor.

38. Support the engine assembly on a suitable stand; do not allow it to remain on the hoist for any length of time.

39. Disconnect the radiator fan temperature switch connector.

40. Disconnect the start injector time switch.

41. Remove the vacuum hoses from the Bimetal Vacuum Switching Valves (BVSV).

42. Remove the hoses from the water bypass valves and remove the water inlet housing assembly.

43. Label and remove the wiring connectors from the reverse switch, the water temperature sensor, and the water temperature switch. If equipped with automatic transaxle, remove the wiring to the neutral safety switch and the transaxle solenoid.

44. If equipped with automatic transaxle, remove the 6 torque converter-to-flexplate bolts.

45. Remove the starter along with its cable and connector.

46. Support the transaxle, remove the retaining bolts in the case and remove the transaxle from the engine. Pull the unit straight off the engine; do not allow it to hang partially removed on the shaft. Keep the automatic transaxle level; if it tilts forward the converter may fall off.

To install:

47. Before reinstalling the engine in the car, several components must be reattached or connected. Install the transaxle to the engine; tighten the 12mm bolts to 47 ft. lbs and the 10mm bolts to 34 ft. lbs

48. Install the starter, its cable and connector. Tighten the mounting bolts to 29 ft. lbs.

49. Install the 6 torque converter-to-flexplate bolts on automatic transaxles. Tighten the bolts to specification.

50. Attach the wiring to the reverse light switch, the water temperature sensor and the water temperature switch.

51. Connect the hoses to the water bypass pipes and the wiring to the start injector time switch and the radiator fan temperature switch.

52. On automatic transaxle vehicles, connect the wiring to the neutral safety switch and the transmission solenoid.

53. Reinstall the water inlet housing assembly and connect all vacuum hoses.

54. Attach the lifting mechanism to the engine; drape the hoses and wires on the chain.

55. Lower the engine and transaxle into place in the vehicle. Be careful not to hit the power steering gear housing or the throttle position sensor.

56. Install the right motor mount and through bolt; tighten it to 58 ft. lbs.

57. Install the left mount and attach it to the transaxle bracket. When the engine is securely mounted in the car, the lifting equipment may be removed.

58. Safely raise and support the vehicle on jackstands.

59. Connect the halfshafts to the transaxle. Tighten the bolts to specifications.

60. Attach the right side control arm to the steering knuckle and tighten the bolts and nuts.

61. Replace the cover under the flywheel.

62. Install the engine mount center crossmember, tightening the bolts to 29 ft. lbs.

63. Install the front and rear mounts onto the crossmember. Tighten the

mount bolts to 35 ft. lbs and the front and rear through bolts to 58 ft. lbs.

64. Using new gaskets and nuts, connect the exhaust pipe to the exhaust manifold.

65. Connect the wiring to the oxygen sensor and attach the oil cooler lines.

66. Lower the vehicle from its stands to the ground.

67. Install the power steering pump and pulley with its bracket. Tighten the lock bolt and the pivot bolt.

68. Connect the wiring to the oil pressure unit.

69. Install the compressor bracket, the compressor and the belt. Tighten the pulley bolt on the power steering pump to 28 ft. lbs.

70. Install the drive belts and adjust them to the proper tension. Make certain each belt is properly fitted on its pulleys.

71. Connect the vacuum hose to the brake booster.

72. Install the wiring to the No. 2 junction block. Connect the cable from the starter to the positive battery terminal and connect the engine and transaxle ground straps. DO NOT connect the negative battery cable at this time.

73. Attach the connectors for the washer change valve, and, if equipped, the cruise control vacuum pump and vacuum switch.

74. Connect the main engine wiring harness as follows:

   a. Feed the two connectors from the engine compartment back into the passenger compartment.

   b. Connect the ECM connector(s) and replace the cover.

   c. Connect the wiring to the No. 4 junction block.

   d. Replace the right side kick panel.

75. Reinstall the ignition coil.

76. If equipped, install the cruise control actuator.

77. Connect or reinstall the cables for the accelerator, the cruise control, the speedometer and the shifter.

78. Install the vacuum hose to the charcoal canister.

79. If equipped with manual transaxle, attach the clutch slave cylinder to the bell housing.

80. Attach the fuel return hose to the pressure regulator, the heater and air hoses to the air valve and the fuel hose to the fuel filter.

81. Connect the heater hoses to the water inlet housing.

82. Reinstall the PCV hose, the coolant reservoir and the air cleaner assembly.

83. Fill the transaxle with the correct amount of oil, and fill the engine with oil.

84. Fill the cooling system with the proper amount of fluid.

85. Double check all installation items, paying particular attention to loose hoses or hanging wires, untightened nuts, poor routing of hoses and wires (too tight or rubbing) and tools left in the engine area.

86. Connect the negative battery cable.

87. Start the engine and allow it to reach normal operating temperature. Check carefully for leaks. Shut the engine off.

88. Raise the front end of the car, support on jackstands and install the splash shields below the car.

89. Lower the car to the ground. With your helper, install the hood and adjust it for proper fit and latching. Road test the vehicle for proper operation.

4A-FE and 7A-FE Engines

1. Remove the hood (mark the hood hinges for correct installation). Have a helper assist you and be careful not to damage the painted bodywork.

2. Relieve the fuel system pressure. Disconnect the negative battery cable, then the positive battery cable and remove the battery.

3. Raise the vehicle and safely support it on jackstands.

4. Remove the left and right splash shields.

5. Drain the engine oil and the transmission oil.

6. Drain the engine coolant and save it in closed containers for reuse.

7. Remove the air cleaner hose and the air cleaner assembly.

8. Remove the coolant reservoir. Remove the radiator and fan assembly.

9. Disconnect the accelerator cable.

10. Disconnect and remove the cruise control actuator.

11. Label and disconnect the main engine wiring harness from its related sensors and switches.

12. Remove the ground strap connector and its bolt. Disconnect the wiring to the vacuum sensor, the oxygen sensor and the air conditioning compressor.

13. Label and disconnect the brake booster vacuum hose, the power steering

84343042

Disconnect the fuel line — 4A-FE engine

1. Engine mount
2. Engine mount bracket

84343043

Removing the engine mount to bracket bolt — 4A-FE and 7A-FE engines

vacuum hose, the charcoal canister vacuum hose and the vacuum switch vacuum hose.

14. Carefully disconnect the fuel inlet and return lines.

NOTE: *The fuel system is under pressure. Release pressure slowly and contain spillage. Observe no smoking/no open flame precautions. Have a Class B-C (dry powder) fire extinguisher within arm's reach at all times.*

15. Disconnect the heater hoses.

16. Loosen the power steering pump mounting bolt and through bolt. Remove the drive belt.

17. Remove the four bolts holding the air conditioner compressor and remove the compressor. DO NOT loosen or remove any lines or hoses. Move the compressor out of the way and hang it from a piece of stiff wire.

18. Disconnect the speedometer cable from the transaxle.

19. If equipped with manual transaxle, unbolt the clutch slave cylinder from the bell housing and move the cylinder out of the way. Don't disconnect any lines or hoses. Disconnect the shift control cables

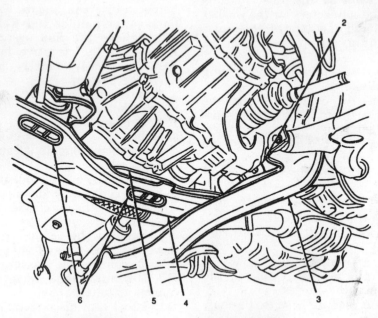

1. Front transaxle mount
2. Rear transaxle mount
3. Main crossmember
4. Center support
5. Center transaxle mount
6. Mount bolt shields

84343044

Detail of the crossmember and center support

by removing the two clips, the washers and retainers.

20. If equipped with automatic transaxle, remove the clip and retainer and separate the control cable from the shift lever.

21. Raise the car and support it safely on jackstands.

22. Remove the two bolts from the exhaust pipe flange and separate the pipe from the exhaust manifold.

23. Remove the nuts and bolts and separate the halfshafts from the transaxle.

24. Remove the through bolt from the rear transaxle mount.

25. Remove the nuts from the center transaxle mount and the rear mount.

26. Lower the vehicle to the ground and attach the lifting equipment to the brackets on the engine. Take tension on the hoist line or chain just enough to support the engine but no more. Hang the engine wires and hoses on the chain or cable.

27. Remove the three exhaust hanger bracket nuts and the hanger. Remove the two center crossmember-to-main crossmember bolts. Remove the three center crossmember-to-radiator support bolts.

CAUTION: *Support the crossmembers with a jack or jackstands when loosening the bolts. The pieces are heavy and could fall on you.*

28. Remove the eight crossmember-to-body bolts, then remove the two bolts holding the control arm brackets to the underbody. Remove the two center mount-to-transaxle bolts and remove the mount. Carefully lower the center mount and crossmember and remove from under the car.

29. At the left engine mount, remove the three bolts and the bracket, then remove the bolt, two nuts, through bolt and mounting. Remove the three bolts and the air cleaner bracket.

30. Loosen and remove the five bolts and disconnect the mounting bracket from the transaxle bracket. Remove the through bolt and mounting.

31. Carefully and slowly raise the engine and transaxle assembly out of the car. Tilt the transaxle down to clear the right engine mount. Be careful not to hit the steering gear housing. Make sure the engine is clear of all wiring, lines and hoses.

32. Support the engine assembly on a suitable stand; do not allow it to remain on the hoist for any length of time.

33. With the engine properly supported, disconnect the reverse light switch and the neutral safety switch (automatic transaxle).

34. Remove the rear end cover plate.

35. If equipped with automatic transaxle, remove the 6 torque converter mounting bolts.

36. Remove the starter.

37. Support the transaxle, remove the retaining bolts in the case and remove the transaxle from the engine. Pull the unit straight off the engine; do not allow it to hang partially removed on the shaft. Keep the automatic transaxle level; if it tilts forward the converter may fall off.

To install:

38. Before reinstalling the engine in the vehicle, several components must be retached or connected. Install the transaxle to the engine; tighten the 12mm bolts to 47 ft. lbs and the 10mm bolts to 34 ft. lbs

39. Install the starter, its cable and connector. Tighten the mounting bolts to 29 ft. lbs.

40. Install the 6 torque converter-to-flexplate bolts if equipped with automatic transaxle. Tighten the bolts to specification.

41. Install the rear cover plate and connect the wiring to the reverse light swich and the neutral safety switch (automatic transaxle).

42. Attach the chain hoist or lift apparatus to the engine and lower it into the engine compartment. Before it is completely in position, attach the power steering pump and its through bolt to the engine.

NOTE: *Tilt the transaxle downward and lower the engine to clear the left motor mount. As before, be careful not to hit the power steering housing (rack) or the throttle position sensor.*

43. Level the engine and align each mount with its bracket.

44. Install the right mounting insulator (bushing) to the engine bracket with the two nuts and bolt. Tighten the bolt temporarily.

45. Align the right insulator with the body bracket and install the through bolt and nut. Temporarily tighten the nut and bolt.

46. Align the left mounting insulator with the transaxle case bracket. Temporarily install the three bracket bolts.

47. With the engine held in place by these mounts, repeat Steps 44, 45 and 46,

tightening the bolts to the following specification: Step 44 — 38 ft. lbs., Step 45 — 64 ft. lbs., Step 46 — 35 ft. lbs.

48. Install the left side mounting support with its two bolts; tighten them to 15 ft. lbs.

49. With the engine securely mounted in the car, the lifting equipment may be removed. Raise the car and support it on jackstands.

50. Install the center mount to the transaxle with its two bolts and tighten them to 45 ft. lbs.

51. Position the center mount over the front and rear studs and start two nuts on the center mount only. Loosely install the three center support-to-radiator support bolts.

52. Loosely install the two front mount bolts. Raise the main crossmember into place over the rear studs and align all the underbody bolts.

53. Install the two rear mount nuts; leave them loose.

54. Loosely install the eight underbody bolts, the lower control arm bracket bolts, the two center support-to-crossmember bolts and the exhaust hanger bracket and nuts.

55. With everything loose, but in place, make a second pass over all the nuts and bolts tightening them to the following specifications:

    Crossmember-to-underbody bolts: 152 ft. lbs.

    Lower control arm bracket-to-underbody bolts: 94 ft. lbs.

    Center support-to-radiator support: 45 ft. lbs.

    Center support-to-crossmember: 45 ft. lbs.

    Front, center and rear mount bolts: 45 ft. lbs.

56. Install the rear transaxle mount and tighten its bolt to 64 ft. lbs

57. Install the nuts on the center transaxle mount and tighten them to 45 ft. lbs

58. Reconnect the halfshafts to the transaxle.

59. Using a new gasket, connect the exhaust pipe to the manifold and install the exhaust pipe bolts.

60. Lower the vehicle to the ground.

61. Either connect the control cables to the shift outer lever and selector lever and attach the control cables, if equipped with a manual transaxle or reconnect the control cable to the shift lever and install the clip and retainer, if equipped with an automatic transaxle. If equipped with a manual transaxle, reattach the clutch slave cylinder to its mount.

62. Attach the speedometer cable to the transaxle.

63. Install the air conditioning compressor and drive belt, if equipped.

64. Install the power steering pump, pivot bolt and drive belt, if equipped. Adjust the belts to the correct tension.

65. Install the fuel inlet and outlet lines.

66. Connect the heater hoses. Make sure they are in the correct positions and that the clamps are in sound condition.

67. Connect the vacuum hoses to the vacuum switch, the charcoal canister, the vacuum sensor, the power steering and the brake booster.

68. Connect the wiring to the air conditioning, the oxygen sensor and the vacuum sensor.

69. Observing the labels made at the time of disassembly, reconnect the main engine harness to its sensors and switches. Work carefully and make sure each connector is properly matched and firmly seated.

70. Install the ground strap connector and its bolt; connect the wiring at the No. 2 junction block in the engine compartment.

71. Install the cruise control actuator, if equipped.

72. Connect the accelerator cable and throttle cable (automatic) to their brackets.

73. Install the radiator and cooling fan assembly. Install the overflow reservoir.

74. Install the air cleaner assembly and the air intake hose.

75. Install the battery. Connect the positive cable to the starter terminal, then to the battery. DO NOT connect the negative battery cable at this time.

76. Fill the transmission with the correct amount of fluid.

77. Refill the engine coolant.

78. Fill the engine with the correct amount of oil.

79. Double check all installation items, paying particular attention to loose hoses or hanging wires, untightened nuts, poor routing of hoses and wires (too tight or rubbing) and tools left in the engine area.

80. Connect the negative battery cable. Start the engine and allow it to idle. As the engine warms up, shift the automatic transmission into each gear range allowing it to engage momentarily. After

each gear has been selected, put the shifter in PARK and check the transmission fluid level.

81. Shut the engine off and check the engine area carefully for leaks, particularly around any line or hose which was disconnected during removal.

82. Raise and support the front end of the car on jackstands. Replace the left and right splash shields and lower the vehicle.

83. With the help of an assistant, reinstall the hood. Adjust the hood for proper fit and latching. Road test the vehicle for proper operation.

Valve Cover (Cam Cover)

REMOVAL & INSTALLATION

4A-GE Engine

1. Disconnect the negative battery cable.

2. Disconnect or remove the PCV valve, the accelerator cable and the wiring harness.

3. Disconnect (mark or label) the spark plug wires at the plugs and disconnect the wiring to the noise filter.

4. Disconnect the oil pressure sender wire and, if equipped with air conditioning, the wire to the compressor.

5. Remove the center cover (between the cam covers) and its gasket.

6. Remove the cap nuts, the rubber seals and remove the valve covers.

NOTE: *If the cover is stuck in place, tap a corner with a plastic or rubber mallet. Don't pry the cover up; it will deform and leak.*

7. Clean the mating surfaces of the head and the covers.

To install:

8. Apply RTV sealant to the cylinder head before reassembly. This step is REQUIRED to prevent oil leakage.

9. Install the covers with new gaskets. Install the seals and the cap nut, making sure everything is properly seated. Tighten the cap nuts in steps to 9 ft. lbs.

10. Install the center cover with its gasket.

11. Connect the wiring to the oil pressure sender and the compressor, if equipped.

12. Connect the wiring to the noise filter and install the spark plug wires.

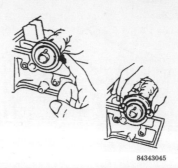

84343045

Apply sealant to these points before reinstalling the valve cover — 4A-GE engine

13. Connect, in this order, the wiring harness, the accelerator cable, the PCV valve and the negative battery cable.

14. Start the engine and check for leaks after the engine has warmed up. Minor leaks may be cured by slightly snugging the cover bolts. Any leak that is still present after about a ¼ turn CANNOT be cured by further tightening. Remove the cover again and either reposition or replace the gasket.

4A-FE and 7A-FE Engines

1. Disconnect the negative battery cable.

2. Disconnect the PCV and the vacuum hose.

3. Loosen the engine wiring harness running over the upper timing belt cover for easier access to the valve cover.

4. Remove the spark plug wires (mark or label) from the spark plugs.

5. Remove the 3 cap nuts, the seals below them and remove the valve cover.

To install:

6. Clean the mating surfaces of the head and the cover. Install a new gasket before installing the valve cover.

7. Apply RTV sealant to the cylinder head before reassembly. This step is REQUIRED to prevent oil leakage.

8. Install the cover with a new gasket. Install the seals and the cap nut, making sure everything is properly seated. Tighten the cap nuts in steps to 6–9 ft. lbs.

9. Reconnect the spark plug wires and reposition the wiring harness over the timing belt cover.

10. Connect the vacuum hose, the PCV hose and the negative battery cable.

11. Start the engine and check for leaks after the engine has warmed up. Minor leaks may be cured by slightly snugging the cover bolts. Any leak that is still pre-

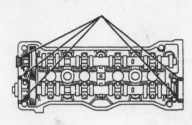

84343046

Apply sealant to these points before reinstalling the valve cover — 4A-FE and 7A-FE engines

sent after about a ¼ turn CANNOT be cured by further tightening. Remove the cover again and either reposition or replace the gasket.

Thermostat

REMOVAL & INSTALLATION

The thermostat is installed on the inlet side of the water pump. Its purpose is to prevent overheating of the coolant by controlling the flow into the engine from the radiator. During warm up, the thermostat remains closed so that the coolant within the engine heats quickly and aids the warming up process.

As the coolant temperature increases, the thermostat gradually opens, allowing a supply of lower temperature coolant (from the radiator) to enter the water pump and circulate through the engine.

NOTE: *A thermostat should never be removed as a countermeasure to an overheating problem. The vehicle cooling system should be serviced, necessary components replaced, correct coolant added and cooling system pressurized.*

1. Drain the cooling system and save the coolant for reuse.

CAUTION: *When draining the coolant, keep in mind that cats and dogs are attracted by the ethylene glycol antifreeze, and are quite likely to drink any that is left in an uncovered container or in puddles on the ground. This will prove fatal in sufficient quantity. Always drain the coolant into a sealable container. Coolant should be reused unless it is contaminated or several years old.*

2. Remove the water inlet (disconnect electrical connection) and remove the thermostat. Carefully observe the positioning of the thermostat within the housing. Clean all mounting surfaces before installation.

To install:

3. On the 4A-FE engine, place the thermostat in the water inlet housing. Install a new gasket to the the thermostat and align the jiggle valve of the thermostat as shown in the water inlet housing. The jiggle valve may be set within 10° of either side of the prescribed position (two types of thermostat are used).

4. On the 7A-FE engine, place the thermostat in the water inlet housing. Install a new gasket to the the thermostat and align the jiggle valve of the thermostat with the upper side of the stud bolt. The jiggle valve may be set within 10° of either side of the prescribed position.

5. On the 4A-GE engine, place the thermostat in the water inlet housing. Install a new gasket to the the thermostat and align the jiggle valve of the thermostat so that it is positioned above the water inlet housing.

6. Install the water inlet (connect electrical connection). Install the two hold-down bolts or nuts and tighten them to 7 ft. lbs. (in steps). Do not overtighten these bolts!

7. Refill the cooling system with coolant.

8. Start the engine. During the warm up period, observe the temperature gauge for normal behavior. Also during this period, check the water inlet housing area for any sign of leakage. Remember to check for leaks under both cold and hot conditions.

Intake Manifold

REMOVAL & INSTALLATION

4A-GE Engine

1. Relieve the fuel pressure. Disconnect the negative battery cable.

2. Remove the air cleaner assembly. Drain the coolant.

3. Tag and remove all wires, hoses or cables in the way of intake manifold removal. Remove the intake manifold stay (bracket).

4. Remove the cold start injector pipe.

5. Disconnect the electrical connectors and remove the fuel delivery pipe (fuel rail) and remove the injectors. During removal, be careful not to drop the injectors.

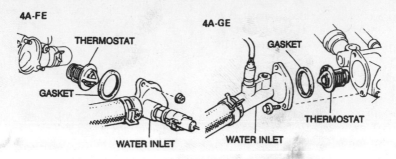

84343047

Thermostat and gasket removal and installation

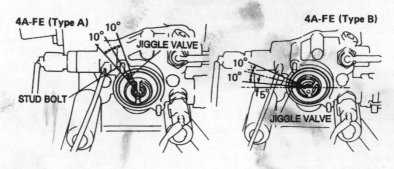

84343048

Thermostat installation — 4A-FE and 4A-GE engines

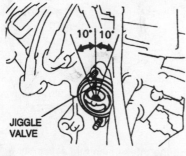

84343049

Thermostat installation — 7A-FE engine

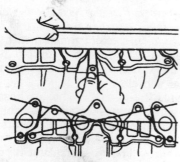

84343050

Measuring the manifold for warpage

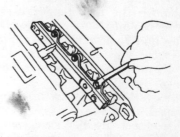

84343051

Removing the fuel rail and injectors — 4A-GE engine

CAUTION: *The fuel system is under pressure. Release pressure slowly and contain spillage. Observe no smoking/no open flame precautions. Have a Class B-C (dry powder) fire extinguisher within arm's reach at all times.*

6. Remove the intake manifold retaining bolts. Remove the intake manifold from the vehicle.

To install:

7. Clean the gasket mating surfaces, being careful not to damage them. Check the mating surfaces for warpage with a straightedge. The specification for maxi-

mum warpage on the intake manifold is
0.0020 in. (0.05 mm). If warpage is
greater than maximum, replace the
manifold.

8. Match the old gasket with the new
one for an exact match. Use a new gasket
when installing the manifold and tighten
the bolts evenly and in several passes
from the center outward to 20 ft. lbs. Install the intake manifold stay (bracket).

9. Install the cold start injector pipe.
Torque the cold start injector union bolt
to 18 ft. lbs.

10. Install all necessary wires, hoses or
cables. Install the air cleaner assembly.

11. Refill the cooling system. Connect
the negative battery cable. Start the engine. Check for leaks and road test for
proper operation.

4A-FE and 7A-FE Engines

NOTE: *On the 1993 4A-FE and 7A-FE
engines, the upper intake air chamber
and intake manifold can be separated.
A metal gasket is used to improve sealing performance. No cold start injector
assembly is used on the 1993 vehicles.*

1. Relieve the fuel pressure. Disconnect the negative battery cable.

2. Remove the air cleaner assembly.
Drain the coolant.

3. Tag and remove all wires, hoses or
cables in the way of intake manifold removal. Remove the intake manifold stay
(bracket).

4. Remove the cold start injector pipe,
if equipped.

5. Disconnect the electrical connectors
and remove the fuel delivery pipe (fuel
rail) and remove the injectors. During removal, be careful not to drop the
injectors.

CAUTION: *The fuel system is under
pressure. Release pressure slowly and
contain spillage. Observe no smok-*

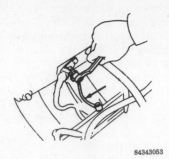

Removing the cold start injector line — 1990–92
4A-FE engine

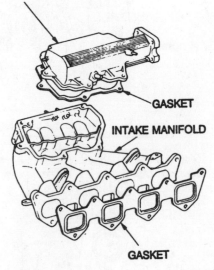

INTAKE AIR CHAMBER
GASKET
INTAKE MANIFOLD
GASKET

Removing the intake manifold assembly — 1993
4A-FE and 7A-FE engines

*ing/no open flame precautions. Have a
Class B-C (dry powder) fire extinguisher within arm's reach at all times.*

6. Remove the intake manifold retaining bolts. Remove the intake manifold
from the vehicle.

To install:

7. Clean the gasket mating surfaces,
being careful not to damage them. Check
the mating surfaces for warpage with a
straightedge. The specification for maximum warpage on the intake manifold is
0.0079 in. (0.20 mm). If warpage is
greater than maximum, replace the
manifold.

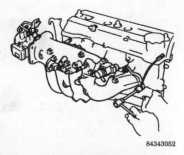

Removing the intake manifold assembly —
1990–92 4A-FE engine

8. Match the old gasket with the new one for an exact match. Use a new gasket when installing the manifold and tighten the bolts evenly and in several passes from the center outward to 20 ft. lbs. Install the intake manifold stay (bracket).

9. Install the cold start injector pipe, if equipped. Torque the cold start injector union bolt to 18 ft. lbs.

10. Install all necessary wires, hoses or cables. Install the air cleaner assembly.

11. Refill the cooling system. Connect the negative battery cable. Start the engine. Check for leaks and road test for proper operation.

Exhaust Manifold

REMOVAL & INSTALLATION

4A-GE Engine

1. Disconnect the negative battery cable. Raise the vehicle and support safely. Remove the right gravel shield from under the vehicle.

2. Remove the front exhaust pipe from the exhaust manifold.

3. Remove the upper heat insulator.

4. Remove the left and right manifold stays (brackets).

5. Remove the manifold retaining nuts. Remove the exhaust manifold from the vehicle.

To install:

6. Clean the gasket mating surfaces, being careful not to damage them. Check the mating surfaces for warpage with a straightedge. The specification for maximum warpage on the exhaust manifold is 0.0118 in. (0.30 mm). If warpage is greater than maximum, replace the manifold.

7. Match the old gasket with the new one for an exact match. Use a new gasket when installing the manifold and tighten the bolts (in steps) from the center outward to 18 ft. lbs.

8. Install the remaining components and torque left and right exhaust manifold stay (bracket) bolts to 29 ft. lbs. Start the engine and check for exhaust leaks.

4A-FE and 7A-FE Engines

NOTE: *On some 7A-FE engine applications, the shape of the exhaust manifold was changed to adopt a manifold cata-lytic converter. On these applications, remove the exhaust manifold assembly, then separate the catalytic converter from the manifold.*

1. Disconnect the negative battery cable. Raise the vehicle and support safely. Remove the right gravel shield from under the vehicle.

2. Remove the front exhaust pipe from the exhaust manifold.

3. Remove the upper heat insulator. Remove the manifold stay (bracket).

4. Remove the manifold retaining nuts. Remove the exhaust manifold from the vehicle.

To install:

5. Clean the gasket mating surfaces, being careful not to damage them. Check the mating surfaces for warpage with a straightedge. The specification for maximum warpage on the exhaust manifold is 0.0118 in. (0.30 mm). If warpage is greater than maximum, replace the manifold.

6. Match the old gasket with the new for an exact match. Use a new gasket when installing the manifold and tighten the bolts (in steps) from the center outward to 18 ft. lbs.

7. Install the remaining components and torque the exhaust manifold stay (bracket) bolts to 29 ft. lbs. Start the engine and check for exhaust leaks.

Radiator

REMOVAL & INSTALLATION

1. Disconnect the negative battery cable. Drain the cooling system.

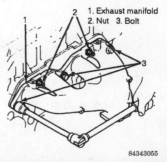

1. Exhaust manifold
2. Nut 3. Bolt

84343055

Location of exhaust manifold retaining bolts — 4A-FE and 7A-FE engines

CAUTION: *When draining the coolant, keep in mind that cats and dogs are attracted by the ethylene glycol antifreeze, and are quite likely to drink any that is left in an uncovered container or in puddles on the ground. This will prove fatal in sufficient quantity. Always drain the coolant into a sealable container. Coolant should be reused unless it is contaminated or several years old.*

2. Disconnect the electric cooling fan connector.

3. Unfasten the clamps and remove the radiator upper and lower hoses. If equipped with an automatic transaxle, remove the oil cooler lines (always use a line wrench).

4. Disconnect the coolant reservoir hose.

5. Remove the 2 bolts and two upper supports. Lift out the radiator. Remove the 2 lower supports. Use care not to damage the radiator fins or the cooling fan.

6. Remove the electric cooling fan assembly from the radiator.

To install:

7. Install the electric cooling fan assembly to the radiator.

8. Place the 2 lower radiator supports in position. Install the radiator and cooling fan as an assembly.

9. Place the radiator in position and install the 2 upper supports with the bolts. Torque the retaining bolts to 9 ft. lbs. Make sure that the rubber cushions are not depressed after installation.

10. Reconnect the transaxle oil cooler lines, if equipped.

11. Connect the coolant reservoir hose and radiator hoses with new hose clamps.

12. Reconnect the electrical connection for the cooling fan. Connect the negative battery cable.

13. Fill the cooling system. Start the engine, check for coolant leaks. Check the automatic transaxle fluid level.

Electric Cooling Fan

REMOVAL & INSTALLATION

1. Disconnect the negative battery cable. Drain the cooling system.

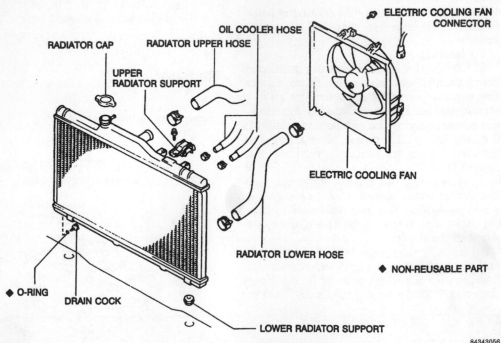

84343056

Radiator assembly and coolant hoses

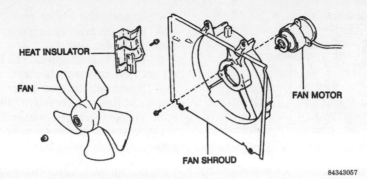

Cooling fan assembly

2. Remove the coolant reservoir tank. Disconnect the upper radiator hose from the radiator.

3. Disconnect the electric cooling fan connector. Remove the 4 bolts and remove the cooling fan and shroud as an assembly.

4. Remove the cooling fan motor from the fan shroud, if necessary.

5. Installation is the reverse of the removal procedure. Reconnect the electrical connection for the cooling fan. Connect the negative battery cable. Fill the cooling system. Start the engine and check for proper cooling fan operation.

TESTING

NOTE: *Always check all fuses and circuit breakers in all junction and relay blocks before troubleshooting the electric cooling fan circuit.*

Inspection Of Cooling Fan

1. Disconnect the cooling fan motor connector.

2. Apply battery voltage to the fan motor connector terminals and check that the fan operates smoothly and the fan housing is cool.

3. If the fan does not rotate with direct battery voltage, replace the fan motor. If

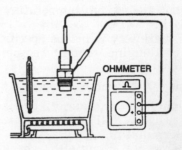

Checking water temperature switch (sending unit)

the fan rotates, check the cooling fan relay, engine main relay and all fuses, temperature switch, or for short circuits in the vehicle wiring.

Inspection Of Engine Coolant Temperature Switch

1. The engine coolant temperature switch is located on the water inlet housing. Using an ohmmeter, check that there is NO CONTINUITY between terminals when the coolant temperature is above 199°F.

2. Using an ohmmeter, check that there is CONTINUITY between termi-

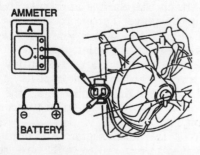

Checking cooling fan

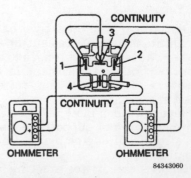

Checking cooling fan relay

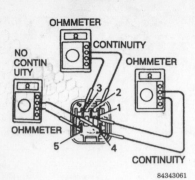

84343061

Checking engine main relay

nals when the coolant temperature is below 181°F.

3. If continuity is not as specified, replace the engine coolant temperature switch.

Inspection Of Cooling Fan Relay

1. Using an ohmmeter, check that there is CONTINUITY between terminal 1 and terminal 2.

2. Using an ohmmeter, check that there is CONTINUITY between terminal 3 and terminal 4.

3. If continuity is not as specified, replace the relay.

Inspection Of Engine Main Relay

1. Using an ohmmeter, check that there is CONTINUITY between terminal 1 and terminal 3.

2. Using an ohmmeter, check that there is CONTINUITY between terminal 2 and terminal 4.

3. Using an ohmmeter, check that there is NO CONTINUITY between terminal 4 and terminal 5.

4. If continuity is not as specified, replace the relay.

Water Pump

REMOVAL & INSTALLATION

4A-GE Engine

1. Disconnect the negative battery cable. Drain the engine coolant by opening the radiator and engine block draincocks. Collect the coolant in clean containers and save for reuse if necessary.

2. Place a wooden block between a jack and the engine and support the engine. Remove the front engine mount (mounting insulator).

3. Remove the power steering drive belt.

4. Loosen the water pump pulley bolts.

5. Loosen the alternator locking bolt and the pivot nut.

6. Move the alternator to its loosest position and remove the belt.

7. Remove the four bolts on the water pump pulley and remove the pulley.

8. Disconnect the water inlet and the water bypass hoses from the water inlet pipe.

9. Disconnect and remove the water inlet pipe by removing the two clamp bolts and the two nuts at the back of the pump. Remove the O-ring from the back of the pump.

10. Remove the mounting bolt for the dipstick tube; remove the tube and dipstick. Immediately plug the hole in block to prevent fluid from contaminating the oil.

NOTE: *During the following steps, if coolant should get by the plug in the dipstick hole and run into the engine, the engine oil MUST be changed before starting the engine.*

11. Remove the No. 3 (upper) and No. 2 (middle) timing belt covers.

12. Remove the water pump bolts and the water pump.

To install:

13. Place the water pump gasket (O-ring) on the block and install the pump. Tighten the mounting bolts evenly to 11 ft. lbs.

14. Install the timing belt covers, making sure they are properly seated and not rubbing on the belt or other moving parts.

15. Install a new seal (O-ring) on the dipstick tube and lightly coat it with engine oil. Remove the plug and install the dipstick tube and dipstick; secure the mounting bolt.

16. Using a new O-ring, install the inlet pipe to the water pump.

17. Attach the clamps and bolts to hold the pipe in place. Torque to 7 ft. lbs.

18. Connect the water inlet and water bypass hoses to the inlet pipe.

19. Install the water pump pulley and temporarily tighten the four pulley bolts.

20. Install the drive belts on all the pulleys and adjust all of them to the correct tension.

21. With the belts in place and adjusted, the water pump pulley will now resist turning. Tighten the pulley bolts to 16–18 ft. lbs.

22. Install the front engine mount (mounting insulator).

23. Confirm that the draincocks are closed on the engine block and radiator. Refill the engine with coolant. Reconnect the negative battery cable. Start the engine and check for leaks.

4A-FE and 7A-FE Engines

1. Disconnect the negative battery cable. Drain the engine coolant from the radiator.

2. Remove all drive belts.

3. Support the engine using suitable equipment. Place a wooden block between the jack and engine. Remove the right engine mount and insulator.

4. Remove the No. 3 (upper) and No. 2 (middle) timing belt covers.

5. If equipped with power steering, raise and safely support the vehicle. Remove the front transaxle mount. Lower the vehicle, remove the cooling fan assembly.

6. Remove the mounting bolt for the dipstick tube; remove the tube and dipstick. Immediately plug the hole in the

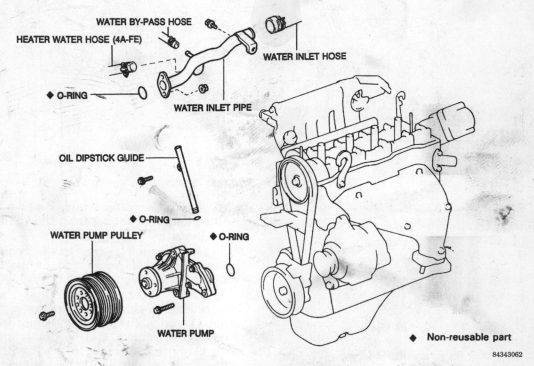

Water pump assembly — 4A-GE and 4A-FE engines

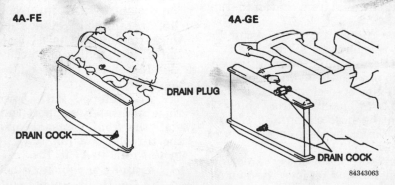

Drain plug locations

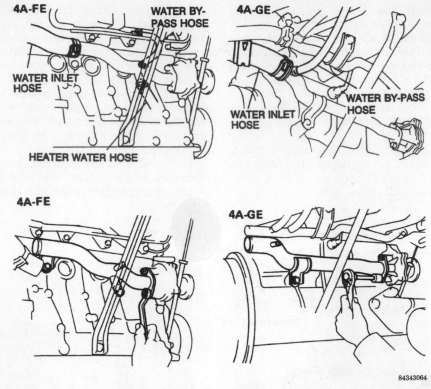

Water inlet hose removal and installation

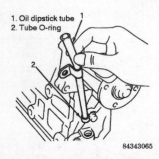

1. Oil dipstick tube
2. Tube O-ring

Removing the oil dipstick tube. Always plug the hole in the engine block when the tube is removed

block to prevent fluid from contaminating the oil.

7. Remove the electrical connector for the coolant temperature sending unit.

8. Remove the 2 nuts securing the engine coolant pipe to the cylinder block.

9. Loosen the hose clamp and remove the coolant inlet pipe from the vehicle.

10. Loosen the hose clamp and remove the coolant inlet hose from the water pump.

11. If equipped with power steering, raise the engine and remove the mount-ing bolts for the water pump. Remove the water pump and O-ring from the vehicle.

To install:

12. Install a new O-ring to the vehicle. Install the water pump and torque the retaining bolts evenly to 11 ft. lbs.

13. Lower the engine if necessary, and connect the coolant hose to the water pump. Reconnect the engine coolant inlet pipe to the vehicle and secure to hose with clamp and secure to block with 2 nuts. Tighten the engine coolant inlet pipe nuts to 11 ft. lbs.

14. Connect the electrical connector for the coolant temperature sending unit.

15. Install the oil guide tube and torque the retaining bolt to 84 inch lbs. Install the oil level indicator to the guide tube.

16. Install the radiator fan assembly, if necessary.

17. If equipped with power steering, raise and safely support the vehicle. Install the front transaxle mount. Torque the through bolt nut to 64 ft. lbs. and 2 mount nuts to 47 ft. lbs.

18. Lower the vehicle (if necessary) and install the No. 3 (upper) and No. 2 (middle) timing belt covers.

19. Support the engine using suitable equipment. Install the right engine mount and insulator.

20. Remove all engine lifting equipment.

21. Install and adjust all drive belts.

22. Reconnect the negative battery cable. Fill the cooling system. Start the engine and check for coolant leaks.

Cylinder Head

REMOVAL & INSTALLATION

4A-FE and 7A-FE Engines

1. Disconnect the negative battery cable at the battery. Drain the cooling system.

2. Remove the engine undercover and then disconnect the exhaust pipe at the manifold.

3. Remove the air cleaner and hoses; disconnect the intake air temperature sensor. Disconnect the accelerator and throttle cables at the bracket on vehicles with automatic transaxle.

4. Remove the cruise control actuator cable.

5. Tag and disconnect all wires, lines and hoses that may interfere with exhaust manifold, intake manifold and cylinder head removal.

6. Disconnect the fuel lines. Disconnect the heater hoses at the engine.

7. Disconnect the water hose and the bypass hose at the rear of the cylinder head. Remove the 2 bolts and pull off the water outlet pipe.

8. Remove the 2 mounting bolts and lift out the exhaust manifold stay. Remove the upper manifold insulator and then remove the exhaust manifold.

9. Remove the distributor.

10. Disconnect the 2 water hoses at the water inlet (front of head) and then remove the inlet housing.

11. Disconnect the PCV, fuel return and vacuum sensing hoses.

12. Remove the fuel inlet pipe and the cold start injector pipe (no cold start injector is used on the 1993 vehicles). Disconnect the 4 vacuum hoses and then remove the EGR vacuum modulator.

13. Remove the fuel delivery pipe along with the injectors, spacers and insulators.

14. Unbolt the engine wire cover at the intake manifold and then disconnect the wire at the cylinder head.

15. Remove the intake manifold assembly.

16. Remove the drive belts and then remove the water pump.

17. Remove the spark plugs, cylinder head cover and semi-circular plug.

18. Remove the No. 3 and No. 2 front covers. Turn the crankshaft pulley and align its groove with the **0** mark on the No. 1 front cover. Check that the camshaft pulley hole aligns with the mark on the No. 1 camshaft bearing cap (exhaust side). If not, rotate the crankshaft 360 degrees until the marks are aligned.

19. Remove the plug from the No. 1 front cover and matchmark the timing belt to the camshaft pulley. Loosen the idler pulley mounting bolt and push the pulley to the left as far as it will go; tighten the bolt. Slide the timing belt off the camshaft pulley and support it so it won't fall into the case.

20. Remove the camshaft pulley and check the camshaft thrust clearance. Remove the camshafts — refer to the necessary service procedures in this Chapter.

21. Gradually loosen the cylinder head mounting bolts in several passes, in the the proper sequence. Remove the cylinder head.

NOTE: *The cylinder head bolts on the intake side of the cylinder head are 3.54 in. (90mm) and the bolts on the exhaust side of the head are 4.25 in. (108mm). Label the bolts to ensure proper installation.*

To install:

22. Position the cylinder head on the block with a new gasket. Lightly coat the cylinder head bolts with engine oil and then install them. On 1990–92 vehicles, tighten the bolts in 3 stages, in the proper sequence. On the final pass, torque the bolts to 44 ft. lbs. (60 Nm). On the 1993 vehicles, coat the head bolts with engine oil and tighten them in several passes, in the sequence shown, to 22 ft. lbs. (29 Nm). Mark the front of each bolt with a dab of paint and then retighten the bolts a further 90 degree turn. The paint dabs should now all be at a 90 degree angle to the front of the head. Retighten the bolts one more time a further 90 degree turn. The paint dabs should now all be pointing toward the rear of the head.

23. Position the camshafts into the cylinder head. Position the bearing caps

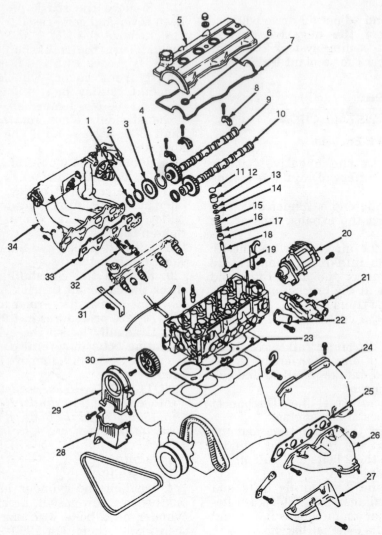

1. Camshaft snapring
2. Wave washer
3. Camshaft sub-gear
4. Camshaft gear spring
5. Valve cover (cylinder head cover)
6. Spark plug tube gasket
7. Valve cover gasket
8. Camshaft bearing cap
9. Instake camshaft
10. Exhaust camshaft
11. Adjusting shim
12. Valve lifter
13. Valve keepers
14. Valve spring retainer
15. Valve spring
16. Valve spring seat
17. Valve stem oil seal
18. Valve guide bushing
19. Valve
20. Distributor
21. Water inlet housing
22. Water outlet housing
23. Head gasket
24. Exhaust manifold upper insulator (heat shield)
25. Exhaust manifold gasket
26. Exhaust manifold
27. Exhaust manifold lower insulator (heat shield)
28. Center timing belt cover
29. Upper timing belt cover
30. Camshaft timing gear
31. Fuel rail
32. Cold-start injector pipe
33. Intake manifold gasket
34. Intake manifold

84343066

Exploded view of the 4A-FE cylinder head assembly

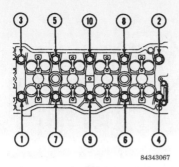

84343067

Cylinder head bolt removal sequence — 4A-FE and 7A-FE engines

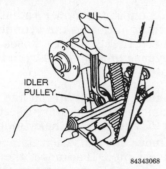

84343068

Loosen the timing belt idler pulley and move it to its loosest position

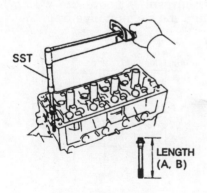

LENGTH (A, B)

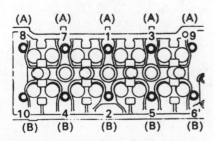

84343069

Cylinder head bolt torque sequence — 4A-FE and 7A-FE engines

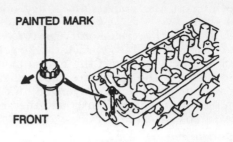

PAINTED MARK

FRONT

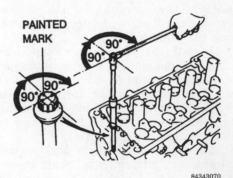

84343070

Cylinder head bolt torque procedure — 4A-FE and 7A-FE engines

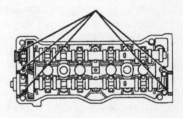

84343071

Apply sealant to these points before reinstalling the valve cover — 4A-FE and 7A-FE engines

over each journal with the arrows pointing forward.

24. Tighten each bearing cap a little at a time and in the reverse of the removal sequence. Tighten to 9 ft. lbs. (13 Nm) and recheck the camshaft end-play.

25. Install the camshaft timing pulley making sure the camshaft knock pins and the matchmarks are in alignment. Lock the camshaft and tighten the pulley bolts to 43 ft. lbs. (59 Nm).

26. Align the matchmarks made during removal and then install the timing belt on the camshaft pulley. Loosen the idler pulley set bolt. Make sure the timing belt

meshing at the crankshaft pulley does not shift.

27. Rotate the crankshaft clockwise 2 revolutions from TDC to TDC. Make sure each pulley aligns with the marks made previously. If the marks are not in alignment, the valve timing is wrong. Shift the timing belt meshing slightly and then repeat Steps 24–26.

28. Tighten the set bolt on the timing belt idler pulley to 27 ft. lbs. (37 Nm). Measure the timing belt deflection at the SIDE span. It should deflect no more than 0.24 in. (6mm) at 4.4 lbs. of pressure. If deflection is greater, readjust by using the idler pulley.

29. Install the remaining components with new gaskets and torque all the following components in several steps from the center position to the ends: the cylinder head cover to 52 inch lbs., intake manifold assembly to 14 ft. lbs. and exhaust manifold to 25 ft. lbs.

30. Check all fluid levels and perform all necessary adjustments. Start the engine and check for leaks. Road test the vehicle for proper operation.

4A-GE Engine

1. Disconnect the negative battery cable. Remove the engine undercover. Drain the cooling system and engine oil.

2. Loosen the clamp and then disconnect the air cleaner hose from the throttle body. Disconnect the actuator and accelerator cables from the bracket on the throttle body.

3. If equipped with power steering, remove the power steering pump and its bracket. Position the pump aside with the hydraulic lines connected.

4. Loosen the water pump pulley set nuts. Remove the drive belt adjusting bolt and then remove the belt. Remove the water pump pulley.

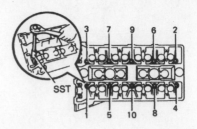

Cylinder head bolt removal sequence — 4A-GE engine

5. Disconnect the upper radiator hose at the water outlet on the cylinder head. Disconnect the 2 heater hoses at the water bypass pipe and the cylinder head rear plate.

6. Remove the ignition coil and distributor. Remove the cold start injector pipe and the PCV hose from the cylinder head.

7. Remove the pulsation damper from the delivery pipe. Disconnect the fuel return hose from the pressure regulator.

8. Tag and disconnect all vacuum hoses which may interfere with cylinder head remvoval. Remove the wiring harness and the vacuum pipe from the No. 3

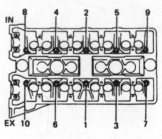

Cylinder head bolt torque sequence — 4A-GE engine

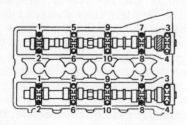

Camshaft bearing cap removal sequence — 4A-GE engine

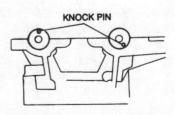

Position the camshafts into the cylinder head as shown — 4A-GE engine

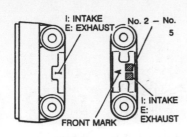

84343076

Camshaft bearing cap positioning — 4A-GE engine

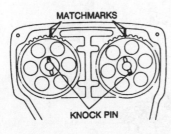

84343077

Align the camshaft knockpin with the camshaft timing pulley — 4A-GE engine

timing cover. Tag and disconnect all wires which might interfere with exhaust manifold, intake manifold and cylinder head removal.

9. Disconnect the exhaust bracket from the exhaust pipe. Disconnect the exhaust manifold from the exhaust pipe.

10. Remove the vacuum tank and the VCV valve. Remove the exhaust manifold.

11. Remove the 2 mounting bolts and remove the water outlet housing from the cylinder head with the No. 1 bypass pipe and gasket. Pull the No. 1 bypass pipe out of the housing.

12. Remove the fuel delivery pipe along with the fuel injectors.

13. Remove the intake manifold stay. Remove the intake manifold along with the air control valve.

14. Remove the cylinder head covers and their gaskets. Remove the spark plugs. Remove the No. 1 and No. 2 timing belt covers and their gaskets.

15. Rotate the crankshaft pulley until its groove is in alignment with the **0** mark on the No. 1 timing belt cover. Check that the valve lifters on the No. 1 cylinder are loose. If not, rotate the

crankshaft 1 complete revolution (360 degrees).

16. Place matchmarks on the timing belt and 2 timing pulleys. Loosen the idler pulley bolts and move the pulley to the left as far as it will go, then retighten the bolt.

17. Remove the timing belt from the camshaft pulleys. When removing the timing belt, support the belt so the meshing of the crankshaft timing pulley and the timing belt does not shift. Never drop anything inside the timing case cover. Be sure the timing belt does not come in contact with dust or oil.

18. Lock the camshafts and remove the timing pulleys. Remove the No. 4 timing belt cover.

19. Using a dial indicator, measure the end-play of each camshaft. If not within specification, replace the thrust bearing.

20. Loosen each camshaft bearing cap bolt a little at a time and in the correct sequence. Remove the bearing caps, camshaft and oil seal.

21. Loosen the cylinder head bolts gradually in 3 stages, and in the proper order using the proper tool.

22. Remove the cylinder head.

NOTE: *The cylinder head bolts on the intake side of the cylinder head are 3.54 in. (90mm) and the bolts on the exhaust side of the head are 4.25 in. (108mm). Label the bolts to ensure proper installation.*

To install:

23. Position the cylinder head on the block with a new gasket.

24. After coating the head bolts with engine oil, install and tighten the head bolts in several passes, in the sequence shown to 22 ft. lbs. (29 Nm). Mark the front of each bolt with a dab of paint and then retighten the bolts a further 90 degree turn. The paint dabs should now all be at a 90 degree angle to the front of the head. Retighten the bolts one more time a further 90 degree turn. The paint dabs should now all be pointing toward the rear of the head.

25. Position the camshafts into the cylinder head. Position the bearing caps over each journal with the arrows pointing forward.

26. Tighten each bearing cap a little at a time and in the reverse of the removal sequence. Tighten to 9 ft. lbs. (13 Nm). Recheck the camshaft end-play.

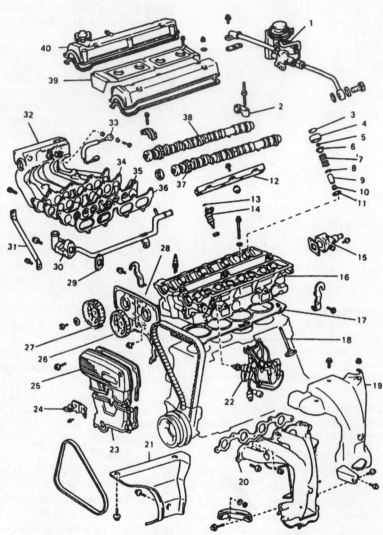

1. EGR valve	15. Cylinder head rear cover	29. Gasket
2. Camshaft bearing cap	16. Cylinder head	30. Water outlet
3. Adjusting shim	17. Cylinder head gasket	31. Intake manifold stay
4. Valve lifter	18. Valve	32. Intake manifold
5. Valve keepers	19. Upper exhaust manifold insulator	33. Cold start injection pipe
6. Valve spring retainer	20. Exhaust manifold	34. Gasket
7. Valve spring	21. Lower exhaust manifold insulator	35. Air control valve
8. Snap ring	22. Distributor	36. Gasket
9. Valve guide bushing	23. No. 2 timing belt cover	37. Exhaust valve camshaft
10. Valve stem oil seal	24. Engine mounting bracket	38. Intake valve camshaft
11. Valve spring seal	25. No. 3 timing belt cover	39. Cylinder head center cover
12. Delivery pipe	26. Exhaust camshaft timing pulley	40. Cylinder head cover
13. O-ring	27. Intake camshaft timing pulley	
14. Injector	28. No. 4 timing belt cover	

84343078

Exploded view of the 4A-GE cylinder head assembly

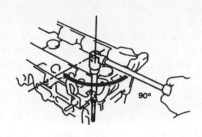

Cylinder head bolt torque procedure — 4A-GE engine

27. Drive the camshaft oil seals onto the end of the camshafts using a suitable seal installer. Be careful not to cock the oil seal in the bore. Install the No. 4 timing belt cover.

28. Install the camshaft timing pulleys, making sure the camshaft knock pins and the matchmarks are in alignment. Lock each camshaft and tighten the pulley bolts to 34 ft. lbs. (47 Nm).

29. Align the matchmarks made during removal and then install the timing belt on the camshaft pulley. Loosen the idler pulley set bolt. Make sure the timing belt meshing at the crankshaft pulley does not shift.

30. Rotate the crankshaft clockwise 2 revolutions from TDC to TDC. Make sure each pulley aligns with the marks made previously. If the marks are not in alignment, the valve timing is wrong. Shift the timing belt meshing slightly and then repeat Steps 28–30.

31. Tighten the set bolt on the timing belt idler pulley to 27 ft. lbs. (37 Nm). Measure the timing belt deflection at the top span between the 2 camshaft pulleys. It should deflect no more than 0.16 in. at 4.4 lbs. of pressure. If deflection is greater, readjust by using the idler pulley.

32. Install the remaining components with new gaskets and torque all the following components in several steps from the center position to the ends: the cylinder head cover to 5.8 ft. lbs., intake manifold assembly to 20 ft. lbs. and exhaust manifold to 18 ft. lbs.

33. Check all fluid levels and perform all necessary adjustments. Start the engine and check for leaks. Road test the vehicle for proper operation.

CLEANING AND INSPECTION

1. With the cylinder head removed from the engine, remove the intake and exhaust manifolds, following procedures outlined earlier in this Chapter, if necessary.

2. Remove the camshafts, if necessary.

3. Remove the valve lifters and the adjusting shims.

4. Remove the spark plug tubes.

5. Remove the engine hoist hooks.

6. Remove the valves, using procedures outlined later in this Chapter.

7. Remove the half-circle plug at the end of the head.

8. Using a wire brush chucked into an electric drill, remove all the carbon from the combustion chambers in the head. Be careful not to scratch the head surface.

9. Use a valve guide brush or a fine-bristled rifle bore brush with solvent to clean the valve guides.

10. Use a clean cloth and a stiff bristle brush with solvent to thoroughly clean the head assembly. Make sure that no material is washed into the bolt holes or passages. If possible, dry the head with

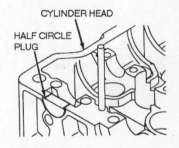

Half circle plug or seal in cylinder head assembly

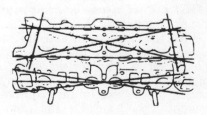

Cylinder head warpage checking points

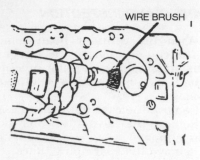

WIRE BRUSH

84343082

Removing combustion chamber carbon

84343083

Checking the cylinder head for warpage

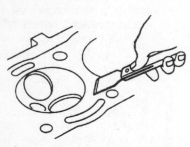

84343084

Do not scratch the head gasket mating surface when removing the old gasket

compressed air to remove fluid and solid matter from all the passages.

NOTE: *Do not clean the head in a hot tank or chemical bath.*

11. With the head clean and dry, use a precision straightedge and a feeler gauge to measure the head for warpage. Also measure the manifold faces. Any warpage in excess of the maximum requires replacement of the head. The maximum allowable warpage is:

- Cylinder block face: 0.05mm
- Intake manifold face: 0.10mm
- Exhaust manifold face: 0.10mm

12. If all is well with the cylinder head to this point, it is highly recommended that it be taken to a professional facility such as a machine shop for sophisticated crack testing. The various procedures are much more reliable than simple examination by eye. The cost is reasonable and the peace of mind is well worth the cost. If any cracks are found, the head must be replaced.

CYLINDER HEAD RESURFACING

The cylinder heads are manufactured to be as light as possible; consequently, there is not much excess metal on the face. Any machining must be minimal. If too much metal is removed, the head becomes unusable. A head which exceeds the maximum warpage specification CANNOT be resurfaced. The machine shop will have a list of minimum head thicknesses; at no time may this minimum be exceeded.

Valve Springs, Valves and Valve Stem Seals

REMOVAL & INSTALLATION

NOTE: *This procedure requires the use of a valve spring compressor. This tool is available at most auto supply stores. It may also be possible to rent one from a tool supplier. It is absolutely essential that all components be kept in order after removal. Old ice trays make excellent holders for small parts. The containers should be labeled so that the parts may be reinstalled in their original location. Keep the valves in numbered order in a holder such as an egg carton or an inverted box with holes punched in it. Label the container so that each valve may be replaced in its exact position. (Example: Exhaust #1, #2 etc.) Toyota does not recommend replacing the valve stem oil seals with the cylinder head installed. Always remove the cylinder head to replace the valve stem oil seals.*

1. Remove the cylinder head following procedures outlined earlier in this Chapter.

2. Remove the intake and exhaust manifolds, if necessary.

3. Remove the camshafts following procedures outlined later in this Chapter. Label the shafts and their retainers.

4. Remove the valve lifters and the adjusting shims.

Lapping a valve in by hand

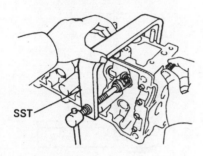

Valve spring compressor tool

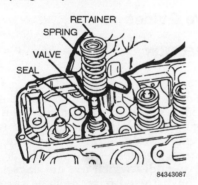

Installing the valve spring (typical)

5. Remove the spark plug tubes from the head.

6. Attach the spring compressor. Make sure the spring compressor tool is compatible with the cylinder head that you are working on.

7. Compress the valve spring and remove the keepers at the top of the valve stem.

8. Slowly release the tension on the compressor and remove it.

9. Remove the spring retainer, the valve spring and the lower spring seat. The valve is then removed from the bottom of the head.

10. Repeat these steps for each valve in the head, keeping them labeled and in order. Remove the half-circle plug at the end of the head. Use needle-nose pliers and remove all oil seals.

11. Thoroughly clean and decarbon each valve. Inspect each valve and spring.

12. Lubricate the the valve stem and guide with engine oil. Install the valve in the cylinder head.

13. Coat the valve face and seat with a light coat of valve grinding compound. Attach the suction cup end of the valve grinding tool to the head of the valve (it helps to moisten it first).

14. Rotate the tool between the palms, changing position and and lifting the tool often to prevent grooving. Lap in the valve until a smooth, evenly polished surface is evident on both the seat and valve face.

15. Remove the valve from the head. Wipe away all traces of grinding compound from the surfaces. Clean out the valve guide with a solvent-soaked rag. Make sure there are NO traces of compound in or on the head.

16. Proceed through the remaining valves, lapping them one at a time to their seats. Clean the area after each valve is done.

17. When all the valves have been lapped, thoroughly clean or wash the head with solvent. There must be NO trace of grinding compound present. Lubricate the new valve oil seals with engine oil and install all in the cylinder head.

18. Install the spring seat, valve spring and the upper retainer, compress the spring and install the two keepers. Relax tension on the compressor and make sure everything is properly placed. Tap on the installed valve stem with a plastic mallet to ensure proper locking of the retainers.

19. Install the valve lifters and the adjusting shims.

20. Coat the half-circle plug with silicone sealant and install it in position.

21. Complete the reassembly of the cylinder head by installing the camshafts and the manifolds if necessary. Check and adjust the valve clearance.

INSPECTION AND MEASUREMENT

NOTE: *Accurate measuring equipment capable of reading to 0.0001 (ten thousandths) inch is necessary for this work. A micrometer and a hole (bore) gauge will be needed.*

Inspect the valve faces and seats for pits, burned spots, and other evidence of poor seating. If necessary, the valves and seats can be ground using suitable valve refacing and seat grinding equipment. These procedures are best left to a qualified machine shop. If the valve is in such poor shape that grinding will not true the valve face, discard the valve. If the valve seat cannot be trued, replace the cylinder head.

Check the valve stem for scoring and/or burned spots. If the stem and head are in acceptable condition, clean the valve thoroughly with solvent to remove all gum and varnish.

Use the micrometer to measure the diameter of the valve stem. Use the hole gauge to measure the inside diameter of the valve guide for that valve. Subtract the stem diameter from the guide diameter and compare the difference. If not within specifications, determine the cause (worn valve or worn guide) and replace the worn part(s).

Using a steel square, check the valve spring for correct height and squareness. If the squareness is not within 2mm, replace the spring. If the free height of the spring is not within specification, replace the spring. The installed height of the spring must be measured with the spring under tension in the head. Assemble the valve and spring with the retainers and clips into the head; modify a small steel ruler to fit and record the distance from the bottom spring seat to the upper retainer. If not within specification, replace the necessary parts.

Valve Seats

REMOVAL & INSTALLATION

The valve seats are not replaceable. A valve seat that cannot be restored by grinding requires replacement of the cylinder head. Valve seat checking and grinding are procedures best left to a qualified machine shop.

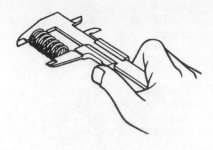

84343089

Checking the valve spring free height

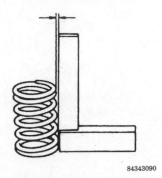

84343090

Checking the valve spring for squareness

Valve Guides

INSPECTION

Valve guides should be cleaned as outlined earlier and checked when the stem-to-guide clearance is measured. As a general rule, if the engine admits oil through the guides and the oil seals are in good condition, the guides are worn.

Valve guides which are not excessively worn or distorted may, in some cases, be knurled rather than replaced. Knurling is a process in which metal inside the valve guide is displaced and raised by a cutter, making a spiral pattern. A reamer passed through the guide then restores the in-

84343088

Measure the diameter of the valve guide and the valve stem — the difference is the stem clearance

side diameter to specification. This process restores the valve stem clearance to specification.

REMOVAL & INSTALLATION

NOTE: *Replacing the valve guides requires heating the head to high temperatures and the use of special tools. Do not attempt this repair if you are not equipped with the proper heating and handling equipment. Do not attempt this repair unless equipped with the correct valve guide tools and a reamer. This repair requires a high level of mechanical skill and machine shop procedures.*

4A-FE and 7A-FE Engines

1. Gradually heat the cylinder head to 212°F (100°C).
2. Carefully remove the head from the heat source.
3. Using the proper tool and a hammer, drive out the guide.
4. With the guide removed, measure the bore (in the head) into which the guide fits. Refer to bore specifications as a new oversized guide or head assembly must be used.

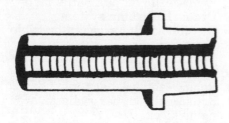

84343091

Cross-section of a knurled valve guide

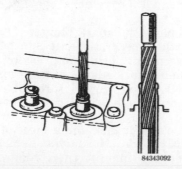

84343092

Use a precision reamer to enlarge new valve guides if necessary

5. Reheat the head to 212°F (100°C) and then remove it from the heat.
6. Using the correct tools, drive in the new guide until it projects to the correct specification (0.500–0.516 in.) above the head.
7. Measure the inner diameter of the guide. Compare this to the stem diameter of the new valve. If the stem to guide clearance is insufficient, ream the new guide with a sharp reamer until the correct clearance is obtained.

4A-GE Engine

1. The part of the old valve guide that protrudes above the cylinder head must be broken off before removing the guide. Wrap an old valve stem in tape to prevent the stem from dropping too far into the guide. Pad the surrounding area with rags. Insert the old valve into the guide and strike the valve with a hammer, to break off the top of the guide.
2. Heat the cylinder head gradually, in water, to 212°F (100°C).
3. Carefully remove the head from water. Use a correct tool and a hammer to drive out the guide.
4. With the guide removed, measure the bore (in the head) into which the guide fits. Refer to bore specifications as a new oversized guide or head assembly must be used.
5. Reheat the head in water to 212°F (100°C), then carefully remove it from the water.
6. Using the removal tool, drive in the new guide until the snapring makes contact with the cylinder head.
7. Measure the inner diameter of the guide. Compare this to the stem diameter of the new valve. If the stem to guide clearance is insufficient, ream the new guide with a sharp reamer until the correct clearance is obtained.

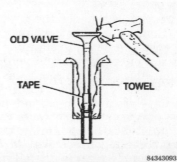

OLD VALVE

TAPE   TOWEL

84343093

Use this method for breaking off the tops of 4A-GE engine valve guides before removal

Valve Lifters

REMOVAL & INSTALLATION

1. Disconnect the negative battery cable.
2. Drain the cooling system.
3. Remove the valve cover(s).
4. Remove the camshafts.
5. Remove the valve lifters and shims, from the cylinder head.
6. Label each lifter and shim with the respective cylinder head bore.
7. Inspect the lifters and shims for excessive wear. Replace worn lifters and shims as required.

To install:

8. Install the lifters and shims into the cylinder head. Make sure the lifter can be rotated freely by hand.
9. Install the camshafts. Check the valve lash, as explained in Chapter 2.
10. Install the valve cover(s) using new gaskets and sealant, as required.
11. Fill the cooling system to the proper level.
12. Connect the negative battery cable.

Oil Pan

REMOVAL & INSTALLATION

NOTE: *On the 1993 7A-FE engine a 2 piece oil pan assembly is used. The No. 1 oil pan (upper) is made of aluminum and the No. 2 oil pan (lower) is made of steel. The upper oil pan section is secured to the cylinder block and the transaxle housing, increasing rigidity.*

1. Disconnect the negative battery cable. Raise and support the vehicle safely. Drain the oil.
2. Remove the splash shield from underneath the engine.
3. Place a jack under the transaxle to support it.
4. Remove the center mounting and stiffener plate.
5. Raise the jack under the transaxle, slightly. Remove the front exhaust pipe.
6. Remove the oil pan retaining bolts. Remove the oil pan from the vehicle. If the oil pan does not come out easily, it may be necessary to unbolt the rear engine mounts from the crossmember. It may be necessary to remove the oil strainer and pick-up assembly to gain clearance for oil pan removal (drop oil strainer assembly right in the oil pan).
7. Installation is the reverse of the removal procedure. Tighten the oil pan

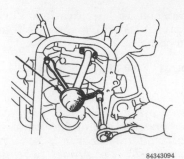

84343094

Arrow indicates the oil strainer and pick-up assembly on the 4A-FE engine

bolts to 5 ft. lbs. (working from the center to the ends). Always replace the oil pan gasket and refill with engine oil. Start the engine and check for leaks.

Oil Pump

REMOVAL & INSTALLATION

NOTE: *When repairing or replacing the oil pump assembly, the oil pan and strainer should be removed and cleaned.*

4A-GE Engine

1. Disconnect the negative battery cable.
2. Remove the oil pan as previously outlined.
3. Remove the oil pick-up and strainer.
4. Remove the oil pan baffle plate.
5. Drain the cooling system.
6. Disconnect the accelerator cable or linkage.
7. Remove the cruise control actuator, if equipped.
8. Remove the washer tank.
9. Remove the upper radiator hose at the engine block.
10. Remove the power steering and/or the air conditioning drive belt(s).
11. Loosen the bolts to the water pump pulley and then remove the alternator drive belt.
12. Remove the spark plugs.
13. Rotate the crankshaft and position the engine at TDC/compression. The crankshaft mark aligns at zero and the camshaft, when viewed through the oil filler cap, has a small cavity pointing upward.
14. Use a floor jack and a piece of wood to slightly elevate the engine. Remove the right engine mount; then remove the three bolts and remove the right reinforcing plate for the engine mount.

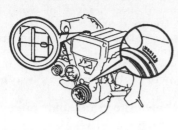

84343095

Aligning the 4A-GE engine at TDC/compression for No. 1 cylinder

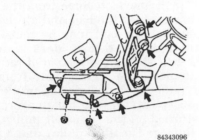

84343096

Arrows indicate the nuts and bolts holding the right engine mount and reinforcing plate on the 4A-GE engine

15. Remove the water pump pulley.

16. Remove the crankshaft pulley.

NOTE: *Counterhold the crankshaft or block the flywheel to prevent the crank from turning.*

17. Remove the timing belt covers.

NOTE: *The timing belt cover bolts are different lengths and MUST be returned to the proper hole at reassembly. During removal, diagram or label each bolt and its correct position.*

18. Remove the timing belt guide.

19. Loosen the idler pulley bolt, push it all the way to the left and tighten the bolt. This removes tension from the belt.

20. Matchmark the belt and all the pulleys so that the belt may be reinstalled exactly as it was before. Mark an arrow on the belt showing direction of rotation.

21. Remove the timing belt from the lower pulley (crankshaft timing pulley). If you are careful, the belt may remain undisturbed on the camshaft pulleys.

22. Remove the idler pulley and spring.

23. Remove the crankshaft timing pulley.

24. Remove the PCV hose.

25. Remove the dipstick and tube.

26. Remove the bolts (note location and length of all bolts) from the oil pump and carefully remove the pump. If it is difficult to remove, tap it lightly with a plastic or rubber mallet. Do not pry it off or strike it with a metal hammer.

To install:

27. Place a new gasket on the block. Install the oil pump to the crankshaft with the spline teeth to the drive gear engaged with the large teeth of the crankshaft.

28. Install the correct retaining bolts and tighten them to 16 ft. lbs.

29. Install the dipstick tube and dipstick.

30. Install the crankshaft timing pulley.

31. Install the timing belt idler pulley.

32. Install the timing belt.

33. Install the timing belt guide. It should install with the cupped side facing outward.

34. Make sure the gaskets are properly seated in the timing belt covers and reinstall the covers. Make sure each bolt is in the correct hole.

35. Install the crankshaft pulley. Again using a counterholding device, tighten the bolt to specifications.

36. Install the water pump pulley and tighten the bolts finger tight. Install the valve covers.

37. Install the right side engine mount. Tighten the nut to 38 ft. lbs. and the through bolt to 64 ft. lbs.

38. Install the reinforcement for the right motor mount and tighten the bolts to 31 ft. lbs.

39. Install the spark plugs.

40. Install the alternator drive belt and tighten the water pump pulley bolts.

41. Install and adjust the power steering and/or the air conditioner drive belts.

42. Connect the upper radiator hose.

43. Install the windshield washer reservoir.

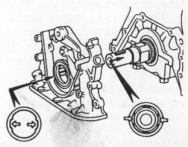

84343097

Correct position for installation of the oil pump

44. If equipped with cruise control, reinstall the cruise control actuator.

45. Connect the accelerator cable or linkage.

46. Install the oil pan baffle plate. Clean the contact surfaces thoroughly, apply a bead of sealer to the baffle plate and press the baffle plate into position. Be very careful not to get any sealant into the oil passages.

47. Install the oil pick-up and strainer assembly. Install the PCV hose.

48. Install the oil pan.

49. Using new gaskets, reconnect the exhaust pipe. Tighten the bolts to the catalytic converter and the bolts to the exhaust manifold.

50. Install the flywheel cover.

51. Install the stiffener plate and the center engine mount.

52. Refill the engine with oil.

53. Refill the cooling system.

54. Start the engine and check for leaks. Allow the engine to warm up to normal operating temperature and check the work area carefully for signs of seepage.

55. With the engine shut off, check the tension of the drive belts and adjust if necessary. Reinstall the splash guards under the car.

4A-FE and 7A-FE Engines

1. Disconnect the negative battery cable and raise the vehicle. Safely support it on jackstands. Remove the splashshield(s).

2. Remove the protectors from the two center engine mount nuts and studs.

3. Remove the two center transaxle mount-to-center crossmember nuts.

4. Remove the two rear transaxle mount-to-main crossmember nuts.

5. Drain the engine oil.

6. Remove the oil pan. Remove the oil pick-up and strainer assembly.

7. Lower the vehicle to the ground.

8. Depending on equipment, loosen the air conditioning compressor bracket, the power steering pump bracket and the alternator bracket as applicable. Remove the drive belts.

9. Remove the alternator from its mounts and place it out of the way. The wiring may be left attached.

10. Lift out the windshield washer fluid reservoir.

11. Support the engine. This may be done from above with a chain hoist or from below with a floor jack. Be very careful of the jack placement (the oil pan is removed); use a piece of wood to distribute the load and protect the engine.

12. Remove the through bolt in the right engine mount.

13. Remove the water pump pulley.

14. Lower the engine to its normal position.

15. Remove the crankshaft pulley.

16. Remove the timing belt covers.

17. Remove the timing belt guide from the crank pulley.

18. Loosen the idler pulley bolt, push it all the way to the left and tighten the bolt. This removes tension from the belt.

19. Matchmark the belt and all the pulleys so that the belt may be reinstalled exactly as it was before. Mark an arrow on the belt showing direction of rotation.

20. Remove the timing belt from the lower pulley (crankshaft timing pulley). If you are careful, the belt may remain undisturbed on the camshaft pulley.

21. Remove the idler pulley and spring.

22. Remove the dipstick and dipstick tube.

23. Remove the crankshaft timing pulley.

24. Raise the vehicle and safely support it on jackstands.

25. Remove the seven bolts holding the oil pump.

26. Remove the seven bolts (note location and length of all bolts) in the oil pump and carefully remove the pump. If it is difficult to remove, tap it lightly with a plastic or rubber mallet. Do not pry it off or strike it with a metal hammer.

To install:

27. Place a new gasket on the block. Install the oil pump to the crankshaft with the spline teeth to the drive gear engaged with the large teeth of the crankshaft.

28. Install the correct retaining bolts and tighten them to 16 ft. lbs.

29. Lower the vehicle to the ground.

30. Install the timing belt idler pulley.

31. Install the dipstick tube and dipstick.

32. Install the timing belt.

33. Install the timing belt guide. It should install with the cupped side facing outward.

34. Make sure the gaskets are properly seated in the timing belt covers and reinstall the covers. Make sure each bolt is in the correct hole.

35. Install the crankshaft pulley. Tighten the bolt to specifications.

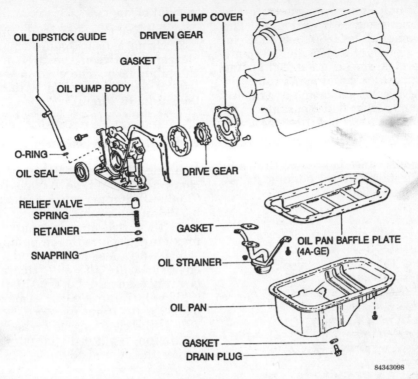

Detail of the oil pump system on the 4A-GE engine. The 4A-FE engine is similar without the baffle plate. Any gasket shown should be replaced before reassembly

36. Elevate the motor to gain access to the water pump.

37. Install the water pump pulley.

38. Install the right engine mount through bolt. Tighten the through bolt to 64 ft. lbs. When the bolt is secure, the engine lifting apparatus may be removed.

39. Position and install the alternator.

40. Reinstall the drive belts for the alternator, power steering and air conditioning as applicable. Adjust the belts to the correct tension.

41. Raise the vehicle and safely support it on jackstands.

42. Install the oil pick-up and strainer assembly.

43. Apply a continuous bead of sealer to both sides of the new pan gasket.

44. Place the gasket on the pan and install the pan to the block. Tighten the bolts and nuts to 5 ft. lbs. from the center to the ends.

45. Install the two rear transaxle mount-to-main crossmember nuts and tighten them to 45 ft. lbs. Install the two center transaxle mount-to-center crossmember nuts and tighten them to 45 ft. lbs.

46. Install the protectors over the nuts and studs for the mounts.

47. Lower the vehicle to the ground.

48. Install the windshield washer fluid reservoir.

49. Refill the engine with the correct amount of oil.

50. Connect the negative battery cable.

51. Start the engine and check for leaks. Allow the engine to warm up to normal operating temperature and check the work area carefully for signs of seepage.

52. With the engine shut off, check the tension of the drive belts and adjust if necessary. Reinstall the splash guard(s) under the vehicle.

INSPECTION AND OVERHAUL

4A-FE and 7A-FE Engines

1. Remove the pump body cover.

2. Using a feeler gauge, measure the clearance between the driven gear and the pump body. The clearance should be 0.0031–0.0071 in. with a maximum of 0.0079 in. (0.20mm).

3. If the clearance is greater than the maximum, replace the oil pump gear set and/or the pump body.

4. Using a feeler gauge, measure the clearance between both gear tips. The clearance should be 0.0010–0.0033 in. with a maximum of 0.0138 in. (0.35mm).

5. If the clearance is greater than the maximum, replace the oil pump rotor set.

6. Using a feeler gauge and a straight-edge, measure the side clearance. The clearance should be 0.0010–0.0033 in. (0.025–0.085mm) with a maximum of 0.0039 in. (0.10mm).

7. If the clearance is greater than the maximum, replace the oil pump gear set and/or the pump body.

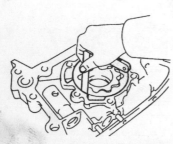

84343099

Checking drive and drive rotor body clearance — oil pump assembly

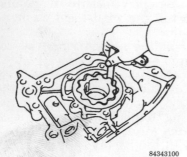

84343100

Checking rotor tip clearance — oil pump assembly

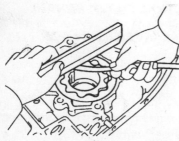

84343101

Checking rotor side clearance — oil pump assembly

4A-GE Engine

1. Remove the pump body cover.

2. Using a feeler gauge, measure the clearance between the driven gear and the pump body. The clearance should be 0.0039–0.0075 in. with a maximum of 0.0079 in. (0.20mm).

3. If the clearance is greater than the maximum, replace the oil pump gear set and/or the pump body.

4. Using a feeler gauge, measure the clearance between both gear tips. The clearance should be 0.0023–0.0071 in. (0.060–0.180mm) with a maximum of 0.0138 in. (0.35mm).

5. If the clearance is greater than the maximum, replace the oil pump rotor set.

6. Using a feeler gauge and a straight-edge, measure the side clearance. The clearance should be 0.0010–0.0030 in. (0.025–0.075mm) with a maximum of 0.0039 in. (0.10mm).

7. If the clearance is greater than the maximum, replace the oil pump gear set and/or the pump body.

Crankshaft Pulley

REMOVAL & INSTALLATION

To remove the crankshaft pulley refer to the "Timing Belt Cover" removal and installation service procedures.

Timing Belt Cover

REMOVAL & INSTALLATION

4A-GE Engine

1. Disconnect the negative battery cable.

2. Raise the vehicle and safely support it on jackstands.

3. Remove the right front wheel.

4. Remove the splash shield from under the car.

5. Drain the coolant into clean containers. Close the draincocks when the system is empty.

6. Lower the car to the ground. Disconnect the accelerator cable and, if equipped, the cruise control cable.

7. Remove the cruise control actuator, if equipped.

8. Carefully remove the ignition coil.

9. Disconnect the radiator hose at the water outlet.

10. Remove the power steering drive belt and the alternator drive belt.

11. Remove the spark plugs.

1. No. 2 timing belt cover
2. No. 3 timing belt cover
3. Exhaust camshaft timing pulley
4. Intake camshaft pulley
5. Gasket
6. Idler pulley
7. Crankshaft timing pulley
8. Timing belt
9. Tension spring

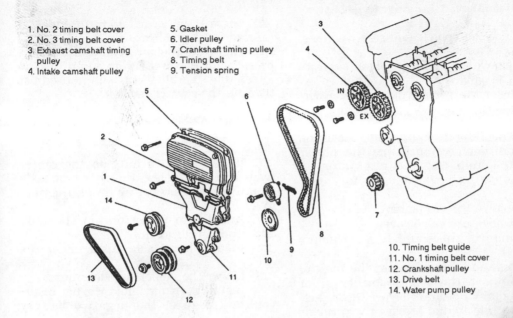

10. Timing belt guide
11. No. 1 timing belt cover
12. Crankshaft pulley
13. Drive belt
14. Water pump pulley

84343102

Timing belt, cover and related components — 4A-GE engine

12. Rotate the crankshaft clockwise and set the engine to TDC/compression on No. 1 cylinder. Align the crankshaft marks at zero; look through the oil filler hole and make sure the small hole in the end of the camshaft can be seen.

13. Raise and safely support the vehicle. Disconnect the center engine mount.

14. Lower the vehicle to the ground.

15. Support the engine either from above or below. Disconnect the right engine mount from the engine.

16. Raise the engine and remove the mount.

17. Remove the water pump pulley.

18. Remove the crankshaft pulley.

19. Remove the 10 bolts and remove the timing belt covers with their gaskets.

NOTE: *The bolts are different lengths; they must be returned to their correct location at reassembly. Label or diagram the bolts during removal.*

To install:

20. When reinstalling, make certain that the gaskets and their mating surfaces are clean and free from dirt and oil. The gasket itself must be free of cuts and deformations and must fit securely in the grooves of the covers.

21. Reinstall the covers and their gaskets and the 10 bolts in their proper positions.

22. Install the crankshaft pulley, again using the counterholding tool. Tighten the bolt to specifications.

23. Install the water pump pulley.

24. Install the right engine mount. Tighten the through bolt to 58 ft. lbs.

25. Reinstall the spark plugs and their wires.

26. Install the alternator drive belt and the power steering drive belt. Adjust the belts to the correct tension.

27. Connect the radiator hose to the water outlet port.

28. Install the ignition coil.

29. Install the cruise control actuator and the cruise control cable, if equipped.

30. Connect the accelerator cable.

31. Refill the cooling system with the correct amount of anti-freeze and water.

32. Connect the negative battery cable.

33. Start the engine and check for leaks. Allow the engine to warm up and check the work areas carefully for seepage.

34. Install the splash shield under the car. Install the right front wheel.

4A-FE and 7A-FE Engines

1. Disconnect the negative battery cable.

2. Raise the vehicle and safely support it on jackstands.

3. Remove the right splash shield from under the car.

4. Lower the vehicle. Remove the wiring harness from the upper timing belt cover.

5. Depending on equipment, loosen the air conditioner compressor, the power steering pump and the alternator on their adjusting bolts. Remove the drive belts.

6. Remove the crankshaft pulley.

7. Remove the valve cover.

8. Remove the windshield washer reservoir.

9. Raise and safely support the vehicle.

10. Support the engine either from above (chain hoist) or below (floor jack and wood block) and remove the through bolt at the right engine mount.

11. If necessary, remove the protectors on the mount nuts and studs for the center and rear transaxle mounts.

12. If necessary, remove the two rear transaxle mount-to-main crossmember nuts. Remove the two center transaxle mount-to-center crossmember nuts.

13. Carefully elevate the engine enough to gain access to the water pump pulley.

14. Remove the water pump pulley. Lower the engine to its normal position.

15. Remove the four bolts and the lower timing cover. Remove the center timing cover and its bolts, then the upper cover with its four bolts.

16. If further work is to be done, the car may be lowered to the ground but the engine must remain supported until the mount(s) are reinstalled.

To install:

17. When reinstalling, make certain that the gaskets and their mating surfaces are clean and free from dirt and oil. The gasket itself must be free of cuts and deformations and must fit securely in the grooves of the covers.

18. Install the covers and the bolts; tighten the bolts to 5–6 ft. lbs.

19. Elevate the engine and install the water pump pulley.

20. Lower the engine to its normal position. Install the through bolt in the right engine mount and tighten it to 64 ft. lbs.

With the bolt secure, the engine lifting apparatus may be removed.

21. Install the valve cover.

22. Install the crankshaft pulley and tighten it to specifications.

23. Reinstall the air conditioning compressor, the power steering pump and the alternator. Install their belts and adjust them to the correct tension.

24. Reconnect the wiring harness to the upper timing belt cover.

25. Raise the vehicle and safely support it on jackstands.

26. Install the two nuts on the center transaxle mount and the rear transaxle mount, if necessary. Tighten all the nuts to 45 ft. lbs.

27. Install the protectors on the nuts and studs, if necessary.

28. Install the splash shield under the car.

29. Lower the vehicle to the ground.

30. Install the windshield washer reservoir and connect the negative battery cable.

Timing Belt and Camshaft Sprockets

REMOVAL & INSTALLATION

NOTE: *Timing belts must always be handled carefully and kept completely free of dirt, grease, fluids and lubricants. This includes any accidental contact from spillage. These same precautions apply to the pulleys and contact surfaces on which the belt rides. The belt must never be crimped, twisted or bent. Never use tools to pry or wedge the belt into place. Such actions will damage the structure of the belt and possibly cause breakage. The timing belt should be replaced at 60,000 miles if the vehicle is used for severe service: towing, repeated short trips in cold weather, extended idling or low speed driving for long distances, etc.*

4A-GE Engine

1. Disconnect the negative battery cable. Remove the timing belt covers.

2. Remove the timing belt guide from the crankshaft pulley.

3. Loosen the timing belt idler pulley, move it to the left (to take tension off the belt) and tighten its bolt.

4. Make matchmarks on the belt and all pulleys showing the exact placement

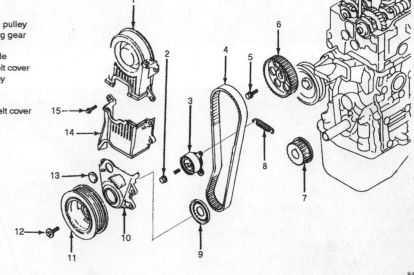

1. Upper timing belt cover
2. Bolt
3. Idler pulley
4. Timing belt
5. Bolt
6. Camshaft timing pulley
7. Crankshaft timing gear
8. Tension spring
9. Timing belt guide
10. Lower timing belt cover
11. Crankshaft pulley
12. Bolt
13. Inspection plug
14. Center timing belt cover
15. Bolt

84343103

Timing belt, cover and related components — 4A-FE and 7A-FE engines

of the belt. Mark an arrow on the belt showing its direction of rotation.

5. Carefully slip the timing belt off the pulleys.

NOTE: *Do not disturb the position of the camshafts or the crankshaft during removal.*

6. Remove the idler pulley bolt, pulley and return spring.

7. Remove the PCV hose and the valve cover.

8. Use an adjustable wrench to counterhold the camshaft. Be careful not to damage the cylinder head. Loosen the center bolt in each camshaft pulley and

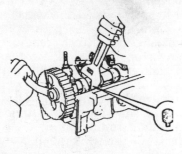

84343104

Make sure the camshaft is firmly held when removing the sprocket

remove the pulley. Label the pulleys and and keep them clean.

9. Check the timing belt carefully for any signs of cracking or deterioration. Pay particular attention to the area where each tooth or cog attaches to the backing of the belt. If the belt shows signs of damage, check the contact faces of the pulleys for possible burrs or scratches.

10. Check the idler pulley by holding it in your hand and spinning it. It should rotate freely and quietly. Any sign of grinding or abnormal noise indicates the pulley should be replaced.

11. Check the free length of the tension spring. Correct length is 43.5mm measured at the inside faces of the hooks. A spring which has stretched during use will not apply the correct tension to the pulley; replace the spring.

12. If you can test the tension of the spring, look for 22 lbs. of tension at 50mm of length. If in doubt, replace the spring.

To install:

13. Align the camshaft knock pin and the pulley. Reinstall the camshaft timing belt pulleys, making sure the pulley fits properly on the shaft and that the timing marks align correctly. Tighten the center

bolt on each pulley to 43 ft. lbs. Be careful not to damage the cylinder head during installation.

14. Before reinstalling the belt, double check that the crank and camshafts are exactly in their correct positions. The alignment marks on the pulleys should align with the cast marks on the head and oil pump.

15. Reinstall the valve covers and the PCV hose.

16. Install the timing belt idler pulley and its tensioning spring. Move the idler to the left and temporarily tighten its bolt.

17. Carefully observing the matchmarks made earlier, install the timing belt onto the pulleys.

18. Slowly release tension on the idler pulley bolt and allow the idler to take up tension on the timing belt. DO NOT allow the idler to slam into the belt; the belt may become damaged.

19. Temporarily install the crankshaft pulley bolt. Turn the engine clockwise through two complete revolutions, stopping at TDC. Check that each pulley aligns with its marks.

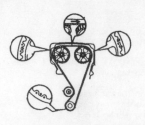

84343107

If reusing the old timing belt, align the marks made during removal and install the belt with the arrow pointing in the direction of rotation

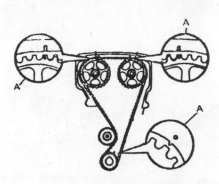

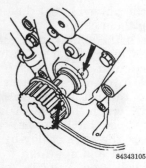

84343105

Crankshaft and oil pump marks must be aligned before installing the timing belt

84343108

Make certain all timing marks are aligned before timing belt is installed — 4A-GE engine

20. Check the tension of the timing belt at a top point halfway between the two camshaft sprockets. The correct deflection is 4mm at 4.4 lbs. pressure. If the belt tension is incorrect, readjust it by repeating steps 18–20. If the tension is correct, tighten the idler pulley bolt to 27 ft. lbs.

21. Remove the crankshaft pulley bolt.

22. Install the timing belt guide onto the crankshaft timing pulley.

23. Reinstall the timing belt covers.

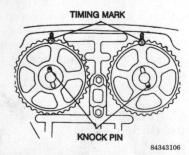

TIMING MARK

KNOCK PIN

84343106

Timing marks and camshaft knock pin locations — 4A-GE engine

4A-FE and 7A-FE Engines

1. Disconnect the negative battery cable. Remove the timing belt covers.

2. Remove the timing belt guide from the crankshaft pulley. If not done as part of the cover removal, rotate the crankshaft clockwise to the TDC/compression position for No. 1 cylinder.

3. Loosen the timing belt idler pulley to relieve the tension on the belt, move the pulley away from the belt and temporarily tighten the bolt to hold it in the loose position.

4. Make matchmarks on the belt and both pulley showing the exact placement of the belt. Mark an arrow on the belt showing its direction of rotation.

5. Carefully slip the timing belt off the pulleys.

NOTE: *Do not disturb the position of the camshafts or the crankshaft during removal.*

6. Remove the idler pulley bolt, pulley and return spring.

7. Remove the valve cover. Use an adjustable wrench mounted on the flats of the camshaft to hold the cam from moving. Loosen the center bolt in the camshaft timing pulley and remove the pulley.

8. Check the timing belt carefully for any signs of cracking or deterioration. Pay particular attention to the area where each tooth or cog attaches to the backing of the belt. If the belt shows signs of damage, check the contact faces of the pulleys for possible burrs or scratches.

9. Check the idler pulley by holding it in your hand and spinning it. It should rotate freely and quietly. Any sign of grinding or abnormal noise indicates replacement of the pulley.

10. Check the free length of the tension spring. Correct length is 38.5mm measured at the inside faces of the hooks, on the 1990–92 vehicles. The correct length for the 1993 vehicles is 35.3mm on the 4A-FE engine and 31.8mm on the 7A-FE engine. A spring which has stretched during use will not apply the correct tension to the pulley; replace the spring.

11. If you can test the tension of the spring, look for 8.4 lbs. of tension at 50mm of length on all except 1993 vehicles. On the 1993 4A-FE engine look for 13.0 lbs. of tension at 50mm of length and on 7A-FE engine look for 26.5 lbs. of tension at 50mm of length. If in doubt, ALWAYS replace the spring.

To install:

12. Reinstall the camshaft timing belt pulley, making sure the pulley fits properly on the shaft and that the timing marks align correctly. Tighten the center bolt to 43 ft. lbs.

13. Before reinstalling the belt, double check that the crank and camshafts are exactly in their correct positions. The alignment mark on the end of the camshaft bearing cap should show through the small hole in the camshaft pulley and the small mark on the crankshaft timing belt pulley should align with the mark on the oil pump.

14. Reinstall the timing belt idler pulley and the tension spring. Pry the pulley to the left as far as it will go and temporarily tighten the retaining bolt. This will hold the pulley in its loosest position.

15. Install the timing belt, observing the matchmarks made earlier. Make sure the belt is fully and squarely seated on the upper and lower pulleys.

16. Loosen the retaining bolt for the timing belt idler pulley and allow it to tension the belt.

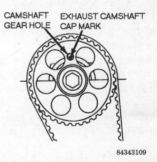

Correct alignment of the camshaft before reinstallation of the timing belt

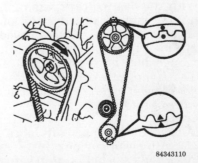

Timing marks — 4A-FE and 7A-FE engines

17. Temporarily install the crankshaft pulley bolt and turn the crank clockwise two full revolutions from TDC to TDC. Ensure that each timing mark realigns exactly.

18. Tighten the timing belt idler pulley retaining bolt to 27 ft. lbs.

19. Measure the timing belt deflection at the SIDE point, looking for 5–6mm of deflection at 4.4 pounds of pressure. If the deflection is not correct, readjust the idler pulley by repeating steps 15 through 18.

20. Remove the bolt from the end of the crankshaft.

21. Install the timing belt guide onto the crankshaft and install the lower timing belt cover.

22. Reinstall the timing belt covers and valve cover following procedures as outlined.

Camshaft and Bearings

REMOVAL & INSTALLATION

NOTE: *Camshaft end-play (thrust clearance) must be checked before the cam is removed. Please refer to the "inspection" section for details of this check.*

4A-GE Engine

1. Remove the valve cover and the timing belt covers.

2. Make certain the engine is set to TDC/compression on No.1 cylinder. Remove the timing belt following procedures outlined earlier in this Chapter.

3. Remove the crankshaft pulley.

4. Remove the camshaft timing belt pulleys.

5. Loosen and remove the camshaft bearing caps in the proper sequence. It is recommended that the bolts be loosened in two or three passes.

6. With the bearing caps removed, the camshaft(s) may be lifted clear of the head. If both cams are to be removed, label them clearly — they are not interchangeable.

NOTE: *Handle the camshaft with care. Do not allow it to fall or hit objects, as it may break into pieces.*

To install:

7. Lubricate the camshaft lobes and journals with clean engine oil.

8. Place the camshaft(s) in position on the head. The exhaust cam has the distributor drive gear on it. Observe the

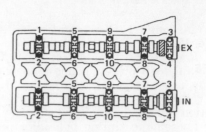

84343111

Camshaft bearing cap removal sequence — 4A-GE engine

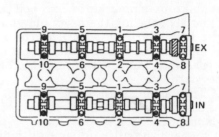

84343112

Camshaft bearing cap installation sequence — 4A-GE engine

markings on the bearing caps and place them according to their numbered positions. The arrow should point to the front of the engine.

9. Tighten the bearing cap bolts in the correct sequence and in three passes to a final tightness of 9 ft. lbs.

10. Position the camshafts so that the guide pins (knock pins) are in the proper position. This step is critical to the correct valve timing of the engine.

11. Install the camshaft timing pulleys and tighten the bolts to 43 ft. lbs.

12. Double check the positioning of the camshaft pulleys and the guide pin.

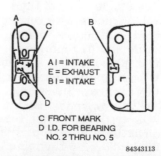

AI = INTAKE
E = EXHAUST
BI = INTAKE

C FRONT MARK
D I.D. FOR BEARING
NO. 2 THRU NO. 5

84343113

Examples of marking on camshaft bearing caps. Note that the bearing cap on the right is for position No. 1 only — 4A-GE engine

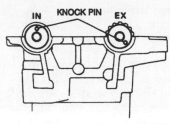

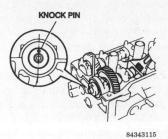

84343114

Correct position of knock pins, the exhaust camshaft has the distributor drive gear — 4A-GE engine

84343115

Correct position of the service bolt hole before removal of the intake camshaft — 4A-FE and 7A-FE engines

13. Install the crankshaft pulley. Tighten its bolt to 101 ft. lbs. and double check its position to be on TDC.

14. Install the timing belt and tensioner. Adjust the belt according to procedures outlined.

15. Install the timing belt covers.

16. Install the valve cover.

4A-FE and 7A-FE Engines

1. Remove the valve cover.

2. Remove the timing belt covers.

3. Remove the timing belt and idler pulley following procedures outlined previously in this Chapter.

4. Hold the exhaust camshaft with an adjustable wrench and remove the camshaft timing belt gear. Be careful not to damage the head or the camshaft during this work.

5. Gently turn the camshafts with an adjustable wrench until the service bolt hole in the intake camshaft end gear is straight up or in the "12 o'clock" position.

6. Alternately loosen the bearing cap bolts in the number 1 position (closest to the pulley) intake and exhaust bearing caps.

7. Attach the intake camshaft end gear to the sub gear with a service bolt. The service bolt should be of the following specifications:

Thread diameter: 6.0mm
Thread pitch: 1.0mm
Bolt length: 16–20mm

8. Uniformly loosen each intake camshaft bearing cap bolt a little at a time and in the correct sequence.

NOTE: *The camshaft must be held level while it is being removed. If the camshaft is not kept level, the portion of the cylinder head receiving the shaft thrust may crack or become damaged. This in turn could cause the camshaft to bind or break.   Before removing the in-*

1. Intake bearing cap bolt
2. Exhaust bearing cap bolt

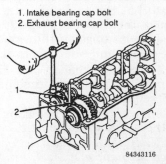

84343116

Alternately loosen the bolts for the No. 1 bearing cap on both the intake and exhaust camshafts

1. Service bolt 2. Sub-gear 3. Main gear

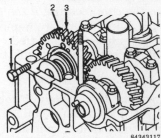

84343117

Always install a service bolt to lock the intake cam gears together

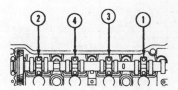

84343118

Remove the camshaft bearing caps in this order. Intake camshaft shown, exhaust camshaft uses identical order — 4A-FE and 7A-FE engines

take camshaft, make sure the torsional spring force of the sub gear has been removed by installing the bolt in Step 7.

9. Remove the bearing caps and remove the intake camshaft.

NOTE: *If the camshaft cannot be removed straight and level, retighten the No.2 bearing cap. Alternately loosen the bolts on the bearing cap a little at a time while pulling upwards on the camshaft gear. DO NOT attempt to pry or force the cam loose with tools.*

10. With the intake camshaft removed, turn the exhaust camshaft approximately 105°, so that the guide pin in the end is just past the "5 o'clock" position. This puts equal loadings on the camshaft, allowing easier and safer removal.

11. Loosen the exhaust camshaft bearing cap bolts a little at a time and in the correct sequence.

12. Remove the bearing caps and remove the exhaust camshaft.

NOTE: *If the camshaft cannot be removed straight and level, retighten the No. 3 bearing cap. Alternately loosen the bolts on the bearing cap a little at a time while pulling upwards on the camshaft gear. DO NOT attempt to pry or force the cam loose with tools.*

13. When reinstalling, remember that the camshafts must be handled carefully and kept straight and level to avoid damage.

To install:

14. Lubricate the camshaft lobes and journals with clean engine oil.

15. Place the exhaust camshaft on the cylinder head so that the cam lobes press evenly on the lifters for cylinders Nos. 1 and 3. This will put the guide pin in the "just past 5 o'clock" position.

16. Place the bearing caps in position according to the number cast into the cap.

The arrow should point towards the pulley end of the engine.

17. Tighten the bearing cap bolts gradually and in the proper sequence to 9 ft. lbs.

18. Apply multi-purpose grease, to a new exhaust camshaft oil seal.

19. Install the exhaust camshaft oil seal using a suitable tool. Be very careful not to install the seal on a slant or allow it to tilt during installation.

20. Turn the exhaust cam until the cam lobes of No. 4 cylinder press down on their lifters.

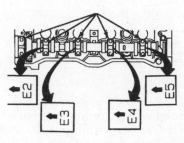

84343120

Examples of bearing cap marking and position (typical)

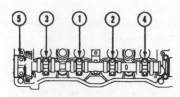

84343121

Install the camshaft bearing caps in this order. Exhaust camshaft shown, intake camshaft uses identical order — 4A-FE and 7A-FE engines

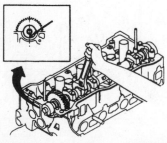

84343119

Setting the engine exhaust camshaft guide pin to just past the 5 o' clock position

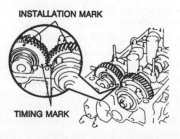

INSTALLATION MARK

TIMING MARK

84343122

Correct camshaft installation — 4A-FE and 7A-FE engines

21. Hold the intake camshaft next to the exhaust camshaft and engage the gears by matching the alignment marks on each gear.

22. Keeping the gears engaged, roll the intake camshaft down and into its bearing journals.

23. Place the bearing caps for Nos. 2, 3, 4 and 5 in position. Observe the numbers on each cap and make certain the arrows point to the pulley end of the engine.

24. Gradually tighten each bearing cap bolt in the same order as the exhaust camshaft bolts. Tighten each bolt to 9 ft. lbs.

25. Remove any retaining pins or bolts in the intake camshaft gears.

26. Install the number 1 bearing cap for the intake camshaft.

NOTE: *If the No. 1 bearing cap does not fit properly, gently push the cam gear towards the rear of the engine by levering between the gear and the head.*

27. Turn the exhaust camshaft one full revolution from TDC/compression on No. 1 cylinder to the same position. Check that the mark on the exhaust camshaft gear matches exactly with the mark on the intake camshaft gear.

28. Counterhold the exhaust camshaft and install the timing belt pulley. Tighten the bolt to 43 ft. lbs.

29. Double check both the crankshaft and camshaft positions, ensuring that they are both set to TDC/compression for No. 1 cylinder.

30. Install the timing belt following the procedures outlined.

31. Install the timing belt covers and the valve cover.

INSPECTION AND MEASUREMENT

The end-play or thrust clearance of the camshaft(s) must be measured with the camshaft installed in the head. It may be checked before removal or after reinstallation. To check the end-play, mount a dial indicator accurate to ten one-thousandths (four decimal places) on the end of the block, so that the tip bears on the end of the camshaft. The timing belt must be removed. It will be necessary to remove the pulleys for unobstructed access to the camshaft. Set the scale on the dial indicator to zero. Using a screwdriver or similar tool, gently lever the camshaft fore-and-aft in its mounts. Record the amount of deflection shown on the gauge and compare this number to the Camshaft Specifications Chart at the beginning of this Chapter.

Excessive end-play may indicate either a worn camshaft or a worn cylinder head; the worn cam is most likely and much cheaper to replace. Chances are good that if the cam is worn in this dimension (axial), substantial wear will show up in other measurements.

Mount the cam in V-blocks and set the dial indicator up on the center bearing journal. Zero the dial and rotate the camshaft. The circular runout should not exceed 0.0016 in. (0.04mm). Excess runout means the camshaft must be replaced.

Using a micrometer or Vernier caliper, measure the diameter of all the journals and the height of all the lobes. Record the readings and compare them to the Camshaft Specifications Chart. Any measurement beyond the stated limits indicates wear and the camshaft must be replaced.

Lobe wear is generally accompanied by scoring or visible metal damage on the lobes. Overhead camshaft engines are very sensitive to proper lubrication with clean, fresh oil. A worn camshaft may be

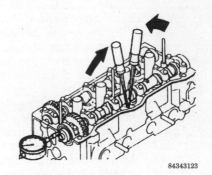

84343123

Checking camshaft end-play

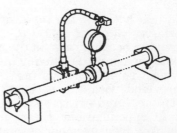

84343124

Use a dial indicator to check the run-out (eccentricity) of the center camshaft bearing

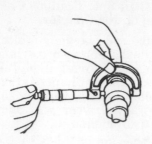

84343125

Use a micrometer to check the camshaft journal diameter

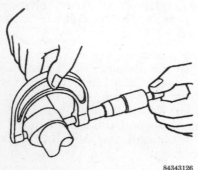

84343126

Measure the height of each camshaft lobe.

your report card for poor maintenance intervals and late oil changes.

On the twin-cam engines, a new camshaft will require readjusting the valves, so new shims are in order.

The clearance between the camshaft and its journals (bearings) must also be measured. Clean the camshaft, the journals and the bearing caps of any remaining oil and place the camshaft in position on the head. Lay a piece of compressable gauging material (Plastigage® or similar) on top of each journal on the camshaft.

Install the bearing caps in their correct order with the arrows pointing towards the front (pulley end) of the engine. Install the bearing cap bolts and tighten them in three passes to the correct tightness of 9 ft. lbs.

NOTE: *Do not turn the camshaft with the gauging material installed.*

Remove the bearing caps (in the correct order) and measure the gauging material at its widest point by comparing it to the scale provided with the package. Compare these measurements to the Camshaft Specifications Chart in this Chapter. Any measurement beyond spec-

ifications indicates wear. If you have already measured the camshaft (or replaced it) and determined it to be usable, excess bearing clearance indicates the need for a new cylinder head.

Remove the camshaft from the head and remove all traces of the gauging material. Check carefully for any small pieces clinging to contact faces.

Pistons and Connecting Rods

REMOVAL & INSTALLATION

NOTE: *These procedures may be performed with the engine in the vehicle. If additional overhaul work is to be performed, it will be easier if the engine is removed and mounted on an engine stand. Most stands allow the block to be rotated, giving easy access to both the top and bottom. These procedures require certain hand tools which may not be in your tool box. A cylinder ridge reamer, a numbered punch set, piston ring expander, snap-ring tools and piston installation tool (ring compressor) are all necessary for correct piston and rod repair.*

1. Remove the cylinder head.
2. Raise and safely support the vehicle on jackstands.
3. Drain the engine oil.
4. Remove any splash shields which are in the way and remove the oil pan.
5. Using a numbered punch set, mark the cylinder number on each connecting rod and bearing cap. Do this BEFORE loosening any bolts.
6. Loosen and remove the rod cap nuts and the rod caps. It will probably be necessary to tap the caps loose; do so with a small plastic mallet or other soft-faced tool. Keep the bearing insert with the cap when it is removed.

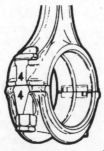

84343127

Use a numbered punch to identify both parts of each connecting rod with its cylinder number

7. Use short pieces of hose to cover the bolt threads; this protects the bolt, the crankshaft and the cylinder walls during removal.

8. One piston will be at the lowest point in its cylinder. Cover the top of this piston with a rag. Examine the top area of the cylinder with your fingers, looking for a noticeable ridge around the cylinder. If any ridge is felt, it must be carefully removed by using the ridge reamer. Work with extreme care to avoid cutting too deeply. When the ridge is removed, carefully remove the rag and ALL the shavings from the cylinder. No metal cuttings may remain in the cylinder or the wall will be damaged when the piston is removed. A small magnet can be helpful in removing the fine shavings.

9. After the cylinder ridge is removed, squirt a liberal coating of engine oil onto the cylinder walls until evenly coated. Carefully push the piston and rod assembly upwards from the bottom by using a wooden hammer handle on the bottom of the connecting rod.

10. The next lowest piston should be gently pushed downwards from above. This will cause the crankshaft to turn and relocate the other pistons as well. When the piston is in its lowest position, repeat Steps 8 and 9. Repeat the procedure for each of the remaining pistons.

To install:

11. When all the pistons are removed, clean the block and cylinder walls thoroughly with solvent.

12. When ready for reassembly, remember that all the pistons, rods and caps must be reinstalled in the correct cylinder. Make certain that all labels and stamped numbers are present and legible. Double check the piston ring end gaps; make certain that the ring gaps are properly spaced around the piston.

Use lengths of vacuum hoses or rubber tubing to protect the crankshaft journals and cylinder walls during piston installation

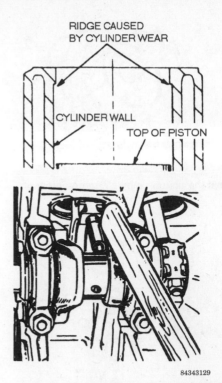

Push the piston out with a hammer handle

Double check the bearing insert at the bottom of the rod for proper mounting. Reinstall the protective rubber hose pieces on the bolts.

13. Liberally coat the cylinder walls and the crankshaft journals with clean, fresh engine oil. Also apply oil to the bearing surfaces on the connecting rod and the cap.

14. Identify the "Front" mark on each piston and rod and position the piston loosely in its cylinder with the marks facing the front (pulley end) of the engine.

NOTE: *Failure to observe the "Front" marking and its correct placement can lead to sudden engine failure.*

15. Install the ring compressor (piston installation tool) around one piston and tighten it gently until the rings are compressed almost completely.

16. Gently push down on the piston top with a wooden hammer handle or similar soft-faced tool and drive the piston into the cylinder bore.

NOTE: *If any resistance or binding is encountered during the installation, DO NOT apply force. Tighten or adjust the ring compressor and/or reposition the piston. Brute force will break the ring(s) or damage the piston.*

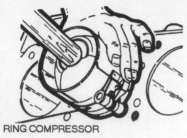

RING COMPRESSOR

84343130

Install the piston using a ring compressor

84343132

Removing the piston rings with a ring expander

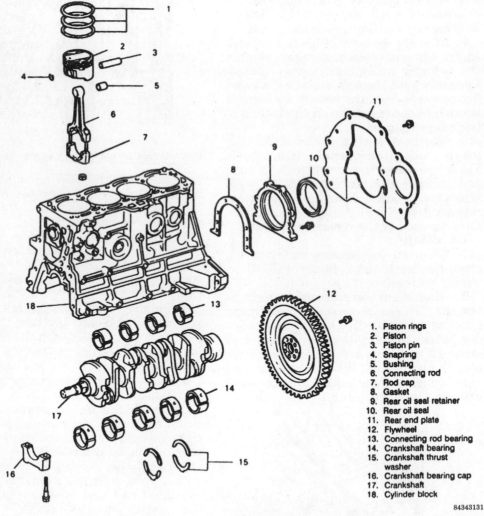

1. Piston rings
2. Piston
3. Piston pin
4. Snapring
5. Bushing
6. Connecting rod
7. Rod cap
8. Gasket
9. Rear oil seal retainer
10. Rear oil seal
11. Rear end plate
12. Flywheel
13. Connecting rod bearing
14. Crankshaft bearing
15. Crankshaft thrust washer
16. Crankshaft bearing cap
17. Crankshaft
18. Cylinder block

84343131

Component detail of 4A-GE engine; other engines similar

17. From underneath, pull the connecting rod into place on the crankshaft. Remove the rubber hoses from the bolts. Check the rod cap to confirm that the bearing is present and correctly mounted, then install the rod cap (observing the correct number and position) and its nuts. Leaving the nuts finger tight will make installation of the remaining pistons and rods easier.

18. Assemble the remaining pistons in the same fashion, repeating Steps 15, 16 and 17.

19. With all the pistons installed and the bearing caps secured finger tight, the retaining nuts may be tightened to their final setting. For each pair of nuts, make three passes alternating between the two nuts on any given rod cap. The intent is to draw each cap up to the crank straight and under even pressure at the nuts.

20. Turn the crankshaft through several clockwise rotations, making sure everything moves smoothly and there is no binding. With the connecting rods installed, the crank may be stiff to turn — try to turn it in a smooth continuous motion so that any binding or stiff spots may be felt.

21. If the engine is to remain apart for other repairs, pack the cylinders with crumpled newspaper or clean rags (to keep out dust and grit) and cover the top of the engine with a large rag. If the engine is on a stand, the whole block can be protected with a large plastic trash bag.

22. If no further work is to be performed, continue reassembly by installing the oil pan, cylinder head, timing belt, etc.

23. When the engine is restarted after reassembly, the exhaust will be somewhat smoky as the oil within the cylinders burns off. This is normal; the smoke should clear quickly during warm up. Depending on the condition of the spark plugs, it may be wise to check for any oil fouling after the engine is shut off.

CLEANING AND INSPECTION

Pistons

With the pistons removed from the engine, use a ring removing tool (ring expander) to remove the rings. Keep the rings labeled and stored by piston number. Clearly label the pistons by number so that they do not get interchanged.

Clean the carbon from the piston top and sides with a stiff bristle brush and cleaning solvent. Do not use a wire brush for cleaning.

CAUTION: *Wear goggles during cleaning; the solvent is very strong and can cause eye damage.*

Clean the ring grooves either with a specially designed tool or with a piece of a broken piston ring. Remove all the carbon from the grooves and make sure that the groove shape (profile) is square all the way around the piston. When all the grooves have been cleaned, again bathe the piston in solvent and clean the grooves with the bristle brush.

Before any measurements are begun, visually examine the piston (a magnifying glass can be handy) for any signs of cracks, particularly in the skirt area, or scratches in the metal. Anything other than light surface scoring disqualifies the piston from further use; the metal will become unevenly heated and the piston may break apart during use.

Hold the piston and rod upright and attempt to move the piston back and forth along the piston pin (wrist pin). There should be NO motion in this axis. If there is, replace the piston and wrist pin.

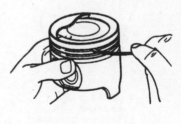

84343133

A piece of a broken ring works well too clean piston ring grooves

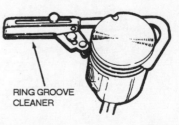

RING GROOVE CLEANER

84343134

The ring grooves can be cleaned and decarboned with a special tool

Accurately measure the cylinder bore diameter in two dimensions (thrust and axial, or if you prefer, left-right and fore-aft) and in three locations (upper, middle and bottom) within the cylinder. That's six measurements in each bore; record them in order. Normal measurements are:

- New: 81.0–81.03mm
- Max Wear limit: 81.23mm

Having recorded the bore measurements, now measure the piston diameter.

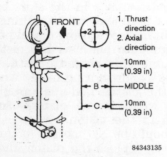

Checking the cylinder bore requires 6 measurements — 3 locations and 2 dimensions in each cylinder

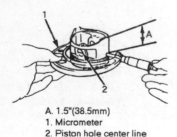

A. 1.5"(38.5mm)
1. Micrometer
2. Piston hole center line

84343136

Measuring the piston diameter — 4A-FE engine

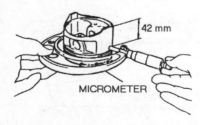

84343137

Measuring the piston diameter — 4A-GE engine

Do this with a micrometer at right angles to the piston pin.

- 4A-GE engine: Measure at a point 42mm from the longest part of the piston skirt.
- 1990–92 4A-FE engine: Measure at a point 38.5mm from the longest part of the piston skirt.
- 1993 4A-FE and 7A-FE engines: Measure at a point 24.5mm from the piston head.

Record each measurement for each piston. Use these specifications as a guide for internal engine component replacement.

The piston-to-cylinder wall clearance is determined by subtracting the piston diameter from the measured diameter of its respective cylinder. The difference will be in thousandths of an inch. Compare this number to the Piston and Ring Specifications Chart at the beginning of this Chapter. Excess clearance may indicate the need for either new pistons and block reboring.

Connecting rods

The connecting rods must be free from wear, cracking and bending. Visually examine the rod, particularly at its upper and lower ends. Look for any sign of metal stretching or wear. The bolts must be firmly mounted and parallel.

The connecting rods should be taken to a machine shop for exact measurement of twist or bend. This is generally easier and cheaper than purchasing a seldom used rod-alignment checking tool.

PISTON PIN REPLACEMENT

4A-GE Engine

NOTE: *The piston and pin are a matched set and must be kept together. Label everything and store parts in identified containers.*

1. Remove the pistons from the engine and remove the rings from the pistons.

2. Remove the snapring at the ends of the piston pin. This may be done with either snapring pliers or needle-nosed pliers; don't try to lever it out with a screwdriver.

3. Place the piston in water and gradually heat the water to the boiling point. DO NOT drop the piston into already hot water. The minimum required temperature is 176°F (80°C); a little hotter makes it a little easier.

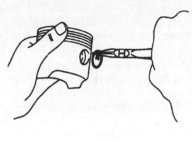

84343138

Remove the circlip — 4A-GE engine

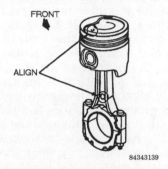

FRONT

ALIGN

84343139

The piston must be heated to install the piston pin — 4A-GE engine

84343140

Align the piston and connecting rod front marks before reassembly

4. Remove the piston from the water. Using a plastic hammer and brass bar, lightly tap out the piston pin and remove the connecting rod.

CAUTION: *You are dealing with hot metal and boiling water. Tongs, thick heat-resistant gloves and towels are required.*

5. When reassembling, identify the front of the piston by its small dot or cavity on the top. Identify the front of the piston rod by the small mark cast into one face of the rod. Make sure the marks

on the piston and rod are both facing the same direction. Also insure that the correct piston pin is to be reinstalled — they are not interchangeable.

6. Install one snapring. Place the piston in water and gradually heat the water to the boiling point. DO NOT drop the piston into already hot water. The minimum required temperature is 176°F (80°C); a little hotter makes it a little easier. This will expand the piston so that the pin will fit smoothly. While the water is heating, apply a coat of clean oil to the piston pin and have the pin at hand when the piston is removed from the water.

7. Remove the piston from the boiling water (carefully) and hold it with gloves or several towels. Making sure the front marks align on the piston and connecting rod, hold the rod in position and press the piston pin into place with your thumb. The pin will bottom against the snapring. Allow the piston to air cool and when it is cool to the touch, install the other snapring. Check that the piston rocks freely on its pin without binding.

4A-FE and 7A-FE Engines

NOTE: *The piston and pin are a matched set and must be kept together. Label everything and store parts in identified containers.*

1. Remove the pistons from the engine and remove the rings from the pistons.

2. Support the piston and rod on its side in a press. Make certain the piston is square to the motion of the press and that the rod is completely supported with blocks. Leave an open space below the piston for the pin to emerge.

3. Line up the press and insert a brass rod of the same or slightly smaller diameter as the piston pin. It is important that

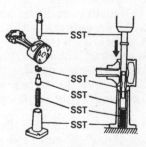

SST
SST
SST
SST
SST

84343141

Pressing the piston pin in the piston — 4A-FE and 7A-FE engines

the rod press evenly on the entire face of the pin, but not on the piston itself.

NOTE: *Toyota special service tools are available for this repair. The special service tool numbers are SST 09221–25024 and SST 09221–00130. Refer to the illustration.*

4. Using smooth and controlled motion, press the pin free of the piston. Do not use sudden or jerky motions; the piston may crack.

5. When reassembling, identify the front of the piston by its small dot or cavity on the top. Identify the front of the piston rod by the small mark cast into one face of the rod. Make sure the marks on the piston and rod are both facing the same direction. Also insure that the correct piston pin is to be reinstalled — they are not interchangeable.

6. Making sure the front marks align on the piston and connecting rod, hold the rod in position and press the piston pin. Check that the piston rocks freely on its pin without binding.

PISTON RING REPLACEMENT

NOTE: *Although a piston ring can be reused if in good condition and carefully removed, it is recommended that the rings be replaced with new ones any time they are removed from the pistons.*

A piston ring expander is necessary for removing piston rings without damaging them; any other method (screwdriver blades, pliers, etc.) usually results in the rings becoming bent, scratched or broken. When the rings are removed, clean the grooves thoroughly with a bristle brush and solvent. Make sure that all traces of carbon and varnish are removed.

NOTE: *Wear goggles during this cleaning; the solvent is very strong and can cause eye damage. Do not use a wire brush or a caustic solvent on the pistons.*

Check the piston condition and diameter following procedures outlined earlier in this Chapter. Piston ring end gap should be checked when the rings are removed from the pistons. Incorrect end gap indicates that the wrong size rings are being used; ring breakage could occur.

Squirt some clean oil into the cylinder so that the top 50–75mm (2–3 in.) of the wall is covered. Gently compress one of the rings to be used and insert it into the cylinder. Use an upside-down piston and push the ring down about 25mm (1 in.) below the top of the cylinder. Using the piston to push the ring keeps the ring square in the cylinder; if it gets crooked, the next measurement may be inaccurate.

Using a feeler gauge, measure the end gap in the ring and compare it to the Piston and Ring Specifications chart at the beginning of this Chapter. If the gap is excessive, either the ring is incorrect or the cylinder walls are worn beyond acceptable limits. If the measurement is too tight, the ends of the ring may be filed to enlarge the gap after the ring is removed form the cylinder. If filing is needed, make certain that the ends are kept square and that a fine file is used.

Check the pistons to see that the ring grooves and oil return holes have been properly cleaned. Slide each piston ring into its groove and check the side clearance with a feeler gauge. Make sure you insert the feeler gauge between the ring and its lower edge; any wear that develops forms a step at the inner portion of the lower land. If the piston ring grooves have worn to the extent that fairly high steps exist on the lower land, the piston must be replaced. Rings are not sold in oversize thicknesses to compensate for ring groove wear.

Install the oil ring expander and the 2 side rails by hand. Using the ring expander, install the 2 compression rings on the piston, lowest ring first. There is a high risk of ring breakage or piston damage if the compression rings are installed by hand or without the expander. When installing the rings, make sure the code mark on the side of the ring faces upward.

The correct spacing of the ring end gaps is critical to oil control. Refer to figure for correct ring gap spacing. Once the rings

84343142

Checking the piston ring end gap

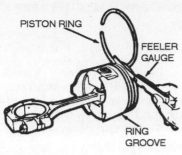

Checking the piston ring side clearance

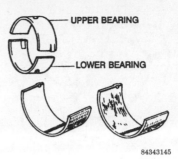

Examples of upper and lower bearing shells —
note the position of the oil hole

are installed, the pistons must be handled carefully and protected from dirt and impact.

CONNECTING ROD BEARING REPLACEMENT

Connecting rod bearings on all engines consist of two halves or shells which are not interchangeable in the rod and cap. When the shells are in position, the ends extend slightly beyond the rod and cap surfaces so that when the bolts are tightened, the shells will be clamped tightly in place. This insures a positive seating and prevents turning. A small tang holds the shells in place within the cap and rod housings.

NOTE: *The ends of the bearing shells must never be filed flush with the mating surface of the rod or cap.*

If a rod becomes noisy or is worn so that its clearance on the crankshaft is sloppy, a new bearing of the correct undersize must be selected and installed. There is no provision for adjustment. Under no circumstances should the rod end or cap be filed to compensate for wear, nor should shims of any type be used.

Inspect the rod bearings while the rods are out of the engine. If the shells are

scored or show flaking they should be replaced. ANY scoring or ridge on the crankshaft means the crankshaft must be ground undersize or replaced.

Standard size rod bearings from Toyota are available in 3 sizes, marked "1", "2" or "3". Do not confuse these markings on the bearing shells with the cylinder number markings on the connecting rod and rod cap.

Measuring the clearance between the connecting rod bearings and the crankshaft (oil clearance) is done with a plastic measuring material such as Plastigage® or similar product.

1. Remove the rod cap with the bearing shell. Completely clean the cap, bearing shells and the journal on the crankshaft. Blow any oil from the oil hole in the crank. The plastic measuring material is soluble in oil and will begin to dissolve if the area is not totally free of oil.

2. Place a piece of the measuring material lengthwise along the bottom center of the lower bearing shell. Install the cap and shell and tighten the bolts in three passes to specifications.

3. Remove the bearing cap with the shell. The flattened plastic material will be found sticking to either the bearing

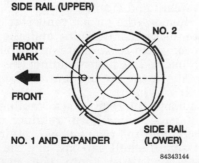

Piston ring positioning

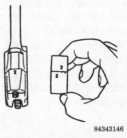

Look for the manufacturer's codes to identify standard bearing sizes. Don't confuse the number on the rod end caps with its position (cylinder) number

84343147

Measure the compressed plastic to determine the bearing clearance

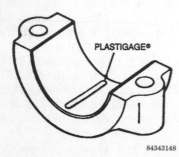

84343148

Plastic measuring material installed on the lower bearing shell

shell or the crank journal. DO NOT remove it yet.

4. Use the scale printed on the packaging for the measuring material to measure the flattened plastic at its widest point. The number within the scale which is closest to the width of the plastic indicates the bearing clearance in thousandths of an inch.

5. Check the specifications chart in the beginning of this Chapter for the proper clearance. If the clearance is incorrect, new or oversize bearings must be used, or the crankshaft should be removed, ground undersize, reinstalled and the clearance rechecked with the corresponding oversize bearings.

6. When the correct bearing is determined, clean off the gauging material, oil the bearing thoroughly on its working face and install it in the cap. Install the other half of the bearing into the rod end and attach the cap to the rod. Tighten the nuts evenly, in three passes to specifications.

Engine Core Plugs (Freeze Plugs)

REMOVAL

Drain the cooling system. Using a blunt tool such as a drift and a hammer, strike the bottom edge of the cup plug. With the cup plug rotated, grasp firmly with pliers and remove the cup plug.

NOTE: *Do not drive the cup plug into the block assembly casting as restricted cooling can result.*

INSTALLATION

Thoroughly clean the inside of the cup plug hole in cylinder block. Be sure to remove old sealer. Lightly coat inside of the cup plug hole with sealer. Make certain the new plug is cleaned of all oil and grease. Using the proper drive tool, drive the cup plug into the hole. Refill the cooling system and check for coolant leaks.

Rear Main Seal

REMOVAL & INSTALLATION

1. Remove the transaxle from the vehicle. Follow procedures outlined in Chapter 7.

2. If equipped with a manual transaxle, perform the following procedures:

   a. Matchmark the pressure plate and flywheel.

   b. Remove the pressure plate-to-flywheel bolts and the clutch assembly from the vehicle.

   c. Remove the flywheel-to-crankshaft bolts and the flywheel. The flywheel is a moderately heavy component. Handle it carefully and protect it on the workbench.

3. If equipped with an automatic transaxle, perform the following procedures:

   a. Matchmark the flexplate or driveplate and crankshaft.

   b. Remove the torque converter drive plate-to-crankshaft bolts and the torque converter drive plate or flexplate.

4. Remove the bolts holding the rear end plate to the engine and the remove the rear end plate.

5. Remove the rear oil seal retainer-to-engine bolts, rear oil seal retainer to oil pan bolts and the rear oil seal retainer.

6. Using a small pry bar, pry the rear oil seal retainer from the mating surfaces.

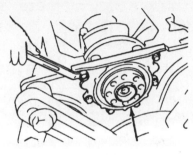

84343149

Removing the rear main oil seal retainer

7. Using a drive punch or a hammer and small screwdriver, drive the oil seal from the rear bearing retainer.

8. Using a putty knife, clean the gasket mounting surfaces. Make certain that the contact surfaces are completely free of oil and foreign matter.

To install:

9. Clean the oil seal mounting surface.

10. Using multi-purpose grease, lubricate the new seal lips.

11. Using a suitable seal installation tool, tap the seal straight into the bore of the retainer.

12. Position a new gasket on the retainer and coat it lightly with gasket sealer. Fit the seal retainer into place on the engine; be careful when installing the oil seal over the crankshaft.

13. Install the six retaining bolts and tighten them to 7 ft. lbs. (84 inch lbs.)

14. Install the rear end plate. Tighten its bolts to 7.5 ft. lbs. (90 inch lbs.).

15. Reinstall either the flexplate (automatic) or the flywheel (manual), carefully observing the matchmarks made earlier. Tighten the flexplate bolts or the flywheel bolts to specifications.

16. Install the clutch disc and pressure plate (manual transaxle).

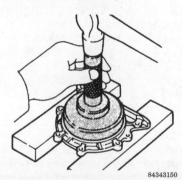

84343150

Installing the new rear main seal

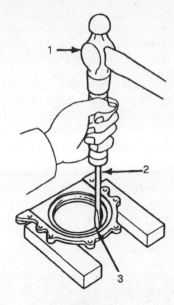

1. Hammer
2. Screwdriver
3. Rear main oil seal

84343151

Removing the rear main oil seal from the retainer — note the supports under the housing

17. Reinstall the transaxle.

Crankshaft and Main Bearings

REMOVAL & INSTALLATION

1. Remove the engine assembly from the vehicle, following procedures outlined earlier in this Chapter. Mount the engine securely on a stand which allows it to be rotated.

2. Remove the timing belt and tensioner assemblies.

3. Turn the engine upside down on the stand. Remove the oil pan and the oil strainer.

4. Remove the oil pump.

5. Remove the clutch and pressure plate (manual transmission/transaxle).

6. Remove either the flywheel (manual) or the drive plate (automatic).

7. Remove the rear end plate.

8. Remove the rear oil seal retainer.

9. Using a numbered punch set, mark each connecting rod cap with its correct cylinder number. Remove the rod caps and their bearings; keep the bearings with their respective caps.

10. Measure the crankshaft endplay (thrust clearance) before removing the crank. Attach a dial indicator to the end

of the block and set the tip to bear on the front end of the crankshaft. With a small prybar, gently move the crankshaft back and forth and record the reading shown on the dial.

- Standard end-play, new: 0.02mm
- Acceptable end-play: 0.02–0.22mm
- Maximum allowable end-play: 0.3mm

If the end-play is excessive, the thrust washers will need to be replaced as a set.

11. Gradually loosen and remove the main bearing cap bolts in three passes and in the correct order. Remove just the bolts, leaving the caps in place.

12. When all the bolts are removed, use two bolts placed in the No. 3 bearing cap to wiggle the cap back and forth. This will loosen the cap and allow it and the thrust washers to be removed. Note and/or label the thrust washers as to their placement and position. If they are to be reused, they must be reinstalled exactly as they were.

13. Remove the remaining caps. Keep the caps in order and keep the bearing shell with its respective cap.

14. Lift the crankshaft out of the block. The crankshaft is a moderately heavy component.

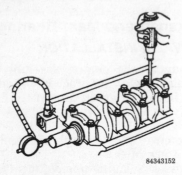

Use a dial indicator to measure crankshaft end-play

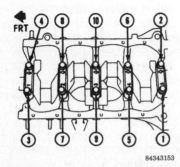

Remove the crankshaft main bearing caps in the correct order

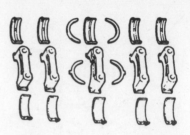

Keep all parts in order — exact reassembly is required

15. Remove the upper bearing shells from the block and place them in order with the corresponding bearing caps.

To install:

16. Check and measure the crankshaft and bearings according to the procedures given in "Cleaning and Inspection" later in this Chapter.

17. When reassembling, clean the bearing caps and journals in the block thoroughly. Coat the bearings with a liberal application of clean motor oil.

18. Fit the upper bearings halves into the block and position the lower bearing halves in the bearing caps.

19. Place the crankshaft into the engine block, making sure it fits exactly into its mounts.

20. Install the upper thrust washers on the center main bearing with the oil grooves facing outward.

21. Install the main bearing caps and the lower thrust washers in the proper sequence. Make sure the arrows on the caps point towards the front (pulley end) of the engine.

22. Tighten the cap bolts in three passes and in the correct sequence to specifications.

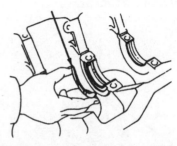

Correct position of the upper thrust washer when reinstalling

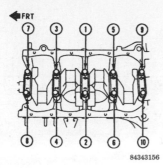

Tighten the crankshaft main bearing caps in the correct order

23. Double check the endplay of the crankshaft by repeating Step 10 of this procedure.

24. Turn the crankshaft through one or two full clockwise rotations, making sure that it turns smoothly and evenly with no binding.

25. Attach the connecting rods, following procedures given earlier in this Chapter. Remember that the rod caps must be reinstalled in their original positions.

26. Install a new rear main oil seal into the retainer and install the retainer onto the block. Tighten the bolts to 7 ft. lbs. (84 inch lbs.).

27. Install the rear end plate on the engine.

28. Install either the driveplate/flexplate (automatic) or the flywheel (manual), observing the matchmarks made during removal.

29. If equipped with a manual transaxle, reinstall the clutch disc and pressure plate.

30. Install the oil pump.

31. Install the oil strainer and oil pan, using new gaskets.

32. Rotate the engine into its upright position and continue reassembly of the timing belt, idler pulley and covers.

33. Reinstall the engine in the car, following procedures outlined earlier in this Chapter.

CLEANING AND INSPECTION

With the crankshaft removed from the engine, clean the crank, bearings and block areas thoroughly. Visually inspect each crankshaft section for any sign of wear or damage, paying close attention to the main bearing journals. ANY scoring or ridge on the crankshaft means the crankshaft must be ground undersize or replaced.

Mount the crankshaft on V-blocks and set a dial indicator to bear on the center main journal. Slowly rotate the crank and record the circular runout as shown on the dial. Runout in excess of 0.0024 in. (0.06mm) on all 1990–92 vehicles or in excess of 0.0012 in. (0.03mm) on 1993 vehicles disqualifies the crankshaft from further use. It must be replaced.

Using a micrometer, measure the diameter of each journal on the crankshaft and record the measurements. The acceptable specifications for both connecting rod and main journals are found in the Crankshaft and Connecting Rod specifications chart at the beginning of this Chapter. If ANY journal is beyond the acceptable range, the crankshaft must be ground undersize or replaced.

Additionally, each journal must be measured at both outer edges. When one measurement is subtracted from the other, the difference is the measurement of journal taper. Any taper beyond 0.2mm is a sign of excess wear on the journal; the crankshaft must be replaced.

BEARING REPLACEMENT

1. With the engine out of the car and inverted on a stand, remove the main bearing caps in the correct sequence.

2. Once the bearing caps are removed, the lower bearing shell may be inspected. Check closely for scoring or abrasion of the bearing surface. If this lower bearing is worn or damaged, both the upper and lower half should be replaced.

3. The bearing shells, the crank throws and the flat surface of the engine block (on the oil pan face) are stamped with numbers (1 through 5) indicating the standard bearing size. This size is determined during the initial manufacturing and assembly process; replacement bearings must be of the same code (thickness)

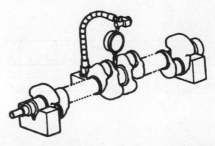

Measure crankshaft runout

if the correct clearances are to be maintained. If the code on the bearing shell is unreadable, use the number on the block and the number on the crank throw to determine the bearing code. Refer to the proper selection chart to find the correct bearing for that position.

4. Lift the crankshaft from the engine block and remove the upper bearing shells. Inspect them for wear or damage. Clean the area thoroughly, allow the surfaces to air dry.

5. Install the new bearing shells in the block, but do not oil them at this time.

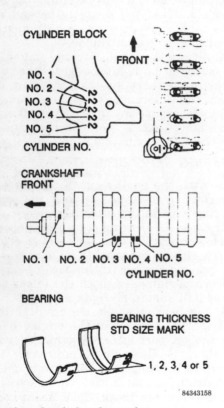

Location of main bearing codes

84343158

Crankshaft Block Mark	1	2	3	1	2	3	1	2	3
Crankshaft	0	0	0	1	1	1	2	2	2
Bearing	1	2	3	3	2	4	3	4	5

84343159

Main bearing selection table — 4A-FE engine

Cylinder Block No.	1	2	3	1	2	3	1	2	3
Crankshaft No.	0	0	0	1	1	1	2	2	2
Bearing No.	1	2	3	2	3	4	3	4	5

Example: Block mark
"2", crankshaft mark
"1" = bearing "3"

84343160

Main bearing selection table — 4A-GE engine

Carefully place the crankshaft in position.

6. Do not oil the lower bearing shells or the caps at this time. Install the bearing shells into the clean, dry caps.

7. Place a piece of plastic gauging material (such as Plastigage® or similar) lengthwise (fore-and-aft) across the full width of each of the five crankshaft main bearing journals. Remember that the measuring material is dissolved by oil. Keep the exposed part of the crank clean and dry.

8. Install the bearing caps with their bearing shells in their correct location and with the arrows pointing towards the front of the engine.

9. Install the bearing cap bolts and tighten them in three passes and in the correct sequence to specifications.

NOTE: *Do not rotate the crankshaft with the measuring plastic installed.*

10. Observing the correct removal sequence, gradually loosen and remove the bearing cap bolts. Carefully remove the bearing caps; the measuring media will be stuck to either the inside of the bearing shell or the face of the crankshaft.

11. Using the scale provided with the package of the measuring media, measure the gauging material at its widest point. This measurement represents the main bearing oil clearance and should be checked against the Crankshaft and Connecting Rod Specifications chart at the beginning of this Chapter.

12. If any clearance is not within specification, oversize bearings must be installed or the crankshaft must be removed, ground undersize and the bearing clearance rechecked.

13. Remove every piece of the plastic gauging material from the crank and bearing caps. Remove the crankshaft, coat the upper bearing shells with clean

	Number marked								
Cylinder block	1			2			3		
Crankshaft	0	1	2	0	1	2	0	1	2
Use bearing	1	2	3	2	3	4	3	4	5

84343161

Main bearing selection table — 7A-FE engine

engine, and reinstall the crankshaft. Coat the lower bearings shells (in the caps) with clean motor oil.

14. Install the main bearing caps and the lower thrust washers in the proper sequence. Make sure the arrows on the caps point towards the front (pulley end) of the engine.

15. Tighten the cap bolts in three passes and in the correct sequence to specifications.

16. Double check the end-play of the crankshaft. Turn the crankshaft through one or two full clockwise rotations, making sure that it turns smoothly and evenly with no binding.

Cylinder Block

Most inspection and service work on the cylinder block should be handled by a machinist or professional engine rebuilding shop. Included in this work are bearing alignment checks, line boring, deck resurfacing, hot-tanking and cylinder block boring. Any or all of this work requires that the block be completely stripped of all components and transported to the shop. A block that has been checked and properly serviced will last much longer than one whose owner cut corners during a repair.

Cylinder de-glazing (honing) can be performed by the owner/mechanic who is careful and takes time to be accurate. The cylinder bores become glazed during normal operation of the engine as the rings ride up and down constantly. This shiny glaze must be removed in order for a new set of piston rings to seat properly.

Cylinder hones are available at most auto tool stores and parts jobbers. With the piston and rod assemblies removed from the block, cover the crankshaft com-

pletely with a rag to keep grit from collecting on it. Install the hone into the chuck of a variable speed drill (preferred in place of a constant speed drill) and insert the hone into the cylinder.

NOTE: *Make sure the drill and hone are kept square to the cylinder bore during the entire honing procedure.*

Start the hone and move it up and down in the cylinder at a rate which will produce approximately a 60° crosshatch pattern. DO NOT extend the hone below the bottom of the cylinder bore. After the crosshatched pattern is established, remove the hone and check the piston fit.

Remove the piston and wash the cylinder with a solution of detergent and water to remove the honing and cylinder grit. Wipe the bores out several times with a clean rag soaked in fresh engine oil. Remove the cover from the crankshaft and check closely to see that NO grit has found its way onto the crankshaft.

Flywheel and Ring Gear

REMOVAL & INSTALLATION

1. Remove the transaxle, following procedures outlined in Chapter 7.

84343162

Cylinders should be honed to look like this

2. For cars equipped with automatic transaxle:

a. Matchmark the driveplate and the crankshaft.

b. Loosen the retaining bolts a little at a time and in a criss-cross pattern. Support the driveplate as the last bolts are removed and then lift the driveplate away from the engine.

3. For manual transaxle cars:

a. Matchmark the pressure plate assembly and the flywheel.

b. Loosen the pressure plate retaining bolts a little at a time and in a criss-cross pattern. Support the pressure plate and clutch assembly as the last bolt is removed and lift them away from the flywheel.

c. Matchmark the flywheel and crankshaft. Loosen the retaining bolts evenly and in a criss-cross pattern. Support the flywheel during removal of the last bolts and remove the flywheel.

4. Carefully inspect the teeth on the flywheel or driveplate for any signs of wearing or chipping. If anything beyond minimal contact wear is found, replace the unit.

NOTE: *Since the flywheel is driven by the starter gear, you would be wise to inspect the starter drive if any wear is found on the flywheel teeth. A worn starter can cause damage to the flywheel.*

To install:

5. Place the flywheel or driveplate in position on the crankshaft and make sure the matchmarks align. Install the retaining bolts finger tight.

6. Tighten the bolts in a diagonal pattern and in three passes. Tighten the flywheel bolts (manual) or the driveplate bolts (automatic) to specifications.

7. Install the clutch and pressure plate assembly. Torque all mounting bolts to specifications.

NOTE: *If the clutch appears worn or cracked in any way, replace it with a new disc, pressure plate and release bearing. The slight extra cost of the parts will prevent having to remove the transaxle again later.*

8. Reinstall the transaxle assembly. Road test the vehicle for proper operation.

RING GEAR REPLACEMENT

If the ring gear teeth on the driveplate or flywheel are damaged, the unit must be replaced. The ring gear cannot be separated or reinstalled individually.

If a flywheel is replaced on a manual transaxle vehicle, the installation of a new clutch disc, pressure plate and release bearing is highly recommended.

EXHAUST SYSTEM

Safety Precautions

For a number of reasons, exhaust system work can be the most dangerous type of work you can do on your car. Always observe the following precautions:

• Support the car extra securely. Not only will you often be working directly under it, but you'll frequently be using a lot of force, say, heavy hammer blows, to dislodge rusted parts. This can cause a car that's improperly supported to shift and possibly fall.

• Wear goggles. Exhaust system parts are always rusty. Metal chips can be dislodged, even when you're only turning rusted bolts. Attempting to pry pipes apart with a chisel makes the chips fly even more frequently.

• If you're using a cutting torch, keep it a GREAT distance from either the fuel tank or lines. Stop what you're doing and feel the temperature of the fuel bearing pipes on the tank frequently. Even slight heat can expand and/or vaporize fuel, resulting in accumulated vapor, or even a liquid leak, near your torch.

• Watch where your hammer blows fall and make sure you hit squarely. You could easily tap a brake or fuel line when you hit an exhaust system part with a glancing blow. Inspect all lines and hoses in the area where you've been working.

CAUTION: *Be very careful when working on or near the catalytic converter. External temperatures can reach 1,500°F (816°C) and more, causing severe burns. Removal or installation should be performed only on a cold exhaust system.*

Special Tools

A number of special exhaust system tools can be rented from auto supply houses or local stores that rent special equipment. A common one is a tail pipe expander, designed to enable you to join pipes of identical diameter.

It may also be quite helpful to use solvents designed to loosen rusted bolts or flanges. Soaking rusted parts the night before you do the job can speed the work of freeing rusted parts considerably. Remember that these solvents are often flammable. Apply only to parts after they are cool.

The exhaust system of most engines consists of four pieces. At the front of the car, the first section of pipe connects the exhaust manifold to the catalytic converter. The catalytic converter is a sealed, non-serviceable unit which can be easily unbolted from the system and replaced if necessary.

An intermediate or center pipe containing a built-in resonator (pre-muffler) runs from the catalytic converter to the muffler at the rear of the car. Should the resonator fail, the entire pipe must be replaced. The muffler and tailpipe at the rear should always be replaced as a unit.

The exhaust system is attached to the body by several welded hooks and flexible rubber hangers; these hangers absorb exhaust vibrations and isolate the system from the body of the car. A series of metal heat shields runs along the exhaust piping, protecting the underbody from excess heat.

When inspecting or replacing exhaust system parts, make sure there is adequate clearance from all points on the body to avoid possible overheating of the floorpan. Check the complete system for broken, damaged, missing or poorly positioned parts. Rattles and vibrations in the exhaust system are usually caused by misalignment of parts. When aligning the system, leave all the nuts and bolts loose until everything is in its proper place, then tighten the hardware working from the front to the rear. Remember that what appears to be proper clearance during repair may change as the car moves down the road. The motion of the engine, body and suspension must be considered when replacing parts.

COMPONENT REMOVAL & INSTALLATION

CAUTION: *DO NOT perform exhaust repairs with the engine or exhaust hot. Allow the system to cool completely before attempting any work. Also, ex-haust systems are noted for sharp edges, flaking metal and rusted bolts. Gloves and eye protection are required.*
NOTE: *ALWAYS use a new gasket at each pipe joint whenever the joint is dis-assembled. Use new nuts, bolts and clamps to hold the joint properly. These low-cost items will serve to prevent future leaks as the system ages.*

Front Pipe

1. Raise and safely support the vehicle on jackstands.
2. Disconnect the oxygen sensor.
3. Remove the two bolts holding the pipe to the exhaust manifold.
4. Remove the two bolts holding the pipe to the catalytic converter.
5. Remove the bolts from the crossmember bracket and remove the pipe from under the car.

To install:
6. Attach the new pipe to the crossmember bracket. Install the bolts at both the manifold and the catalyst ends, leaving them finger tight until the pipe is correctly positioned. Make certain the gaskets are in place and straight.
7. Tighten the pipe-to-manifold bolts to 46 ft. lbs.
8. Tighten the bolts at the converter to 32 ft. lbs.
9. Reconnect the oxygen sensor.
10. Lower the vehicle to the ground, start the system and check for leaks.

Catalytic Converter

With the car safely supported on jackstands, the converter is removed simply by removing the two bolts at either end. When reinstalling the converter, install it with new gaskets and tighten the end bolts to 32 ft. lbs.

Intermediate Pipe (Resonator Pipe)

1. Raise and safely support the vehicle on jackstands.
2. Remove the two bolts holding the pipe to the catalytic converter.
3. Remove the bolts holding the intermediate pipe to the muffler inlet pipe.
4. Disconnect the rubber hangers and remove the pipe.

To install:
5. Install the new pipe by suspending it in place on the rubber hangers. Install the gaskets at each end and install the bolts finger tight.

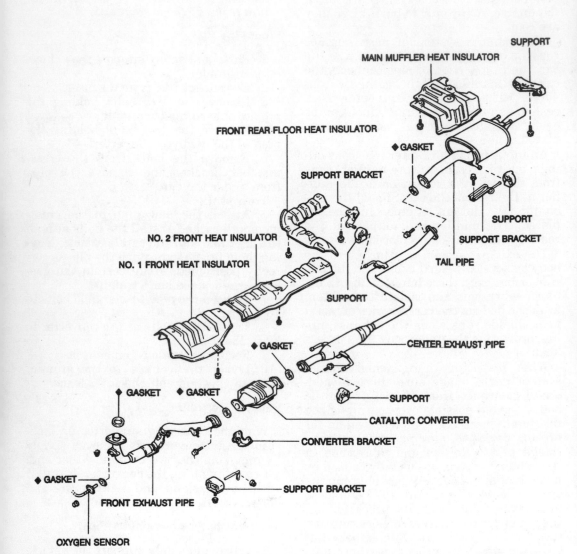

SUPPORT

MAIN MUFFLER HEAT INSULATOR

FRONT REAR FLOOR HEAT INSULATOR

◆ GASKET

SUPPORT BRACKET

SUPPORT

SUPPORT BRACKET

NO. 2 FRONT HEAT INSULATOR

TAIL PIPE

NO. 1 FRONT HEAT INSULATOR

SUPPORT

◆ GASKET

CENTER EXHAUST PIPE

◆ GASKET   ◆ GASKET

SUPPORT

CATALYTIC CONVERTER

CONVERTER BRACKET

◆ GASKET

SUPPORT BRACKET

FRONT EXHAUST PIPE

OXYGEN SENSOR

84343163

Exhaust system components-2WD 4A-FE engine

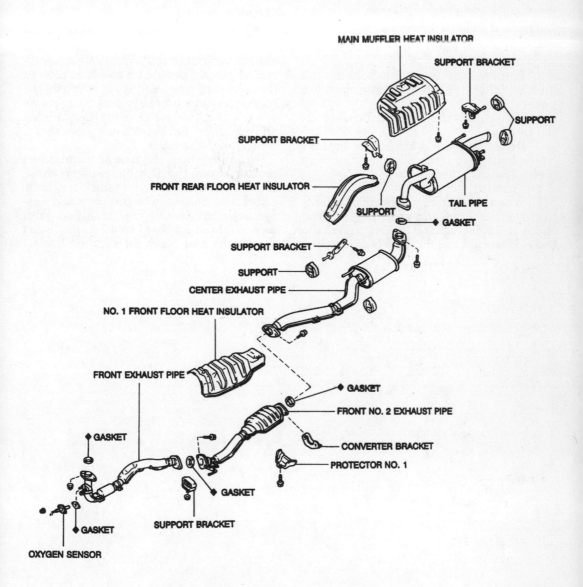

MAIN MUFFLER HEAT INSULATOR

SUPPORT BRACKET

SUPPORT

SUPPORT BRACKET

FRONT REAR FLOOR HEAT INSULATOR

TAIL PIPE

SUPPORT

◆ GASKET

SUPPORT BRACKET

SUPPORT

CENTER EXHAUST PIPE

NO. 1 FRONT FLOOR HEAT INSULATOR

FRONT EXHAUST PIPE

◆ GASKET

FRONT NO. 2 EXHAUST PIPE

CONVERTER BRACKET

PROTECTOR NO. 1

◆ GASKET

◆ GASKET

SUPPORT BRACKET

◆ GASKET

OXYGEN SENSOR

84343164

Exhaust system components-4WD 4A-FE engine

6. Double check the placement of the pipe and insure proper clearance to all body and suspension components.

7. Tighten the bolts holding the pipe to the catalytic converter to 32 ft. lbs., then tighten the bolts to the muffler inlet pipe to 32 ft. lbs.

8. Lower the car to the ground. Start the engine and check for leaks.

Muffler and Tailpipe Assembly

1. Raise and safely support the vehicle on jackstands.

2. Remove the two bolts holding the muffler inlet pipe to the intermediate pipe.

3. Disconnect the forward bracket on the muffler.

4. Disconnect the rear muffler bracket (three bolts) and remove the muffler from under the car.

To install:

5. When reinstalling, suspend the muffler from its front and rear hangers and check it for correct positioning under the body. If the old muffler had been rattling or hitting the body it is possible that the hangers and brackets have become bent from a light impact.

6. Attach the inlet pipe to the intermediate pipe and tighten the bolts to 32 ft. lbs.

7. Lower the vehicle to the ground, start the engine and check for leaks.

Complete System

If the entire exhaust system is to be replaced, it is much easier to remove the system as a unit than remove each individual piece. Disconnect the first pipe at the manifold joint and work towards the rear removing brackets and hangers as you go. Remove the rear muffler bracket and slide the entire exhaust system out form under the car.

When installing the new assembly, suspend it from the flexible hangers first, then attach the fixed (solid) brackets. Check the clearance to the body and suspension and install the manifold joint bolts, tightening them to 46 ft. lbs. Start the engine and check for exhaust leaks.

EMISSION CONTROLS

Component location and vacuum routing diagrams are located at the end of this Chapter. Please refer to them before beginning any disassembly or testing.

Due to varying state, federal, and provincial regulations, specific emission control equipment may vary by area of sale. The U.S. emission equipment is divided into two categories: California and 49 State. In this Chapter, the term "California" applies only to cars originally built to be sold in California. Some California emissions equipment is not shared with equipment installed on cars built to be sold in the other 49 states. Models built to be sold in Canada also have specific emissions equipment, although in many cases the 49 State and Canadian equipment is the same.

Positive Crankcase Ventilation (PCV) System

SYSTEM OPERATION

A closed positive crankcase ventilation system is used on all Toyota models. This system cycles incompletely burned fuel which works its way past the piston rings back into the intake manifold for reburning with the fuel/air mixture. The oil filler cap is sealed and the air is drawn from the top of the crankcase into the intake manifold through a valve with a variable orifice.

This valve (commonly known as the PCV valve) regulates the flow of air into the manifold according to the amount of manifold vacuum.

A plugged valve or hose may cause a rough idle, stalling or low idle speed, oil leaks in the engine and/or sludging and

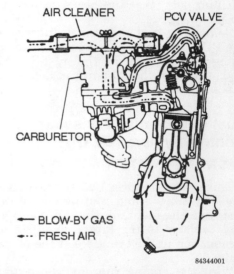

Typical positive crankcase ventilation (PCV) system

oil deposits within the engine and air cleaner. A leaking valve or hose could cause an erratic idle or stalling.

INSPECTION AND TESTING

The PCV is easily checked with the engine running at normal idle speed (warmed up). Remove the PCV valve from the valve cover, but leave it connected to its hose. Place your thumb over the end of the valve to check for vacuum. If there is no vacuum, check for plugged hoses or ports. With the engine off, remove the PCV valve completely. Shake it end to end, listening for the rattle of the needle inside the valve. If no rattle is heard, the needle is jammed (probably with oil sludge) and the valve should be replaced.

An engine which is operated without crankcase ventilation can be damaged very quickly. It is important to check and change the PCV valve (check PCV valve hose also) at regular maintenance intervals.

REMOVAL & INSTALLATION

Remove the PCV valve from the valve (camshaft) cover. Remove the hose from the valve. Take note of which end of the valve was in the manifold. This one-way valve must be reinstalled correctly or it will not function. While the valve is removed, the hoses should be checked for splits, kinks and blockages. Check the vacuum port (that the hoses connect to) for any clogging.

Remember that the correct function of the PCV system is based on a sealed engine — an air leak at the oil filler cap and/or around the oil pan can defeat the design of the system.

Fuel Evaporative Emission Control System (EVAP)

SYSTEM OPERATION

This system reduces hydrocarbon emissions by storing and routing evaporated fuel from the fuel tank through the charcoal canister to the intake manifold for combustion in the cylinders at the proper time.

With the engine running above 1500 rpm, the fuel vapors are purged from the canister into the intake manifold. If deceleration occurs, the throttle position switch opens (disconnects) and the ECM detects the change. The control valve is closed and the purging of vapor is stopped. This eliminates the delivery of excess fuel vapor during periods of poor or reduced combustion.

When there is pressure in the fuel tank (such as from summer heat or long periods of driving) the canister valve opens, allowing vapor to enter the canister and be stored for future delivery to the engine.

INSPECTION AND TESTING

Before embarking on component removal or extensive diagnosis, perform a complete visual check of the system. Every vacuum line and vapor line (including the lines running to the tank) should be inspected for cracking, loose clamps, kinks and obstructions. Additionally, check the tank for any signs of deformation or crushing. Each vacuum port on the engine or manifold should be checked for restriction by dirt or sludge.

The evaporative control system is generally not prone to component failure in normal circumstances; most problems can be tracked to the causes listed above.

Fuel Filler Cap

Check that the filler cap seals effectively. Replace the filler cap if the seal is defective.

Charcoal Canister

1. Label and disconnect the lines running to the canister. Remove the charcoal canister from the vehicle.
2. Visually check the charcoal canister for cracks or damage.
3. Check for a clogged filter and stuck check valve. Using low pressure compressed air, blow into the tank pipe and check that the air flows without resistance from the other pipes. If this does not test positive replace the canister.

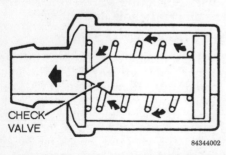

CHECK VALVE

84344002

Cross section of a PCV valve-the valve should rattle when shaken

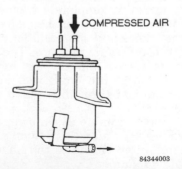

COMPRESSED AIR

84344003

Checking for clogged filter and stuck valve in the charcoal canister — all engines

COMPRESSED AIR

84344004

Cleaning filter in the charcoal canister — all engines

4. Clean the filter in the canister by blowing no more than 43 psi of compressed air into the pipe to the outer vent control valve while holding the other upper canister pipes closed.

NOTE: *Do not attempt to wash the charcoal canister. Also be sure that no activated carbon comes out of the canister during the cleaning process.*

5. Replace or reinstall the canister as needed.

Inspection of Bimetal Vacuum Switching Valve (BVSV)

1. Drain the engine coolant from the radiator into a suitable container.
2. Remove the BVSV.
3. Cool the BVSV to below 104° with cool water. Blow air into pipe and check that the BVSV is closed.
4. Heat the BVSV to above 129° with hot water. Blow air into pipe and check that the BVSV is open. If a problem is found, replace the valve.
5. Apply liquid sealer to the threads of the BVSV and reinstall.
6. Fill the radiator with coolant.

REMOVAL & INSTALLATION

Removal and installation of the various evaporative emission control system components consists of labeling or marking and unfastening hoses, loosening retaining screws or removing a threaded vacuum valve and removing the part which is to be replaced.

NOTE: *When replacing any EVAP system hoses, always use hoses that are fuel-resistant or are marked EVAP. Use of hose which is not fuel-resistant will lead to premature hose failure.*

Dash Pot (DP) System
SYSTEM OPERATION

The operation of this system reduces the HC and CO emissions. When decelerating, the dash pot opens the throttle valve slightly more than at idle. This causes the air-fuel mixture to burn completely.

ADJUSTMENT
4A-GE Engine

1. Warm up and stop engine.
2. Check idle speed.
3. Remove the cap, filter and separator from the dash pot.
4. Adjust DP setting speed as follows:
   a. Race the engine at 2500 rpm for a few seconds. Plug the VTV hole with your finger in the dash pot assembly.
   b. Release the throttle valve.
   c. Check the DP setting speed. The DP setting speed is 1800 rpm with cooling fan OFF.
   d. Adjust the DP setting speed by turning the DP adjusting screw.
5. Reinstall the DP separator, filter and cap.
6. Check system operation by racing the engine at 2500 rpm for a few seconds, release the throttle valve and check that the engine returns to idle speed in a few seconds.

4A-FE Engine

NOTE: *The 1993 4A-FE and 7A-FE engines do not use this system.*

1. Warm up and stop engine.
2. Check idle speed and adjust, if necessary.
3. Remove the cap, filter and separator from the dash pot.
4. Adjust DP setting speed as follows:
   a. Connect terminals TE_1 and E_1 in the check connector.
   b. On 2WD California and 4WD, disconnect the EGR VSV connector.
   c. Race the engine at 3000 rpm (2WD) or 3500 rpm (4WD) for a few seconds. Plug the VTV hole with your finger in the dash pot assembly.
   d. Release the throttle valve.
   e. Check the DP setting speed. The DP setting speed should be 1500 rpm on 2WD, 1800 rpm on 4WD with M/T or 2200 rpm on 4WD with A/T, with cooling fan OFF.
   f. Adjust the DP setting speed by turning the DP adjusting screw.

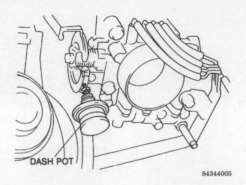

84344005

Dash pot (DP) system — 4A-GE and 4A-FE engines

g. Connect the EGR VSV connector if so equipped. Remove the SST or jumper from the check connector.

5. Reinstall the DP separator, filter and cap.

6. Check system operation by racing the engine at 3000 rpm (2WD) or 3500 rpm (4WD) for a few seconds, release the throttle valve and check that the engine returns to idle speed in a few seconds.

REMOVAL & INSTALLATION

On all engine applications, to remove the dash pot assembly disconnect dash pot mounting bracket from the throttle body. Replace the dash pot assembly and adjust if necessary.

Exhaust Gas Recirculation (EGR) System

SYSTEM OPERATION

The EGR system reduces oxides of nitrogen. This is accomplished by recirculating some of the exhaust gases through the EGR valve to the intake manifold, lowering peak combustion temperatures.

INSPECTION AND TESTING

4A-GE Engine

1. Check and clean the filter in the EGR vacuum modulator. Use compressed air (if possible) to blow the dirt out of the filters and check the filters for contamination or damage.

2. Using a tee (3-way connector), connect a vacuum gauge to the hose between the EGR valve and the vacuum modulator.

3. Check the seating of the EGR valve by starting the engine and seeing that it runs at a smooth idle. If the valve is not completely closed, the idle will be rough.

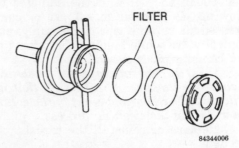

84344006

Check and clean filters in the EGR vacuum modulator — all engines

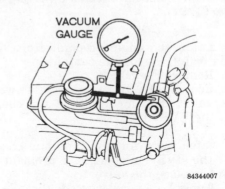

84344007

Check operation of EGR valve — 4A-GE engine

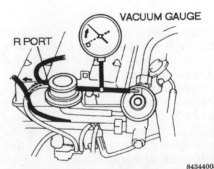

84344008

Check operation of EGR valve — 4A-GE engine

4. With the engine coolant temperature below 129°F (54°C), the vacuum gauge should read 0 at 2500 rpm. This indicates that the Vacuum Switching Valve (VSV) is functioning correctly at this temperature range.

5. Warm the engine to normal operating temperature. Check the vacuum gauge and confirm low vacuum at 3500 rpm. This indicates the VSV and the EGR vacuum modulator are working correctly in this temperature range.

6. Disconnect the vacuum hose from the **R** port on the EGR vacuum modulator and, using another piece of hose, connect the **R** port directly to the intake manifold. Check that the vacuum gauge indicates high vacuum at 2500 rpm.

NOTE: *As a large amount of exhaust gas enters, the engine will misfire slightly at this time.*

7. Disconnect the vacuum gauge and reconnect the vacuum hoses to their proper locations.

8. Check the EGR valve by applying vacuum directly to the valve with the engine at idle. (This may be accomplished either by bridging vacuum directly from the intake manifold or by using a hand-held vacuum pump.) The engine should falter and die as the full load of recirculated gasses enters the engine.

9. If no problem is found with this inspection, the system is OK; otherwise inspect each part.

EGR VALVE

1. Remove the EGR valve.
2. Check the valve for sticking and heavy carbon deposits. If a problem is found, replace the valve.
3. Reinstall the EGR valve with a new gasket.

EGR VACUUM MODULATOR

1. Label and disconnect the vacuum hoses from ports **P**, **Q**, and **R** of the EGR vacuum modulator.
2. Plug the **P** and **R** ports with your fingers.
3. Blow air into port **Q**. Check that the air passes freely through the sides of the air filter.
4. Start the engine and maintain 2500 rpm.
5. Repeat the test above. Check that there is a strong resistance to air flow.
6. Reconnect the vacuum hoses to the proper locations.

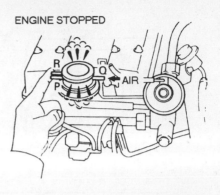

ENGINE STOPPED

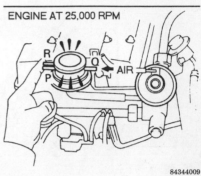

ENGINE AT 25,000 RPM

84344009

Inspection of the EGR valve modulator — 4A-GE engine

VACUUM SWITCHING VALVE

1. The vacuum switching circuit is checked by blowing air into the pipe under the following conditions:
   a. Connect the vacuum switching valve terminals to the battery.
   b. Blow into the tube and check that the VSV switch is open.
   c. Disconnect the positive battery terminal.
   d. Blow into the tube and check that the VSV switch is closed (no flow).

2. Check for a short circuit within the valve. Using an ohmmeter, check that there is no continuity between the positive terminal and the VSV body. If there is continuity, replace the VSV.

3. Check for an open circuit. Using an ohmmeter, measure the resistance (ohms) between the two terminals of the valve. The resistance should be 33–39 ohms at 68°F (20°C). If the resistance is not within specifications, replace the VSV.

NOTE: *The resistance will vary slightly with temperature. It will decrease in cooler temperatures and increase with heat. Slight variations due to temperature range are not necessarily a sign of a failed valve.*

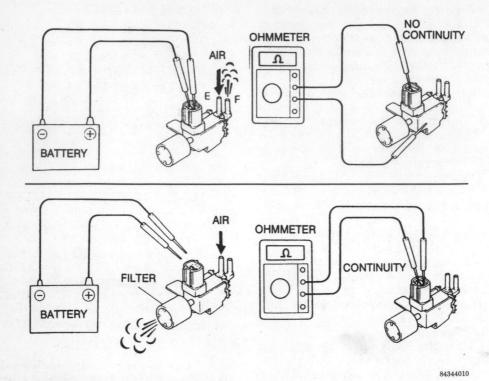

84344010

Inspection and testing of the Vacuum Switching Valve (VSV) — 4A-GE engine

4A-FE And 7A-FE Engines

NOTE: *The EGR system is used only on 1993 7A-FE California vehicles.*

1. Check and clean the filter in the EGR vacuum modulator. Use compressed air (if possible) to blow the dirt out of the filters and check the filters for contamination or damage.

2. Using a tee (3-way connector), connect a vacuum gauge to the hose between the EGR valve and the vacuum modulator.

3. Check the seating of the EGR valve by starting the engine and seeing that it runs at a smooth idle. If the valve is not completely closed, the idle will be rough.

4. Connect terminals TE_1 and E_1 in the check connector. Inspect VSV operation with cold engine. With the engine coolant temperature below 104°F (47°C), the vacuum gauge should read 0 at 2500 rpm.

5. Connect terminals TE_1 and E_1 in the check connector. Inspect VSV and EGR vacuum modulator operation with hot engine. With the engine coolant temperature above 127°F (53°C), check the vacuum gauge and confirm low vacuum at 2500 rpm. This indicates the VSV and the EGR vacuum modulator are working correctly in this temperature range.

6. Disconnect the vacuum gauge, SST or jumper wire and reconnect the vacuum hoses to their proper locations.

7. Connect terminals TE_1 and E_1 in the check connector. Check the EGR valve by applying vacuum directly to the valve with the engine at idle. (This may be accomplished either by bridging vacuum directly from the intake manifold or by using a hand-held vacuum pump.) The engine should falter and die as the full

load of recirculated gasses enters the engine.

8. If no problem is found with this inspection, the system is OK; otherwise inspect each part.

EGR VALVE

1. Remove the EGR valve.
2. Check the valve for sticking and heavy carbon deposits. If a problem is found, replace the valve.
3. Reinstall the EGR valve with a new gasket.

EGR VACUUM MODULATOR

1. Label and disconnect the vacuum hoses from ports **P**, **Q**, and **R** of the EGR vacuum modulator.
2. Plug the **P** and **R** ports with your fingers.
3. Blow air into port **Q**. Check that the air passes freely through the sides of the air filter.
4. Start the engine and maintain 2500 rpm.
5. Repeat the test above. Check that there is a strong resistance to air flow.
6. Reconnect the vacuum hoses to the proper locations.

VACUUM SWITCHING VALVE

1. The vacuum switching circuit is checked by blowing air into the pipe under the following conditions:
   a. Connect the vacuum switching valve terminals to the battery.
   b. Blow into the tube and check that the VSV switch is open.
   c. Disconnect the positive battery terminal.
   d. Blow into the tube and check that the VSV switch is closed (no flow).
2. Check for a short circuit within the valve. Using an ohmmeter, check that there is no continuity between the positive terminal and the VSV body. If there is continuity, replace the VSV.
3. Check for an open circuit. Using an ohmmeter, measure the resistance (ohms) between the two terminals of the valve. The resistance (cold) should be 37–44 ohms. If the resistance is not within specifications, replace the VSV.

REMOVAL & INSTALLATION

Exhaust emission control equipment is generally simple to work on and easy to get to on the engine. The air cleaner assembly will need to be removed. Always label each vacuum hose before removing

ENGINE STOPPED

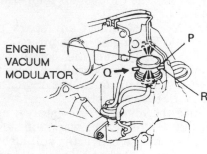

ENGINE AT 25,000 RPM

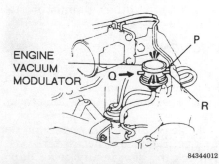

84344012

Inspection of the EGR valve modulator — 4A-FE and 7A-FE California engines

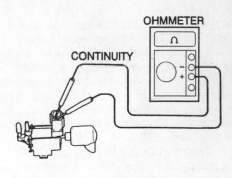

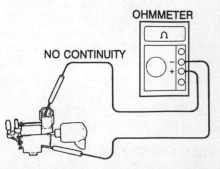

84344013

Testing of the vacuum switching valve (VSV) — 4A-FE and 7A-FE California engines

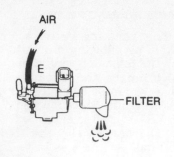

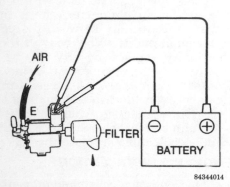

84344014

Inspection of the vacuum switching valve (VSV) — 4A-FE and 7A-FE California engines

it — they must be replaced in the correct position.

Most of the valves and solenoids are made of plastic, particularly at the vacuum ports. Be very careful during removal not to break or crack the ports; you have NO chance of regluing a broken fitting. Remember that the plastic has been in a hostile environment (heat and vibration); the fittings become brittle and less resistant to abuse or accidental impact.

The EGR valve is held in place by mounting bolts. The bolts can be difficult to remove due to corrosion. Remove the air cleaner assembly and all necessary components for access to the EGR valve mounting bolts. Once the EGR is off the engine, clean the bolts and the bolt holes of any rust or debris. Always replace the gasket any time the EGR valve is removed.

Three-Way and Oxidation Catalyst (TWC) System

SYSTEM OPERATION

The catalytic converter is a muffler-like container built into the exhaust system to aid in the reduction of HC, CO and NOx

emissions by changing them into nitrogen, carbon dioxide and water vapor through the action of the catalyst upon the exhaust gas.

The 3-way catalytic convertor is the best type to use since it can change all three types of emissions into non-polluting gases. In this type of converter nitrous oxides are chemically reduced by the catalyst and reformed into the molecules of oxygen and nitrogen. The oxygen formed by the reduction reaction is then used to oxidize carbon monoxide and the hydrocarbons, forming carbon dioxide and water vapor.

For the catalytic converter to work most efficiently, the following conditions must be met:

• Operating temperature must be over 500°F (260°C).

• Air/fuel ratio must be held closely at 14.7:1.

PRECAUTIONS

• Use only unleaded fuel.

• Avoid prolonged idling; the engine should run no longer than 20 minutes at curb idle, nor longer than 10 minutes at fast idle.

• Reduce the fast idle speed, by quickly depressing and releasing the accelerator pedal, as soon as the coolant temperature reaches 120°F (49°C).

• DO NOT disconnect any spark plug leads while the engine is running.

• Always make engine compression checks as quickly as possible. Excess fuel can be pumped through the motor and build up in the converter.

• Since the inside of the catalyst must reach 500°F (260°C) to work efficiently, the outside of the converter will also become very hot. Always be aware of what may be under the car when you park. Parking a hot exhaust system over dry grass, leaves or other flammable items may lead to a fire.

INSPECTION

1. Inspect the exhaust pipe assembly for looseness or damage.
2. Check exhaust clamps for cracks or damage.
3. Check catalytic converter for dents or damage. Replace if necessary.
4. Check the heat insulator for damage and adequate clearance between catalytic converter and heat insulator.

VACUUM DIAGRAMS

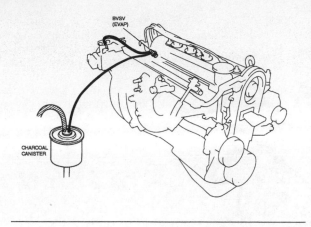

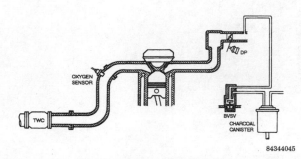

84344045

Emission control system — 1990–92 4A-FE 2WD Federal and Canada

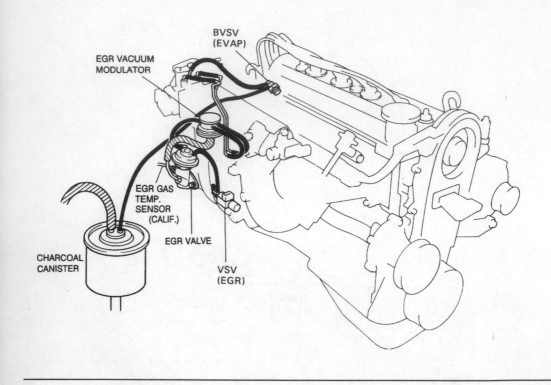

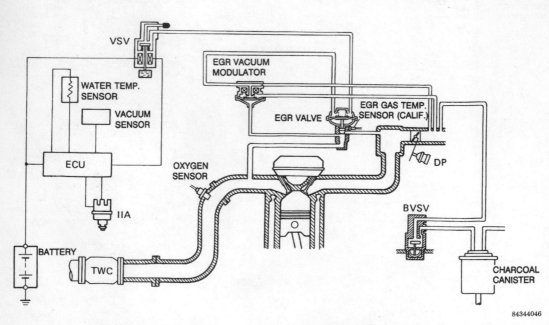

Emission control system — 1990–92 4A-FE 2WD California and 4WD

84344046

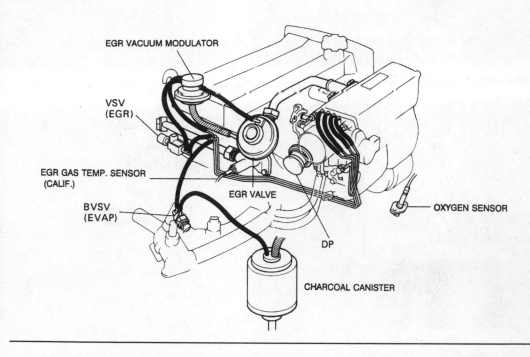

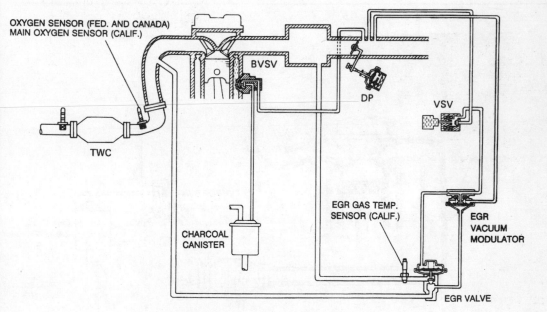

Emission control system — 1990–91 4A-GE

84344047

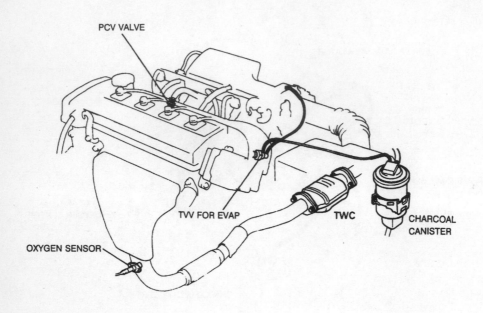

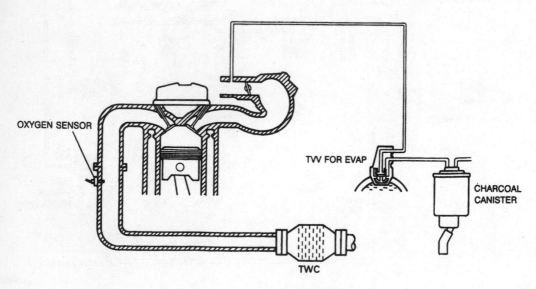

84344048

Emission control system — 1993 4A-FE and 7A-FE except California

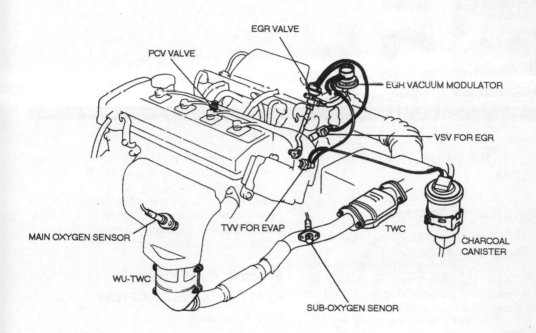

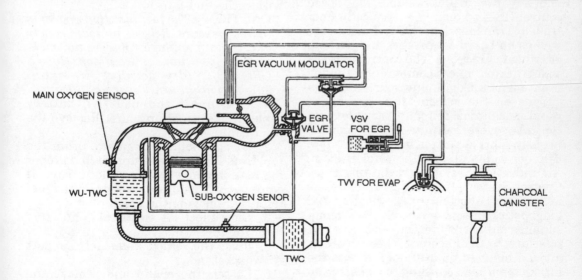

84344049

Emission control system — 1993 4A-FE and 7A-FE California

Fuel System

ELECTRONIC FUEL INJECTION SYSTEM

Description of System

Fuel injected engines are equipped with the Toyota Computer Control System (TCCS). This integrated control system allows the Engine Control Unit (ECU) to control other systems as well as the fuel injection. On earlier systems, the fuel management was performed by the EFI computer; in the current system, the control unit also oversees ignition timing and advance, EGR function, idle speed control (ISC system), Electronically Controlled Transmission (ECT) function as well as on-board diagnostics and back-up or fail-safe functions. The control unit is a sophisticated micro-computer, receiving input signals from many sources and locations on the vehicle. It is capable of rapid calculation of many variables and controls several output circuits simultaneously. This system is broken down into 3 major sub-systems: the Fuel System, Air Induction System and the Electronic Control System. Keeping these divisions in mind will shorten troubleshooting and diagnostic time. An electric fuel pump supplies sufficient fuel, under a constant pressure, to the injectors. These injectors allow a metered quantity of fuel into the intake manifold according to signals from the ECU. The air induction system provides sufficient air for the engine operation. This system includes the throttle body, air intake device and idle control system components.

Relieving Fuel Pressure

1. Disconnect the negative battery cable.

2. Unbolt the retaining screws and remove the protective shield for the fuel filter (if so equipped).

3. Place a large pan under the delivery pipe (large connection) to catch the dripping fuel and SLOWLY loosen the union bolt to bleed off the fuel pressure.

Electric Fuel Pump

REMOVAL & INSTALLATION

1990–92 Models

The electric fuel pump used on all vehicles covered in this manual are contained within the fuel tank.

CAUTION: *The fuel injection system is under pressure. Release pressure slowly and contain spillage. Observe no smoking/no open flame precautions. Have a Class B-C (dry powder) fire extinguisher within arm's reach at all times.*

1. Disconnect the negative battery cable. Relieve fuel pressure. Remove the filler cap.

2. Using a siphon or pump, drain the fuel from the tank and store it in a proper metal container with a tight cap. If equipped with a drain plug drain the fuel tank by removing the drain plug.

3. Disconnect all electrical connectors from the fuel tank.

4. Raise the vehicle and safely support it on jackstand.

5. Loosen the clamp and remove the filler neck and overflow pipe or hose from the tank.

6. Remove all lines from the fuel tank. Wrap a rag around the fitting to collect escaping fuel if necessary. Disconnect the vent hose if so equipped from the tank.

7. Cover or plug the end of each disconnected line to keep dirt out and fuel in.

8. Support the fuel tank with a floor jack or transmission jack. Use a broad

1. Fuel pump bracket
2. Electrical connector
3. Gasket
4. Fuel hose
5. Pump
6. Fuel pump filter
7. Clip
8. Rubber cushion

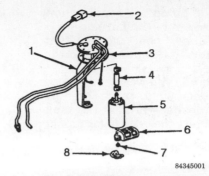

84345001

Fuel pump assembly — 1990–92

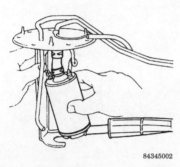

84345002

Removing the fuel pump from the bracket assembly — 1990–92

piece of wood to distribute the load. Be careful not to deform the bottom of the tank.

9. Remove the fuel tank support strap bolts.

10. Swing the straps away from the tank and lower the jack. Balance the tank with your other hand or have a helper assist you. The tank is bulky and may have some fuel left in it. If its balance changes suddenly, the tank may fall.

11. Remove the fuel filler pipe extension assembly, the vent pipe assembly and the sending unit assembly if necessary.

12. Keep these items in a clean, protected area away from the car.

13. To remove the electric fuel pump:

   a. Remove the fuel pump bracket (7 retaining bolts) and gasket from the fuel tank.

   b. Disconnect the two pump-to-harness wires.

   c. Loosen the pump outlet hose clamp at the bracket pipe.

   d. Remove the pump from the bracket and the outlet hose from the bracket pipe.

   e. Separate the outlet hose and the filter from the pump.

14. While the tank is out and disassembled, inspect it for any signs of rust, leakage or metal damage. If any problem is found, replace the tank. Clean the inside of the tank with water and a light detergent and rinse the tank thoroughly several times.

To install:

15. Inspect all of the lines, hoses and fittings for any sign of corrosion, wear or damage to the surfaces. Check the pump outlet hose and the filter for restrictions.

16. When reassembling, ALWAYS replace the sealing gaskets with new ones. Also replace any rubber parts showing any sign of deterioration.

17. Assemble the outlet hose and filter onto the pump; then attach the pump to the bracket.

18. Connect the outlet hose clamp to the bracket pipe and connect the pump wiring to the harness wire.

19. Install the fuel pump and bracket assembly onto the tank with a NEW gasket.

20. Install the sending unit assembly.

21. Connect the vent pipe assembly and the filler pipe extension assembly.

NOTE: *Tighten the vent pipe screw to 17 INCH lbs. and all other fuel tank attaching screws to 30 INCH lbs.*

22. Place the fuel tank on the jack and elevate it into place within the car. Attach the straps and install the strap bolts, tightening them (in even steps) to 29 ft. lbs.

23. Connect the vent hose to the tank pipe, the return hose to the tank pipe and the supply hose to its tank pipe. Tighten the supply hose fitting to 22 ft. lbs.

24. Connect the filler neck and overflow pipe to the tank. Make sure the clamps are properly seated and secure.

25. Lower the vehicle to the ground.

26. Connect the pump and sending unit electrical connectors to the harness.

27. Using a funnel, pour the fuel that was drained from its container into the fuel filler.

28. Install the fuel filler cap.

29. Start the engine and check carefully for any sign of leakage around the tank and lines. Road test the vehicle for proper operation.

1993 Models

CAUTION: *The fuel injection system is under pressure. Release pressure slowly and contain spillage. Observe no smoking/no open flame precautions. Have a Class B-C (dry powder) fire extinguisher within arm's reach at all times.*

1. Disconnect the negative battery cable. Relieve fuel pressure.

2. Remove the rear seat cushion.

3. Remove the 4 retaining screws and floor service hole cover.

4. Disconnect the electrical fuel pump connection at the fuel pump assembly.

5. Disconnect the fuel pipe and hose from the fuel pump bracket. Remove the fuel pump bracket assembly from the fuel tank. Remove the fuel pump from the fuel bracket.

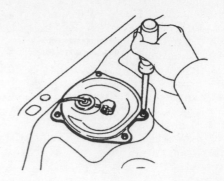

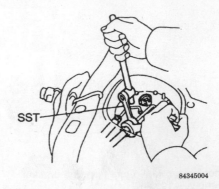

84345004

Removing the fuel pump assembly — 1993

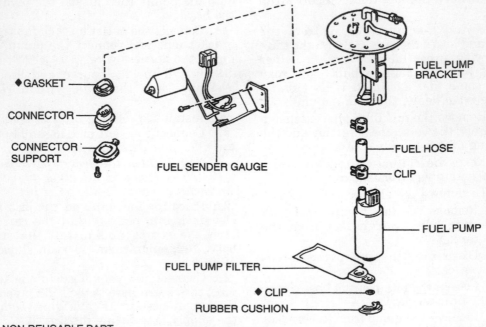

◆ GASKET

CONNECTOR

CONNECTOR SUPPORT

FUEL SENDER GAUGE

FUEL PUMP BRACKET

FUEL HOSE

CLIP

FUEL PUMP

FUEL PUMP FILTER

◆ CLIP

RUBBER CUSHION

◆ NON-REUSABLE PART

84345003

Fuel pump assembly — 1993

6. To remove the electric fuel pump:

a. Pull off the lower side of the fuel pump from the pump bracket.

b. Disconnect the pump connector.

c. Loosen the pump outlet hose clamp at the bracket pipe.

d. Remove the pump from the bracket and the outlet hose from the bracket pipe.

e. Separate the outlet hose and the filter from the pump.

To install:

7. Install the fuel pump to the fuel pump bracket. Make sure to install rubber cushion.

8. Install the fuel pump bracket assembly with NEW gasket in the tank. Torque pump bracket retaining screws 34 inch lbs.

9. Connect the fuel pipe (torque the fuel outlet pipe to 25 ft. lbs.) and fuel hose to fuel pump bracket.

10. Connect battery cable and start engine and check for fuel leaks.

11. Install floor service hole cover.

12. Install rear seat cushion.

TESTING

On-Vehicle Inspection

Since the fuel pump is concealed within the tank, it is difficult to test directly at the pump. It is possible to test the pump from under the hood, listening for pump function and feeling the fuel delivery lines for the build-up of pressure.

1. Turn the ignition switch **ON**, but do not start the engine.

2. Using a jumper wire, short both terminals of the fuel pump check connector. The check connector is located near the air cleaner. Connect the terminals lableled **FP** and **+B**.

3. Check that there is pressure in the hose running to the delivery pipe. You should hear fuel pressure noise and possibly hear the pump at the rear of the car.

4. Remove the jumper wire.

5. Turn the ignition to OFF. If the fuel pump failed to function, it may indicate a faulty pump, but before removing the fuel pump, check the following items within the pump system:

a. All fusible links

b. All fuses (EFI/15amp and IGN/10.0amp)

c. EFI main relay

d. Circuit opening relay

e. All wiring connections and grounds.

Checking Fuel Pressure

NOTE: *Do not operate the fuel pump unless it is immersed in gasoline and connected to its resistor.*

1. Check that the battery voltage is above 12 volts. With the ignition switch in the **OFF** position, disconnect the negative battery terminal.

2. Relieve the fuel pressure and disconnect the fuel connection at the fuel filter or cold start injector, using a shop towel to catch spilled fuel.

3. Install a fuel pressure guage, using 2 new gasket.

4. Reconnect the negative battery terminal.

5. Using a jumper wire, connect terminals +B and FP at the check connector.

NOTE: *The check connector is a small plastic box with a flip-up lid; it is found near the strut tower or battery.*

6. Turn the ignition switch **ON** and read the fuel pressure guage.

7. The fuel pressure should read 38–44 psi. on all engines. If the pressure is high, replace the fuel pressure regulator. If the fuel pressure is low, check the following: fuel hoses and connections, fuel pump, fuel filter or pressure regulator.

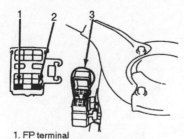

1. FP terminal
2. Battery positive (+) terminal
3. Jumper wire

84345005

Checking the fuel pump at the check connector

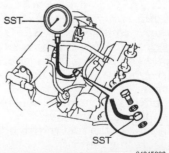

SST

84345006

Installing a fuel pressure test gauge

8. Turn the ignition switch **OFF** and remove the jumper wire.

9. Relieve the fuel pressure and remove the guage, catching the spilled fuel with a shop towel. Use new gaskets and connect the fuel line as necessary.

Fuel Injectors

The injectors — electrically triggered valves — deliver a measured quantity of fuel into the intake manifold according to signals from the ECM. As driving conditions change, the computer signals each injector to stay open a longer or shorter period of time, thus controlling the amount of fuel introduced into the engine. An injector, being an electric component, is either on or off (open or closed); there is no variable control for an injector other than duration.

Cleanliness equals success when working on a fuel injected system. Every component must be treated with the greatest care and be protected from dust, grime and impact damage. The miniaturized and solid state circuitry is easily damaged by a jolt. Additionally, care must be used in dealing with electrical connectors. Look for and release any locking mechanisms on the connector before separating the connectors. When reattaching, make sure each pin is properly lined up and seated before pushing the connector closed.

REMOVAL & INSTALLATION

4A-GE Engine

CAUTION: *The fuel system is under pressure. Release pressure slowly and contain spillage. Observe no smoking/no open flame precautions. Have a Class B-C (dry powder) fire extinguisher within arm's reach at all times.*

1. Disconnect the negative battery cable.

NOTE: *If you are diagnosing a driveability problem, check the ECM for any stored trouble codes BEFORE disconnecting the cable. The codes will be lost after the battery is disconnected.*

2. Disconnect the PCV hose from the valve cover.

3. Remove the vacuum sensing hose from the pressure regulator.

4. Disconnect the fuel return hose from the pressure regulator.

5. Place a towel or container under the cold start injector pipe. Loosen the two union bolts at the fuel line and remove the pipe with its gaskets.

6. Remove the fuel inlet pipe mounting bolt and disconnect the fuel inlet hose by removing the fuel union bolt, the two gaskets and the hose.

7. Disconnect the injector electrical connections.

8. At the fuel delivery pipe (rail), remove the three bolts. Lift the delivery pipe and the injectors free of the engine. DON'T drop the injectors.

9. Remove the four insulators and three collars from the cylinder head.

84345007

Removing the fuel delivery pipe hose — 4A-GE engine

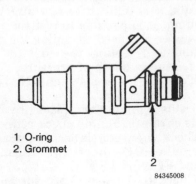

1. O-ring
2. Grommet

84345008

Injector seals — 4A-GE engine

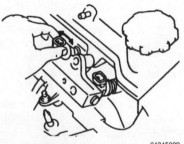

84345009

Make certain the fuel injector can be rotated in place after installation

10. Pull the injectors free of the delivery pipe.

To install:

11. Before installing the injectors back into the fuel rail, install a NEW O-ring on each injector.

12. Coat each O-ring with a light coat of gasoline (NEVER use oil of any sort) and install the injectors into the delivery pipe. Make certain each injector can be smoothly rotated. If they do not rotate smoothly, the O-ring is not in its correct position.

13. Install the insulators into each injector hole. Place the three spacers on the delivery pipe mounting holes in the cylinder head.

14. Place the delivery pipe and injectors on the cylinder head and again check that the injectors rotate smoothly. Install the three bolts and tighten them to 13 ft. lbs.

15. Connect the electrical connectors to each injector.

16. Install two new gaskets and attach the inlet pipe and fuel union bolt. Tighten the bolt to 22 ft. lbs. Install the mounting bolt.

17. Install new gaskets and connect the cold start injector pipe to the delivery pipe and cold start injector. Install the fuel line union bolts and tighten them to 13 ft. lbs.

18. Connect the fuel return hose and the vacuum sensing hose to the pressure regulator. Attach the PCV hose to the valve cover.

19. Connect the battery cable to the negative battery terminal. Start the engine and check for leaks.

CAUTION: *If there is a leak at any fitting, the line will be under pressure and the fuel may spray in a fine mist. This mist is extremely explosive. Shut the engine off immediately if any leakage is detected. Use rags to wrap the leaking fitting until the pressure diminishes and wipe up any fuel from the engine area.*

4A-FE Engine (1990–92)

CAUTION: *The fuel system is under pressure. Release pressure slowly and contain spillage. Observe no smoking/no open flame precautions. Have a Class B-C (dry powder) fire extinguisher within arm's reach at all times.*

1. Disconnect the negative battery cable.

2. Disconnect the PCV hose from the valve cover.

3. Remove the vacuum sensing hose from the pressure regulator.

4. Disconnect the fuel return hose from the pressure regulator.

5. Place a towel or container under the cold start injector pipe. Loosen the two union bolts at the fuel line and remove the pipe with its gasket.

6. Remove the fuel inlet pipe mounting bolt and disconnect the fuel inlet hose by removing the fuel union bolt, the two gaskets and the hose.

7. Disconnect the injector electrical connection.

8. At the fuel delivery pipe (rail), remove the two bolts. Lift the delivery pipe and the injectors free of the engine. DON'T drop the injector.

9. Remove the 4 insulators and 2 collars from the cylinder head.

10. Pull the injectors free of the delivery pipe.

To install:

11. Before installing the injectors back into the fuel rail, install a NEW O-ring on each injector.

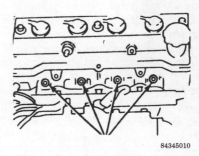

Placement of injectors insulators — 4A-FE engine 1990–92

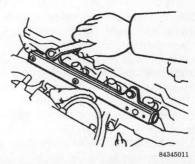

Removing the fuel delivery pipe — 4A-FE engine 1990–92

12. Coat each O-ring with a light coat of gasoline (NEVER use oil of any sort) and install the injectors into the delivery pipe. Make certain each injector can be smoothly rotated. If they do not rotate smoothly, the O-ring is not in its correct position.

13. Install the insulators into each injector hole. Place the two spacers on the delivery pipe mounting holes in the cylinder head.

14. Place the delivery pipe and injectors on the cylinder head and again check that the injectors rotate smoothly. Install the two bolts and tighten them to 11 ft. lbs.

15. Connect the electrical connectors to each injector.

16. Install two new gaskets and attach the inlet pipe and fuel union bolt. Tighten the bolt to 22 ft. lbs. Install the mounting bolt.

17. Install new gaskets and connect the cold start injector pipe to the delivery pipe and cold start injector. Install the fuel line union bolts and tighten them to 13 ft. lbs.

18. Connect the fuel return hose and the vacuum sensing hose to the pressure regulator. Attach the PCV hose to the valve cover.

19. Connect the battery cable to the negative battery terminal. Start the engine and check for leaks.

> CAUTION: *If there is a leak at any fitting, the line will be under pressure and the fuel may spray in a fine mist. This mist is extremely explosive. Shut the engine off immediately if any leakage is detected. Use rags to wrap the leaking fitting until the pressure diminishes and wipe up any fuel from the engine area.*

4A-FE And 7A-FE Engine (1993)

> CAUTION: *The fuel system is under pressure. Release pressure slowly and contain spillage. Observe no smoking/no open flame precautions. Have a Class B-C (dry powder) fire extinguisher within arm's reach at all times.*

1. Disconnect the negative battery cable. Relieve the fuel pressure.

2. Remove the air cleaner hose and cap.

3. Disconnect the accelerator cable bracket from the throttle body.

4. Disconnect the throttle body from the air intake chamber.

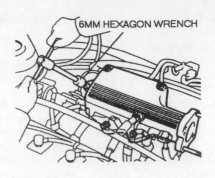

6MM HEXAGON WRENCH

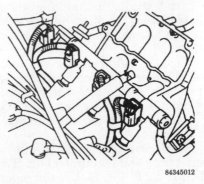

84345012

Removing the fuel injectors — 4A-FE and 7A-FE engine 1993

5. Remove the engine hanger and air intake chamber stay and EGR vacuum modulator if so equipped.

6. Remove the EGR valve and pipe if so equipped.

7. Remove all necessary hoses/electrical connections and remove the air intake chamber cover and gasket.

8. Disconnect the injector electrical connection.

9. Disconnect the fuel inlet hose from the delivery pipe.

10. Disconnect the fuel return hose from the fuel pressure regulator.

11. At the fuel delivery pipe (rail), remove the two bolts. Lift the delivery pipe and the injectors free of the engine. DON'T drop the injectors.

12. Remove the 4 insulators and 2 collars from the intake manifold. Pull the injectors free of the delivery pipe.

To install:

13. Before installing the injectors back into the fuel rail, install a NEW O-ring on each injector.

14. Coat each O-ring with a light coat of gasoline (NEVER use oil of any sort) and install the injectors into the delivery pipe. Make certain each injector can be smoothly rotated. If they do not rotate

smoothly, the O-ring is not in its correct position.

15. Install the insulators into each injector hole. Place the two spacers on the delivery pipe mounting holes in the intake manifold.

16. Place the delivery pipe and injectors on the intake manifold and again check that the injectors rotate smoothly. Position the injector connector upward. Install the two bolts and tighten them to 11 ft. lbs.

17. Connect the electrical connectors to each injector.

18. Install two new gaskets and attach the inlet pipe and fuel union bolt. Tighten the bolt to 22 ft. lbs. Install the mounting bolt.

19. Install the air intake chamber cover with a NEW gasket. Torque the retaining bolts in steps to 14 ft. lbs.

20. Install all necessary hoses and electrical connections.

21. Install the EGR valve and pipe if so equipped.

22. Install the engine hanger and air intake chamber stay and EGR vacuum modulator if so equipped.

23. Install a new gasket on the air intake chamber stay, facing the protrusion downward. Install the throttle body and torque the bolts evenly (in a X-pattern) to 16 ft. lbs.

24. Connect the accelerator cable bracket to the throttle body.

25. Install the air cleaner hose and cap.

26. Connect the battery cable to the negative battery terminal. Start the engine and check for leaks.

CAUTION: *If there is a leak at any fitting, the line will be under pressure and the fuel may spray in a fine mist. This mist is extremely explosive. Shut the engine off immediately if any leakage is detected. Use rags to wrap the leaking fitting until the pressure diminishes and wipe up any fuel from the engine area.*

TESTING

The simplest way to test the injectors is simply to listen to them with the engine running. Use either a stethoscope-type tool or the blade of a long screw driver to touch each injector while the engine is idling. You should hear a distinct clicking as each injector opens and closes.

Additionally, the resistance of the injector can be easily checked. Disconnect the negative battery cable and remove the electrical connector from the injector to be tested. Use an ohmmeter to check the resistance across the terminals of the injector. Correct ohmmage is approximately 13.8 ohms at 68°F (20°C); slight variations are acceptable due to temperature conditions.

Never attempt to check a removed injector by hooking it directly to the battery. The injector runs on a much smaller voltage and the 12 volts from the battery will destroy it internally.

Cold Start Injector

REMOVAL & INSTALLATION

4A-GE and 4A-FE Engines (1990–92)

CAUTION: *The fuel system is under pressure. Release pressure slowly and contain spillage. Observe no smoking/no open flame precautions. Have a Class B-C (dry powder) fire extinguisher within arm's reach at all times.*

1. Disconnect the negative battery cable.

2. Remove the wiring connector at the cold start injector.

3. Wrap the fuel pipe connection in a rag or towel. Remove the two union bolts and the cold start injector pipe with its gaskets. Slowly loosen the union bolt.

4. Remove the two retaining bolts and remove the cold start injector with its gasket.

5. When reinstalling, always use a new gasket for the injector. Install it with the injector and tighten the two mounting bolts to 7 ft. lbs. (82 inch lbs.).

6. Again using new gaskets, connect the cold start injector pipe to the delivery pipe (fuel rail) and to the cold start injector. Tighten the bolts to 13 ft. lbs.

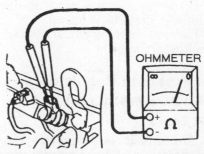

84345013

Testing fuel injector resistance

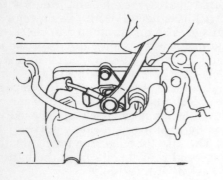

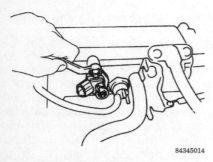

84345014

Removing cold start injector — 4A-GE engine

7. Install the wiring to the cold start injector.

8. Connect the negative battery cable. Start the engine and check for leaks.

TESTING

1. Switch the ignition OFF.

2. Disconnect the electrical connector from the cold start injector

3. Use an ohmmeter to check the resistance of the injector. Correct resistance is 2–4 ohms. at 68°F (20°C) on the 4A-FE engine and 3–5 ohms. at 68°F (20°C) on the 4A-GE engine. The resistance specification may vary slightly with the temperature of the injector. Use common sense and good judgement when testing.

4. If the resistance is not within specifications, it must be replaced.

5. Reconnect the electrical connector to the cold start injector.

Fuel Pressure Regulator

REMOVAL & INSTALLATION

4A-GE Engine

1. Disconnect the negative battery cable. Relieve the fuel pressure. Remove the vacuum sensing hose from the fuel pressure regulator.

2. Remove the fuel hose from the regulator.

3. Remove the two retaining bolts and pull the regulator out of the fuel rail.

4. When reinstalling (replace O-ring) the two retaining bolts are tightened to 5.5 ft. lbs. (65 inch lbs.) Connect the two hoses (fuel and vacuum).

5. Start the engine and check carefully for leaks.

4A-FE AND 7A-FE Engines

1. Disconnect the negative battery cable. Relieve the fuel pressure.

2. Disconnect the vacuum hose from the regulator.

3. Disconnect the fuel return line from the regulator.

4. Remove the two retaining bolts and remove the fuel pressure regulator.

5. When reinstalling, place the new regulator on the fuel rail (with new O-ring) install the bolts and tighten them to 7 ft. lbs. (84 inch lbs.).

6. Connect the fuel return line, making sure the clamp is properly placed and secure.

7. Connect the vacuum hose, then connect the negative battery cable.

Air Flow Meter

REMOVAL & INSTALLATION

4A-GE Engine

1. Disconnect the negative battery cable. Disconnect the air cleaner hose.

2. Remove the VSV (idle up) assembly.

3. Disconnect the air flow meter connector.

4. Pry off the lock plate and remove the 4 nuts, lock plate, air flow meter and gasket.

5. Installation is the reverse of the removal procedure. Make absolutely sure that the air flow meter and its gasket are correctly positioned. No air leaks are acceptable. Install and tighten the four nuts. Road test the vehicle for proper operation.

TESTING

Using an ohmmeter, measure the resistance between each terminal by moving the measuring plate. Resistance between terminals E2 and VS will change in a wave pattern as the measuring plate slowly opens. If the resistance is not as specified-refer to test chart, replace the air flow meter.

CHILTON'S
FUEL ECONOMY
& TUNE-UP TIPS

Tune-up • Spark Plug Diagnosis • Emission Controls

Fuel System • Cooling System • Tires and Wheels

General Maintenance

55 WAYS TO IMPROVE FUEL ECONOMY

CHILTON'S FUEL ECONOMY & TUNE-UP TIPS

Fuel economy is important to everyone, no matter what kind of vehicle you drive. The maintenance-minded motorist can save both money and fuel using these tips and the periodic maintenance and tune-up procedures in this Repair and Tune-Up Guide.

There are more than 130,000,000 cars and trucks registered for private use in the United States. Each travels an average of 10-12,000 miles per year, and, and in total they consume close to 70 billion gallons of fuel each year. This represents nearly ⅔ of the oil imported by the United States each year. The Federal government's goal is to reduce consumption 10% by 1985. A variety of methods are either already in use or under serious consideration, and they all affect you driving and the cars you will drive. In addition to "down-sizing", the auto industry is using or investigating the use of electronic fuel delivery, electronic engine controls and alternative engines for use in smaller and lighter vehicles, among other alternatives to meet the federally mandated Corporate Average Fuel Economy (CAFE) of 27.5 mpg by 1985. The government, for its part, is considering rationing, mandatory driving curtailments and tax increases on motor vehicle fuel in an effort to reduce consumption. The government's goal of a 10% reduction could be realized — and further government regulation avoided — if every private vehicle could use just 1 less gallon of fuel per week.

How Much Can You Save?

Tests have proven that almost anyone can make at least a 10% reduction in fuel consumption through regular maintenance and tune-ups. When a major manufacturer of spark plugs sur-

TUNE-UP

1. Check the cylinder compression to be sure the engine will really benefit from a tune-up and that it is capable of producing good fuel economy. A tune-up will be wasted on an engine in poor mechanical condition.

2. Replace spark plugs regularly. New spark plugs alone can increase fuel economy 3%.

3. Be sure the spark plugs are the correct type (heat range) for your vehicle. See the Tune-Up Specifications.

Heat range refers to the spark plug's ability to conduct heat away from the firing end. It must conduct the heat away in an even pattern to avoid becoming a source of pre-ignition, yet it must also operate hot enough to burn off conductive deposits that could cause misfiring.

The heat range is usually indicated by a number on the spark plug, part of the manufacturer's designation for each individual spark plug. The numbers in bold-face indicate the heat range in each manufacturer's identification system.

Periodically, check the spark plugs to be sure they are firing efficiently. They are excellent indicators of the internal condition of your engine.

Manufacturer	Typical Designation
AC	R **45** TS
Bosch (old)	WA **145** T30
Bosch (new)	HR **8** Y
Champion	RBL **15** Y
Fram/Autolite	**415**
Mopar	P-**62** PR
Motorcraft	BRF-**42**
NGK	BP **5** ES-15
Nippondenso	W **16** EP
Prestolite	14GR **5** 2A

On AC, Bosch (new), Champion, Fram/Autolite, Mopar, Motorcraft and Prestolite, a higher number indicates a hotter plug. On Bosch (old), NGK and Nippondenso, a higher number indicates a colder plug.

4. Make sure the spark plugs are properly gapped. See the Tune-Up Specifications in this book.

5. Be sure the spark plugs are firing efficiently. The illustrations on the next 2 pages show you how to "read" the firing end of the spark plug.

6. Check the ignition timing and set it to specifications. Tests show that almost all cars have incorrect ignition timing by more than 2°.

veyed over 6,000 cars nationwide, they found that a tune-up, on cars that needed one, increased fuel economy over 11%. Replacing worn plugs alone, accounted for a 3% increase. The same test also revealed that 8 out of every 10 vehicles will have some maintenance deficiency that will directly affect fuel economy, emissions or performance. Most of this mileage-robbing neglect could be prevented with regular maintenance.

Modern engines require that all of the functioning systems operate properly for maximum efficiency. A malfunction anywhere wastes fuel. You can keep your vehicle running as efficiently and economically as possible, by being aware of your vehicle's operating and performance characteristics. If your vehicle suddenly develops performance or fuel economy problems it could be due to one or more of the following:

PROBLEM	POSSIBLE CAUSE
Engine Idles Rough	Ignition timing, idle mixture, vacuum leak or something amiss in the emission control system.
Hesitates on Acceleration	Dirty carburetor or fuel filter, improper accelerator pump setting, ignition timing or fouled spark plugs.
Starts Hard or Fails to Start	Worn spark plugs, improperly set automatic choke, ice (or water) in fuel system.
Stalls Frequently	Automatic choke improperly adjusted and possible dirty air filter or fuel filter.
Performs Sluggishly	Worn spark plugs, dirty fuel or air filter, ignition timing or automatic choke out of adjustment.

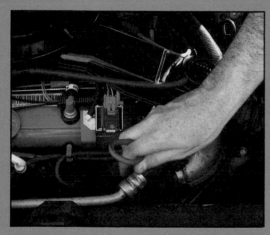

Check spark plug wires on conventional point type ignition for cracks by bending them in a loop around your finger.

Be sure that spark plug wires leading to adjacent cylinders do not run too close together. (Photo courtesy Champion Spark Plug Co.)

7. If your vehicle does not have electronic ignition, check the points, rotor and cap as specified.

8. Check the spark plug wires (used with conventional point-type ignitions) for cracks and burned or broken insulation by bending them in a loop around your finger. Cracked wires decrease fuel efficiency by failing to deliver full voltage to the spark plugs. One misfiring spark plug can cost you as much as 2 mpg.

9. Check the routing of the plug wires. Misfiring can be the result of spark plug leads to adjacent cylinders running parallel to each other and too close together. One wire tends to pick up voltage from the other causing it to fire "out of time".

10. Check all electrical and ignition circuits for voltage drop and resistance.

11. Check the distributor mechanical and/or vacuum advance mechanisms for proper functioning. The vacuum advance can be checked by twisting the distributor plate in the opposite direction of rotation. It should spring back when released.

12. Check and adjust the valve clearance on engines with mechanical lifters. The clearance should be slightly loose rather than too tight.

SPARK PLUG DIAGNOSIS

Normal

APPEARANCE: This plug is typical of one operating normally. The insulator nose varies from a light tan to grayish color with slight electrode wear. The presence of slight deposits is normal on used plugs and will have no adverse effect on engine performance. The spark plug heat range is correct for the engine and the engine is running normally.

CAUSE: Properly running engine.

RECOMMENDATION: Before reinstalling this plug, the electrodes should be cleaned and filed square. Set the gap to specifications. If the plug has been in service for more than 10-12,000 miles, the entire set should probably be replaced with a fresh set of the same heat range.

Oil Deposits

APPEARANCE: The firing end of the plug is covered with a wet, oily coating.

CAUSE: The problem is poor oil control. On high mileage engines, oil is leaking past the rings or valve guides into the combustion chamber. A common cause is also a plugged PCV valve, and a ruptured fuel pump diaphragm can also cause this condition. Oil fouled plugs such as these are often found in new or recently overhauled engines, before normal oil control is achieved, and can be cleaned and reinstalled.

RECOMMENDATION: A hotter spark plug may temporarily relieve the problem, but the engine is probably in need of work.

Incorrect Heat Range

APPEARANCE: The effects of high temperature on a spark plug are indicated by clean white, often blistered insulator. This can also be accompanied by excessive wear of the electrode, and the absence of deposits.

CAUSE: Check for the correct spark plug heat range. A plug which is too hot for the engine can result in overheating. A car operated mostly at high speeds can require a colder plug. Also check ignition timing, cooling system level, fuel mixture and leaking intake manifold.

RECOMMENDATION: If all ignition and engine adjustments are known to be correct, and no other malfunction exists, install spark plugs one heat range colder.

Carbon Deposits

APPEARANCE: Carbon fouling is easily identified by the presence of dry, soft, black, sooty deposits.

CAUSE: Changing the heat range can often lead to carbon fouling, as can prolonged slow, stop-and-start driving. If the heat range is correct, carbon fouling can be attributed to a rich fuel mixture, sticking choke, clogged air cleaner, worn breaker points, retarded timing or low compression. If only one or two plugs are carbon fouled, check for corroded or cracked wires on the affected plugs. Also look for cracks in the distributor cap between the towers of affected cylinders.

RECOMMENDATION: After the problem is corrected, these plugs can be cleaned and reinstalled if not worn severely.

MMT Fouled

APPEARANCE: Spark plugs fouled by MMT (Methycyclopentadienyl Maganese Tricarbonyl) have reddish, rusty appearance on the insulator and side electrode.

CAUSE: MMT is an anti-knock additive in gasoline used to replace lead. During the combustion process, the MMT leaves a reddish deposit on the insulator and side electrode.

RECOMMENDATION: No engine malfunction is indicated and the deposits will not affect plug performance any more than lead deposits (see Ash Deposits). MMT fouled plugs can be cleaned, regapped and reinstalled.

High Speed Glazing

APPEARANCE: Glazing appears as shiny coating on the plug, either yellow or tan in color.

CAUSE: During hard, fast acceleration, plug temperatures rise suddenly. Deposits from normal combustion have no chance to fluff-off; instead, they melt on the insulator forming an electrically conductive coating which causes misfiring.

RECOMMENDATION: Glazed plugs are not easily cleaned. They should be replaced with a fresh set of plugs of the correct heat range. If the condition recurs, using plugs with a heat range one step colder may cure the problem.

Ash (Lead) Deposits

APPEARANCE: Ash deposits are characterized by light brown or white colored deposits crusted on the side or center electrodes. In some cases it may give the plug a rusty appearance.

CAUSE: Ash deposits are normally derived from oil or fuel additives burned during normal combustion. Normally they are harmless, though excessive amounts can cause misfiring. If deposits are excessive in short mileage, the valve guides may be worn.

RECOMMENDATION: Ash-fouled plugs can be cleaned, gapped and reinstalled.

Detonation

APPEARANCE: Detonation is usually characterized by a broken plug insulator.

CAUSE: A portion of the fuel charge will begin to burn spontaneously, from the increased heat following ignition. The explosion that results applies extreme pressure to engine components, frequently damaging spark plugs and pistons.

Detonation can result by over-advanced ignition timing, inferior gasoline (low octane) lean air/fuel mixture, poor carburetion, engine lugging or an increase in compression ratio due to combustion chamber deposits or engine modification.

RECOMMENDATION: Replace the plugs after correcting the problem.

Photos Courtesy Champion Spark Plug Co.

EMISSION CONTROLS

13. Be aware of the general condition of the emission control system. It contributes to reduced pollution and should be serviced regularly to maintain efficient engine operation.

14. Check all vacuum lines for dried, cracked or brittle conditions. Something as simple as a leaking vacuum hose can cause poor performance and loss of economy.

15. Avoid tampering with the emission control system. Attempting to improve fuel econ-

FUEL SYSTEM

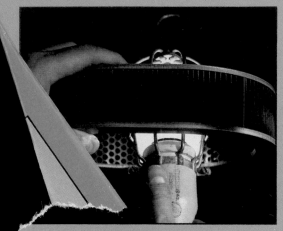

Check the air filter with a light behind it. If you can see light through the filter it can be reused.

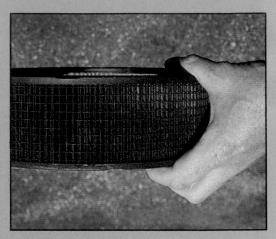

Extremely clogged filters should be discarded and replaced with a new one.

18. Replace the air filter regularly. A dirty air filter richens the air/fuel mixture and can increase fuel consumption as much as 10%. Tests show that 1/3 of all vehicles have air filters in need of replacement.

19. Replace the fuel filter at least as often as recommended.

20. Set the idle speed and carburetor mixture to specifications.

21. Check the automatic choke. A sticking or malfunctioning choke wastes gas.

22. During the summer months, adjust the automatic choke for a leaner mixture which will produce faster engine warm-ups.

COOLING SYSTEM

29. Be sure all accessory drive belts are in good condition. Check for cracks or wear.

30. Adjust all accessory drive belts to proper tension.

31. Check all hoses for swollen areas, worn spots, or loose clamps.

32. Check coolant level in the radiator or expansion tank.

33. Be sure the thermostat is operating properly. A stuck thermostat delays engine warm-up and a cold engine uses nearly twice as much fuel as a warm engine.

34. Drain and replace the engine coolant at least as often as recommended. Rust and scale

TIRES & WHEELS

38. Check the tire pressure often with a pencil type gauge. Tests by a major tire manufacturer show that 90% of all vehicles have at least 1 tire improperly inflated. Better mileage can be achieved by over-inflating tires, but never exceed the maximum inflation pressure on the side of the tire.

39. If possible, install radial tires. Radial tires deliver as much as 1/2 mpg more than bias belted tires.

40. Avoid installing super-wide tires. They only create extra rolling resistance and decrease fuel mileage. Stick to the manufacturer's recommendations.

41. Have the wheels properly balanced.

omy by tampering with emission controls is more likely to worsen fuel economy than improve it. Emission control changes on modern engines are not readily reversible.

16. Clean (or replace) the EGR valve and lines as recommended.

17. Be sure that all vacuum lines and hoses are reconnected properly after working under the hood. An unconnected or misrouted vacuum line can wreak havoc with engine performance.

23. Check for fuel leaks at the carburetor, fuel pump, fuel lines and fuel tank. Be sure all lines and connections are tight.

24. Periodically check the tightness of the carburetor and intake manifold attaching nuts and bolts. These are a common place for vacuum leaks to occur.

25. Clean the carburetor periodically and lubricate the linkage.

26. The condition of the tailpipe can be an excellent indicator of proper engine combustion. After a long drive at highway speeds, the inside of the tailpipe should be a light grey in color. Black or soot on the insides indicates an overly rich mixture.

27. Check the fuel pump pressure. The fuel pump may be supplying more fuel than the engine needs.

28. Use the proper grade of gasoline for your engine. Don't try to compensate for knocking or "pinging" by advancing the ignition timing. This practice will only increase plug temperature and the chances of detonation or pre-ignition with relatively little performance gain.

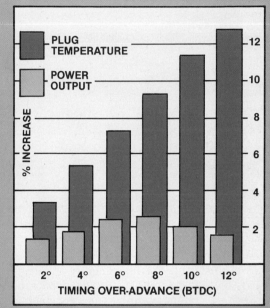

Increasing ignition timing past the specified setting results in a drastic increase in spark plug temperature with increased chance of detonation or preignition. Performance increase is considerably less. (Photo courtesy Champion Spark Plug Co.)

that form in the engine should be flushed out to allow the engine to operate at peak efficiency.

35. Clean the radiator of debris that can decrease cooling efficiency.

36. Install a flex-type or electric cooling fan, if you don't have a clutch type fan. Flex fans use curved plastic blades to push more air at low speeds when more cooling is needed; at high speeds the blades flatten out for less resistance. Electric fans only run when the engine temperature reaches a predetermined level.

37. Check the radiator cap for a worn or cracked gasket. If the cap does not seal properly, the cooling system will not function properly.

42. Be sure the front end is correctly aligned. A misaligned front end actually has wheels going in differed directions. The increased drag can reduce fuel economy by .3 mpg.

43. Correctly adjust the wheel bearings. Wheel bearings that are adjusted too tight increase rolling resistance.

Check tire pressures regularly with a reliable pocket type gauge. Be sure to check the pressure on a cold tire.

GENERAL MAINTENANCE

Check the fluid levels (particularly engine oil) on a regular basis. Be sure to check the oil for grit, water or other contamination.

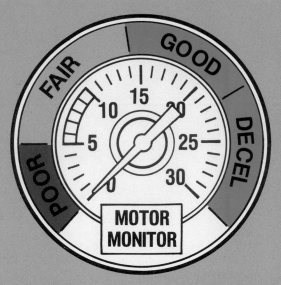

A vacuum gauge is another excellent indicator of internal engine condition and can also be installed in the dash as a mileage indicator.

44. Periodically check the fluid levels in the engine, power steering pump, master cylinder, automatic transmission and drive axle.

45. Change the oil at the recommended interval and change the filter at every oil change. Dirty oil is thick and causes extra friction between moving parts, cutting efficiency and increasing wear. A worn engine requires more frequent tune-ups and gets progressively worse fuel economy. In general, use the lightest viscosity oil for the driving conditions you will encounter.

46. Use the recommended viscosity fluids in the transmission and axle.

47. Be sure the battery is fully charged for fast starts. A slow starting engine wastes fuel.

48. Be sure battery terminals are clean and tight.

49. Check the battery electrolyte level and add distilled water if necessary.

50. Check the exhaust system for crushed pipes, blockages and leaks.

51. Adjust the brakes. Dragging brakes or brakes that are not releasing create increased drag on the engine.

52. Install a vacuum gauge or miles-per-gallon gauge. These gauges visually indicate engine vacuum in the intake manifold. High vacuum = good mileage and low vacuum = poorer mileage. The gauge can also be an excellent indicator of internal engine conditions.

53. Be sure the clutch is properly adjusted. A slipping clutch wastes fuel.

54. Check and periodically lubricate the heat control valve in the exhaust manifold. A sticking or inoperative valve prevents engine warm-up and wastes gas.

55. Keep accurate records to check fuel economy over a period of time. A sudden drop in fuel economy may signal a need for tune-up or other maintenance.

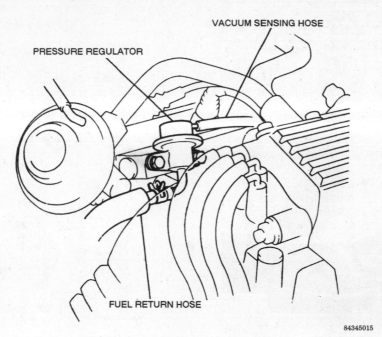

Fuel pressure regulator — 4A-GE engine

Between Terminals	Resistance Ω	Measuring plate Opening
FC - E1	Infinity	Fully closed
	Zero	Other than closed position
VS - E2	20 - 400	Fully closed
	20 - 3,000	Fully closed

Inspection chart for air flow meter — 4A-GE engine

Throttle Body

REMOVAL & INSTALLATION

4A-GE Engine

1. Disconnect the negative battery cable. Either drain the coolant from the throttle body by disconnecting a coolant hose or open the engine draincock.
2. Disconnect the throttle return spring.
3. Disconnect the throttle cable.
4. Label and disconnect the vacuum hose.
5. Carefully remove the throttle position sensor wiring connector.
6. Remove the air cleaner hose.
7. Remove the water hoses from the air valve.
8. Remove the two bolts and two nuts and the throttle body with its gasket.
9. Wash and clean the cast metal parts with a soft brush and carburetor cleaner. Use compressed air to blow through all the passages and openings.
10. Check the throttle valve to see that there is NO clearance between the stop

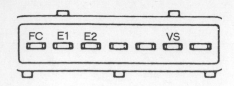

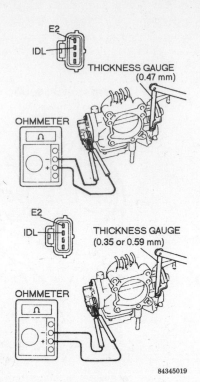

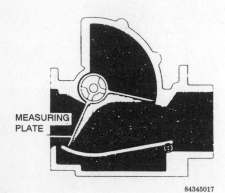

84345017

Terminal identification for air flow meter — 4A-GE engine

Throttle position sensor adjustment — 4A-GE engine

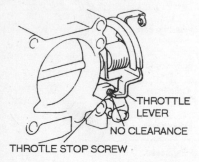

84345018

Throttle body inspection — 4A-GE engine

screw and the throttle lever when the throttle plate is fully closed.

11. Check the throttle position sensor (TPS). Insert a 0.47mm feeler gauge between the throttle stop screw and the lever. Connect an ohmmeter between terminal **IDL** and **E$_2$**. Loosen the two screws holding the TPS and gradually turn the TPS clockwise until the ohmmeter deflects, but no more. Secure the TPS screws at this point. Double check the clearance at the lever and stop screw. Additional resistance tests may be made on the TPS using the chart.

Clearance between lever and stop screw	Continuity IDL - E2
0.35 MM (0.0138 IN.)	Continuity
0.59 MM (0.0232 IN.)	No continuity

84345020

Check chart for throttle position sensor — 4A-GE engine

To install:

12. Place a new gasket in position and install the throttle body with its two nuts and two bolts. Make certain everything is properly positioned before securing the unit. Tighten the bolts to 16 ft. lbs.

13. Connect the water hoses to the air valve.

14. Install the air cleaner hose and the vacuum hoses.

15. Connect the wiring to the throttle position sensor.

16. Connect the accelerator cable and its return spring.

17. Refill the coolant to the proper level.

4A-FE And 7A-FE Engines

1. Disconnect the negative battery cable. Drain the coolant from the throttle body.

2. Disconnect the throttle return spring.

3. Disconnect the throttle cable.

4. Label and disconnect the vacuum hose.

5. Carefully remove the throttle position sensor wiring connector.

6. Remove the air cleaner hose.

7. Remove the water hoses from the air valve.

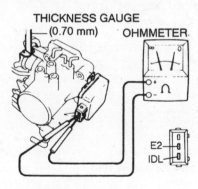

THICKNESS GAUGE (0.70 mm) OHMMETER

E2
IDL

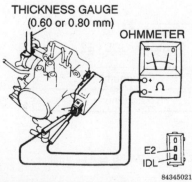

THICKNESS GAUGE (0.60 or 0.80 mm) OHMMETER

E2
IDL

84345021

Throttle position sensor adjustment — 4A-FE engine 1990–92

8. Remove the two bolts and two nuts and the throttle body with its gasket.

9. Wash and clean the cast metal parts with a soft brush and carburetor cleaner. Use compressed air to blow through all the passages and openings.

10. Check the throttle valve to see that there is NO clearance between the stop screw and the throttle lever when the throttle plate is fully closed.

NOTE: *On 1993 4A-FE and 7A-FE California engine equipped vehicles, apply vacuum to the throttle opener before inserting the feeler gauge between the throttle stop screw and the lever.*

11. Check the throttle position sensor (TPS). Insert a 0.70mm feeler gauge between the throttle stop screw and the lever. Connect an ohmmeter between terminal **IDL** and **E$_2$**. Loosen the two screws holding the TPS and gradually turn the TPS clockwise until the ohmmeter deflects, but no more. Secure the TPS screws at this point. Double check the clearance at the lever and stop screw. Additional resistance tests may be made on the TPS using the chart.

To install:

12. Place a new gasket in position and install the throttle body with its two nuts and two bolts. On the 1993 4A-FE and 7A-FE engines install the throttle body (with new gasket facing the protrusion downward) with the 2 bolts and 2 nuts and tighten in the correct sequence. Make certain everything is properly positioned before securing the unit. Tighten the bolts to 16 ft. lbs. on all engines.

13. Connect the water hoses to the air valve.

14. Install the air cleaner hose and the vacuum hoses.

15. Connect the wiring to the throttle position sensor.

16. Connect the accelerator cable and its return spring.

17. Refill the coolant to the proper level.

Auxiliary Air Valve

REMOVAL & INSTALLATION

4A-GE Engine

1. Remove the throttle body.

2. Remove the retaining screws and remove the air valve. Remove the O-ring and gasket.

3. Use a new O-ring and/or gasket; install the air valve to the throttle body.

Clearance between lever and stop screw	Continuity IDL - E2
0.60 MM (0.0236 IN.)	Continuity
0.80 MM (0.0315 IN.)	No continuity

84345022

Check chart for throttle position sensor — 4A-FE engine 1990–92

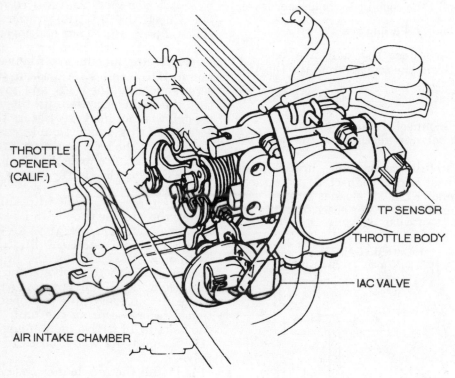

84345023

Throttle body assembly — 4A-FE and 7A-FE engine 1993

Clearance between lever and stop screw	Continuity IDL - E2
0.40 mm (0.016 in.)	Continuity
0.90 mm (0.035 in.)	No continuity

84345024

Check chart for throttle position sensor — 4A-FE and 7A-FE engine 1993

4. Reinstall the throttle body.

4A-FE (1990-92) Engine

1. Remove the throttle body.
2. Remove the retaining screws and remove the air valve. Remove the O-ring and gasket.
3. Use a new O-ring and/or gasket; install the air valve to the throttle body.
4. Reinstall the throttle body.

TESTING

4A-GE Engine

1. Check the engine rpm by fully screwing in the idle speed adjusting screw.
2. When the idle speed adjusting screw is in, the engine rpm should drop.

4A-FE (1990–92) Engine

1. Check the engine rpm by closing the air valve port on the throttle body.
2. When the port is closed, check the engine rpm does not drop more than 100 rpm. If operation is not as specified, replace the air valve.

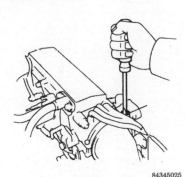

84345025

Idle speed adjusting screw — 4A-GE engine

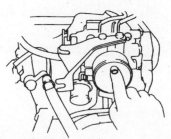

84345026

Throttle body air port location — 4A-FE engine 1990–92

Idle Air Control Valve

REMOVAL & INSTALLATION

4A-FE And 7A-FE (1993) Engines

1. Remove the throttle body.
2. Remove the retaining screws and remove the air valve. Remove the gasket.
3. Use a new gasket and install the air valve to the throttle body.
4. Reinstall the throttle body.

TESTING

To inspect the IAC valve operation connect the positive (+) lead from the battery to terminal +B and negative (-) lead to terminal RSC and check that the valve is closed.

Connect the positive (+) lead from the battery to terminal +B and negative (-) lead to terminal RSO and check that the valve is opened. If operation is not as specified, replace the air valve.

Throttle Position Sensor

REMOVAL, INSTALLATION AND ADJUSTMENT

4A-GE Engine

1. Disconnect the negative battery cable. Remove the air cleaner hose.
2. Disconnect the electrical connection for sensor.
3. Remove the 2 screws and remove the sensor.
   To install:
4. Check that the throttle valve is fully closed.
5. Place the sensor on the throttle body. Turn the sensor clockwise and install the 2 screws.
6. Adjust the throttle position sensor. Insert a 0.47mm or 0.0185 in. feeler gauge between the throttle stop screw and the lever. Connect an ohmmeter between terminal **IDL** and E_2. Loosen the two screws holding the TPS and gradually turn the TPS clockwise until the ohmmeter deflects, but no more. Secure the TPS screws at this point.
7. Reconnect electrical connector. Install air cleaner hose. Start engine and check for proper operation.

4A-FE And 7A-FE Engines

1. Disconnect the negative battery cable. Remove the air cleaner hose.
2. Disconnect sensor connector.

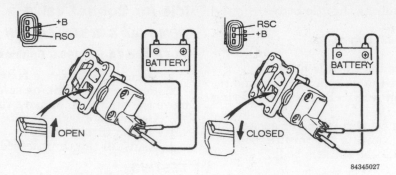

84345027

Testing the IAC valve — 4A-FE and 7A-FE engine 1993

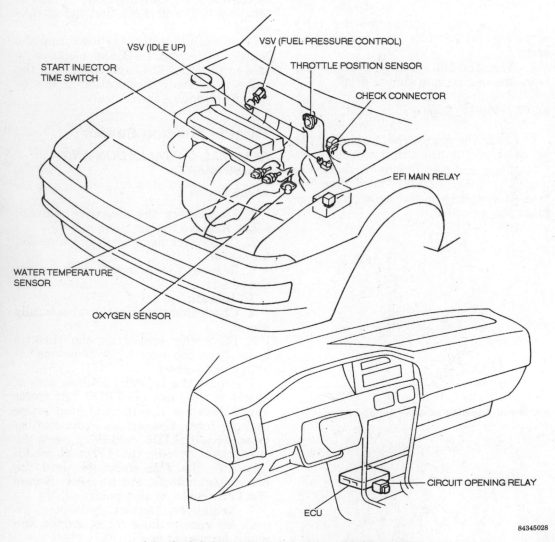

84345028

Location of electronic control parts — 4A-GE engine

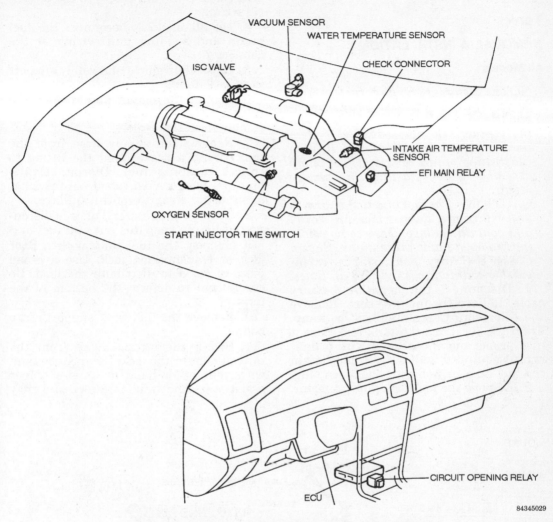

VACUUM SENSOR

WATER TEMPERATURE SENSOR

ISC VALVE

CHECK CONNECTOR

INTAKE AIR TEMPERATURE SENSOR

EFI MAIN RELAY

OXYGEN SENSOR

START INJECTOR TIME SWITCH

CIRCUIT OPENING RELAY

ECU

84345029

Location of electronic control parts — 4A-FE engine 1990–92

3. Hold the throttle valve opening angle at 45 degrees. Remove the 2 screws and remove the sensor.

To install:

4. Place the TPS sensor over the throttle valve shaft in correct alignment.

5. Install the 2 screws. Adjust the throttle position sensor. Insert a 0.70mm or 0.0276 in. feeler gauge between the throttle stop screw and the lever. Connect an ohmmeter between terminal **IDL** and **E₂** . Loosen the two screws holding the TPS and gradually turn the TPS clockwise until the ohmmeter deflects, but no more. Secure the TPS screws at this point.

NOTE: *On 1993 4A-FE and 7A-FE California engine equipped vehicles, apply vacuum to the throttle opener before inserting the feeler gauge between the throttle stop screw and the lever.*

6. Reconnect electrical connector. Install air cleaner hose. Start engine and check for proper operation.

FUEL TANK

Tank

REMOVAL & INSTALLATION

All Models

NOTE: *Before removing fuel system parts, clean them with a spray-type engine cleaner. Follow the instructions on the cleaner. Do not soak fuel system parts in liquid cleaning solvent. Refer to illustration of fuel tank and fuel pump assembly before starting this service repair.*

CAUTION: *The fuel injection system is under pressure. Release pressure slowly and contain spillage. Observe no smoking/no open flame precautions. Have a Class B-C (dry powder) fire extinguisher within arm's reach at all times.*

1. Disconnect the negative battery cable. Relieve the fuel pressure. Remove the filler cap. Using a siphon or pump, drain the fuel from the tank and store it in a proper metal container with a tight cap. If equipped with a drain plug drain the fuel tank by removing the drain plug.

2. Remove the fuel tank pipe protector.

3. On the 1993 model, remove the rear seat cushion to gain access to the electrical wiring.

4. On all models, disconnect the fuel pump and sending unit wiring at the connector.

5. Raise the vehicle and safely support it on jackstands.

6. Loosen the clamp and remove the filler neck assembly and overflow pipe assembly from the tank.

7. Remove the supply hose from the tank. Wrap a rag around the fitting to collect escaping fuel. Disconnect the breather hose or vent tube from the tank, again using a rag to control spillage.

8. Cover or plug the end of each disconnected line to keep dirt out and fuel in.

9. Support the fuel tank with a floor jack or transmission jack. Use a broad piece of wood to distribute the load. Be careful not to deform the bottom of the tank.

10. Remove the fuel tank support strap bolts.

11. Swing the straps away from the tank and lower the jack. Balance the tank with your other hand or have a helper assist you. The tank is bulky and may

COUPE

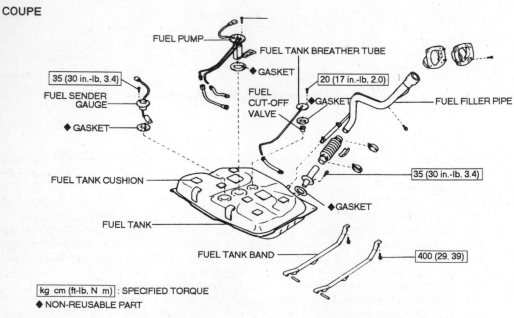

kg cm (ft-lb, N m) : SPECIFIED TORQUE
◆ NON-REUSABLE PART

84345030

Fuel tank assembly — 1990–92 models

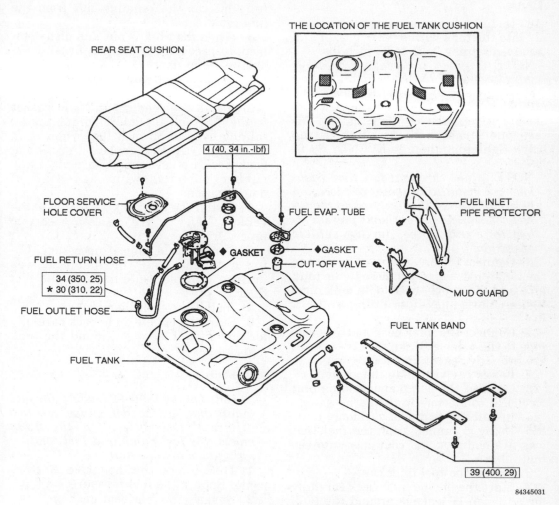

REAR SEAT CUSHION

THE LOCATION OF THE FUEL TANK CUSHION

4 (40, 34 in.-lbf)

FLOOR SERVICE
HOLE COVER

FUEL EVAP. TUBE

FUEL INLET
PIPE PROTECTOR

FUEL RETURN HOSE

♦ GASKET

♦GASKET

CUT-OFF VALVE

34 (350, 25)
★ 30 (310, 22)

FUEL OUTLET HOSE

MUD GUARD

FUEL TANK BAND

FUEL TANK

39 (400, 29)

84345031

Fuel tank assembly — 1993 models

ave some fuel left in it. If its balance changes suddenly, the tank may fall.

12. Remove the fuel filler pipe extension, the vent pipe assembly, fuel pump and or the sending unit assembly. Keep these items in a clean, protected area away from the car.

NOTE: *On the 1990–92 models, the fuel pump and fuel sender gauge are two different assemblies. On the 1993 model, the fuel pump and fuel sender gauge are one unit.*

13. While the tank is out and disassembled, inspect it for any signs of rust, leakage or metal damage. If any problem is found, replace the fuel tank. Clean the inside of the tank with water and a light detergent and rinse the tank thoroughly several times.

14. Inspect all of the lines, hoses and fittings for any sign of corrosion, wear or damage to the surfaces. Check the pump outlet hose and the filter for restrictions.

15. When reassembling, ALWAYS replace the sealing gaskets with new ones. Also replace any rubber parts showing any sign of deterioration.

16. Connect the vent pipe assembly and the filler pipe extension to the fuel tank. Always use new hose clamps as necessary.

17. Install the fuel pump and bracket assembly into the tank with a NEW gasket and torque retaining bolts to 30 inch lbs.

18. Install the fuel sending unit assembly into the tank with a NEW gasket and torque retaining bolts to 30 inch lbs.

NOTE: *Tighten the vent or breather tube screw to 17 INCH lbs. and all other attaching screws to 30 INCH lbs.*

19. Place the fuel tank on the jack and elevate it into place within the car. Attach the straps and install the strap bolts, tightening them to EVENLY 29 ft. lbs.

NOTE: *Make sure that fuel tank cushions are installed in the correct location before installing the fuel tank to the vehicle. The fuel tank cushions prevent vibration and noise during vehicle operation.*

20. Connect the breather hose or vent to the tank pipe, the return hose to the tank pipe and the supply hose to its tank pipe. tighten the supply hose fitting to 21 ft. lbs.

21. Connect the filler neck and overflow pipe to the vehicle. Make sure the clamps are properly seated and secure.

22. Lower the vehicle to the ground.

23. Connect the pump and sending unit electrical connectors to the harness.

24. Install the rear seat cushion.

25. Using a funnel, pour the fuel that was drained from its container into the fuel filler.

26. Install the fuel filler cap.

27. Start the engine and check carefully for any sign of leakage around the tank and lines.

SENDING UNIT REPLACEMENT

1990–92 Models

NOTE: *On the 1990–92 models, the fuel pump and fuel sender gauge are two different assemblies. On the 1993 model, the fuel pump and fuel sender gauge are one unit.*

1. Disconnect the negative battery cable. Relieve the fuel pressure. Remove the filler cap. Using a siphon or pump, drain the fuel from the tank and store it in a proper metal container with a tight cap. If equipped with a drain plug drain the fuel tank by removing the drain plug.

2. Remove the fuel tank assembly from the vehicle. Refer to the necessary service procedures.

3. With the fuel tank drained and on a suitable work bench remove the fuel sending unit retaining screws and carefully lift the the sending unit from the fuel tank.

4. While the tank is out and disassembled, inspect it for any signs of rust, leakage or metal damage. If any problem is found, replace the tank.

To install:

5. Install the sending unit and gasket in the fuel tank assembly. Torque the retaining bolts to 30 inch lbs. When reassembling, ALWAYS replace the sealing gasket with a new one. Also replace any rubber parts showing any sign of deterioration.

6. Install the fuel tank assembly to the vehicle. Refer to the necessary service procedures.

7. Install drain plug if necessary. Using a funnel, pour the fuel that was drained from its container into the fuel filler.

8. Install the fuel filler cap.

9. Start the engine and check carefully for any sign of leakage around the tank and lines.

1993 Models

NOTE: *On the 1990–92 models, the fuel pump and fuel sender gauge are two different assemblies. On the 1993 model, the fuel pump and fuel sending unit gauge are one unit.*

1. Disconnect the negative battery cable. Relieve the fuel pressure.

2. Remove the rear seat cushion.

3. Remove the 4 retaining screws and floor service hole cover.

4. Disconnect the electrical fuel pump connection at the fuel pump/sending unit gauge assembly.

5. Disconnect the fuel pipe and hose from the fuel pump/sending unit gauge bracket. Remove the fuel pump/sending unit gauge bracket assembly from the fuel tank.

6. Remove the 3 side retaining screws for the sending unit gauge from the fuel pump/sending unit gauge bracket. Remove the fuel sender gauge.

To install:

7. Install the 3 side retaining screws for the sending unit gauge to the fuel pump/sending unit gauge bracket.

8. Install the fuel pump/sending unit gauge bracket assembly with NEW gas-

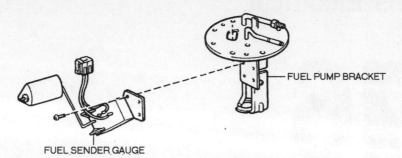

FUEL PUMP BRACKET

FUEL SENDER GAUGE

84345032

Fuel sender gauge assembly — 1993 models

ket in the fuel tank. Torque pump bracket retaining screws 34 inch lbs.

9. Connect fuel pipe (torque fuel outlet pipe to 25 ft. lbs.) and hose to the fuel pump/sending unit bracket.

10. Install drain plug if necessary. Using a funnel, pour the fuel that was drained from its container into the fuel filler.

11. Install the fuel filler cap.

12. Connect battery cable and start engine and check for fuel leaks.

13. Install floor service hole cover.

14. Install rear seat cushion.

Chassis Electrical

SUPPLEMENTAL RESTRAINT SYSTEM (SRS)

General Information

The air bag system used on the 1993 Corolla is referred to as Supplemental Restraint System (SRS). The SRS provides additional protection for the driver, if a forward collision of sufficient force is encountered. The SRS assists the normal seatbelt restraining system by deploying an air bag, via the steering column.

The center air bag sensor is the heart of the SRS. It consists of safing sensors, ignition control and drive circuit, diagnosis circuit, etc. The center air bag receives signals from the air bag sensors and determines whether the air bag must be activated or not. The center air bag sensor is also used to diagnose system malfunctions.

The air bag warning light circuit is equipped with an electrical connection check mechanism which detects when the connector to the center air bag sensor assembly is not properly connected.

All connectors in the air bag system are colored yellow. These connectors use gold-plated terminals with twin-lock mechanism. This design assures positive locking; there-by, preventing the terminals from coming apart.

SYSTEM OPERATION

When the ignition switch is turn to the **ON** or **ACC** position, the air bag warning lamp will turned ON for approximately 6 seconds. If no malfunctions are detected in the system, after the 6 second period have elapse, the warning light will go **OFF** .

The safing sensors are designed to go ON at a lower deceleration rate than the front or center air bag sensor. When the vehicle is involved in a frontal collision, the shock is great enough to overcome the predetermine level of the front or center air bag sensor. When a safing sensor and a front air bag sensor and/or the center air bag sensor go ON simultaneously, it causes the squib of the air bag to ignite and the air bag is deployed automatically. The inflated bag breaks open the steering wheel pad.

After air bag deployment have occurred, the gas is discharged through the discharge holes provided behind the bag. The bag become deflated as a result.

The connector of the air bag contains a short spring plate, which provides an activation prevention mechanism. When the connector is disconnected, the short spring plate automatically connects the power source and grounding terminals of the inflator module (squib).

SYSTEM COMPONENTS

Front Air Bag Sensor

The front sensors, located inside each front fenders, detects deceleration force above a predetermined limit.

Center Air Bag Sensor

The center air bag sensor is mounted on the floor inside the rear of the center cluster. The center sensor determines whether or not the air bag should be deployed and is also used to diagnose system malfunction.

Spiral Cable

The spiral cable, part of the combination switch, is used as an electrical joint from the vehicle body to the steering wheel. The spiral cable is referred to as a clock spring.

Air Bag

The air bag, located in the steering wheel pad, contains a gas generant which will rapidly inflate the bag in a case of frontal collision.

Warning Lamp

The air bag warning lamp, located on the combination meter, is used to alert the driver of any malfunctions within the air bag system.

SERVICE PRECAUTIONS

CAUTION: *To avoid deployment when servicing the SIR system or components in the immediate area, do not use electrical test equipment such as battery or A.C. powered voltmeter, ohmmeter, etc. or any type of tester other than specified. Do not use a non-powered probe tester. To avoid personal injury, all precautions must be strictly adhered to.*

• Do not disassemble any air bag system components.

• Always carry an inflator module with the trim cover pointed away.

• Always place an inflator module on the workbench with the pad side facing upward, away from loose objects.

• After deployment, the air bag surface may contain sodium hydroxide dust. Always wear gloves and safety glasses when handling the assembly. Wash hands with mild soap and water afterwards.

• The center air bag sensor assembly contains mercury. If replacement of the center air bag sensor is necessary, dispose of it as toxic waste.

• When servicing any SRS parts, discard the old bolts and replace with new ones.

• The SRS must be inspected 10 years after the vehicle's manufacture date shown on the certification label located on the left front door latch post.

• Always inspect the air bag sensors and steering wheel pad, when the vehicle has been involved in a collision (even in cases of minor collision) where the air bag did not deploy.

• Always use a fine needle test lead for testing, to prevent damaging the connector terminals.

• Never measure the resistance of the air bag module. This may cause the air bag to deploy.

• Never disconnect any electrical connection with the ignition switch **ON** unless instructed to do so in a test.

• Before disconnecting the negative battery cable, make a record of the contents memorized by each memory system like the clock, audio, etc. When service or repairs are completed make certain to reset these memory systems.

• Always wear a grounded wrist static strap when servicing any control module or component labeled with a Electrostatic Discharge (ESD) sensitive device symbol.

• Avoid touching module connector pins.

• Leave new components and modules in the shipping package until ready to install them.

• Always touch a vehicle ground after sliding across a vehicle seat or walking across vinyl or carpeted floors to avoid static charge damage.

• All sensors are specifically calibrated to a particular series. The sensors, mounting brackets and wiring harness must never be modified from original design.

• Never strike or jar a sensor, or deployment could happen.

• The inflator module must be deployed before it is scrapped.

• Any visible damage to sensors requires component replacement.

• Never bake dry paint on vehicle or subject the vehicle to temperatures exceeding 200°F (93°C), without disabling the air bag system and removing the inflator module, crash zone sensors, SRS diagnosis unit and the spiral cable.

• Do not interchange sensors between models or years.

• Do not install used air bag system parts from another vehicle.

• Never allow welding cables to lay on, near or across any vehicle electrical wiring.

• When ever any SRS parts are removed, always use new retaining bolts.

• Caution labels are important when servicing the air bag system in the field. If they are dirty or damaged, replace them with new ones.

DISARMING THE SYSTEM

On models with an airbag, wait at least 90 seconds from the time that the ignition switch is turned to the LOCK position and the battery is disconnected before performing any further work.

ENABLING THE SYSTEM

Reconnect the negative battery cable and preform the airbag warning light check by turning to the **ON** or **ACC** position, the air bag warning lamp will turned ON for approximately 6 seconds. If no malfunctions are detected in the system, after the 6 second period have elapse, the warning light will go **OFF** .

HEATER

Blower Motor

The blower motor is located under the dashboard on the far right side of the car. The blower motor turns the fan, which circulates the heated, cooled or fresh air within the car. Aside from common electrical problems, the blower motor may need to be removed to clean out leaves or debris which have been sucked into the casing.

REMOVAL & INSTALLATION

1. Disconnect the negative battery cable.
2. Remove the glove box assembly.
3. Disconnect the wiring from the blower motor.
4. Remove the three screws holding the blower motor and remove the blower motor.
To install:
5. With the blower motor removed, check the heater case for any debris or signs of fan contact. Inspect the fan for wear spots, cracked blades or hub, loose retaining nut or poor alignment.
6. Place the blower motor in position, making sure it is properly aligned within the case. Install the three screws and tighten them EVENLY.
7. Connect the wiring to the blower motor.
8. Connect the negative battery cable. Check operation of blower motor for all speeds and heater A/C system for proper operation.

Heater Unit

REMOVAL & INSTALLATION

1. Disconnect the negative battery cable. Drain the cooling system.
   CAUTION: *On models with an airbag, wait at least 90 seconds from the time that the ignition switch is turned to the LOCK position and the battery is disconnected before performing any further work.*
2. Remove the cooling unit-refer to the necessary service procedures.
3. Remove the heater hose clamps. Disconnect the heater hoses from the heater core. Remove the heater core pipe grommet.
4. Remove the instrument panel-refer to the necessary service procedure.
5. Remove the instrument panel reinforcement No. 1 and No. 2 bracket.
6. Remove the duct heater to register No. 3 and remove the front defroster nozzle.
7. Remove the heater unit.
To install:
8. Install the heater unit in the vehicle.
9. Install the front defroster nozzle and duct heater to register No. 3.
10. Install the instrument panel reinforcement No. 1 and No. 2 braces.
11. Install the instrument panel assembly.
12. Install the heater core pipe grommets. Push the water hoses onto the heater core pipes as far as the ridge on the pipes. Reconnect the heater hoses use NEW hose clamps if necessary.
13. Install the cooling unit assembly. Refill the cooling system.

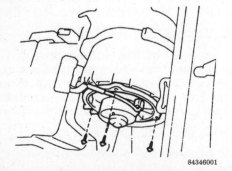

84346001

Blower motor removal

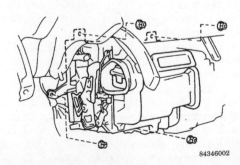

84346002

Remove the heater unit assembly

14. Connect the negative battery cable. Check operation of heater and A/C system.

Heater Core

The heater core is simply a small heat exchanger (radiator) within the heater housing assembly in the car. If the driver selects heat on the control panel, a water valve is opened allowing engine coolant to circulate through the heater core. The blower fan circulates air through the fins, picking up the heat from the engine coolant. The heated air is ducted into the car and the cool.

1. Remove the heater unit assembly-refer to the necessary service procedure.

2. Remove the screws and 2 heater core retaining clip.

3. Remove the heater core from the heater unit.

4. Installation is the reverse of the removal procedure. Push the water hoses onto the heater core pipes as far as the ridge on the pipes. Refill the cooling system. Connect the negative battery cable. Check operation of heater and A/C system.

Heater Water Control Valve

REMOVAL & INSTALLATION

1. Disconnect the negative battery cable. Drain the cooling system.

2. Disconnect the water valve control cable.

3. Disconnect the heater hoses from the heater core and water valve.

4. Remove the water valve.

5. Installation is the reverse of the removal procedure. Push the water hose onto the heater core pipe as far as the ridge on the pipe. Refill the cooling system. Adjust control cable if necessary.

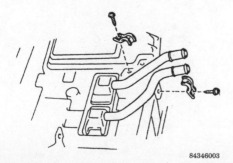

84346003

Remove the heater core from the heater unit assembly

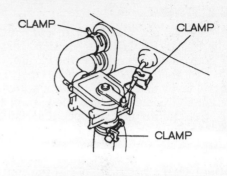

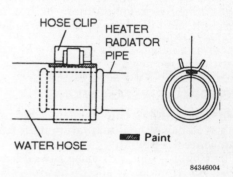

84346004

Water valve installation

Connect the negative battery cable. Check operation of the system.

Control Cables

REMOVAL, INSTALLATION AND ADJUSTMENT

For removal, installation and adjustment of "Control Cables" refer to the "Control Assembly" service procedures.

Control Assembly

REMOVAL & INSTALLATION

1. Disconnect the negative battery cable. Remove the center cluster finish lower panel and stereo opening cover.

2. Remove the center cluster finish panel and radio.

3. Disconnect the control cables from the heater unit and water valve.

4. Remove the 4 screws and the control assembly. Disconnect the air inlet control cable from the control assembly. Disconnect the blower switch connector. Remove the control assembly.

5. Installation is the reverse of the removal procedure. Adjust control cables as necessary. Connect the negative battery cable. Check operation of the system.

ADJUSTMENT

1. Set the air inlet damper and control lever to the **RECIRC** position, install the control cable and lock the clamp.

2. Set the mode selector damper and control lever to the **DEF** position, install the control cable and lock the clamp.

3. Set the air mix damper and control lever to the **COOL** position, install the control cable and lock the clamp.

4. Set the water valve and control lever to the **COOL** position, install the control cable and lock the clamp.

5. Move the control levers left and right and check for stiffness or binding through the full range of the levers. Test control cable operation.

Blower Speed Control Switch

REMOVAL & INSTALLATION

1. Disconnect the negative battery cable. Remove the illumination light from the control assembly.

2. Using a tool, pry loose the clip and push out the blower speed control switch to the rear of the control assembly.

3. Installation is the reverse of the removal procedure. Connect the negative battery cable. Check operation of the system.

Blower Motor Resistor

REMOVAL & INSTALLATION

1. Disconnect the negative cable.

2. Disconnect the electrical connector from the blower resistor assembly.

3. Remove the cowl side panel and glove box assembly. Remove mounting screw and remove the blower resistor assembly from the heater case.

4. Installation is the reverse of the service removal procedure. Reconnect the negative battery cable. Check the blower motor for proper operation at all speeds after installation.

AIR CONDITIONER

Compressor

REMOVAL & INSTALLATION

1. Run the engine at idle with the air conditioning on for approximately 10 minutes.

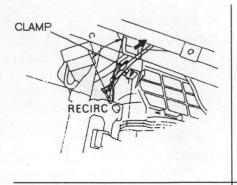

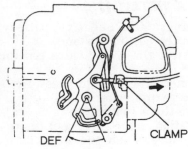

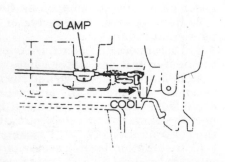

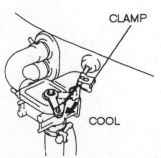

84346005

Control cable adjustment

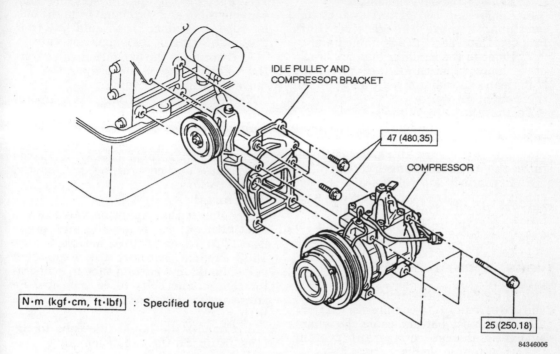

IDLE PULLEY AND
COMPRESSOR BRACKET

47 (480,35)

COMPRESSOR

| N·m (kgf·cm, ft·lbf) | : Specified torque

25 (250,18)

84346006

A/C compressor removal — 1993 models

2. Stop engine and disconnect the negative battery cable.

3. Remove the washer reserve tank.

4. Disconnect all electrical connection.

5. Recover refrigerant (discharge system) from refrigeration system.

6. Disconnect hoses from the compressor service valves. Cap open fittings immediately.

7. Remove engine undercover, if necessary. Loosen the compressor mounting bolts. Remove the compressor drive belt.

8. Remove the compressor mounting bolts. Remove the compressor from the vehicle.

To install:

9. Install compressor with mounting bolts and torque retaining bolts evenly to 18 ft. lbs. (25 Nm) Install and adjust the drive belt. Install engine undercover, if necessary.

10. Reconnect hoses to the compressor service valves.

11. Reconnect all electrical connections. Install the washer reserve tank.

12. Reconnect the battery cable.

13. Evacuate, charge and test refrigerant system. Check system for leaks.

Condenser

REMOVAL & INSTALLATION

1. Disconnect the negative battery cable.

2. Recover refrigerant (discharge system) from refrigeration system.

3. Remove the following parts:
   a. radiator grille
   b. horn
   c. hood lock
   d. center brace
   e. battery
   f. radiator reserve tank

4. Remove the condenser fan assembly.

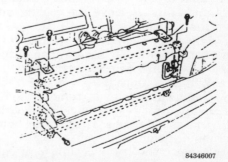

84346007

A/C condenser installation

5. Remove the oxygen sensor.

6. Remove all refrigerant system connections. Remove the receiver with bracket. Cap open fittings immediately.

7. Remove the radiator support brackets--remove the condenser mounting bolts lean the radiator back and pull out the condenser.

To install:

8. Install the condenser assembly to the vehicle. Install radiator support brackets. Make sure all rubber cushions fit on the mounting flanges correctly.

9. Reconnect all refrigerant system connections. Install receiver with bracket. Replace O-rings, as required.

10. Install the oxygen sensor, torque the nuts to 15 ft. lbs. Install condenser fan.

11. Install all other remaining components in reverse order of removal procedure.

12. If condenser assembly was replaced, add 1.4–1.7 fl. oz. of compressor oil.

13. Reconnect battery cable. Evacuate, charge and test refrigerant system. Check system for leaks.

Cooling Unit (Evaporator)

REMOVAL & INSTALLATION

1. Disconnect the negative battery cable. Recover refrigerant (discharge system) from refrigeration system.

2. Disconnect the suction flexible hose from the cooling unit outlet fitting.

3. Disconnect the liquid line from the cooling unit inlet fitting. Cap the open fittings immediately to keep the moisture out of the system.

4. Remove the grommets from the inlet and outlet fittings.

5. Remove the front door scuff plate and glove box assembly. Disconnect all necessary connectors and the air conditioning harness.

6. Remove the cooling unit attaching nuts and bolts. Remove the cooling unit from the vehicle.

7. Place the cooling unit on a suitable work bench and remove control amplifier, relay assemblies or power transistor assembly if so equipped.

8. Using suitable tools, remove the upper cooling unit case clamps and retaining screws. Remove thermistor with thermistor holder.

9. Remove the lower cooling unit case from the evaporator. Remove the evaporator from the cooling unit.

10. Remove the heat insulator (heat sensing tube) and the clamp from the outlet tube. Disconnect the liquid line from the inlet fitting of the expansion valve.

11. Disconnect the expansion valve from the inlet fitting of the evaporator. Remove the expansion valve.

NOTE: *Before installing the evaporator, check the evaporator fins for blockage. If the fins are clogged, clean them with compressed air. Never use water to clean the evaporator. Check the fittings for cracks and or scratches and replace, as necessary.*

To install:

12. Connect the expansion valve to the inlet fitting of the evaporator and torque it to 17 ft. lbs. on 1990–92 models. On the 1993 models, connect the expansion valve, liquid and suction tube to evaporator tighten the bolts to 48 inch lbs. Be sure the O-ring is positioned on the tube fitting.

13. Connect the liquid line tube to the inlet fitting on the expansion valve. Torque the nut to 10 ft. lbs.

14. Install the clamp and heat insulator (heat sensing tube) to the outlet tube.

15. Install the upper and lower cases on the evaporator. Install the thermistor. Install control amplifier, relay assemblies or power transistor assembly, if equipped.

16. Install the air conditioning wiring harness to the cooling unit and all other necessary components.

17. Install the cooling unit assembly in the vehicle. Be careful not to pinch the wiring harness while installing the cooling unit.

18. Install the glove box assembly, front door scuff plate and the grommets on the inlet and outlet fittings.

19. Connect the liquid line to the cooling unit inlet fittings and torque to 10 ft. lbs.

20. Connect the suction tube to the cooling unit outlet fitting and torque to 24 ft. lbs.

21. If the evaporator was replaced, add 1.4–1.7 oz. of compressor oil to the compressor. Connect the negative battery cable.

22. Evacuate, charge and test the refrigeration system.

NOTE: *If the drain hose on the cooling unit assembly becomes clogged or blocked with debris the cooling unit will leak water on the front floor rug area.*

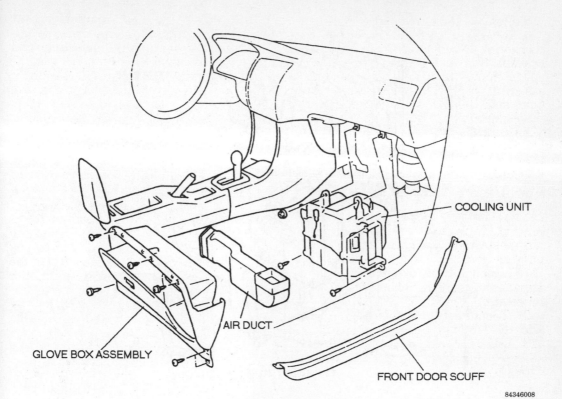

COOLING UNIT

AIR DUCT

GLOVE BOX ASSEMBLY

FRONT DOOR SCUFF

84346008

Cooling unit removal

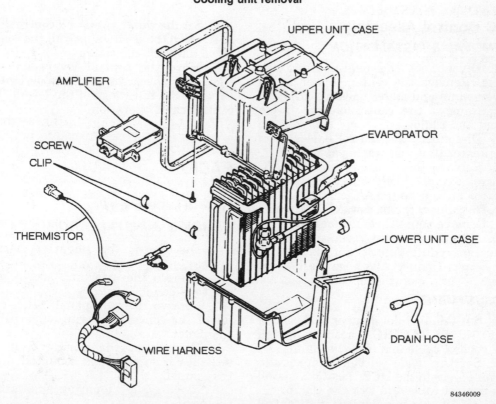

UPPER UNIT CASE

AMPLIFIER

EVAPORATOR

SCREW

CLIP

THERMISTOR

LOWER UNIT CASE

WIRE HARNESS

DRAIN HOSE

84346009

Exploded view of cooling unit — 1990–92 models

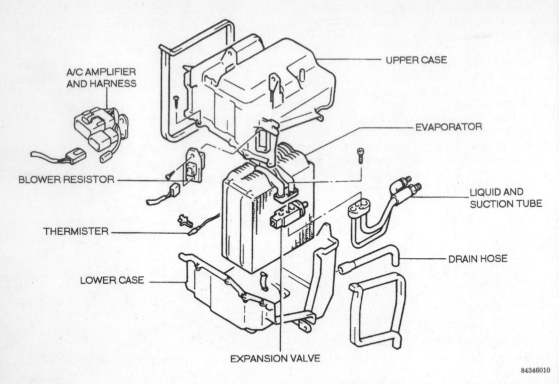

A/C AMPLIFIER AND HARNESS

BLOWER RESISTOR

THERMISTER

LOWER CASE

UPPER CASE

EVAPORATOR

LIQUID AND SUCTION TUBE

DRAIN HOSE

EXPANSION VALVE

84346010

Exploded view of cooling unit — 1993 models

A/C Control Assembly

REMOVAL & INSTALLATION

1. Disconnect the negative battery cable. Remove the center cluster finish lower panel and stereo opening cover.
2. Remove the center cluster finish panel and radio.
3. Disconnect the control cables from the heater unit and water valve.
4. Remove the 4 screws and the A/C control assembly. Disconnect the air inlet control cable from the A/C control assembly. Disconnect the blower switch connector. Remove the A/C control assembly.
5. Installation is the reverse of the removal procedure. Adjust control cables as necessary. Connect the negative battery cable. Check operation of the system.

ADJUSTMENT

1. Set the air inlet damper and control lever to the **RECIRC** position, install the control cable and lock the clamp.
2. Set the mode selector damper and control lever to the **DEF** position, install the control cable and lock the clamp.
3. Set the air mix damper and control lever to the **COOL** position, install the control cable and lock the clamp.

4. Set the water valve and control lever to the **COOL** position, install the control cable and lock the clamp.
5. Move the control levers left and right and check for stiffness or binding through the full range of the levers. Test control cable operation.

RADIO

Radio/Tape Player

REMOVAL & INSTALLATION

1. Disconnect the negative battery cable.
2. Remove the attaching screws from the trim panel.
3. Remove the trim panel, being careful of the concealed spring clips behind the panel.
4. Disconnect the wiring from the switches if so equipped mounted in the trim panel.
5. Remove the mounting screws from the radio.
6. Remove the radio from the dash until the wiring connectors are exposed.

7. Disconnect the electrical connectors and the antenna cable from the body of the radio and remove the radio from the car.

To install:

8. Reconnect all the wiring and antenna cable first, then place the radio in position within the dash.

9. Install the attaching screws.

10. Reconnect the wiring harnesses to the switches if so equipped in the trim panel and make sure the switches if so equipped are secure in the panel.

11. Install the trim panel (make sure all the spring clips engage) and install the screws.

12. Check radio system for proper operation.

Speakers

REMOVAL & INSTALLATION

1. Remove the speaker cover.

2. Remove the attaching screws for the speaker. Note location of speaker wires Remove the speaker.

3. Installation is the reverse of the removal procedure. Make sure that the speaker wires are installed in the correct location. Check radio system for proper operation.

WINDSHIELD WIPERS

Blade and Arm

REMOVAL & INSTALLATION

1. To remove the wiper blades lift up on the spring release tab on the wiper blade-to-wiper arm connector.

2. Pull the blade assembly off the wiper arm.

3. Press the old wiper blade insert down, away from the blade assembly, to free it from the retaining clips on the blade ends. Slide the insert out of the blade. Slide the new insert into the blade assembly and bend the insert upward slightly to engage the retaining clips.

4. To replace a wiper arm, unscrew the acorn nut (a cap covers this retaining nut at the bottom of the wiper arm) which secures it to the pivot and carefully pull the arm upward and off the pivot. Install the arm by placing it on the pivot and

tightening the nut. Remember that the arm MUST BE reinstalled in its EXACT previous position or it will not cover the correct area during use.

NOTE: *If one wiper arm does not move when turned on or only moves a little bit, check the retaining nut at the bottom of the arm. The extra effort of moving wet snow or leaves off the glass can cause the nut to come loose--the pivot will turn without moving the arm.*

Windshield Wiper Motor

REMOVAL & INSTALLATION

Front Wiper Assembly

1. Disconnect the negative battery terminal.

2. Disconnect the electrical connector from the wiper motor.

3. Remove the mounting bolts and remove the motor from the firewall.

4. Remove the wiper linkage from the wiper motor assembly.

5. Installation is the reverse of removal. Check wiper system for proper operation.

Rear Wiper Assembly

1. Remove the wiper arm from the pivot and remove the spacer and washer on the pivot.

2. Remove the cover (trim) panel on the inside of the hatch lock.

3. Remove the plastic cover on the wiper motor and disconnect the wiring connector from the motor.

4. Remove the mounting nuts and bolts and remove the wiper motor.

To install:

5. Position the motor and secure it in the hatch lid.

6. Connect the wiring harness and install the plastic cover.

7. Install the inner trim panel on the hatch lid.

8. Install the wiper arm with its washer and spacer, making sure the arm is correctly positioned before tightening the nut.

Front Wiper Linkage

REMOVAL & INSTALLATION

1. Remove the windshield wiper motor as previously outlined.

2. Loosen the wiper arm retaining nuts and remove the arms.

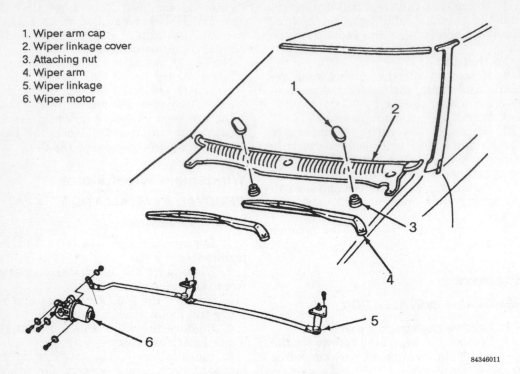

1. Wiper arm cap
2. Wiper linkage cover
3. Attaching nut
4. Wiper arm
5. Wiper linkage
6. Wiper motor

84346011

Front wiper assembly — 1990–92

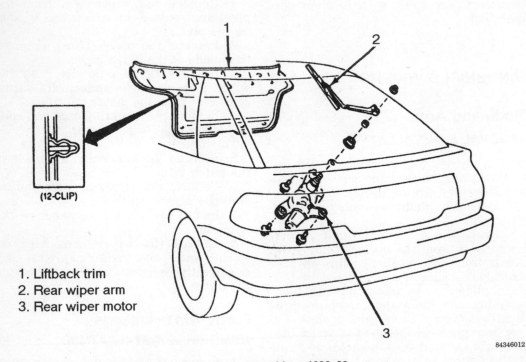

(12-CLIP)

1. Liftback trim
2. Rear wiper arm
3. Rear wiper motor

84346012

Rear wiper assembly — 1990–92

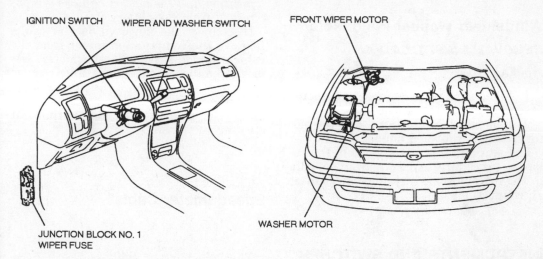

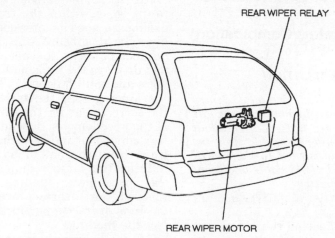

Wiper and washer parts location — 1993

3. Unfasten the large wiper pivot retaining nuts and remove the linkage assembly through the access hole.

To install:

4. Place the linkage through the access hole and line up the pivots in their holes.

5. Install the two large pivot retaining nuts onto the pivots. Before final tightening, make sure the linkage is aligned in all its holes.

6. Reinstall the wiper motor. Check wiper system for proper operation.

Windshield Washer Fluid Reservoir

REMOVAL & INSTALLATION

Front And Rear

1. Disconnect the negative battery terminal and fluid reservoir electrical connection.

2. Disconnect the fluid tube from the washer motor.

3. Remove the reservoir retaining bolts and slide out of the bracket.

4. Installation is the reverse of the removal procedure. Apply petroleum jelly

to the motor nipple before installing the washer tube.

Windshield Washer Fluid Motor

REMOVAL & INSTALLATION

Front And Rear

1. Remove the washer reservoir/motor assembly from the vehicle.
2. Remove all connections. Pull the motor from the rubber grommet.
3. Installation is the reverse of the removal procedure. Apply petroleum jelly to the motor before installing. Reconnect all connections.

INSTRUMENTS AND SWITCHES

Instrument Cluster (Combination Meter)

REMOVAL & INSTALLATION

CAUTION: *To avoid personal injury and accidental deployment of the air bag, work must be started after about 90 seconds or longer from the time the ignition switch is turned to the LOCK position and the battery cable is disconnected from the battery.*

1. Disconnect the negative battery cable.
2. Remove the steering column covers. Removing the steering wheel is not required, but may make the job easier.
NOTE: *Be careful not to damage the collapsible steering column mechanism.*
3. Remove the cluster finish panel.
4. Remove the combination meter attaching screws and pull the unit forward.
5. Disconnect the speedometer and any other electrical connections that are necessary.
6. Remove the instruments from the combination meter as required.
7. Installation is the reverse of the removal procedure.

Speedometer

REMOVAL & INSTALLATION

CAUTION: *To avoid personal injury and accidental deployment of the air bag, work must be started after about 90 seconds or longer from the time the ignition switch is turned to the LOCK position and the battery cable is disconnected from the battery.*

Disconnect the negative battery cable. Remove the combination meter from the vehicle and disassemble the meter. Remove the retaining screws and remove the speedometer from the meter lens. Keep the indicator needle horizontal. Remove the indicator needle without it striking the lens.

Speedometer Cable

The speedometer cable connects a rotating gear within the transaxle to the dashboard speedometer/odometer assembly. The dashboard unit interprets the number of turns the made by the cable and displays the information as miles per hour and total mileage.

Assuming that the transaxle contains the correct gear for the car, the accuracy of the speedometer depends primarily on tire condition and tire diameter. Badly worn tires (too small in diameter) or over-inflation (too large in diameter) can affect the speedometer reading. Replacement tires of the incorrect overall diameter (such as oversize snow tires) can also affect the readings.

Generally, manufacturers state that speedometer/odometer error of 10% is considered normal due to wear and other variables. Stated another way, if you drove the car over a measured 1 mile course and the odometer showed anything between 0.9 and 1.1 miles, the error is considered normal. If you plan to do any checking, always use a measured course such as mileposts on an Interstate highway or turnpike. Never use another car for comparison--the other car's inherent error may further cloud your readings.

The speedometer cable can become dry or develop a kink within its case. As it turns, the ticking or light knocking noise it makes can easily lead an owner to chase engine related problems in error. If such a noise is heard, carefully watch the speedometer needle during the speed range in which the noise is heard. Generally, the needle will jump or deflect each time the cable binds.

NOTE: *The slightest bind in the speedometer cable can cause unpredictable behavior in the cruise control system. If the cruise control exhibits intermittent surging or loss of set speed symptoms, check the speedometer cable first.*

To replace the speedometer cable and housing:

1. Follow the appropriate procedure given previously for removal of the instrument cluster. The cluster need not be fully removed, but only loosened to the point of being able to disconnect the speedometer cable.

2. Disconnect the speedometer cable and check that any retaining clamps or clips between the dash and the firewall are released.

3. Safely raise the car and support it on jackstands.

4. Disconnect the cable fitting at the transaxle and lift the cable and case away from the transaxle.

5. Follow the cable back to the firewall, releasing any clips or retainers.

6. From inside the car, work the speedometer cable through the grommet in the firewall into the engine compartment. It may be necessary to pop the grommet out of the firewall and transfer it to the new cable.

7. When reinstalling, track the new cable into position, remembering to attach the grommet to the firewall securely. Make absolutely certain that the cable is not kinked, or routed near hot or moving parts. All curves in the cable should be very gentle and not located near the ends. Note the speedometer cable inside the housing must be lubricated with the proper lubricant before installing it to the vehicle.

8. Attach any retaining clips, brackets or retainers, beginning from the middle of the cable and working towards each end.

9. Attach the cable to the transaxle. Remember that the cable has a formed, square end on it; this shaped end must fit into a matching hole in the transaxle mount. Don't try to force the cable collar (screw fitting) into place if the cable isn't seated properly.

10. Inside the car, hold the other end of the cable with your fingers or a pair of tapered-nose pliers. Gently attempt to turn the cable; if it's properly seated at the other end, the cable will NOT turn more than about ¼ turn. If the cable turns freely, the other end is not correctly seated.

11. Lower the car to the ground.

12. Attach the speedometer cable to the instrument cluster, again paying close attention to the fit of the square-cut end into the square hole. Don't force the cable retainer.

13. Reinstall the instrument cluster following procedures outlined previously. Road test the vehicle for proper operration.

Windshield Wiper/Washer Switch
REMOVAL & INSTALLATION

The windshield wiper/washer switch is part of the Combination Switch Assembly--refer to Turn Signal/Combination Switch services procedures in Chapter 8 for additional information.

Rear Window Wiper/Washer Switch
REMOVAL & INSTALLATION

1. Disconnect the negative battery cable.

2. Disconnect wiring from the switch assembly.

3. Remove the switch from the panel.

4. Installation is the reverse of the removal procedure. Check system for proper operation.

Headlight Switch
REMOVAL & INSTALLATION

The headlight switch is part of the Combination Switch Assembly--refer to Turn Signal/Combination Switch services procedures in Chapter 8 for additional information.

Clock
REMOVAL & INSTALLATION

1. Disconnect the negative battery cable.

2. Remove all necessary trim panels- remove the clock assembly mounting screws/or push in retaining clips.

3. Disconnect the electrical connection from the rear of the clock assembly, then remove it.

4. Installation is the reverse of the removal procedure.

LIGHTING

Headlights

REMOVAL & INSTALLATION

Sealed Beam Type

NOTE: *If vehicle is equipped with retractable headlights raise the headlights and turn the lights off with the headlights raised. Then pull out the "RTR 30 AMP" fuse. Unless power is disconnected, headlights could suddenly retract causing injury.*

1. Remove the headlight bezel (trim).

2. The sealed beam is held in place by a retainer and either 2 or 4 small screws. Identify these screws before applying any tools.

NOTE: *DO NOT confuse the small retaining screws with the larger aiming screws! There will be two aiming screws or adjustors for each lamp. (One adjustor controls the up/down motion and the other controls the left/right motion.)*

Identify the adjustors and avoid them during removal. If they are not disturbed, the new headlamp will be in identical aim to the old one.

3. Using a small screwdriver (preferably magnetic) and a pair of taper-nose pliers if necessary, remove the small screws in the headlamp retainer. DON'T drop the screws.

4. Remove the retainer and the headlamp may be gently pulled free from its mounts. Detach the connector (if the connector is tight wiggle it) from the back of the sealed beam unit and remove the unit from the car.

5. Place the new headlamp in position (single protrusion on the glass face upward) and connect the wiring harness. Remember to install the rubber boot on the back of the new lamp--its a water seal. Make sure the headlight is right-side up.

6. Turn on the headlights and check the new lamp for proper function, checking both high and low beams before final assembly.

7. Install the retainer and the small screws that hold it.

8. Reinstall the headlight bezel.

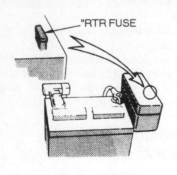

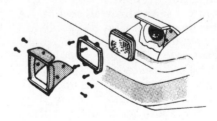

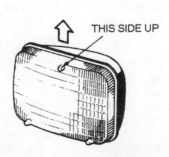

84346014

Removing and correct installation of headlight

Replaceable Bulb (Semi-Sealed Beam)/Fixed Lens Type

1990–92 MODELS

NOTE: *This type of light is replace from behind the unit. The lens is not removed or loosened.*

1. Open and support the hood.
2. Remove the wiring connector from the back the lamp. Be careful to release the locking tab completely before removal.
3. Grasp the base of the bulb holder and collar, twist it counterclockwise (as viewed from the engine compartment) and carefully remove the bulb holder and bulb from the housing.
4. Using gloves or a rag, hold the bulb and release the clip on the holder. Remove the bulb.
5. Install the new bulb in the holder and make sure the clip engages firmly.

NOTE: *Hold the new bulb with a clean cloth or a piece of paper. DO NOT touch or grasp the bulb with your fingers. The oils from your skin will produce a hot spot on the glass envelope, shortening bulb life. If the bulb is touched accidentally, clean it with alcohol and a clean rag before installation.*

6. Install the holder and bulb into the housing. Note that the holder has guides which must align with the housing. When the holder is correctly seated, turn the collar clockwise to lock the holder in place.
7. Connect the wiring harness. Turn on the headlights and check the function of the new bulb on both high and low beam.

Replaceable Bulb (Semi-Scaled Beam)/Fixed Lens Type

1993 MODELS

NOTE: *This type of light is replace from behind the unit. The lens is not removed or loosened.*

1. Open and support the hood.
2. Remove the wiring connector from the back the lamp. Be careful to release the locking tab completely before removal.
3. Grasp the base of the bulb holder, twist it counterclockwise (as viewed from the engine compartment) and carefully remove the bulb holder and bulb from the housing.
4. Using gloves or a rag, hold the bulb and release the clip on the holder. Remove the bulb.

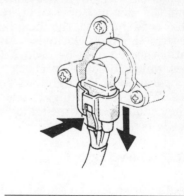

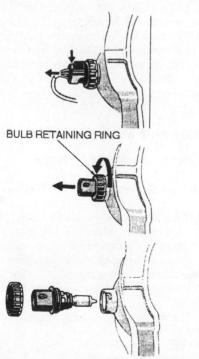

BULB RETAINING RING

84346015

Replacing semi-sealed beam headlight bulb — 1990–92

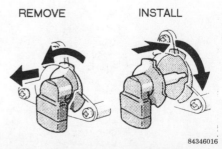

REMOVE   INSTALL

84346016

Replacing semi-sealed beam headlight bulb — 1993

5. Install the new bulb in the holder and make sure the clip engages firmly.

NOTE: *Hold the new bulb with a clean cloth or a piece of paper. DO NOT touch or grasp the bulb with your fingers. The oils from your skin will produce a hot spot on the glass envelope, shortening bulb life. If the bulb is touched accidentally, clean it with alcohol and a clean rag before installation.*

6. Install the holder and bulb into the housing. Note that the holder has guides which must align with the housing. When the holder is correctly seated, turn the clockwise to lock the holder in place.

7. Connect the wiring harness. Turn on the headlights and check the function of the new bulb on both high and low beam.

MANUAL OPERATION OF RETRACTABLE HEADLIGHTS

The retractable headlights can be manually operated if their electrical mechanism fails. To raise or lower the lights, Turn the ignition and headlight switches OFF and pull out the "RTR MTR 30A" fuse. Unless the power is disconnected, there is a danger of the headlights suddenly retracting. Remove the rubber cover from the manual operation knob (under the hood next to the headlight unit) and turn the knob clockwise. Manual operation should only be used if the system has failed; be sure to check the electrical operation of the lights as soon as possible. When the headlights are retracted, they should match the silhouette of the vehicle body.

HEADLIGHT AIMING

The headlamps should be aimed with a special alignment tool, state regulations

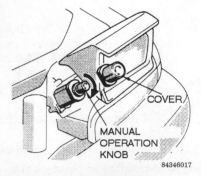

Manual operation of headlight doors

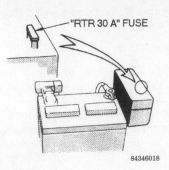

Remove this fuse-before manual operation of headlight doors

may vary this procedure, use this procedure below for temporary adjustments.

1. Inspect and correct all components that could interfere with proper headlamp alignment.

2. Verify proper tire pressure. Clean headlamp lenses and make sure that there is no heavy loads in the trunk or hatch luggage area. The gas tank should be filled.

3. Position the vehicle on a level surface perpendicular to flat wall 25 feet away.

4. Rock the vehicle side to side and up and down a few times to allow the suspension to stabilizer.

5. Turn lights On, adjust the horizontal direction of headlamps to achieve a straight and high intensity pattern. Adjust the vertical direction of headlamps to achieve a straight and high intensity pattern. Refer to the adjustment illustrations.

Signal and Marker Lights

REMOVAL & INSTALLATION

Front Turn Signals

NOTE: *This can be done with the car on the ground. Access is improved if the car is safely supported on jackstands.*

1. From behind the bumper, disconnect the electrical connector.

2. Remove the two nuts from the housing.

3. Remove the turn signal lamp housing.

NOTE: *If only the bulb is to be changed, the lens may be removed from the front.*

4. Reassemble the housing in reverse order of disassembly procedure.

COUPE

FOR ADJUSTMENT IN HORIZONTAL
DIRECTION

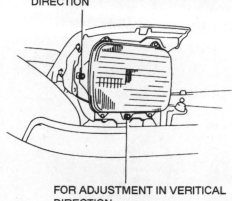

FOR ADJUSTMENT IN VERITICAL
DIRECTION

SEDAN AND WAGON

FOR ADJUSTMENT IN VERTICAL
DIRECTION

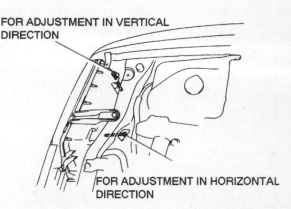

FOR ADJUSTMENT IN HORIZONTAL
DIRECTION

84346019

Headlight adjustment — 1990–92

FOR ADJUSTMENT IN HORIZONTAL
DIRECTION

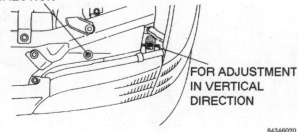

FOR ADJUSTMENT
IN VERTICAL
DIRECTION

84346020

Headlight adjustment — 1993

Side Marker Lights (Parking Lights)

FRONT

1. Remove the retaining screws. On some models, the screws are visible at the rear corner of the lens. On other models, the screw is under the hood.

2. Gently remove the lighting assembly from the body of the car.

3. Disconnect the bulb and socket(s) from the housing.

4. Reassemble in reverse order of removal procedure.

REAR

1. Some models incorporates the sidelights into the taillight assemblies. Remove the two screws in the sidemarker lens.

2. Remove the lighting assembly from the bodywork.

3. Disconnect the bulb and socket from the lighting assembly.

4. Reassemble in reverse order of the removal procedure.

No.	Light Bulbs	Bulb No.	W
1.	Parking and front side marker lights**	194	38
2.	Front turn signal lights	1156	27
3.	Rear turn signal lights	1156	27
4.	Stop and tail lights	1157	27/8
5.	Rear side marker, stop and tail lights	1157	27/8
6.	Back-up lights	1156	27
7.	High mounted stop-light	-	18
8.	License plate lights**	-	5
9.	Interior light*	-	10
10.	Personal light	-	10
11.	Luggage compartment light*		
12.	Trunk room light**	194	3.8

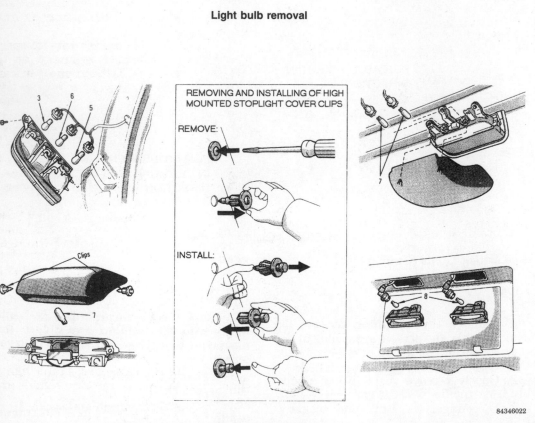

84346021

Light bulb removal

REMOVING AND INSTALLING OF HIGH MOUNTED STOPLIGHT COVER CLIPS

REMOVE:

INSTALL:

84346022

Light bulb removal

Rear Turn Signal, Brake and Parking Lights

1. Raise the trunk lid and remove or fold back the trunk carpeting.

2. Disconnect the wiring from the bulb holder(s).

3. If a bulb is to be changed, remove the bulb holder from the housing by pressing the tab and lifting out the holder assembly. Replace the bulb and reinsert the housing.

4. Remove the nuts holding the taillight assembly in place. Some may be difficult to reach.

5. Remove the lens assembly from the outside of the car.

6. When reinstalling the lens assembly, pay close attention to the placement of the gasket. It must be correctly positioned and evenly positioned to prevent water from entering the lens or trunk area. Double check the holes through which the threaded studs pass; caulk them with sealer if needed.

7. Install the retaining nuts and tighten them evenly. Do not overtighten them or the lens may crack.

8. Install the electrical connectors. Operate the lights while you check the function at the rear of the car. Replace the trunk carpet.

High Mounted Stoplight

REMOVAL & INSTALLATION

1. Remove the high mounted stoplight cover by pressing the center portion of the clip in while removing it--see illustration.

2. Remove the bulb from the high mounted stoplight holder.

3. Reassemble in reverse order of the removal procedure. Before installing retaining clips position center of clip correctly before installation.

Dome Light

REMOVAL & INSTALLATION

1. Remove the dome light cover.
2. Remove the bulb from holder.
3. Reassemble in reverse order of the removal procedure.

License Plate Lights

REMOVAL & INSTALLATION

1. Remove the lighting assembly from the bodywork.

2. Disconnect the bulb and socket from the lighting assembly.

3. Remove the bulb from the holder.

4. Reassemble in reverse order of the removal procedure.

TRAILER WIRING

Wiring the car for towing is fairly easy. There are a number of good wiring kits available and these should be used, rather than trying to design your own. All trailers will need brake lights and turn signals as well as tail lights and side marker lights. Most states require extra marker lights for overly wide trailers. Also, most states have recently required back-up lights for trailers, and most trailer manufacturers have been building trailers with back-up lights for several years.

Additionally, some trailers have electric brakes. Others can be fitted with them as an option, depending on the weight to be carried.

Add to this an accessories wire, to operate trailer internal equipment or to charge the trailer's battery, and you can have as many as seven wires in the harness.

Determine the equipment on your trailer and buy the wiring kit necessary. The kit will contain all the wires needed, plus a plug adapter set which includes the female plug, mounted on the bumper or hitch, and the male plug to be wired into the trailer harness.

When installing the kit, follow the manufacturer's instructions. The color coding of the wires is standard throughout the industry.

One point to note: some domestic vehicles, and most imported vehicles, have separate turn signals at the rear. On most domestic vehicles, the brake lights and rear turn signals operate with the same bulb. For those vehicles with separate turn signals, you can purchase an isolation unit so that the brake lights won't blink whenever the turn signals are operated.

You can also go to your local electronics supply house and buy four diodes to wire in series with the brake and turn signal bulbs. Diodes will isolate the brake and turn signals. The choice is yours. The isolation units are simple and quick to install, but far more expensive than the diodes. The diodes, however, require more work to install properly, since they require the cutting of each bulb's wire and soldering the diode into place.

The best wiring kits are those with a spring loaded cover on the vehicle mounted socket. This cover prevents dirt and moisture from corroding the terminals. Never let the vehicle socket hang loosely. Always mount it securely to the bumper or hitch. If you don't get a connector with a cover, at least put a piece of tape over the end of the connector when not in use. Most trailer lighting failures can be traced to corroded connectors and/or poor grounds.

CIRCUIT PROTECTION

Fuses And Fusible Links

REPLACEMENT

NOTE: *Vehicle fuses, fusible links and or relays are found in relay or junction blocks. Refer to the illustrations for location of relay and or junction block locations. The covers for the relay or junction blocks identify each fuse, fusible link or relay.*

All models have fuses, fusible links and relays found in various locations. One junction block (No. 1) is located within the cabin of the car, just under the extreme left side of the dashboard. This fuse block generally contains the fuses for body and cabin electrical circuits such as the wipers, rear defogger, ignition, cigarette lighter, etc. In addition, various relays and circuit breakers for other equipment are also mounted on or around this fuse block.

The second junction block (No. 2) is found under the hood on the forward part of the left wheelhouse (driver's side). The fuses, fusible links and relays in this junction block generally control the engine and major electrical systems on the car, such as headlights (separate fuses for left and right), air conditioning, horns, fuel injection, ECM, and fans.

All models have an additional small panel (relay/junction block No. 4) at the right kick panel area containing a fuse

(air conditioner or heater) and a relay and circuit breaker for the heater system.

All models have a relay block (No. 5) near junction block (No. 2) which is found under the hood. On 1993 Canada vehicles, relay block No. 6 is located in the front right engine compartment (passenger's side). These relay blocks contain various fuses, fusible links and relays for the vehicle. The covers for the relay or junction blocks identify each fuse, fusible link or relay for your vehicle.

Each fuse and fusible link location is labeled on the fuseblock cover identifying its primary circuit, but designations such as "Engine", "CDS Fan" or "ECU-B" may not tell you what you need to know. A fuse and fusible link can control more than one circuit, so check related fuses. The sharing of fuses is necessary to conserve space and wiring.

The individual fuses are of the plastic or "slip-fuse" type. They connect into the fusebox with two small blades, similar to a household wall plug. Removing the fuse with the fingers can be difficult; there isn't a lot to grab onto. For this reason, the fuseblock contains a small plastic fuse remover which can be clipped over the back of the fuse and used as a handle to pull it free.

Once the fuse is out, view the fusible element through the clear plastic of the fuse case. An intact fuse will show a continuous horseshoe-shaped wire within the plastic. This element simply connects one blade with the other; if it's intact, power can pass. If the fuse is blown, the link inside the fuse will show a break, possibly accompanied by a small black mark. This shows that the link broke when the electrical current exceeded the wires ability to carry it.

It is possible for the link to become weakened (from age or vibration) without

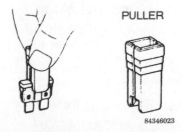

PULLER

84346023

Use the fuse puller to remove a fuse

breaking. In this case, the fuse will look good but fail to pass the proper amount of current, causing some electrical item to not work.

Once removed, any fuse may be checked for continuity with an ohmmeter. A reliable general rule is to always replace a suspect fuse with a new one. So doing eliminates one variable in the diagnostic path and may cure the problem outright. Remember, however, that a blown fuse is rarely the cause of a problem; the fuse is opening to protect the circuit from some other malfunction either in the wiring or the component itself. Always replace a fuse or other electrical component with one of equal amperage rating; NEVER increase the ampere rating of the circuit. The number on the back of the fuse body (5, 7.5, 10, 15 ,etc.) indicates the rated amperage of the fuse.

Circuit Breakers

REPLACEMENT

The circuit breakers found on the junction and relay blocks mount to the blocks with blades similar to the fuses. Before removing a breaker, always disconnect the negative battery cable to prevent potentially damaging electrical "spikes" within the system. Simply remove the breaker by pulling straight out from the block. Do not twist the circuit breaker, because damage may occur to the connectors inside the housing.

NOTE: *Some circuit breakers do not reset automatically. Once tripped, they must be reset by hand. Use a small screwdriver or similar tool; insert it in the hole in the back of the breaker and*

push gently. Once the breaker is reset, either check it for continuity with an ohmmeter or reinstall it and check the circuit for function.

Reinstall the circuit breaker by pressing it straight in to its mount. Make certain the blades line up correctly and that the circuit breaker is fully seated. Reconnect the negative battery cable and check the circuit for function.

Turn Signal and Hazard Flasher

The combination turn signal and hazard flasher unit is located under the dash on the left side near junction block (No. 1). The flasher unit is not the classic round "can" found on many domestic cars; instead, it is a small box-shaped unit easily mistaken for another relay. Depending on the year of your vehicle, the flasher may be plugged directly into the junction block (No.1) or it may be plugged into its own connector and mounted near junction block (No. 1). The flasher unit emits the familiar ticking sound when the signals are in use and may be identified by touching the case and feeling the "click" as the system functions.

The flasher unit simply unplugs from its connector and a replacement may be installed. Assuming that all the bulbs on the exterior of the car are working properly, the correct rate of flash for the turn signals or hazard lights is 60–75 flashes per minute. Very rapid flashing on one side only or no flashing on one side generally indicates a failed bulb rather than a failed flasher.

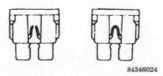

84346024

A blown fuse (left) compared with an intact fuse- the fuse cannot be inspected without removing it

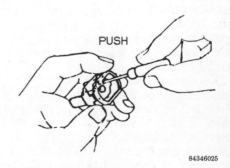

PUSH

84346025

Resetting a circuit breaker

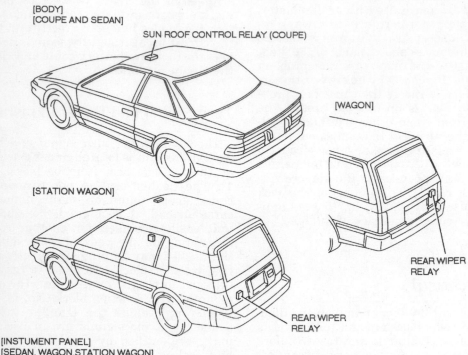

[BODY]
[COUPE AND SEDAN]

SUN ROOF CONTROL RELAY (COUPE)

[WAGON]

[STATION WAGON]

REAR WIPER
RELAY

REAR WIPER
RELAY

[INSTUMENT PANEL]
[SEDAN, WAGON, STATION WAGON]

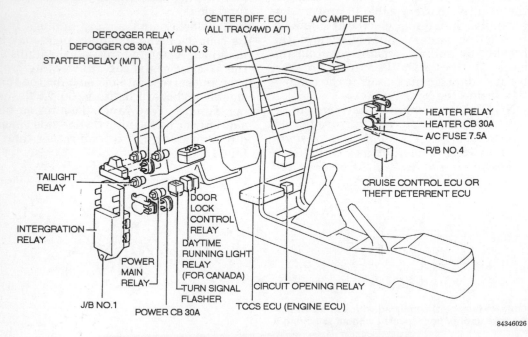

CENTER DIFF. ECU
(ALL TRAC/4WD A/T)   A/C AMPLIFIER

DEFOGGER RELAY
DEFOGGER CB 30A
STARTER RELAY (M/T)   J/B NO. 3

HEATER RELAY
HEATER CB 30A
A/C FUSE 7.5A
R/B NO.4

TAILIGHT
RELAY

CRUISE CONTROL ECU OR
THEFT DETERRENT ECU

INTERGRATION
RELAY

DOOR
LOCK
CONTROL
RELAY

DAYTIME
RUNNING LIGHT
RELAY
(FOR CANADA)

POWER
MAIN
RELAY

TURN SIGNAL
FLASHER

CIRCUIT OPENING RELAY

J/B NO.1

POWER CB 30A   TCCS ECU (ENGINE ECU)

84346026

Electronic component locations 1991 — other years similar

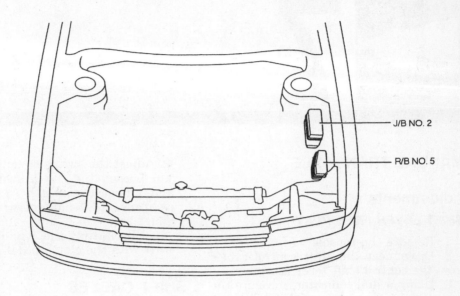

J/B NO. 2

R/B NO. 5

[INSTRUMENT PANEL]
[COUPE]

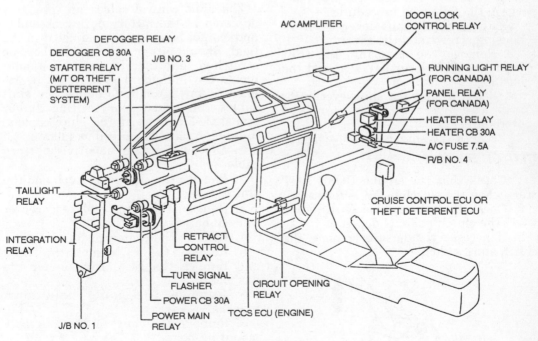

A/C AMPLIFIER

DOOR LOCK
CONTROL RELAY

DEFOGGER RELAY

DEFOGGER CB 30A

STARTER RELAY
(M/T OR THEFT
DERTERRENT
SYSTEM)

J/B NO. 3

RUNNING LIGHT RELAY
(FOR CANADA)

PANEL RELAY
(FOR CANADA)

HEATER RELAY

HEATER CB 30A

A/C FUSE 7.5A

R/B NO. 4

TAILLIGHT
RELAY

CRUISE CONTROL ECU OR
THEFT DETERRENT ECU

INTEGRATION
RELAY

RETRACT
CONTROL
RELAY

TURN SIGNAL
FLASHER

POWER CB 30A

POWER MAIN
RELAY

CIRCUIT OPENING
RELAY

TCCS ECU (ENGINE)

J/B NO. 1

84346027

Electronic component locations 1991 — other years similar

Drive Train

MANUAL TRANSAXLE

Adjustments

SHIFT LEVER FREE PLAY

1. Remove the console.
2. Disconnect the shift control cables from the control shift lever assembly.
3. Using a dial indicator, measure the up and down movement of the shift lever; it should be 0.0059 in. (0.15mm).
4. If necessary to adjust the free-play, perform the following procedures:
   a. Remove the shift lever cover-to-housing screws and the cover.
   b. Remove the snapring, the shift lever, the shift lever ball seat and the bushing.
   c. Select the correct shift lever bushing and reverse the removal procedures.
5. Recheck the shift lever movement.

CLUTCH SWITCH

1. Check that the engine DOES NOT start when the clutch pedal is released.
2. Check that the engine DOES start when the clutch pedal is depress
3. If necessary, adjust or replace the clutch start switch.

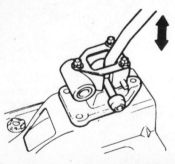

84347001

Checking shifter play

4. Adjust the switch as follows:
   a. Loosen the clutch switch locknut and adjust the switch to the proper clearance (2.0–6.0mm) with a feeler gauge set.
   b. Check that the engine does not start with the clutch pedal released.

SHIFT CABLES

REMOVAL & INSTALLATION

The shift control cables are precisely adjusted at the factory during assembly and cannot be accurately adjusted in the field. Should either of the cables become stretched and therefore out of adjustment, the individual cable must be replaced. Any attempt to adjust the shift cables can cause poor shifting and/or transaxle damage. If the shift cable(s) must be replaced, proceed as follows:

1. Disconnect the negative battery cable.
2. Remove the shift lever knob and the shifter boot.
3. Remove the front and rear center console halves.
4. Remove the center air ducts.
5. Remove the ECM mounting nuts and remove the ECM from under the dashboard.
6. Remove the cable hold-down bracket.
7. Remove the four shifter assembly mounting bolts.
8. Remove the shift cable retainer and end clips from the shifter assembly.
9. Remove the shifter control assembly.
10. Disconnect the cable retainers at the transaxle.
11. Remove the shift cables by pulling them from the outside of the firewall.

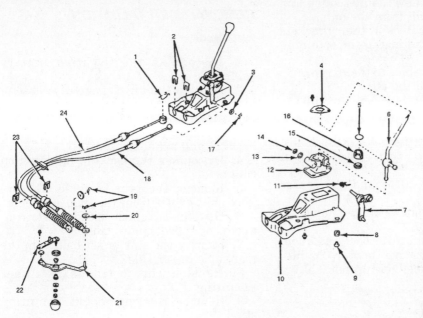

1. Cable end clips
2. Retainer clips
3. Plate washer
4. Shift lever cover
5. Snap ring
6. Shift lever
7. Selecting bellcrank
8. Bushing No. 2
9. Bushing No.1
10. Control shift lever retainer plate
11. Torsion spring
12. Shift lever housing
13. Plate washer
14. E-clip
15. shift lever seat bushing
16. Shift lever ball seat
17. Clip
18. Shift select cable
19. Clips
20. Plate washer
21. Selecting bellcrank
22. Selecting bellcrank support
23. Retainer clips
24. Shift control cable

84347002

Shifter and cable assembly

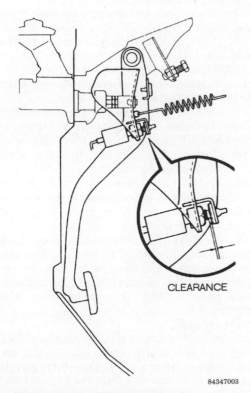

CLEARANCE

84347003

Clutch start switch adjustment

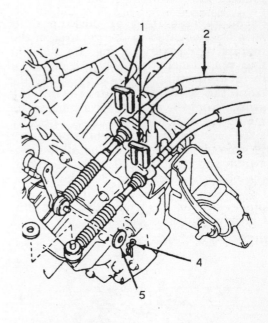

1. Cable retainer
2. Shift control cable
3. Shift select cable

4. Cable end clip
5. Cable end washer

84347004

Shift cables-typical

To install:

12. Install the new cables by going through the firewall from the outside.

13. Position the cables in their brackets at the transaxle and install the retaining clips.

14. Connect the cables to their transaxle mounts and install the clips.

15. Connect the cables and install the clips at the shifter assembly.

16. Install the shifter assembly and its four bolts. Tighten the bolts to 15 ft. lbs.

17. Install the cable hold-down brackets.

18. Reinstall the ECM and the center air duct.

19. Install the front and rear halves of the console.

20. Install the shift lever boot and knob. Connect the negative battery cable. roadtest the vehicle for proper shifter operation.

Back-up Light Switch

REMOVAL & INSTALLATION

The reverse light or back-up light switch is mounted in the top area of the manual transaxle housing. Its removal and replacement is easily accomplished by disconnecting the wiring connector from the switch and unscrewing the switch from the case (always replace the mounting gasket below it). A specially sized socket or its equivalent is necessary for this service operation. Install the new switch and tighten it 30 ft. lbs. Reinstall the electrical connector. Turn key to the ON position, depress clutch pedal and place shifter in REVERSE position. Check operation of back-up lights.

BACK-UP
LIGHT SWITCH

84347005

Back-up light switch

Transaxle

REMOVAL & INSTALLATION

2WD Models

1. Disconnect the negative battery cable.

2. Remove the air cleaner case assembly with hose. Remove the coolant reservoir tank.

3. Remove clutch release cylinder tube bracket and cylinder assembly.

4. Disconnect the back-up light switch connector.

5. Remove the ground cable. Disconnect shift cables from the transaxle.

6. Disconnect vehicle speed sensor connector or speedometer cable.

7. Remove the starter set bolt from the transaxle upper side.

8. Remove the 2 transaxle upper mounting bolts.

9. Remove the engine left mounting stay.

10. Install engine support fixture. Raise and safely support the vehicle.

11. Remove the front wheels. Remove the engine under covers.

12. Drain the transaxle oil.

13. Disconnect the lower ball joint from the lower arm.

14. Remove the halfshafts-refer to the necessary service procedures.

15. Remove the front exhaust pipe.

16. Remove the hole cover. Remove the engine front mounting set bolts.

17. Disconnect engine rear mounting. Remove the engine center support member.

18. Remove the starter. Remove stiffener plate if so equipped.

19. Raise the transaxle and engine slightly with a jack. Remove the engine left mounting set bolts from the front side.

20. Remove the transaxle mounting bolts from the engine front side. Remove the transaxle mounting bolts from the engine rear side. Lower the engine left side and remove the transaxle from the engine.

To install:

21. Align the input shaft with the clutch disc and install the transaxle to the engine and torque the engine-to-transaxle bolts to 47 ft. lbs. (64 Nm) for 12mm bolts and 34 ft. lbs. (46 Nm) for 10mm bolts.

22. Raise the transaxle and engine slightly and install the left engine mount-

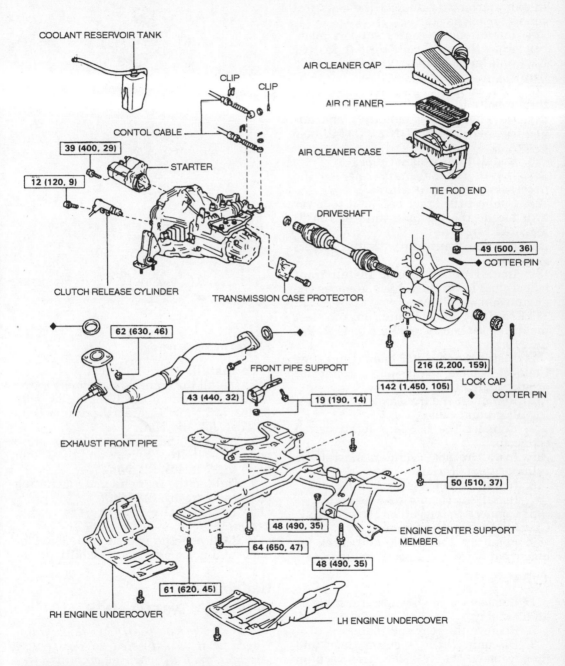

COOLANT RESERVOIR TANK

CLIP

CLIP

CONTOL CABLE

AIR CLEANER CAP

AIR CI FANER

AIR CLEANER CASE

39 (400, 29)

STARTER

12 (120, 9)

TIE ROD END

DRIVESHAFT

49 (500, 36)

◆ COTTER PIN

CLUTCH RELEASE CYLINDER

TRANSMISSION CASE PROTECTOR

62 (630, 46)

FRONT PIPE SUPPORT

43 (440, 32)

19 (190, 14)

216 (2,200, 159)

142 (1,450, 105)

LOCK CAP

◆ COTTER PIN

EXHAUST FRONT PIPE

50 (510, 37)

48 (490, 35)

ENGINE CENTER SUPPORT MEMBER

64 (650, 47)

48 (490, 35)

61 (620, 45)

RH ENGINE UNDERCOVER

LH ENGINE UNDERCOVER

N·m (kgf·cm, ft·lbf) : SPECIFIED TORQUE

◆ NON-REUSABLE PART

84347006

Manual transaxle removal

ing. Install the left engine-to-transaxle mount bolts torque to 41 ft. lbs. (56 Nm).

23. Install stiffener plate if so equipped. Install starter and connect the electrical connector to the starter.

24. Install engine center support member torque the small bolts to 45 ft. lbs. (61 Nm) and larger bolts to 152 ft. lbs. (206 Nm).

25. Connect the engine rear mounting torque bolts to 35 ft. lbs. (48 Nm). Connect the engine front mounting and torque bolts 47 ft. lbs. (64 Nm). Install hole covers.

26. Install front exhaust pipe.

27. Install the halfshafts-refer to the necessary service procedures.

28. Connect the lower ball joint to lower arm torque the bolt and nuts to 105 ft. lbs. (142 Nm).

29. Fill the transaxle with the correct gear oil.

30. Install under covers. Install front wheels and lower the vehicle. Remove the engine support fixture.

31. Install and torque engine left mounting set bolt to rear side to 41 ft. lbs. (56 Nm).

32. Install engine left mounting stay. Connect vehicle speed sensor connector or speedometer cable.

33. Reconnect the transaxle shift cables. Install ground cable.

34. Connect the back-up light switch connector.

35. Install release cylinder and release cylinder tube bracket.

36. Install coolant reservoir tank.

37. Install air cleaner case assembly.

38. Connect the negative battery cable. Check front wheel alignment.

39. Road test the vehicle and check for abnormal noise and smooth shifting.

4WD Models

1. Remove the engine and transaxle as an assembly.

2. Remove the rear end plate.

3. Disconnect the vacuum lines and then remove the transfer case vacuum actuator.

4. Remove the right and center transfer case stiffener plate.

5. Pull the transaxle out slowly until there is approximately 2.36–3.15 in. (60–80mm) clearance between the transaxle and the engine.

6. Turn the output shaft in a clockwise direction and then remove the transaxle.

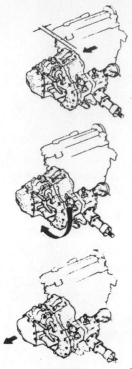

84347007

All-Trac transaxle removal

To install:

7. Install the transaxle assembly to the engine and tighten the 10mm bolts to 34 ft. lbs. (46 Nm). Tighten the 12mm bolts to 47 ft. lbs. (64 Nm).

8. Tighten the 8mm stiffener plate bolts to 14 ft. lbs. (20 Nm) and the 10mm bolts to 27 ft. lbs. (37 Nm).

9. Tighten the rear end plate mounting bolts to 17 ft. lbs. (23 Nm).

10. Install the engine/transaxle assembly.

11. Road test the vehicle and check for abnormal noise and smooth shifting.

Halfshafts

REMOVAL & INSTALLATION

NOTE: *The hub bearing could be damaged if it is subjected to the vehicle weight, such as when moving the vehicle with the halfshaft removed. If it is necessary to place the vehicle weight on the hub bearing, support it with a special tool SST 09608–16041. Refer to the illustrations.*

1. Remove the wheel cover.

2. Remove the cotter pin, lock nut cap, and bearing lock nut.

3. Loosen the wheel nut.

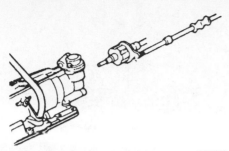

84347008

Using a tool to remove halfshaft from the transaxle

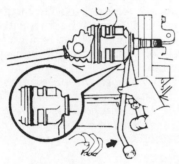

84347009

Removing the halfshaft

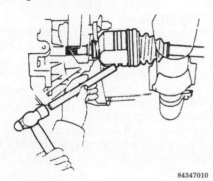

84347010

Removing the halfshaft

4. Raise and safely support the car. Remove the engine under covers and drain gear oil or transaxle fluid.

5. Remove the wheel.

6. Disconnect the lower control arm to steering knuckle attaching nuts and bolts.

7. Use a ball joint separator or equivalent to remove the tie rod ball joint from the steering knuckle.

8. Remove the bolts holding the brake caliper bracket to the steering knuckle. Use stiff wire to suspend the caliper out of the way; do not let the caliper hang by its hose. Remove the brake disc.

9. Using a puller or equivalent, push the axle from the hub.

NOTE: *The axle can be separated from the hub using a brass or plastic hammer some others may require the use of a puller.*

10. Use a slide hammer and appropriate end fitting or equivalents to pull the halfshaft from the transaxle. Remove the halfshaft from the car.

To install:

11. Install halfshaft into transaxle. If necessary, use a long brass drift and a hammer to drive the housing ribs onto the inner joint.

NOTE: *Before installing the halfshaft, position the snapring opening side facing downward.*

12. Install the halfshaft into the wheel hub.

13. Install the lower control arm to the steering knuckle. Tighten the nuts and bolts to 105 ft. lbs.

14. Install the tie rod end to the steering knuckle and tighten the nut to 36 ft. lbs.

15. Install the brake disc; install the brake caliper and tighten the bolts.

16. Install the wheel.

17. Install the hub nut and washer.

18. Lower the vehicle to the ground.

19. Tighten the wheel lugs to 76 ft. lbs. Tighten the hub nut to 137 ft. lbs.

20. Install the lock nut cap and NEW cotter pin. Fill transaxle with gear oil or transaxle fluid if necessary.

21. Install engine cover. Check front wheel alignment.

OVERHAUL

The halfshaft assembly is a flexible unit consisting of an inner and outer constant velocity (cv) joint joined by an axle shaft. Care must be taken not to overextend the joint assembly during repairs or handling. When either end of the shaft is disconnected from the car, any overextension could result in separation of the internal components and possible joint failure.

The CV joints are protected by rubber boots or seals, designed to keep the high-temperature grease in and the road grime and water out. The most common cause of joint failure is a ripped boot (tow hooks on halfshaft when car is being towed) which allows the lubricant to leave the joint, thus causing heavy wear.

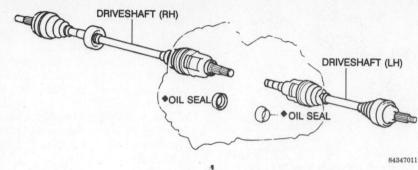

Halfshaft assembly

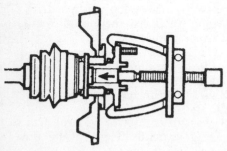

Using a tool to remove halfshaft from the front hub

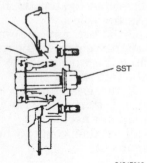

Toyota special tool number 09608–16041

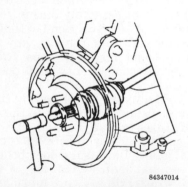

Removing halfshaft from the front hub

The boots are exposed to road hazards all the time and should be inspected frequently. Any time a boot is found to be damaged or slit, it should be replaced immediately.

NOTE: *Whenever the halfshaft is held in a vise, use pieces of wood in the jaws to protect the components from damage or deformation. Refer to the illustrations.*

DISASSEMBLY

1. Mount the driveshaft in a vise and check that there is no play in the inboard and outboard joint.

2. Make sure that the inboard joint slides smoothly in the thrust direction.

3. Make sure that there is no excessive play in the radial direction of the inboard joint.

4. Inspect the boots for damage (rips, punctures and cracks).

5. Remove the inboard joint boot clips.

6. With chalk or paint, matchmark the inboard joint tulip and tripod. DO NOT use a punch.

7. Remove the inboard joint tulip from the driveshaft.

8. Remove the snapring.

9. Using a brass rod and hammer, evenly drive the tripod joint off the driveshaft without hitting the joint roller.

10. Remove the inboard joint boot.

11. Remove the clamp and driveshaft damper.

12. Remove the clamps and the outboard drive boot. DO NOT disassemble the outboard joint.

REASSEMBLY

NOTE: *Before installing the boot, wrap the spline end of the shaft with masking tape to prevent damage to the boot.*

1. Install the driveshaft damper with a new clamp.

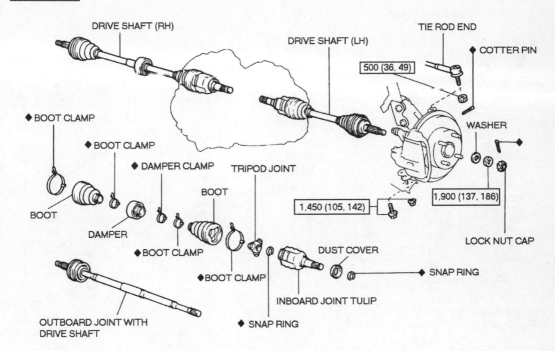

TOYOTA TYPE

DRIVE SHAFT (RH)

DRIVE SHAFT (LH)

TIE ROD END

◆ COTTER PIN

500 (36, 49)

◆ BOOT CLAMP

WASHER

◆ BOOT CLAMP

◆ DAMPER CLAMP

TRIPOD JOINT

BOOT

1,900 (137, 186)

BOOT

BOOT

DAMPER

1,450 (105, 142)

◆ BOOT CLAMP

LOCK NUT CAP

DUST COVER

◆ BOOT CLAMP

◆ SNAP RING

INBOARD JOINT TULIP

OUTBOARD JOINT WITH
DRIVE SHAFT

◆ SNAP RING

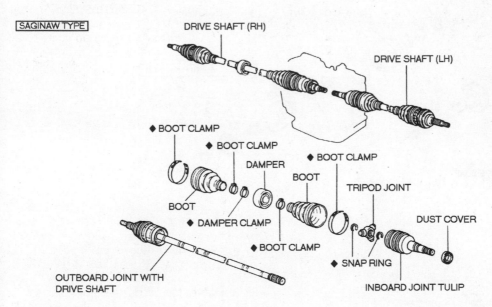

SAGINAW TYPE

DRIVE SHAFT (RH)

DRIVE SHAFT (LH)

◆ BOOT CLAMP

◆ BOOT CLAMP

DAMPER

◆ BOOT CLAMP

BOOT

TRIPOD JOINT

BOOT

DUST COVER

◆ DAMPER CLAMP

◆ BOOT CLAMP

◆ SNAP RING

INBOARD JOINT TULIP

OUTBOARD JOINT WITH
DRIVE SHAFT

kg-cm (ft-lb, Nm) : SPECIFIED TORQUE

◆ NON-REUSABLE PART

84347015

Halfshaft components-2WD

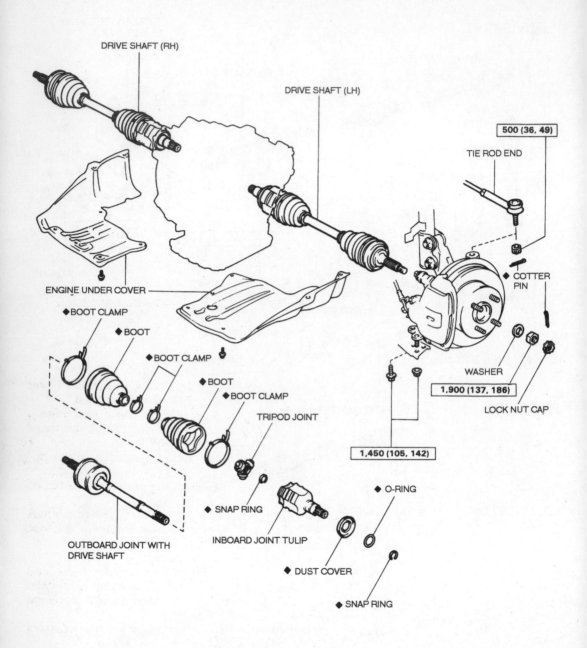

DRIVE SHAFT (RH)

DRIVE SHAFT (LH)

500 (36, 49)

TIE ROD END

ENGINE UNDER COVER

◆ COTTER
   PIN

◆ BOOT CLAMP

◆ BOOT

◆ BOOT CLAMP

◆ BOOT

◆ BOOT CLAMP

TRIPOD JOINT

WASHER

1,900 (137, 186)

LOCK NUT CAP

1,450 (105, 142)

◆ SNAP RING

◆ O-RING

OUTBOARD JOINT WITH
DRIVE SHAFT

INBOARD JOINT TULIP

◆ DUST COVER

◆ SNAP RING

kg-cm (ft-lb, Nm) : SPECIFIED TORQUE

◆ NON-REUSABLE PART

84347016

Halfshaft components-4WD

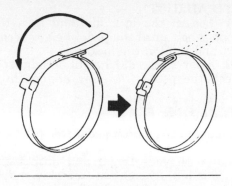

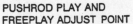

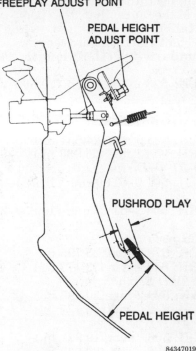

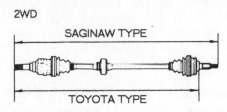

84347017

Halfshaft clamp installation

Clutch pedal adjustment

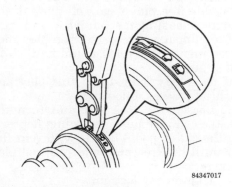

2WD

SAGINAW TYPE

TOYOTA TYPE

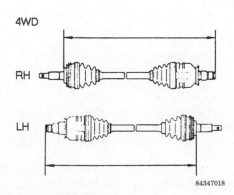

4WD

RH

LH

84347018

Halfshaft standard length

2. Temporarily install the inboard boot with new clamp to the drive joint.

NOTE: *The inboard boot and clamp are larger than those of the outboard boot.*

3. Position the beveled side of the tripod spline towards the outboard joint.

4. Align the matchmarks on the tripod and driveshaft.

5. Tap the tripod onto the driveshaft with a brass rod and hammer without hitting the joint roller.

6. Install the snapring.

7. Pack the outboard tulip joint and the outboard boot with about 0.26–0.33 lbs. ounces of grease that was supplied with the boot kit.

8. Install the boot onto the outboard joint.

9. Pack the inboard tulip joint and boot with ½ lb. of grease that was supplied with the boot kit.

10. Align the matchmarks on the tulip joint and tripod.

11. Install the inboard tulip joint onto the driveshaft.

12. Install the boot onto the driveshaft.

13. Make sure that the boot is properly installed on the driveshaft.

14. Before checking the standard length, bend the band and lock it.

15. Make sure that the boot is not stretched or squashed when the driveshaft is at standard length.

Standard driveshaft length:*1990–91 Toyota type*
- LH: 523.2–533.2 mm (20.598–20.992 in.)
- RH:837.7–847.7mm(32.980–33.374in.)

1990–91 2WD Saginaw type
- LH: 623.6 mm (24.551 in.)
- RH: 938.1 mm (36.933 in.)

1990–91 4WD type
- LH: 501.0–511.0 mm (19.724–20.118 in.)
- RH: 504.2–514.2 mm (19.850–20.244 in.)

1992 Toyota type
- LH: 528.2 mm (20.795 in.)
- RH: 842.7 mm (33.177 in.)

1992 2WD Saginaw type
- LH: 528.2 mm (20.795 in.)
- RH: 842.7 mm (33.177 in.)

1992 4WD type
- LH: 506.0 mm (19.921 in.)
- RH: 509.2 mm (20.047 in.)

1993 2WD type
- LH: 540.2 mm (21.268 in.)
- RH: 857.4 mm (33.756 in.)

CLUTCH

CAUTION: *The clutch driven disc contains asbestos which has been determined to be a cancer causing agent. Never clean clutch surfaces with compressed air. Avoid inhaling any dust from any clutch area! When cleaning clutch surfaces, use commercially available brake cleaning fluids.*

Adjustments

LINKAGE

No external adjustments are needed or possible.

PEDAL HEIGHT

Check that the height of the clutch pedal is correct by measuring from the top of the pedal to the asphalt sheet on the kick panel. The pedal height should be within these specifications:
- 1990–93: 5.71–6.10 in. (145–155 mm)
- 1993: 5.61–6.00 in. (142.5–152.5 mm)

TO ADJUST

1. Loosen the lock nut and turn the stopper bolt until the pedal height is correct and tighten the lock nut.

2. After the pedal height is adjusted, check the pedal free play and pushrod play.

PEDAL FREE PLAY

Measure the clutch pedal free play and pushrod play by pressing on the clutch pedal with your finger and until resistance is felt. The clutch free play should be between 5–15mm (0.197–0.591 in.). Inadequate free play wears all parts of the clutch releasing mechanisms and may cause slippage. Excessive free play may cause inadequate release and hard shifting of gears.

If necessary, adjust the free play and pushrod play as follows:

1. Loosen the lock nut and turn the master cylinder push rod while depressing the clutch pedal lightly with your finger until the free play and pushrod play is correct.

2. Tighten the lock nut.

3. Check the pedal height.

PUSH ROD PLAY

Push in on the pedal with a finger softly until the resistance begins to increase somewhat. The push rod play at the pedal top should be: 1.0–5.0mm (0.039–0.197 in.).

Driven Disc and Pressure Plate

REMOVAL & INSTALLATION

1. Remove the transaxle from the vehicle.

2. Matchmark the flywheel and the clutch cover with paint or chalk.

3. Loosen each set bolt one at a time until the spring tension is relieve.

4. Remove the set bolts completely and pull off the clutch cover with the clutch disc.

NOTE: *Do not drop the clutch disc. Do not allow grease or oil to get on any of the disc, pressure plate, or flywheel surfaces.*

5. Unfasten the release fork bearing clips. Withdraw the release bearing assembly with the fork and then separate them.

6. Remove the release fork boot.

7. Using calipers, measure the rivet head depth. Minimum depth is 0.30mm.

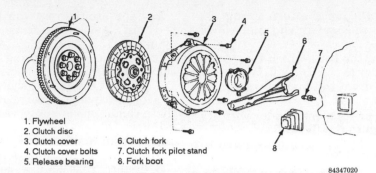

1. Flywheel
2. Clutch disc
3. Clutch cover
4. Clutch cover bolts
5. Release bearing
6. Clutch fork
7. Clutch fork pilot stand
8. Fork boot

84347020

Clutch components

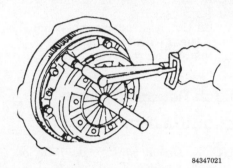

84347021

Use a pilot tool when installing the clutch assembly

If not within the limit, replace the clutch disc.

8. Using a dial indicator and V-blocks, measure the clutch disc runout. Maximum allowable runout is 0.8mm. If the runout is excessive, replace the clutch disc.

9. Using a dial indicator, measure the flywheel runout. Maximum runout is 0.10mm. If the runout is excessive, machine or replace the flywheel.

10. Using calipers, measure the diaphragm spring for depth and width and wear. Maximum depth is 0.60mm and maximum width is 5mm. Replace the clutch cover as necessary.

11. Grasp the release bearing and turn it while applying force in the axial direction. Replace the bearing and hub as required.

To install the clutch:

12. Insert proper alignment tool into the clutch disc and set them and the clutch cover in position.

13. Install the clutch disc bolts and tighten them evenly and gradually in a criss-cross pattern in several passes around the cover until they are snug.

14. Once the bolts are snug, torque them in sequence to 14 ft. lbs.

15. Using a dial indicator with a roller attachment, measure the diaphragm spring tip alignment. Maximum non-alignment is 0.05mm. Adjust the alignment as necessary using SST No. 09333–00013.

16. Apply molybdenum disulphide lithium base grease (NLGI No.2) to the following parts:

    a. Release fork and hub contact point.

    b. Release fork and push rod contact point.

    c. Release fork pivot point.

    d. Clutch disc spline.

    e. Inside groove of the release bearing hub.

17. Install the bearing assembly on the fork and then install them to the transaxle.

18. Install the boot.

19. Install the transaxle to the engine.

Clutch Master Cylinder

NOTE: *When inspecting the clutch hydraulic system for leakage or impaired function, check the inside of the firewall (under the carpet) below the clutch master cylinder. A master cylinder leak may not show up under the cylinder on the engine side of the firewall.*

REMOVAL & INSTALLATION

1. Drain or siphon the fluid from the master cylinder. On the 4A-GE engine equipped vehicles, remove the brake booster.

2. Disconnect the hydraulic line to the clutch from the master cylinder.

NOTE: *Do not spill brake fluid on the painted surfaced of the vehicle.*

3. Inside the car, remove the underdash panel and the air duct.

4. Remove the pedal return spring.

5. Remove the spring clip and clevis pin.

6. Unfasten the bolts which secure the master cylinder to the firewall. Withdraw the assembly from the firewall side.

To install:

7. Install the master cylinder with its retaining nuts to the firewall.

8. Connect the line from the clutch to the master cylinder.

9. Connect the clevis and install the clevis pin and spring clip.

10. Install the pedal return spring.

11. Fill the reservoir with clean, fresh brake fluid and bleed the system.

12. Check the cylinder and the hose connection for leaks. Install brake booster if necessary.

13. Bleed and adjust the clutch pedal.

14. Reinstall the air duct and underdash cover panel.

OVERHAUL

1. Refer to the exploded view of clutch master cylinder components. Clamp the master cylinder body in a vise with protected jaws.

2. Separate the reservoir (remove slotted pin) assembly from the master cylinder.

3. Remove the snapring and remove the pushrod/piston assembly.

4. Inspect the master cylinder bore for scoring, grooving or corrosion. If any of these conditions are observed, replace the cylinder. Inspect piston, spring, push rod and boot for damage or wear replace any parts which are worn or defective.

5. Before reassembly, coat all parts with clean brake fluid.

6. Install the piston assembly in the cylinder bore.

7. Fit the pushrod over the washer and secure them with the snapring.

8. Install the reservoir tank.

Clutch Release Cylinder

REMOVAL & INSTALLATION

NOTE: *Do not spill brake fluid on the painted surface of the vehicle.*

1. Raise the vehicle and safely support it with jackstands or equivalent.

2. If necessary, remove the under covers to gain access to the release cylinder.

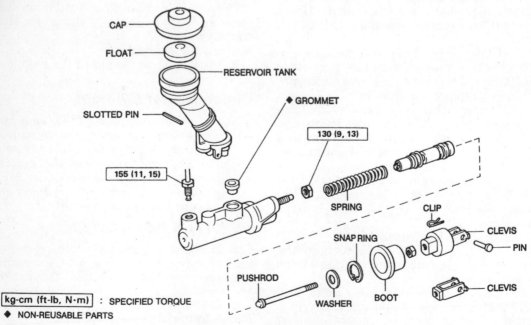

kg-cm (ft-lb, N·m) : SPECIFIED TORQUE
◆ NON-REUSABLE PARTS

84347022

Clutch master cylinder components

3. Remove the clutch fork return spring.

4. Unfasten the hydraulic line from the release cylinder by removing its retaining nut.

5. Remove the release cylinder retaining nuts and remove the cylinder.

To install:

6. Reinstall the cylinder to the clutch housing and tighten the bolts to 9 ft. lbs.

7. Connect the hydraulic line and tighten it to 11 ft. lbs.

8. Install the clutch release spring.

9. Bleed the system and remember to top up the fluid in the master cylinder when finished.

10. Install the under covers as necessary. Lower the car to the ground.

OVERHAUL

1. Refer to the exploded view of clutch release cylinder components. Remove the pushrod assembly and the rubber boot.

2. Withdraw the piston, complete with its cup; don't remove the cup unless it is being replace.

3. Wash all the parts in brake fluid.

4. Replace any worn or damaged parts. Inspect the cylinder bore carefully for any sign of damage, wear or corrosion.

5. Before reassembly, coat all the parts in clean brake fluid. Insert the spring and piston into the cylinder.

6. Install the boot and insert the pushrod.

HYDRAULIC SYSTEM BLEEDING

NOTE: *If any maintenance on the clutch system was performed or the system is suspected of containing air, bleed the system. Brake fluid will remove the paint from any surface. If the brake fluid spills onto any painted surface, wash it off immediately with soap and water.*

1. Fill the clutch reservoir with brake fluid. Check the reservoir level frequently and add fluid as needed.

2. Connect one end of a vinyl tube to the clutch release cylinder bleeder plug and submerge the other end into a container half-filled with brake fluid.

3. Slowly pump the clutch pedal several times.

4. Have an assistant hold the clutch pedal down and loosen the bleeder plug until fluid starts to run out of the bleeder plug. You will notice air bubbles mixed in with the fluid.

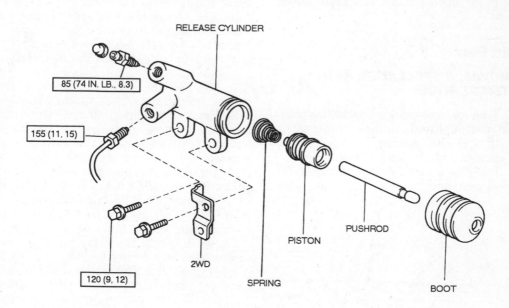

RELEASE CYLINDER

85 (74 IN. LB., 8.3)

155 (11, 15)

2WD

120 (9, 12)

SPRING

PISTON

PUSHROD

BOOT

KG-CM (FT. LB., NM) : SPECIFIED TORQUE

84347023

Clutch release cylinder components

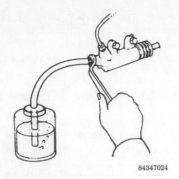

84347024

Bleeding the clutch system

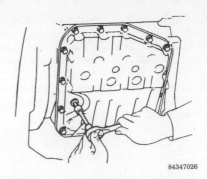

84347026

Removing the automatic transaxle oil pan

5. Repeat Steps 3 and 4 until all the air bubbles are removed from the system.

6. Tighten the bleeder plug when all the air is gone.

7. Refill the master cylinder to the proper level as required.

8. Check the system for leaks.

AUTOMATIC TRANSAXLE

Identification

The automatic transaxle identification code is stamped on the VIN plate under the hood.

Fluid Pan

REMOVAL, INSTALLATION AND FILTER SERVICE

1. To avoid contamination of the transaxle, thoroughly clean the exterior of the oil pan and surrounding area to remove any deposits of dirt and grease.

2. Position a suitable drain pan under the oil pan and remove the drain plug.

OIL STRAINER

84347025

Removing the automatic transaxle oil filter (strainer)

Allow the oil to drain from the pan. Set the drain plug aside.

3. Loosen and remove all but two of the oil pan retaining bolts.

4. Support the pan by hand and slowly remove the remaining two bolts.

5. Carefully lower the pan to the ground.

CAUTION: *There will be some fluid still inside the pan and it may be hot. Allow the fluid to cool down before removing the pan and wear eye protection to avoid personal injury.*

6. Remove the 3 oil strainer (filter) attaching bolts and carefully remove the strainer. The strainer will also contain some fluid.

NOTE: *One of the 3 oil strainer bolts is slightly longer than the other 2. Make a note of where the longer bolt goes so that it may be reinstalled in the original position.*

7. Discard the strainer. Remove the gasket from the pan and discard it.

8. Drain the remainder of the fluid from the oil pan and wipe the pan clean with a lint-free rag. With a gasket scraper, remove any old gasket material from the flanges of the pan and the transaxle. Remove the gasket from the drain plug and replace it with a new one.

NOTE: *There may be from one to three small magnets on the bottom of the pan. These magnets were installed by the manufacturer at the time the transaxle was assembled. The magnets function to collect metal chips and filings from clutch plates, bushings and bearings that accumulate during the normal break-in process that a new transaxle experiences. Clean the magnets and reinstall them. They can be useful tools for determining transaxle component wear.*

To install the filter and pan:

9. Install the new oil strainer. Install and tighten the retaining bolts to 7–8 ft lbs. (10–11 Nm) in their proper locations.

10. Install the new gasket onto the oil pan making sure that the holes in the gasket are aligned evenly with those of the pan. Position the magnets so that they will not interfere with the oil tubes.

11. Raise the pan and gasket into position on the transaxle and install the retaining bolts. Torque the retaining bolts in a criss-cross pattern to 43 inch lbs. (4.9 Nm).

12. Install and tighten the drain plug.

13. Fluid is added only through the dipstick tube. Use only the proper automatic transmission fluid.

NOTE: *Do not overfill the transaxle. Do not race the engine when adding fluid.*

14. Replace the dipstick after filling. Start the engine and allow it to idle.

15. After the engine has idled for a few minutes, shift the transmission slowly through the gears and then return it to **P**. With the engine still idling, check the fluid level on the dipstick. If necessary, add more fluid to raise the level to where it is supposed to be.

NOTE: *Before discarding the used fluid, check the color of the fluid. It should always be a bright red color. It if is discolored (brown or black), or smells burnt, serious transmission troubles, possibly due to overheating, should be suspected. The transmission should be inspected to locate the cause of the burnt fluid.*

Adjustments

THROTTLE CABLE

To inspect the throttle cable operation, remove the air cleaner assembly and depress the accelerator cable all the way. Check that the throttle valve opens fully. If the throttle valve does not open fully, adjust the accelerator link as follows:

1. Remove the air cleaner.
2. Fully depress the accelerator cable.
3. Loosen the adjustment nut.
4. Adjust the cable housing so that the distance between the end of boot and the stopper is 0–0.04 in. (0–1mm).
5. Tighten the adjusting nuts.
6. Recheck the adjustment.

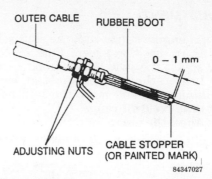

Throttle cable adjustment

SHIFT CABLE

1. Loosen the control cable lever swivel nut.
2. Push the control lever to the right as far as it will go.
3. Bring the lever back two notches to the Neutral position.
4. Place the shift lever in Neutral.
5. Hold the lever, lightly, toward the **R** range side and tighten the swivel nut.

Neutral Safety Switch

The neutral safety switch in addition to preventing the vehicle from starting with the transaxle in gear also actuates the back-up warning lights.

REMOVAL & INSTALLATION

1. Disconnect the neutral start switch connector.
2. With a pair of needle nose pliers, remove the clip that connects the manual control cable to the manual shift lever.
3. Unstake the lock nut and remove the manual shift lever.
4. Remove the neutral start switch with the seal gasket.

To install:

5. Install the neutral start switch making sure that the lip of the seal gasket is facing inward.
6. Install the manual shift lever.
7. Install the locknut and torque to 61 inch lbs. (6.9 Nm). Stake the nut with the locking plate.
8. Connect the switch connector.
9. Adjust the neutral start switch.
10. Connect the transaxle shift cable and install the clip.
11. Adjust the transaxle shift cable.
12. Check the operation of the switch and adjust as necessary.

ADJUSTMENT

If the engine starts with the shift selector in any position except Park or Neutral, adjust the switch as follows:

1. Loosen the two neutral start switch retaining bolts and move the shift selector to the Neutral range.

2. Align the groove and the neutral basic line. Maintain the alignment and torque the bolts to 48 inch lbs. (5.4 Nm).

Back-Up light Switch

The neutral safety switch functions as the back-up light switch. See removal, installation and adjustment procedures for the neutral safety switch as previously detailed in this Chapter.

Transaxle

REMOVAL & INSTALLATION

NOTE: *On All-Trac vehicles, the automatic transaxle unit must be removed with the engine as an assembly.*

1. Disconnect the negative battery cable. Remove the air cleaner assembly.

2. Disconnect the neutral start switch. Disconnect the speedometer cable or speed sense.

3. Disconnect the shift control cable and throttle cable (at engine compartment).

4. Disconnect the oil cooler hose. Plug the end of the hose to prevent leakage.

5. Drain the radiator and remove the water inlet pipe if so equipped.

6. Raise and support the vehicle safely. Drain the transaxle fluid. As required remove the exhaust front pipe.

7. Remove the engine undercover. Remove the front and rear transaxle mounts.

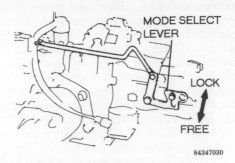

Mode select lever position — All Trac

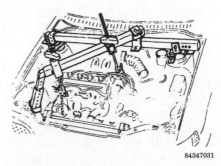

Using a tool to support the engine-transaxle removal and installation

8. Support the engine and transaxle using the proper equipment. Remove the engine center and lower crossmember.

9. Remove the halfshafts. Remove the starter assembly. Remove filler tube.

10. Remove the flywheel cover plate. Remove the torque converter bolts.

11. Remove the left engine mount. Remove the transaxle-to-engine bolts. Slowly back the transaxle away from the engine. Lower the assembly to the floor.

To install:

12. Check torque converter installation. Transaxle installation is the reverse of the removal procedure. When installing

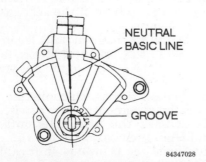

Neutral safety switch adjustment

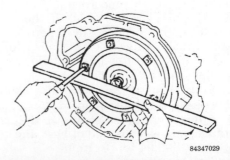

Checking torque converter installation

the automatic transaxle on the 4WD All-Trac vehicles, be sure the mode selector lever is positioned in the **FREE** mode and attach the lock bolt. Refer to the illustration.

13. To check torque converter installation measure from the installed surface to the front surface of the transaxle housing. The correct distance on 1990–92 vehicles should be 0.906 inch (23.0mm). On the 1993 vehicle, the correct distance is 0.898 inch (22.8mm).

14. Torque the transaxle retaining bolts--12mm bolts to 47 ft. lbs. and 10mm bolts to 34 ft. lbs.

15. Torque the converter bolts (coat threads with loctite or equivalent) evenly to 20 ft. lbs. on 2WD vehicles and 34 ft. lbs. on 4WD vehicles.

16. Fill transaxle to the correct level, roadtest the vehicle, check fluid level.

Halfshafts

REMOVAL & INSTALLATION

Refer to the "Manual Transaxle Halfshaft Removal and Installation" in this Chapter for the necessary service procedures.

OVERHAUL

Refer to the "Manual Transaxle Halfshaft Overhaul" in this Chapter for the necessary service procedures.

TRANSFER CASE

Transfer Vacuum Actuator

REMOVAL & INSTALLATION

All-Trac Models

1. Remove and tag the 4 vacuum hoses from the actuator.

2. Remove the stiffener center plate and the actuator bracket bolts and then remove the actuator.

To install:

3. Install the transfer vacuum actuator, tightening the 3 bolts, then install the stiffener center plate and actuator bracket bolts and torque to 27 ft. lbs. (37 Nm).

4. Reinstall the vacuum hoses in their proper positions.

Rear Output Shaft Seal

REMOVAL & INSTALLATION

All-Trac Models

The following procedure can be accomplished while the transfer case is in the vehicle.

1. Drain the transaxle oil.

2. Remove the propeller shaft.

3. Drive out the output shaft oil seal using SST 09308–00010.

To install:

4. Drive in a new seal using SST 09325–20010 to a depth of 0.043–0.075 in. (1.1–1.9mm).

5. Install the propeller shaft and fill the transaxle with the proper lubricant.

Transfer Case

REMOVAL & INSTALLATION

All-Trac Models

For ease of removal, the entire transaxle assembly should be removed first.

1. Remove the 3 bolts and the 5 nuts.

2. Using a plastic hammer, remove the transfer assembly from the transaxle.

To install:

3. Make sure that the contact surfaces are clean and oil-free.

4. Apply seal packing (part No. 08826–00090 or equivalent) to the transfer and install the transfer as soon as the packing is applied.

NOTE: *Shift into 4th gear, and install the transfer assembly while turning the input shaft of the transaxle.*

5. Apply sealant (part No. 08833–00080) to the bolt threads.

6. Torque the 3 bolts and the 5 nuts to 51 ft. lbs. (69 Nm).

DRIVELINE

Propeller Shaft

REMOVAL & INSTALLATION

All-Trac Models

1. Matchmark the both front driveshaft flanges.

2. Remove the four bolts, nuts and washers and disconnect the front driveshaft.

3. Withdraw the yoke from the transfer.

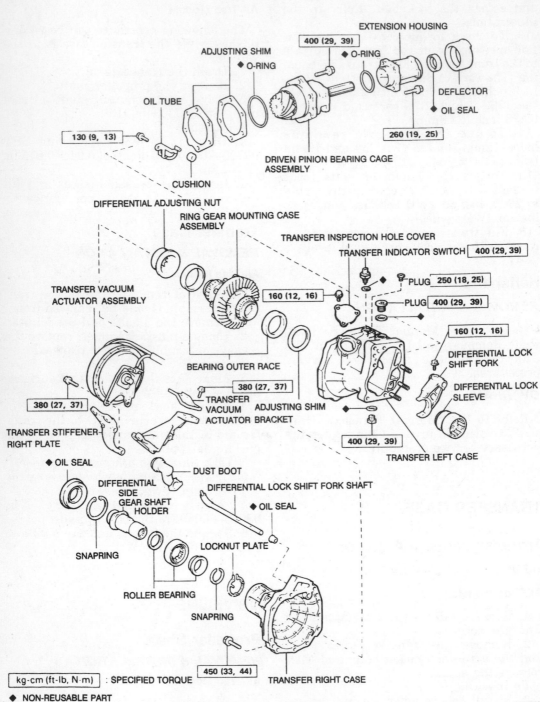

kg-cm (ft-lb, N·m) : SPECIFIED TORQUE

◆ NON-REUSABLE PART

84347032

Transfer case components

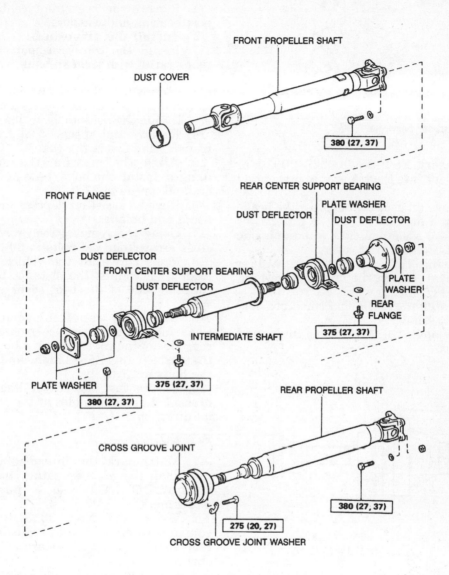

FRONT PROPELLER SHAFT

DUST COVER

380 (27, 37)

FRONT FLANGE

REAR CENTER SUPPORT BEARING

PLATE WASHER

DUST DEFLECTOR

DUST DEFLECTOR

DUST DEFLECTOR

FRONT CENTER SUPPORT BEARING

DUST DEFLECTOR

PLATE WASHER

REAR FLANGE

INTERMEDIATE SHAFT

375 (27, 37)

PLATE WASHER

375 (27, 37)

380 (27, 37)

REAR PROPELLER SHAFT

CROSS GROOVE JOINT

380 (27, 37)

275 (20, 27)

CROSS GROOVE JOINT WASHER

kg·cm (ft-lb, N·m) : SPECIFIED TORQUE

◆ NON-REUSABLE PART

84347033

Propeller shaft components

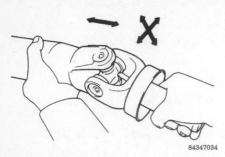

84347034

Inspect spider bearings

4. Insert SST No. 09325–20010 or equivalent into the transfer to prevent oil leaks.

5. Have an assistant depress the brake pedal and hold .

6. Place a piece of cloth into the inside of the universal joint cover.

7. Using SST No. 09325–20010 or equivalent, loosen the cross groove joint set bolts ½ turn.

8. Matchmark the intermediate and rear driveshaft.

9. Remove the four bolts, nuts and washers.

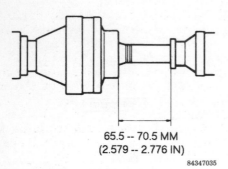

65.5 -- 70.5 MM
(2.579 -- 2.776 IN)

84347035

Correct installation of propeller shaft — Step 1

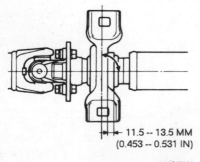

11.5 -- 13.5 MM
(0.453 -- 0.531 IN)

84347036

Correct installation of propeller shaft — Step 2

10. Remove the two bolts from the front center support bearing and remove the bearing and the washer.

11. Remove the rear front center support bearing and washers.

To install the driveshaft:

12. Install the center support bearing temporarily with the two bolts.

13. Align the matchmarks on the rear and intermediate flanges and connect the shafts with the four nuts, bolts and washers. Torque the bolts to 27 ft. lbs.

14. Remove the special tool from the transfer and insert the yoke.

15. Align the matchmarks on both flanges. Install the bolts, nuts and washers and torque to 27 ft. lbs.

16. Have an assistant depress the brake pedal and hold it.

17. Using the removal tool, torque the cross groove joint set bolts to 20 ft. lbs.

18. Make sure that the vehicle is unloaded, and adjust the distance between the rear side of the boot cover and the shaft.

19. Under the same unloaded conditions, adjust the distance between the rear side of the center bearing housing of the cushion to 11.5–13.5mm and torque the bolts to 27 ft. lbs.

20. Ensure that the center line of the bracket is at right angles at the shaft axial direction.

INSPECTION

1. Matchmark the intermediate and rear shaft flanges. Use paint, chalk or a scribe. DO NOT use a punch to matchmark.

2. Using SST No. 09313–30021 or equivalent, remove the intermediate and rear flange bolts and separate the two shafts.

3. Place the propeller and intermediate shafts on V-blocks and check the run out with a dial indicator. If the run out exceeds 0.08mm replace the shaft.

4. Measure the run out of the face of the intermediate shaft flange. If the runout exceeds 0.1mm, replace the shaft.

5. Measure the run out of the rear face of the intermediate flange in the vertical direction.

6. Check the front shaft spider bearings for axial play by turning the flange while holding the shaft tightly.

7. Mount the rear propeller shaft in a vise and check the cross groove joint play. Check the joint for damage or signs of

grease leakage around the boot. If damaged, replace the joint.

OVERHAUL

DISASSEMBLY

1. Using a ball-peen hammer and a small cold chisel, loosen the staked part of the locking nut located on the rear center support bearing front flange.

2. Using SST No. 09330–0021 or equivalent, hold the front flange and remove the nut and plate washer.

3. Match mark the rear flange and the front shaft.

4. Using SST No. 09950–20017 or equivalent, remove the rear flange.

5. Remove the rear center support bearing (note front and back location for correct installation) and plate washer.

6. Repeat Steps 1–5 to remove the front center support bearing (note front and back location for correct installation).

7. Turn the center support bearing by hand while applying force in the direction of rotation. Check the bearing smooth play.

8. Inspect both support seals for cracks and damage.

REASSEMBLY

1. Set the front center support bearing onto the intermediate shaft.

2. Install the plate washer.

3. Align the matchmark and install the bearing flange onto the shaft.

4. Using SST No. 09330–00021 or equivalent to hold the flange, press the bearing into place by tightening the new locking nut and washer to 134 ft. lbs.

5. Loosen the locking nut.

6. Torque the nut again to 51 ft. lbs. and stake the nut with a ball-peen hammer and small cold chisel.

7. Repeat Steps 1–6 to install the rear center support bearing.

8. Mount the rear propeller shaft in a vise and check the cross groove joint play.

9. Using SST No. 09313–30021 or equivalent, temporarily tighten the six bolts and three washers using a piece of cloth on the inside of the joint cover.

Center Support Bearings

Two center support bearings are used on All-Trac 4-Wheel Drive vehicles to control driveshaft noise and vibration and as a means of support for the intermediate driveshaft assembly.

REMOVAL & INSTALLATION

Refer to the service procedures under the "Propeller Shaft" Chapter.

REAR AXLE

Axle Shaft, Bearing and Seal

REMOVAL & INSTALLATION

All-Trac Models

NOTE: *This service procedures requires use of special tools-machine shop press and oil bath or equivalent-it is best to remove axle shaft and send it out to a machine shop to replace the axle bearing assembly.*

1. Raise and safely support the vehicle.

2. Remove the wheel cover, unfasten the lug nuts, and remove the wheel.

3. Punch matchmarks on the brake drum and the axle shaft to maintain rotational balance.

4. Remove the brake drum or disc brake caliper, disc rotor and related component.

5. Remove the backing plate attachment nuts through the access holes in the rear axle shaft flange.

6. Use a slide hammer with a suitable adaptor to withdraw the axle shaft from its housing. Use care not to damage the oil seal when removing the axle shaft.

7. Disconnect the brake line, remove the backing plate and remove the end gasket from the axle housing.

To install:

8. To replace the axle bearing, cut the axle bearing retainer and press the bearing off the axle shaft.

9. Position bearing outer retainer and new bearing on shaft using a press install it to the correct location.

10. Heat the inner bearing retainer to about 150 °C in an oil bath-press the inner retainer on the axle shaft. Face the non-beveled side of the inner retainer toward the bearing.

11. Remove the oil seal from the axle housing.

NOTE: *The oil seal can be removed from the axle housing by using the end of the rear axle shaft for a puller by placing the outmost lip of the axle shaft against the oil seal inner lip and prying it downward.*

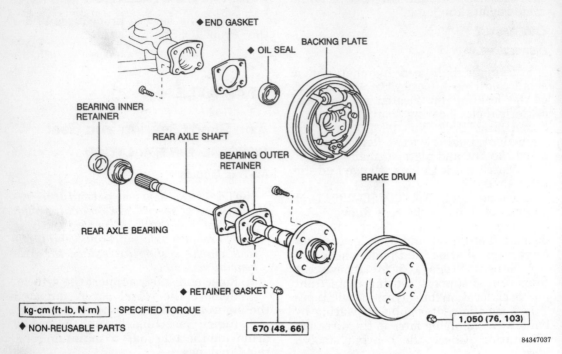

◆ END GASKET

◆ OIL SEAL

BACKING PLATE

BEARING INNER
RETAINER

REAR AXLE SHAFT

BEARING OUTER
RETAINER

BRAKE DRUM

REAR AXLE BEARING

◆ RETAINER GASKET

| kg-cm (ft-lb, N·m) | : SPECIFIED TORQUE
◆ NON-REUSABLE PARTS

670 (48, 66)

1,050 (76, 103)

84347037

Rear axle shaft components-4WD All-Trac Models

12. Install the oil seal in the axle housing housing. Drive the oil seal into the axle housing to a depth of 0.220 in. (5.6mm) using the proper tools.

13. Clean flange of the axle housing and backing plate. Apply sealer to the end gasket and retainer gasket as necessary.

14. Place end gasket onto end of axle housing with the notch of gasket facing downward. Align the notches of the 2 gaskets and bearing outer retainer with the oil hole of the backing plate.

15. Install the backing plate to the axle housing and all necessary components.

16. Install the retainer gasket on the axle shaft. Install the rear axle shaft with 4 NEW SELF-LOCKING NUTS torque to 48 ft. lbs. (66Nm).

17. Install all other necessary parts in reverse order of removal.

18. Bleed brake system, install wheel and roadtest for proper operation.

Differential Carrier

REMOVAL & INSTALLATION

All-Trac Models

1. Raise and safely support the vehicle. Remove drain plug and drain differential oil.

2. Remove the rear axle shafts as outlined in this Chapter.

3. Disconnect the propeller shaft or driveshaft (matchmark flange for correct installation) form the differential assembly.

4. Remove the differential carrier assembly retaining bolts. Remove the carrier assembly.

5. Installation is the reverse of the removal procedures. Torque the differential carrier retaining bolts to 23 ft. lbs. the driveshaft flange bolts 27 ft. lbs. Refill the unit with 1–1.2 qts. as necessary of API GL-5 gear oil and install drain plug.

Pinion Seal

REMOVAL & INSTALLATION

All-Trac Models

1. Matchmark the differential and driveshaft flanges.

2. Remove the four flange bolts, nuts and washers.

3. Disconnect the driveshaft from the differential.

4. With a hammer and a cold chisel, loosen the staked part of the locking nut.

5. Using SST No. 09330–00021 or equivalent to hold the flange, remove the locking nut.

6. Remove the plate washer.

7. Using SST No. 09557–22022 or equivalent, remove the companion flange.

8. Using SST No. 09308–10010 or equivalent seal puller, remove the front oil seal and then remove the oil slinger.

9. Using SST No. 09556–22010 or equivalent bearing puller, remove the front bearing.

10. Remove the front bearing spacer.

To install the front seal and bearing

11. Install a new bearing spacer and bearing onto the shaft.

12. Install the oil slinger onto the shaft.

13. Using SST No. 09554–22010 or equivalent, drive in the new oil seal to a depth of 0.157 in. (4mm).

14. Coat the lip of the new oil seal with multi-purpose grease.

15. Using the removal tool, install the companion flange.

16. Install the plate washer.

17. Coat the threads of the new nut with gear oil.

18. Using the removal tool to hold the flange, torque the companion flange to 80 ft. lbs.

19. Check and adjust the drive pinion preload as follows:

   a. Using a inch lb. torque wrench, measure the preload of the backlash between the drive pinion and the ring gear. Preload for a new bearing is 8.7–13.9 inch lbs. and 4.3–6.9 inch lbs. for a used bearing.

   b. If the preload is greater that the specified limit, replace the bearing spacer.

   c. If the preload is less than specification, re-torque the nut in 9 ft. lb. incre-

ments until the specified preload is reached. Do not exceed a maximum torque of 174 ft. lbs.

   d. If the maximum torque is exceeded, replace the bearing spacer and repeat the bearing preload procedure. Preload CANNOT be reduced by simply backing off on the pinion nut.

20. Stake the drive pinion nut.

21. Align the driveshaft and differential flange matchmarks.

22. Install the flange bolts and torque to 27 ft. lbs.

23. Remove the differential FILL plug and check the oil level. Fill the differential to the proper level (about 1.2 quarts) with new API GL-5 hypoid gear oil.

24. Install and tighten the fill plug with a new gasket if so equipped.

Axle Housing

REMOVAL & INSTALLATION

All-Trac Models

1. Raise and safely support the vehicle. Remove drain plug and drain differential oil.

2. Remove the rear axle shafts as outlined in this Chapter. Disconnect and reposition all lines or vacuum hoses that are necessary to remove the axle housing assembly from the vehicle.

3. Disconnect the propeller shaft or driveshaft (matchmark flange for correct installation) form the differential assembly.

4. Support the rear axle assembly with proper equipment. Disconnect the rear shock absorbers, upper and lower control arms, rear stabilizer bar.

5. Slowly lower the rear axle assembly, remove the rear coil springs. Remove the axle assembly from the vehicle.

6. Installation is the reverse of the removal procedure. Refill the unit (refill to the proper level) with 1–1.2 qts. as necessary of API GL-5 gear oil. Install the drain plug.

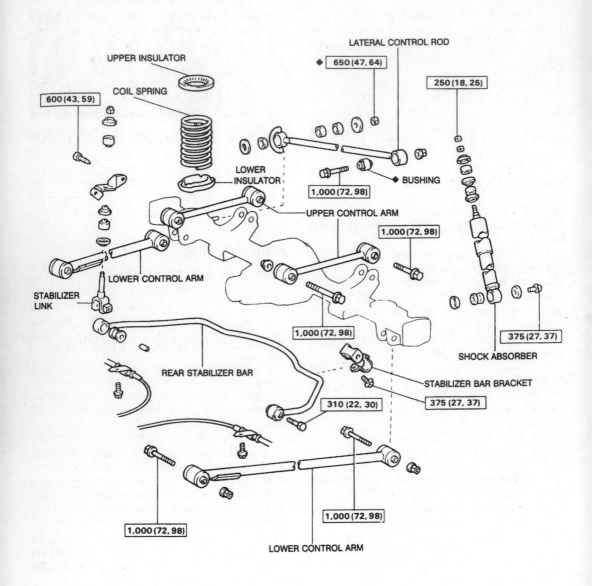

UPPER INSULATOR

LATERAL CONTROL ROD

◆ 650 (47, 64)

250 (18, 25)

COIL SPRING

600 (43, 59)

LOWER
INSULATOR

1,000 (72, 98)

◆ BUSHING

UPPER CONTROL ARM

1,000 (72, 98)

LOWER CONTROL ARM

STABILIZER
LINK

1,000 (72, 98)

375 (27, 37)

SHOCK ABSORBER

REAR STABILIZER BAR

STABILIZER BAR BRACKET

375 (27, 37)

310 (22, 30)

1,000 (72, 98)

1,000 (72, 98)

LOWER CONTROL ARM

kg-cm (ft-lb, N·m) : SPECIFIED TORQUE

◆ NON-REUSABLE PARTS

84347038

Rear axle housing-4WD All-Trac Models

FRONT SUSPENSION

Wheels

REMOVAL & INSTALLATION

1. If using a lug wrench, loosen the lug nuts before raising the vehicle.
2. Raise the vehicle and support safely.
3. Remove the lug nuts and wheel from the vehicle.
   To install:
4. Install the wheel and hand tighten the lug nuts until they are snug.

84348001

Inspection and cleaning of wheel

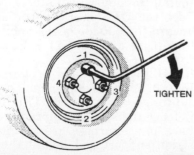

84348002

Wheel lug torque sequence

5. Lower the vehicle and torque the lug nuts EVENLY to 76 ft. lbs in a crisscross pattern.

INSPECTION

Before putting on wheels, check for any cracks on wheels or enlarged mounting holes, remove any corrosion on the mounting surfaces with a wire brush. Installation of wheels without a good metal-to-metal contact at the mounting surface can cause wheel nuts to loosen. Recheck the wheel nuts after 1,000 miles of driving.

Wheel Lug Studs

REPLACEMENT

Front Wheel

1. Raise and support the vehicle safely. Remove the front wheel.
2. Remove the front brake caliper and disc rotor.
3. Remove the hub bolt.
   To install:
4. Install the new hub bolt and draw into place using the nut and a stack of washers. The new hub bolt must be fully seated in the hub assembly.
5. Install front brake disc and front brake caliper. Torque the brake caliper to 65 ft. lbs.
6. Install front wheel and lower the vehicle.

McPherson Struts

REMOVAL & INSTALLATION

1. Raise and support the vehicle safely. Remove the front wheel.
2. Disconnect brake hose from the shock absorber.
3. Disconnect the ABS sensor wire from the shock absorber if so equipped.

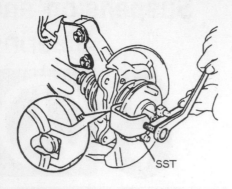

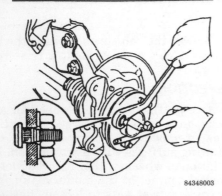

84348003

Hub bolt or lug bolt replacement

4. Remove the two bolt nuts and bolts and disconnect shock absorber from the steering knuckle.

5. Remove the three nuts on the upper side of the shock absorber. Remove the shock absorber with coil spring from the vehicle.

To install:

6. Install the shock absorber with coil spring to the vehicle. Install the three nuts and torque to 29 ft. lbs. (39 Nm).

7. Connect the shock absorber assembly to the steering knuckle. Install the two bolts (with bolt heads--to the rear of the vehicle) and torque the bolts 203 ft. lbs. (275 Nm).

8. Connect the ABS sensor wire to the shock absorber if so equipped.

9. Reconnect the brake hose to the shock absorber, torque the retaining bolt to 22 ft. lbs. (29 Nm).

10. Install front wheel and lower the vehicle. Check the front wheel alignment.

OVERHAUL

Disassembly

1. Remove the strut from the vehicle.

2. Position a bolt and two nuts between the bracket at the lower portion of the shock absorber shell and clamp shock absorber in a vise. The bolt acts as a spacer to allow for clamping without crushing the bracket.

3. Using SST No. 09727-22032 or a suitable spring compressor, compress the coil spring.

CAUTION: *Failure to fully compress the spring and hold it securely is extremely hazardous.*

4. Using SST No. 09727-22032 or suitable clamping device, hold the spring seat so that it will not turn and remove the center nut. Discard the nut.

5. Slowly release the coil spring tension.

6. Remove the suspension support, dust seal, spring seat, spring insulators, coil spring and bumper.

7. While pushing on the piston rod, make sure that the pull stroke is even and that there is no unusual noise or resistance.

8. Push the piston rod in and then release it. Make sure that the return rate is constant.

9. If the shock absorber does not operate as described, replace it.

If a shock absorber is replaced, the old one should be drilled at the center to vent the internal gas. Wear safety goggles and drill a small hole (2–3mm) into the base of the shock absorber (not through bracket). The gas within the strut is colorless, odorless and non-toxic, but should be vented to make the unit safe for disposal.

Assembly

1. Install the lower insulator.

2. Install the spring bumper onto the piston rod.

3. Compress the coil spring with the spring compressor.

4. Align the coil spring end with the lower seat hollow and install.

5. Install the upper insulator.

6. Face the **OUT** mark of the spring seat toward the outside of the vehicle.

7. Install the dust seal onto the spring seat.

8. Install the suspension support.

9. Install a new suspension support nut and torque to 34 ft. lbs. (47 (Nm).

10. Release the spring compressor.

11. Pack multi-purpose grease into the suspension support and install the dust cover.

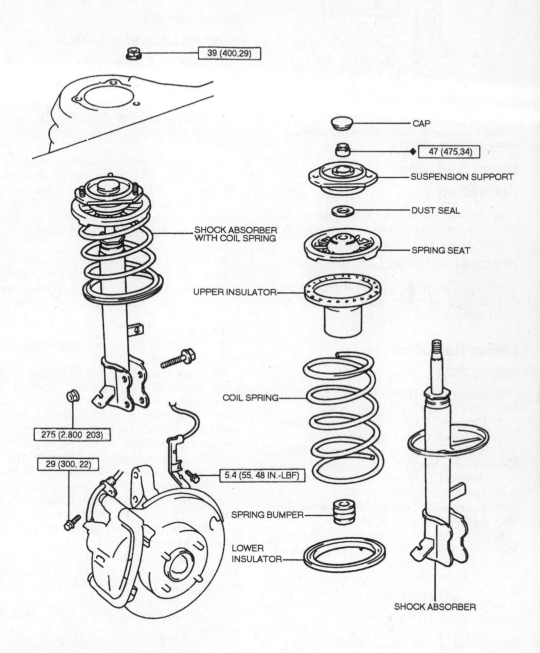

39 (400,29)

CAP

47 (475,34)

SUSPENSION SUPPORT

DUST SEAL

SHOCK ABSORBER
WITH COIL SPRING

SPRING SEAT

UPPER INSULATOR

COIL SPRING

275 (2,800 203)

29 (300, 22)

5.4 (55, 48 IN.-LBF)

SPRING BUMPER

LOWER
INSULATOR

SHOCK ABSORBER

N·m (kgf·cm, ft·lbf)   : SPECIFIED TORQUE

◆ NON-REUSABLE PART

84348004

Front shock absorber components

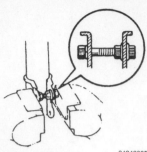

84348005

Install a bolt in the lower bracket to secure shock absorber in a vice

Upper Ball Joint

INSPECTION

All vehicles cover in this repair manual do not use an upper ball joint assembly as a front suspension component.

REMOVAL & INSTALLATION

All vehicles cover in this repair manual do not use a upper ball assembly as a front suspension component.

Lower Ball Joint

INSPECTION

1. Make the front wheels straight and jack up the front of the vehicle.
2. Place an 7.09–7.87 in. (180–200mm) wooden block under one front tire.
3. Slowly lower the jack until there is about half a load on the front coil spring.
4. Support the front of the vehicle with jackstands for safety.
5. Make sure that the front wheels are still straight and block them.
6. Move the lower suspension arm up and down and check that there is no vertical play in the joint.
7. If there is play in the joint, replace it.
8. Repeat the procedure for the other side.

REMOVAL & INSTALLATION

1. Remove the steering knuckle with axle hub and mount in a vise-refer to the necessary service procedures.
2. Remove the dust deflector.
3. Remove the cotter pin and nut. Using a puller remove the lower ball joint.
To install:
4. Install the lower ball joint and tighten the nut to 87 ft. lbs. (118 Nm).
5. Install a NEW cotter pin.

6. Install dust deflector. Install steering knuckle with axle hub.

Stabilizer Bar

REMOVAL & INSTALLATION

1. Raise and support the vehicle safely. Remove the front wheels.
2. Disconnect stabilizer links from stabilizer bar.
3. Disconnect the stabilizer bar brackets (note position of bushing) from the bolt.
4. Disconnect the exhaust system or center pipe (2WD vehicles) or driveshaft assembly (4WD vehicles) as necessary.
5. Remove the stabilizer bar from the vehicle. Examine the insulators (bushings) carefully for any sign of wear and replace them if necessary.
NOTE: *Check the bushings inside the brackets for wear or deformation. A worn bushing can cause a distinct noise as the bar twists during cornering operation.*
To install:
6. Install stabilizer bar bushings in the correct position.
7. Place the bar in position and reconnect the exhaust system. Install the driveshaft assembly if necessary.
8. Temporarily install stabilizer bar brackets. Install both stabilizer bar links torque link nuts to 33 ft. lbs. (44 Nm).
9. Stabilize suspension. Bounce the vehicle up and down several times to stabilize the suspension.
10. Jack up vehicle and support the body with stands. Remove the front wheels. Support the lower arm with a jack and block of wood.
11. Torque stabilizer bar bracket bolts and nuts--bolt A to 108 ft. lbs. (147 Nm), bolt B to 37 ft. lbs (50 (Nm) and torque nut C to 14 ft. lbs. (19 Nm).
12. Install front wheels and lower the vehicle.
13. Check front wheel alignment.

Lower Control Arm

REMOVAL & INSTALLATION

1. Raise and safely support the vehicle. Remove the front wheels. Do not place the stands under the control arms or the suspension crossmember. Refer to exploded view of front suspension components.

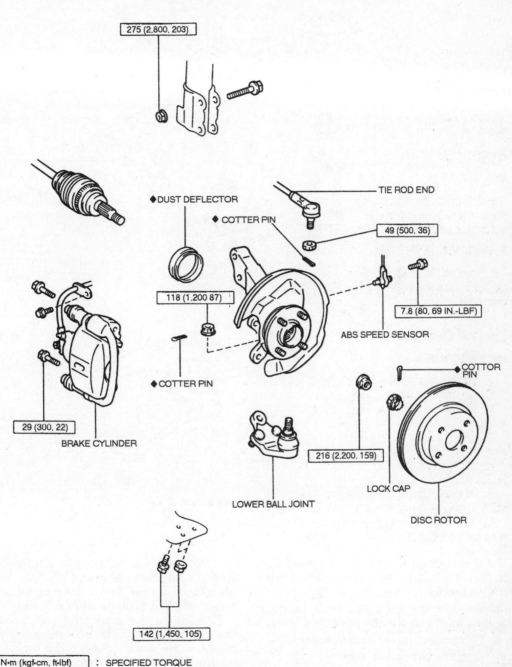

275 (2,800, 203)

◆ DUST DEFLECTOR

TIE ROD END

◆ COTTER PIN

49 (500, 36)

118 (1,200 87)

7.8 (80, 69 IN.-LBF)

ABS SPEED SENSOR

◆ COTTER PIN

29 (300, 22)

BRAKE CYLINDER

LOWER BALL JOINT

216 (2,200, 159)

◆ COTTER PIN

LOCK CAP

DISC ROTOR

142 (1,450, 105)

N•m (kgf•cm, ft•lbf) : SPECIFIED TORQUE

◆ NON-REUSABLE PART

84348006

Lower ball joint components

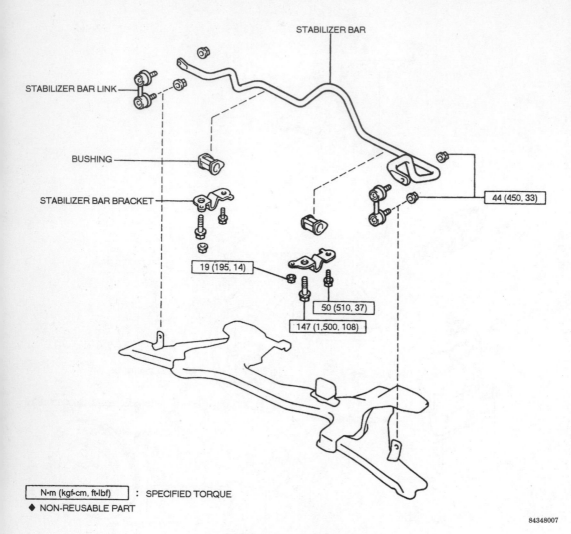

STABILIZER BAR

STABILIZER BAR LINK

BUSHING

STABILIZER BAR BRACKET

44 (450, 33)

19 (195, 14)

50 (510, 37)

147 (1,500, 108)

N·m (kgf·cm, ft·lbf) : SPECIFIED TORQUE

◆ NON-REUSABLE PART

84348007

Stabilizer bar components

2. If equipped with stabilizer bar, disconnect stabilizer bar link from lower arm assembly.

3. Remove the nuts and bolts holding the ball joints to the lower control arms.

4. Disconnect lower arm brackets.

5. Remove the lower arm.

6. On automatic transaxle left side with stabilizer bar, remove the center of exhaust system. Remove the stabilizer bar.

7. Place a floor jack under the suspension crossmember. Use a broad piece of wood between the jack and crossmember to evenly distribute the loading.

8. Remove the bolts/nuts holding the suspension crossmember. Carefully lower the crossmember (with the control arms attached) and remove from the car.

9. Remove the mounting bolt holding the control arm to the crossmember and remove the arm. Inspect the arm and bushing for damage, deformation or corrosion damage.

To install:

10. Install lower arm bracket-temporarily install the nut.

11. Temporarily install control arm.

12. On automatic transaxle left side with stabilizer bar, install lower arm to suspension member-temporarily install

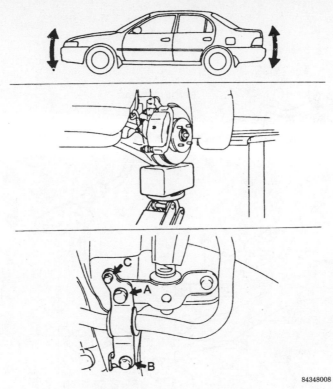

84348008

Stabilize suspension procedure

the bolt. Jack up the suspension cross-member-temporarily install the six bolt torque to 152 ft. lbs. (206 Nm) and nuts 45 ft. lbs. (61 Nm). Install stabilizer bar and exhaust system.

13. Temporarily install lower arm bracket.

14. Connect lower arm to lower ball joint torque bolt and nuts to 105 ft. lbs (142 Nm).

15. If equipped with stabilizer bar, connect stabilizer bar link to lower arm assembly. Torque link nut to 33 ft. lbs. (44 Nm).

16. Install front wheels. Stabilize suspension. Lower the vehicle to the ground. Bounce the front end up and down several times to stabilize the suspension.

17. Jack up vehicle and support the body with stands. Remove the front wheels. Support the lower arm with a jack and block of wood.

18. Torque bolt A to 108 ft. lbs. (147 Nm), bolt B to 37 ft. lbs (50 (Nm) and torque nut C to 14 ft. lbs. (19 Nm). Torque lower arm to bracket main retaining nut to 101 ft. lbs. (137 Nm). Torque lower arm to crossmember bolt to 161 ft. lbs (218 Nm).

19. Install front wheels and lower the vehicle.

20. Check front wheel alignment.

CONTROL ARM BUSING REPLACEMENT

If lower control arm bushings are worn or damaged replace the complete assembly.

Steering Knuckle, Hub And Bearing

REMOVAL & INSTALLATION

1. Loosen the wheel nuts and the center axle nut.

2. Raise the vehicle and safely support it.

3. Remove the wheel. Remove the ABS speed sensor if so equipped.

4. Remove the center axle nut.

5. Remove the brake caliper and hang it out of the way on a piece of stiff wire. Do not disconnect the brake line; do not allow the caliper to hang by the hose.

6. Remove the brake disc.

7. Remove the cotter pin and nut from the tie rod end.

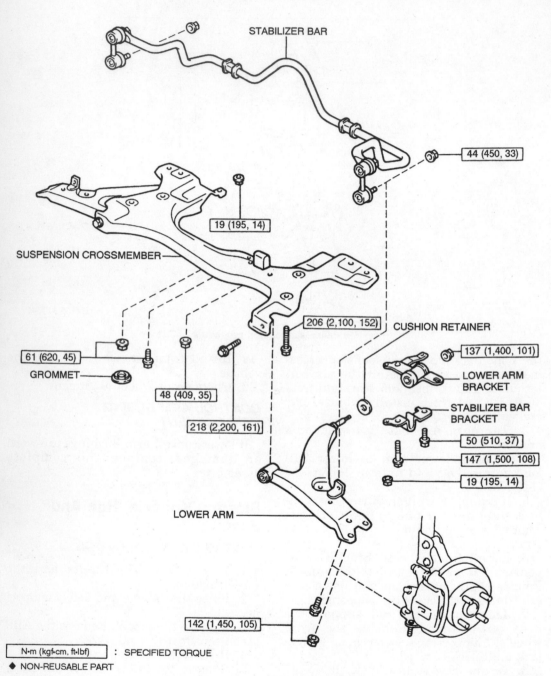

STABILIZER BAR

44 (450, 33)

19 (195, 14)

SUSPENSION CROSSMEMBER

206 (2,100, 152)

CUSHION RETAINER

137 (1,400, 101)

61 (620, 45)

LOWER ARM
BRACKET

GROMMET

STABILIZER BAR
BRACKET

48 (409, 35)

50 (510, 37)

147 (1,500, 108)

218 (2,200, 161)

19 (195, 14)

LOWER ARM

142 (1,450, 105)

N·m (kgf·cm, ft·lbf) : SPECIFIED TORQUE

◆ NON-REUSABLE PART

84348009

Lower suspension arm

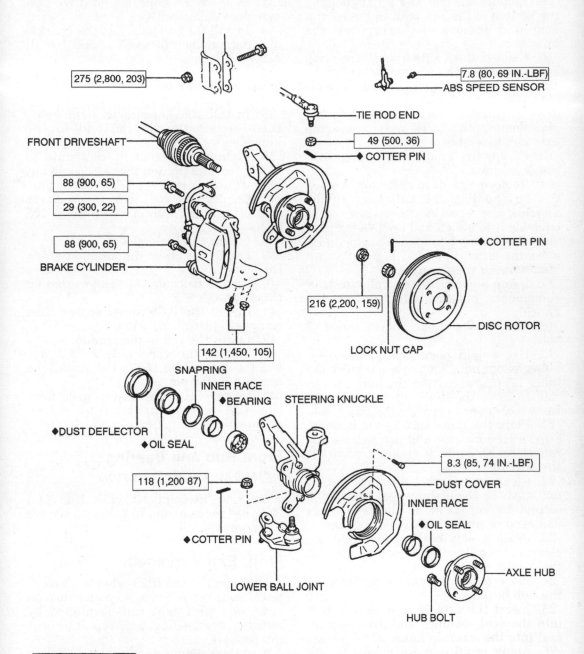

275 (2,800, 203)

7.8 (80, 69 IN.-LBF)
ABS SPEED SENSOR

TIE ROD END

FRONT DRIVESHAFT

49 (500, 36)
◆ COTTER PIN

88 (900, 65)

29 (300, 22)

88 (900, 65)

◆ COTTER PIN

BRAKE CYLINDER

216 (2,200, 159)

DISC ROTOR

LOCK NUT CAP

142 (1,450, 105)

SNAPRING

INNER RACE

◆ BEARING

STEERING KNUCKLE

◆ DUST DEFLECTOR

◆ OIL SEAL

8.3 (85, 74 IN.-LBF)

DUST COVER

INNER RACE

118 (1,200 87)

◆ OIL SEAL

◆ COTTER PIN

AXLE HUB

LOWER BALL JOINT

HUB BOLT

N·m (kgf·cm, ft·lbf) : SPECIFIED TORQUE

◆ NON-REUSABLE PART

84348010

Front axle hub components

8. Remove the tie rod end from the knuckle using a joint separator or equivalent.

9. Remove the bolt and 2 nuts holding the bottom of the ball joint to the control arm and remove the arm from the knuckle.

10. Remove the 2 nuts from the steering knuckle. Place a protective cover or shield over the CV boot on the driveshaft.

11. Using a plastic mallet, tap the driveshaft free of the hub assembly.

12. Remove the bolts and remove the axle hub assembly.

13. Clamp the knuckle in a vise with protected jaws.

14. Remove the dust deflector. Loosen the nut holding the ball joint to the knuckle. Use a ball joint separator tool or equivalent to loosen and remove the joint.

15. Use a slide hammer/extractor to remove the outer oil seal.

16. Remove the snapring.

17. Using a hub puller and pilot tools or equivalents, pull the axle hub from the knuckle.

18. Remove the brake splash shield (3 bolts).

19. Use a split plate bearing remover, puller pilot and a shop press, remove the inner bearing race from the hub.

20. Remove the inner oil seal with the same tools used to remove the outer seal.

21. Place the inner race in the bearing. Support the knuckle and use an axle hub remover with a plastic mallet to drive out the bearing.

22. Clean and inspect all parts but do not wash or clean the wheel bearing; it cannot be repacked. If the bearing is damaged or noisy, it must be replaced.

23. Press a new bearing race into the steering knuckle using a bearing driver of the correct size.

24. Place a new bearing inner race on the hub bearing.

25. Insert the side lip of a new oil seal into the seal installer and drive the oil seal into the steering knuckle.

26. Apply multi-purpose grease to the oil seal lip.

27. Apply sealer to the brake splash shield and install the shield.

28. Use a hub installer to press the hub into the steering knuckle.

29. Install a new snapring into the hub.

30. Using a seal installer of the correct size, install a new outer oil seal into the steering knuckle.

31. Apply multi-purpose grease to the seal surfaces which will contact the driveshaft.

32. Support the knuckle and drive in a new dust deflector.

33. Install the ball joint into the knuckle and tighten the nut to 87 ft. lbs. Install NEW cotter pin.

34. Temporarily install the hub assembly to the lower control arm and fit the driveaxle into the hub.

35. Install the knuckle to strut bolts, then install the tie rod end to the knuckle.

36. Tighten the strut bracket nuts to 203 ft. lbs. and tighten the tie rod end nut to 36 ft. lbs. Install the NEW cotter pin.

37. Connect the ball joint to the lower control arm and tighten the nuts to 105 ft. lbs.

38. Install the brake disc.

39. Install the brake caliper and tighten the bolts.

40. Install the center nut and washer on the drive axle.

41. Install the ABS speed sensor if so equipped. Install the wheel

42. Lower the car to the ground.

43. Tighten the wheel nuts to 76 ft. lbs. and the axle bolt to 159 ft. lbs. Install the cap and cotter pin.

44. Remove the protective cover from the CV boot. Check front wheel alignment.

Front Hub and Bearing

REMOVAL & INSTALLATION

Refer to "Steering Knuckle, Hub And Bearing" removal and installation service procedures.

Front End Alignment

Alignment of the front wheels is essential if your car is to go, stop and turn as designed. Alignment can be altered by collision, overloading, poor repair or bent components.

If you are diagnosing bizarre handling and/or poor road manners, the first place to look is the tires. Although the tires may wear as a result of an alignment problem, worn or poorly inflated tires can make you chase alignment problems which don't exist.

Once you have eliminated all other causes (always check and repair front end parts BEFORE wheel alignment), unload everything from the trunk except the spare tire, set the tire pressures to the correct level and take the car to a reputable alignment facility. Since the alignment settings are measured in very small increments, it is almost impossible for the home mechanic to accurately determine the settings. The explanations that follow will help you understand the three dimensions of alignment: caster, camber and toe.

CASTER

Caster is the tilting of the steering axis either forward or backward from the vertical, when viewed from the side of the vehicle. A backward tilt is said to be positive and a forward tilt is said to be negative.

CAMBER

Camber is the tilting of the wheels from the vertical (leaning in or out) when viewed from the front of the vehicle. When the wheels tilt outward at the top, the camber is said to be positive. When the wheels tilt inward at the top the camber is said to be negative. The amount of tilt is measured in degrees from the vertical. This measurement is called camber angle.

TOE

Toe is the turning in or out (parallelism) of the wheels. The actual amount of toe setting is normally only a fraction of an inch. The purpose of toe-in (or out) specification is to ensure parallel rolling of the wheels. Toe-in also serves to offset the small deflections of the steering support system which occur when the vehicle is rolling forward or under braking.

Changing the toe setting will radically affect the overall "feel" of the steering, the behavior of the car under braking, tire wear and even fuel economy. Exces-

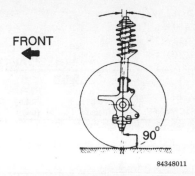

FRONT

84348011

Caster angle affects the tracking of the steering

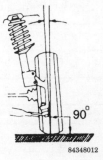

84348012

Camber is the inward or outward tilt of the wheel on the road

sive toe (in or out) causes excessive drag or scrubbing on the tires.

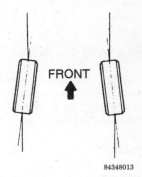

FRONT

84348013

Toe can affect tire wear and fuel economy

WHEEL ALIGNMENT SPECIFICATIONS

Year	Model	Caster		Camber		Toe-in (in.)	Steering Axis Inclination (deg.)
		Range (deg.)	Preferred Setting (deg.)	Range (deg.)	Preferred Setting (deg.)		
1990	Corolla (2WD)	$^9/_{16}$P–$2^1/_{16}$P	$1^5/_{16}$P	1N–$^1/_2$P	$^1/_4$N	0–$^5/_{32}$	$12^{13}/_{16}$
	Corolla (4WD)	$^3/_4$P–$1^3/_4$P	$1^1/_4$P	$^5/_{16}$N–$^{11}/_{16}$P	$^3/_{16}$P	0–$^5/_{32}$	12
1991	Corolla (2WD)	$^9/_{16}$P–$2^1/_{16}$P	$1^5/_{16}$P	1N–$^1/_2$P	$^1/_4$N	0–$^5/_{64}$	$12^5/_8$
	Corolla (4WD)	$^3/_4$P–$1^3/_4$P	$1^1/_4$P	$^5/_{16}$N–$^{11}/_{16}$P	$^3/_{16}$P	0–$^5/_{64}$	12
1992	Corolla (2WD)	$^2/_3$P–$2^1/_6$P	$1^5/_{12}$P	$^{11}/_{12}$N–$^7/_{12}$P	$^1/_6$N	0.04 out–0.12 in	$12^2/_3 \pm ^3/_4$
	Corolla (4WD)	$^3/_4$P–2P	$1^1/_4$P	$^1/_3$N–$^2/_3$P	$^1/_6$P	0.04 out–0.12 in	$12^1/_{12} \pm ^1/_2$
1993	Corolla (2WD)	$^2/_3$P–$2^1/_6$P	$1^5/_{12}$P	$^{11}/_{12}$N–$^7/_{12}$P	$^1/_6$N	0.04 out–0.12 in	$12^2/_3 \pm ^3/_4$

NOTE: Camber, caster and steering axis inclination are not adjustable. If measurements are not within specification, inspect the suspension parts for damaged and/or worn out parts and replace them as necessary.
N—Negative
P—Positive

84348014

REAR SUSPENSION

Wheels

REMOVAL & INSTALLATION

1. If using a lug wrench, loosen the lug nuts before raising the vehicle.
2. Raise the vehicle and support safely.
3. Remove the lug nuts and wheel from the vehicle.
To install:
4. Install the wheel and hand tighten the lug nuts until they are snug.
5. Lower the vehicle and torque the lug nuts EVENLY to 76 ft. lbs in a crisscross pattern.

INSPECTION

Before putting on wheels, check for any cracks on wheels or enlarged mounting holes, remove any corrosion on the mounting surfaces with a wire brush. Installation of wheels without a good metal-to-metal contact at the mounting surface can cause wheel nuts to loosen. Recheck the wheel nuts after 1,000 miles of driving.

Wheel Lug Studs

REPLACEMENT

Drum Brakes

1. Raise the vehicle and support safely.
2. Remove the wheel.
3. Remove the brake drum from the vehicle.
4. Drive the lug bolt out of the axle hub.
To install:
5. Draw the lug bolt into the axle hub using the nut and a stack of washers.
6. Install the brake drum onto the vehicle.
7. Install the wheel and lower the vehicle.

Rear Disc Brakes

1. Raise the vehicle and support safely.
2. Remove the rear wheel.
3. Remove the rear caliper and brake rotor.
4. Remove the wheel lug bolt by tapping bolt through hub with a hammer.
To install:
5. Draw the new lug bolt into the hub using the nut and a stack of washers.

6. Install the brake rotor. Install rear brake caliper and torque to 25 ft. lbs. (14 Nm).

7. Install the rear wheel and lower the vehicle.

Coil Springs

REMOVAL & INSTALLATION

4WD Models

1. Remove the hubcap and loosen the lug nuts.

2. Jack up the rear axle housing and support the frame (not rear axle housing) with jackstands. Leave the jack in place under the rear axle housing.

CAUTION: *Support the car securely. Remember; you will be working underneath it.*

3. Remove the lug nuts and wheel.

4. Unfasten the lower shock absorber end.

5. Remove stabilizer bar bracket bolts.

6. Remove lateral control rod--disconnect the rod from the rear axle housing.

7. Slowly lower the jack under the rear axle housing until the axle is at the bottom of its travel.

8. Withdraw the coil spring, complete with its insulator.

9. Inspect the coil spring and insulator for wear and cracks, or weakness; replace either or both as necessary.

10. Installation is performed in the reverse order of removal procedure (install the lower insulator or spring seat in the correct position). Tighten shock absorber mounting nut to 27 ft. lbs. When reconnecting the lateral control rod, tighten the bolt finger tight. When the car is lowered, bounce it a few times to stabilize the rear suspension. Raise the rear axle housing until the body is free and then tighten the nut to 47 ft. lbs.

84348015

Make sure that the spring is installed correctly in the lower insulator (spring seat)

Lateral Control Rod Upper And Lower Control Arms

REMOVAL & INSTALLATION

4WD Models

1. Raise the rear of the vehicle and support the axle housing with jackstands.

2. Disconnect the lateral rod or arm from the rear axle housing.

3. Disconnect the lateral rod or from the body and remove the rod.

4. Install the arm-to-body nut and finger tighten it.

5. Position the rod or arm on the axle housing and install a washer, bushing, spacer, the arm, bushing, washer and then the nut. Finger tighten the nut.

6. Lower the vehicle and bounce it a few times to stabilize the suspension.

7. Raise the rear of the vehicle again then tighten the lateral control rod-to-body nut to 72 ft. lbs. and the control rod-to-axle housing nut to 47 ft. lbs. Torque upper and lower control arms to 72 ft. lbs.

Rear Stabilizer Bar

REMOVAL & INSTALLATION

4WD Models

1. Remove all necessary components to gain access for removal and installation of stabilizer bar. Remove the stabilizer bar brackets.

2. Remove the nuts, cushions and links holding both sides of the stabilizer bar from the suspension arms. Remove the stabilizer bar.

3. To install assemble the stabilizer link sub-assembly and install the link to the arm.

4. Install the stabilizer bar to the link.

5. Install the stabilizer bar bracket to the differential support member-torque to 27 ft. lbs.

6. Install all necessary components that were removed for removal access of stabilizer bar.

Shock Absorbers

TESTING

4WD Models

Shock absorbers require replacement if the car fails to recover quickly after hitting a large bump or if it sways excessively following a directional change.

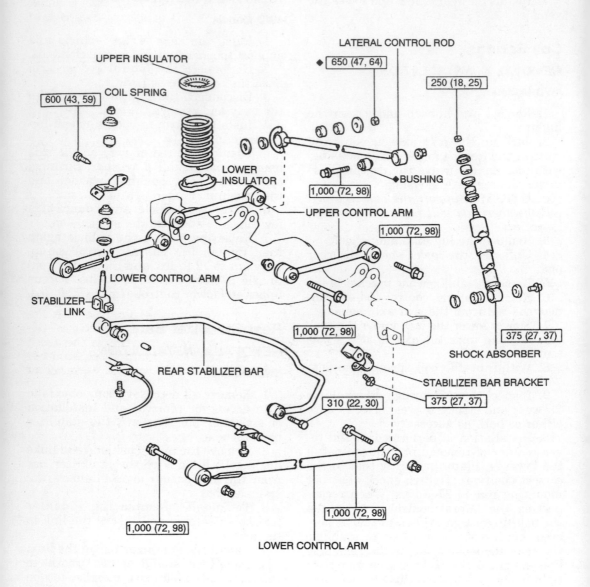

LATERAL CONTROL ROD

◆ 650 (47, 64)

250 (18, 25)

UPPER INSULATOR

COIL SPRING

600 (43, 59)

LOWER
INSULATOR

1,000 (72, 98)

◆BUSHING

UPPER CONTROL ARM

1,000 (72, 98)

LOWER CONTROL ARM

STABILIZER
LINK

1,000 (72, 98)

375 (27, 37)

SHOCK ABSORBER

REAR STABILIZER BAR

STABILIZER BAR BRACKET

310 (22, 30)

375 (27, 37)

1,000 (72, 98)

1,000 (72, 98)

LOWER CONTROL ARM

kg·cm (ft-lb, N·m)   : SPECIFIED TORQUE
◆ NON-REUSABLE PART

84348016

Rear suspension — 4WD models

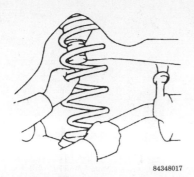

Removing the coil spring

A good way to test the shock absorbers is to intermittently apply downward pressure to the side of the car until it is moving up and down for almost its full suspension travel. Release it and observe its recovery. If the car bounces once or twice after having been released and then comes to a rest, the shocks are all right. If the car continues to bounce, the shocks will probably require replacement.

NOTE: *On McPherson strut shock absorbers and conventional rear shock absorbers if oil is leaking from the cylinder portion of the assembly the shock absorber must be replaced.*

REMOVAL & INSTALLATION

4WD Models-Conventional Rear Shock Absorber

1. Raise the rear of the car and support the rear axle with jackstands.
2. Unfasten the upper shock absorber retaining nuts. Use a tool to keep the shaft from spinning.
NOTE: *Always remove and install the shock absorbers one at a time. Do not allow the rear axle to hang.*
3. Remove the lower shock retaining nut where it attaches to the rear axle housing.
4. Remove the shock absorber.
5. Inspect the shock for wear, leaks or other signs of damage.
6. Installation is in the reverse order of removal procedure. Make sure when you are installing the rear shock absorbers that rubber bushings (cushions) and washers (retainers) are installed in the correct position. Tighten the upper shock mounting retaining nut to 18 ft. lbs. Tighten the lower shock mounting retaining nut to 37 ft. lbs.

McPherson Struts (2WD Models)

REMOVAL

1. Remove the seat back side cushion or the rear sill side panel to gain access to the upper strut mount.
2. Raise the rear of the vehicle and support it with jackstands (do not place stands under suspension arms). Remove the wheel.
3. Disconnect the brake hose from the shock absorber. Disconnect the ABS wire harnesses if so equipped.
4. Disconnect the stabilizer bar link from the strut assembly as necessary. Remove the 2 lower bolts holding the strut to the axle carriage.
5. Remove the 3 upper strut mounting nuts and carefully remove the strut assembly.
WARNING: *Do not loosen the center nut on the top of the shock absorber piston.*

DISASSEMBLY

1. Place the strut assembly in vise. Position a bolt and two nuts between the bracket at the lower portion of the shock absorber shell and clamp shock absorber in a vise. The bolt acts as a spacer to

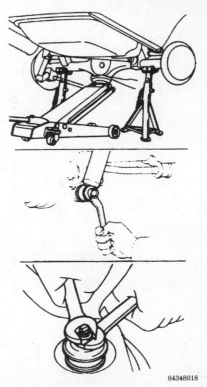

Removing rear shock absorber

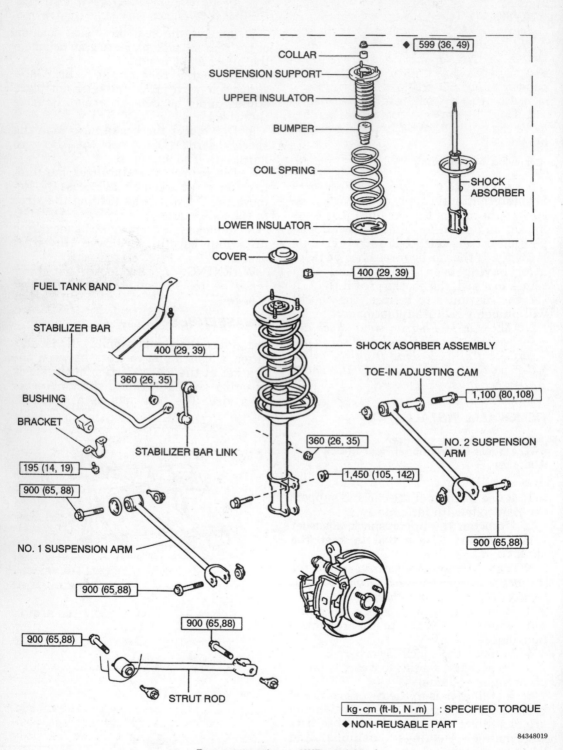

COLLAR — ◆ 599 (36, 49)

SUSPENSION SUPPORT

UPPER INSULATOR

BUMPER

COIL SPRING

SHOCK ABSORBER

LOWER INSULATOR

COVER — 400 (29, 39)

FUEL TANK BAND

STABILIZER BAR — 400 (29, 39)

360 (26, 35)

BUSHING

BRACKET

195 (14, 19)

900 (65, 88)

STABILIZER BAR LINK

SHOCK ASORBER ASSEMBLY

TOE-IN ADJUSTING CAM — 1,100 (80,108)

NO. 2 SUSPENSION ARM

360 (26, 35)

1,450 (105, 142)

900 (65,88)

NO. 1 SUSPENSION ARM

900 (65,88)

900 (65,88)

900 (65,88)

STRUT ROD

kg·cm (ft-lb, N·m) : SPECIFIED TORQUE
◆ NON-REUSABLE PART

84348019

Rear suspension — 2WD models

allow for clamping without crushing the bracket.

NOTE: *Do not attempt to clamp the strut assembly in a flat jaw vise as this will result in damage to the strut tube.*

2. Attach a spring compressor and compress the spring until the upper suspension support is free of any spring tension. Do not over-compress the spring.

3. Hold the upper support and then remove the nut on the end of the shock piston rod.

4. Remove the support, coil spring, insulator and bumper.

INSPECTION

Check the shock absorber by moving the piston shaft through its full range of travel. It should move smoothly and evenly throughout its entire travel without any trace of binding or notching. Use a small straightedge to check the piston shaft for any bending or deformation. If a shock absorber is replaced, the old one should be drilled at the center to vent the internal gas. Wear safety goggles and drill a small hole (2–3mm) into the center of the shock absorber. The gas within the strut is colorless, odorless and non-toxic, but should be vented to make the unit safe for disposal.

ASSEMBLY AND INSTALLATION

1. Loosely assemble all components onto the the strut assembly. Make sure the spring end aligns with the hollow in the lower seat.

2. Align the upper suspension support with the piston rod and install the support.

3. Align the suspension support with the strut lower bracket. This assures the spring will be properly seated top and bottom.

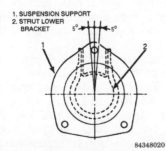

1. SUSPENSION SUPPORT
2. STRUT LOWER BRACKET

84348020

Correct position of upper and lower mounts when reassembling rear strut assembly — 2WD models

4. Compress the spring slightly by pushing on the suspension support with one hand to expose the strut piston rod threads.

5. Install a new strut piston nut and tighten it to 36 ft. lbs.

6. Place the complete strut assembly into the lower mount and mount it in position with the bolts.

7. Use a floor jack to gently raise the suspension and guide the upper strut mount into position.

CAUTION: *The car is on jackstands. Elevate the floor jack only enough to swing the strut into position; do not raise the car.*

8. Tighten the lower strut retaining nuts and bolts to 105 ft. lbs.

9. Tighten the 3 upper retaining bolts to 29 ft. lbs.

10. Reconnect the stabilizer bar link to the strut assembly as necessary.

11. Reconnect the brake hose to the shock absorber. Connect the ABS wire harnesses if so equipped.

12. Install the wheel. Lower the vehicle to the ground.

13. Reinstall the interior components as necessary.

Control Arms

REMOVAL

1990–92 2WD Models

These vehicles use two control arms on each rear wheel. To avoid the obvious confusion they are referred to as No. 1 and No. 2, with arm No.1 being the closest to the front of the car.

No. 1 ARM

1. Raise and safely support the vehicle.

2. Disconnect the sway bar link if so equipped.

3. Remove the bolt holding the arm to the body.

4. Remove the bolt holding the arm to the suspension knuckle.

5. Remove the arm.

No. 2 ARM

1. Raise and safely support the vehicle.

2. Observe and matchmark the position of the adjusting cam at the body mount.

3. Disconnect the bolt holding the arm to the suspension knuckle.

4. Disconnect the bolt holding the arm to the body.

5. Remove the arm.

6. Inspect the arms for any bending or cracking. If the arm is not true in all dimensions, it must be replaced. Any attempt to straighten a bent arm will damage it. Also check the bushings within the ends of the arms and replace any which are deformed or too spongy. If a bushing must be replaced, do not grease it before installation.

INSTALLATION

1. Place the arm in position, install the arm to body bolts and partially tighten them. If installing arm No. 2, make sure the matchmarks for the adjusting cam are aligned.

2. Install the arm to the knuckle and partially tighten the bolts.

3. Reconnect the stabilizer bar link if it was removed. Use a new nut and tighten it to 26 ft. lbs.

4. Lower the car to the ground. Bounce the car rear and front several times to position the suspension.

5. Tighten the retaining bolts at the body and the knuckle to 65 ft. lbs. and No. 2 arm toe-in adjusting cam bolt and nut to 80 ft. lbs.

6. Check rear wheel alignment.

Lower Suspension Arm and Strut Rod

REMOVAL & INSTALLATION

1993 2WD Models

1. Jack up vehicle and remove the rear wheel.

2. Remove the strut r

3. Remove the No. 2 suspension arm.

4. Remove the exhaust system.

5. Remove the No. 1 suspension arm and lower suspension member.

6. Installation is the reverse of the removal procedure. Torque suspension member to body to 55 ft. lbs. Lower the car to the ground. Bounce the car rear and front several times to position the suspension. Tighten the retaining bolts at the body and the knuckle to 87 ft. lbs. and strut rod retaining bolts to 67 ft. lbs.

7. Check rear wheel alignment--after rear alignment tighten lock nuts on No. 2 suspension arm.

Rear Stabilizer Bar

REMOVAL & INSTALLATION

2WD Models

1. Jack up vehicle and remove the rear wheel.

2. Remove the left and right stabilizer bar bushing brackets.

3. Remove the exhaust system. Remove the right fuel tank band only.

4. If so equipped, remove the lower suspension member (1993 models only). Remove the rear stabilizer bar.

5. Installation is the reverse of the removal procedure. Torque suspension member to body to 55 ft. lbs. Torque left and right stabilizer bar bushing brackets to 14 ft. lbs. and bar links to 33 ft. lbs.

Rear Axle Hub, Carrier And Bearing

REMOVAL & INSTALLATION

2WD Models

1. Raise and safely support the vehicle.

2. Remove the brake drum or disc rotor. Disconnect the hydraulic brake line.

3. Remove the 4 axle hub and carrier mounting bolts. Remove the axle hub and brake assembly.

NOTE: *The bearing assembly can be replaced by removing staked nut, bearing races, seal and pressing bearing in and out. Torque the bearing assembly retaining nut to 90 ft. lbs. then stake nut.*

4. At this point of the service remove the rear axle carrier by following this procedure:

   a. Remove the strut rod mounting bolt from the axle carrier.

   b. Remove all rear suspension arm mounting bolts from the axle carrier.

   c. Remove the 2 axle carrier mounting bolts from the shock absorber. Remove the rear axle carrier assembly from vehicle.

5. Installation is the reverse of the removal procedure. Install new O-ring in axle carrier. Torque the rear axle carrier to shock absorber to 105 ft. lbs. and the 4 axle hub retaining bolts to 59 ft. lbs.

6. Bounce the car rear and front several times to position the suspension. torque strut rod to axle carrier to 65 ft. lbs. and No. 1 and No. 2 arm to axle carrier to 65 ft. lbs. Check rear wheel alignment.

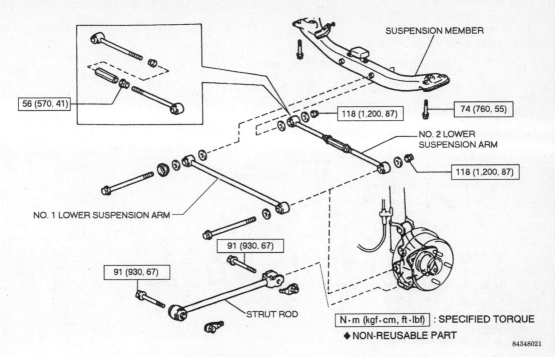

56 (570, 41)

118 (1,200, 87)

SUSPENSION MEMBER

74 (760, 55)

NO. 2 LOWER
SUSPENSION ARM

118 (1,200, 87)

NO. 1 LOWER SUSPENSION ARM

91 (930, 67)

91 (930, 67)

STRUT ROD

N·m (kgf·cm, ft·lbf) : SPECIFIED TORQUE
◆ NON-REUSABLE PART

84348021

Lower suspension arm and strut rod — 1993 models

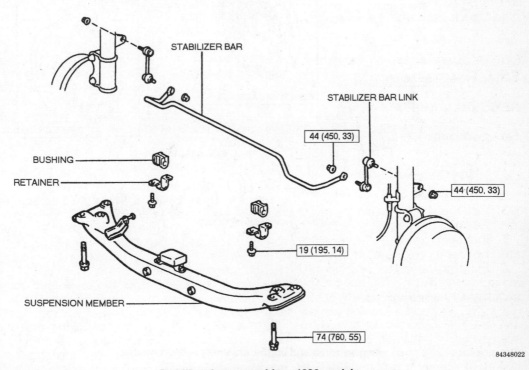

STABILIZER BAR

STABILIZER BAR LINK

44 (450, 33)

BUSHING

RETAINER

44 (450, 33)

19 (195, 14)

SUSPENSION MEMBER

74 (760, 55)

84348022

Stabilizer bar assembly — 1993 models

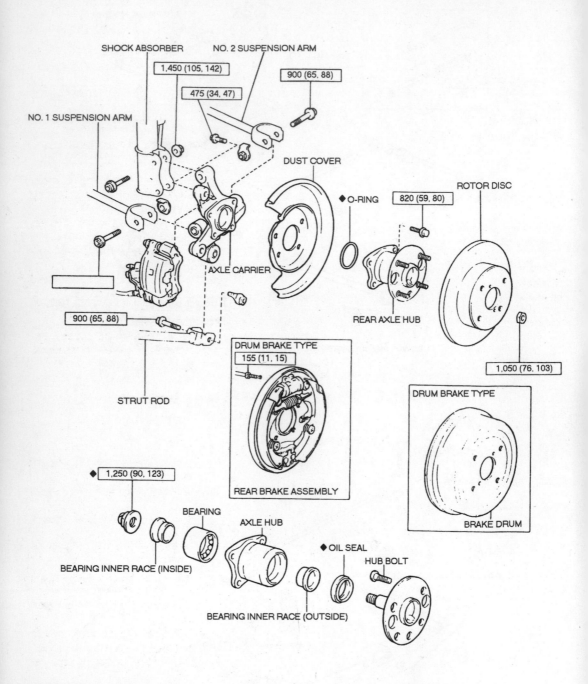

SHOCK ABSORBER

NO. 2 SUSPENSION ARM

1,450 (105, 142)

475 (34, 47)

900 (65, 88)

NO. 1 SUSPENSION ARM

DUST COVER

◆ O-RING

820 (59, 80)

ROTOR DISC

AXLE CARRIER

REAR AXLE HUB

900 (65, 88)

DRUM BRAKE TYPE

155 (11, 15)

1,050 (76, 103)

DRUM BRAKE TYPE

STRUT ROD

REAR BRAKE ASSEMBLY

BRAKE DRUM

◆ 1,250 (90, 123)

BEARING

AXLE HUB

◆ OIL SEAL

HUB BOLT

BEARING INNER RACE (INSIDE)

BEARING INNER RACE (OUTSIDE)

kg·cm (ft-lb, N·m) : SPECIFIED TORQUE

◆NON-REUSABLE PART

84348023

Rear axle hub and carrier assembly — 2WD models

Rear Wheel Alignment

The proper alignment of the rear wheels is as important as the alignment of the front wheels and should be checked periodically. If the rear wheels are misaligned the car will exhibit unpredictable handling characteristics. This behavior is particularly hazardous on slick surfaces; the back wheels of the car may attempt to go in directions unrelated to the front during braking or turning maneuvers.

NOTE: *Rear wheel alignment (toe-in adjustment) is only necessary on 2WD models. Camber is not adjustable-if not within specifications replace the suspension parts as necessary.*

DISARMING THE AIR BAG SYSTEM

On models with an airbag, wait at least 90 seconds from the time that the ignition switch is turned to the LOCK position and the battery is disconnected before performing any further work.

STEERING

Steering Wheel

REMOVAL & INSTALLATION

NOTE: *Do not attempt to remove or install the steering wheel by hammering on it. Damage to the energy-absorbing steering column could result.*

1. Disconnect the negative battery cable.

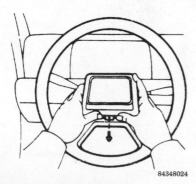

84348024

Removing the steering wheel pad

84348025

Use a steering wheel puller to remove the steering wheel

2. Loosen the trim pad retaining screws from the back side of the steering wheel.

3. Lift the trim pad and horn button assembly from the wheel.

4. Remove the steering wheel hub retaining nut and washer.

5. Scratch matchmarks on the hub and shaft to aid in correct installation.

6. Use a steering wheel puller to remove the steering wheel.

7. Installation is performed in the reverse order of removal. Tighten the wheel retaining nut to 25 ft. lbs.

Combination Switch

REMOVAL & INSTALLATION

Without Airbag System

1. Disconnect the negative battery cable.

2. Remove the lower dash cover and the air duct.

3. Remove the upper and lower steering column covers.

4. Remove the steering wheel. Refer to the necessary service procedure.

5. Disconnect the wiring at the connector.

6. Unscrew the mounting screws and remove the switch.

7. When reinstalling, place the switch in correct position and tighten the bolts.

8. Connect the wiring harness and reinstall the steering wheel.

9. Reinstall the column cover(s).

10. Install the lower dash trim panel.

11. Connect the negative battery cable. Check system for proper operation.

With Airbag System

1. Disconnect the negative battery cable. Wait at least 90 seconds before working on the vehicle.

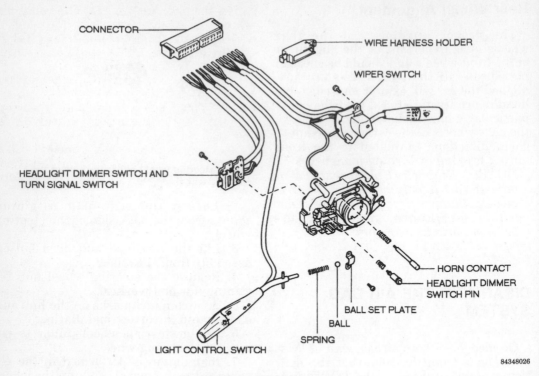

CONNECTOR

WIRE HARNESS HOLDER

WIPER SWITCH

HEADLIGHT DIMMER SWITCH AND
TURN SIGNAL SWITCH

HORN CONTACT

HEADLIGHT DIMMER
SWITCH PIN

BALL SET PLATE

BALL

LIGHT CONTROL SWITCH

SPRING

84348026

Combination switch components

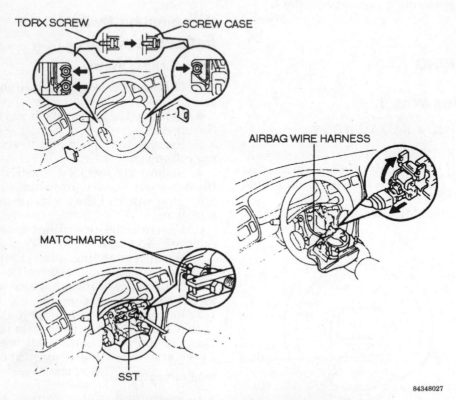

TORX SCREW

SCREW CASE

AIRBAG WIRE HARNESS

MATCHMARKS

SST

84348027

Steering wheel removal with air bag system

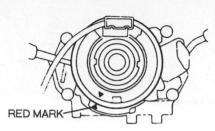

RED MARK

84348028

Center spiral cable

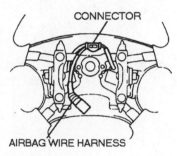

CONNECTOR

AIRBAG WIRE HARNESS

84348029

Steering wheel installation with air bag system

2. Remove (matchmark before removal) the steering wheel, as outlined in this Chapter.

3. Remove the instrument lower finish panel (as required), air duct and upper and lower column covers.

4. Disconnect the combination switch connector.

5. Disconnect the cable connectors, remove the spiral cable housing attaching screws and slide the cable assembly from the front of the combination switch.

6. Remove the screws that attach the combination switch to its mounting brackets and remove the combination switch from the vehicle.

To install:

7. Position the combination switch onto the mounting bracket and install the retaining screws.

8. Connect the electrical connector.

9. Install the upper/lower column covers, air duct and instrument lower finish panel.

10. Turn the spiral cable on the combination switch counterclockwise by hand until it becomes harder to turn. Then rotate the cable clockwise about 3 turns to

align the alignment mark. The connector should be straight up.

11. Install the steering wheel (align matchmarks) onto the shaft and torque nut to 26 ft. lbs. (35 Nm).

12. Connect the air bag connector and install the steering pad.

13. Connect the battery cable, check operation and the steering wheel center point.

14. Connect the negative battery cable. Check all combination switch functions for proper operation. Check the steering wheel center point.

Ignition Switch/Ignition Lock Cylinder

REMOVAL & INSTALLATION

1. Disconnect the negative battery cable.

2. Unscrew the retaining screws and remove the upper and lower steering column covers.

3. Remove the 2 retaining screws and remove the steering column trim.

4. Turn the ignition key to the **ACC** position.

5. Push the lock cylinder stop in with a small, round object (cotter pin, punch, etc.) and pull out the ignition key and the lock cylinder.

NOTE: *You may find that removing the steering wheel and the combination switch makes the job easier.*

6. Loosen the mounting screw and withdraw the ignition switch from the lock housing.

To install:

7. Position the ignition switch so that the recess and the bracket tab are properly aligned. Install the retaining screw.

8. Make sure that both the lock cylinder and the column lock are in the ACC position. Slide the cylinder into the lock housing until the stop tab engages the hole in the lock.

9. Make certain the stop tab is firmly seated in the slot. Turn the key to each switch position, checking for smoothness of motions and a positive feel. Remove and insert the key a few times, each time turning the key to each switch position.

10. Reinstall the combination switch and the steering wheel if they were removed.

11. Install the steering column trim and the upper and lower column covers.

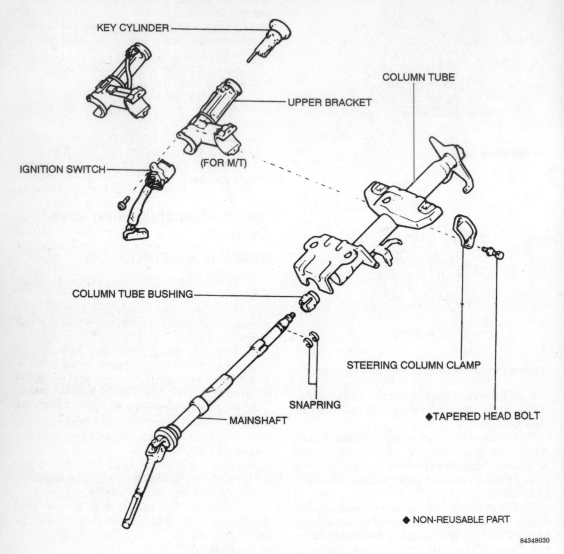

KEY CYLINDER

UPPER BRACKET

COLUMN TUBE

IGNITION SWITCH

(FOR M/T)

COLUMN TUBE BUSHING

STEERING COLUMN CLAMP

SNAPRING

MAINSHAFT

◆TAPERED HEAD BOLT

◆ NON-REUSABLE PART

84348030

Steering column components

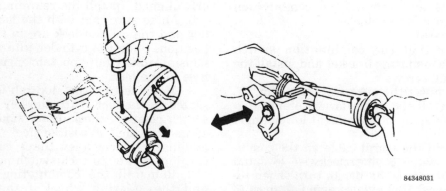

84348031

Removing key cylinder from the assembly

12. Connect the negative battery cable.

Steering Column

REMOVAL & INSTALLATION

CAUTION: *Air bag equipped vehicles: Work must be started after 90 seconds or longer from the time the ignition switch is turned to the LOCK and the negative battery terminal is disconnected. If the air bag system is disconnected with the ignition switch at the ON or ACC, diagnostic codes will be recorded.*

1. Disconnect the negative battery cable.
2. Remove the set bolt(s) from the universal joint.
3. Disengage the universal joint from the gear housing.
4. Remove the steering wheel as outlined in this Chapter.
5. Remove the instrument lower finish panel (as required), air duct and upper and lower column covers.
6. Disconnect all electrical connections for ignition switch and combination switch. Remove the combination switch as outlined in this Chapter.
7. Loosen or remove the column hole cover.
8. Remove the four column mounting nuts. Remove the steering column assembly from the vehicle.

To install:
9. Position the steering column inside the vehicle so that the main shaft can be inserted in the hole cover. Then, position the main shaft so that the ends of the steering support holes touch the mounting holes.
10. Support the column while installing the mounting nuts finger tight. Torque the nuts evenly to 19 ft. lbs.
11. Tighten or install the column hole cover.
12. Connect the switch connectors and install the combination switch, if removed.
13. Install the column covers, air duct and lower instrument panel finish panel.
14. Engage the universal joint with the steering gear housing spline, secure with the set bolt(s). Torque the set bolt(s) to 26 ft. lbs.
15. Install the steering wheel.
16. Connect the negative battery cable.

Tie Rod Ends

REMOVAL & INSTALLATION

1. Raise the front of the vehicle and support it safely. Remove the wheel.
2. Remove the cotter pin and nut holding the tie rod to the steering knuckle.
3. Using a tie rod separator, press the tie rod out of the knuckle.

NOTE: *Use only the correct tool to separate the tie rod joint. Replace the joint if the rubber boot is cracked or ripped.*

4. Matchmark the inner end of the tie rod to the end of the steering rack.
5. Loosen the locknut and remove the tie rod (count the number turns out to remove the tie rod) from the steering rack.

To install:
6. Install the tie rod end (count the same amount of turns in for correct installation) onto the rack ends and align the matchmarks made earlier.
7. Tighten the locknut to 41 ft. lbs.
8. Connect the tie rod to the knuckle. Tighten the tie rod to steering knuckle nut to 36 ft. lbs. and install a NEW cotter pin. Wrap the prongs of the cotter pin firmly around the flats of the nut.

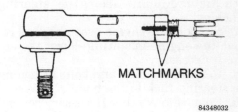

MATCHMARKS

84348032

Tie rod end removal

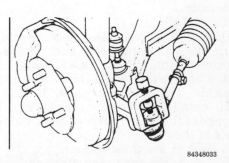

84348033

Removing the tie rod end from the steering knuckle

9. Install the wheel and lower the vehicle to the ground. Have the alignment checked at a reputable repair facility. The toe adjustment may have to be reset.

Manual Steering Gear

ADJUSTMENTS

Adjustments to the manual steering gear (rack and pinion) are not necessary during normal service. Adjustments are preformed only as part of overhaul.

REMOVAL & INSTALLATION

2WD Models

NOTE: *If vehicle is equipped with an air bag system, after repair is complete remove the steering wheel and make sure that the spiral cable is aligned properly. Refer to the necessary service procedures in this Chapter.*
1. Disconnect the negative battery cable. Remove the steering column cover.
2. Disconnect universal joint from the gear housing. Place matchmarks before removing set bolts.
3. Raise and safely support the vehicle.
4. Remove both front wheels.
5. Remove the cotter pins from both tie rod joints and remove the nuts.
6. Using a tie rod separator, remove both tie rod joints from the steering knuckles.
7. Support the engine assembly and remove the engine mounting--lower the engine if necessary.
8. Remove the nuts and bolts attaching the steering rack to the body.
9. Remove any other necessary component to gain working access (if possible slide assembly out the wheel well opening) to remove the rack and pinion assembly from the vehicle. Remove the rack assembly.
   To install:
10. Install the rack assembly. Secure it with the retaining bolts and nuts and tighten them EVENLY to 43 ft. lbs.
11. Connect the tie rods to each steering knuckle. Tighten the nuts to 36 ft. lbs. and install NEW cotter pins. Wrap the prongs of the cotter pin firmly around the flats of the nuts.
12. Install the front wheels.
13. Lower the car to the ground.
14. Align matchmarks and connect universal joint to the steering gear housing.

Tighten the upper and lower set bolts to 26 ft. lbs.
15. Install the steering column cover. Reconnect the negative battery cable. Check front wheel alignment.

4WD Models

1. Disconnect the negative battery cable. Remove the steering column cover.
2. Disconnect universal joint from the gear housing. Place matchmarks before removing set bolts.
3. Raise and safely support the vehicle.
4. Remove both front wheels and engine undercovers.
5. Install an engine support and tension it to support the engine without raising it.
   CAUTION: *The engine hoist is in place and under tension. Use care when repositioning the vehicle and make necessary adjustments to the engine support.*
6. Remove the bolts holding the center crossmember to the radiator support.
7. Remove the covers from the front and center mount bolts.
8. Remove the front mount bolts, then the center mount bolts.
9. Support the crossmember (disconnect the stabilizer bar as necessary) and remove the rear mount bolts.
10. Remove the bolts holding the center crossmember to the main crossmember.
11. Use a floor jack and a wide piece of wood to support the main crossmember.
12. Remove the bolts holding the main crossmember to the body.
13. Remove the bolts holding the lower control arm brackets to the body.
14. Slowly lower the main crossmember while holding onto the center crossmember.
15. Remove the cotter pins from both tie rod joints and remove the nuts.
16. Using a tie rod separator, remove both tie rod joints from the knuckles.
17. Lower the engine assembly if necessary, remove the nuts and bolts attaching the steering rack to the body.
18. Remove the steering rack.
    To install:
19. Place the steering rack in position and tighten the bracket bolts EVENLY to 43 ft. lbs.
20. Attach the tie rods to the knuckles. Tighten the nuts to 36 ft. lbs. and install NEW cotter pins. Wrap the prongs of the cotter pin firmly around the flats of the nut.

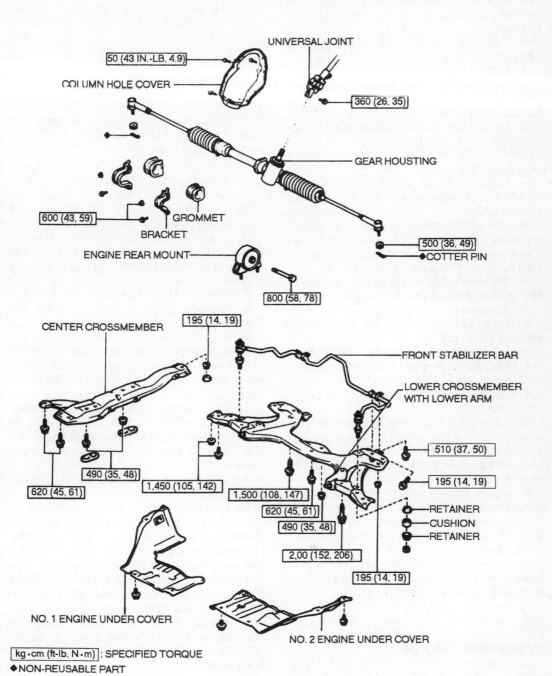

50 (43 IN.-LB, 4.9)

COLUMN HOLE COVER

UNIVERSAL JOINT

360 (26, 35)

GEAR HOUSING

600 (43, 59)

GROMMET

BRACKET

ENGINE REAR MOUNT

500 (36, 49)
◆COTTER PIN

800 (58, 78)

CENTER CROSSMEMBER

195 (14, 19)

FRONT STABILIZER BAR

LOWER CROSSMEMBER
WITH LOWER ARM

510 (37, 50)

195 (14, 19)

490 (35, 48)

620 (45, 61)

1,450 (105, 142)

1,500 (108, 147)

620 (45, 61)

490 (35, 48)

RETAINER
CUSHION
RETAINER

2,00 (152, 206)

195 (14, 19)

NO. 1 ENGINE UNDER COVER

NO. 2 ENGINE UNDER COVER

kg・cm (ft-lb, N・m) : SPECIFIED TORQUE
◆NON-REUSABLE PART

84348034

Manual steering gear/rack and pinion-4WD models

21. Position the center crossmember over the center and rear transaxle mount studs; start nuts on the center mount.

22. Loosely install the bolts holding the center crossmember to the radiator support.

23. Loosely install the front mount bolts.

24. Raise the main crossmember into position over the rear mount studs and align all underbody bolts. Install the rear mount nuts loosely.

25. Install the main crossmember to underbody bolts loosely.

26. Install the lower control arm bracket bolts loosely.

27. Loosely install the bolts holding the center crossmember to the main crossmember.

28. The crossmembers, bolts and brackets should now all be in place and held loosely by their nuts and bolts. If any repositioning is necessary, do so now.

29. Tighten the components below in the order listed to the correct torque specification:
- Main crossmember to underbody bolts: 152 ft. lbs.
- Lower control arm bolts: 105 ft. lbs.
- Center crossmember to radiator support bolts: 45 ft. lbs.
- Front, center and rear mount bolts: 58 ft. lbs.

30. Reconnect the stabilizer bar as necessary. Install the covers on the front and center mount bolts.

31. Install the front wheels and engine undercovers.

32. Lower the vehicle to the ground.

33. Align matchmarks and connect universal joint to the steering gear housing. Tighten the upper and lower set bolts to 26 ft. lbs.

34. Install the steering column cover. Reconnect the negative battery cable. Check front wheel alignment.

Power Steering Gear

ADJUSTMENTS

Adjustments to the power steering gear (rack and pinion) are not necessary during normal service. Adjustments are preformed only as part of overhaul.

REMOVAL & INSTALLATION

2WD Models

NOTE: *If vehicle is equipped with an air bag system, after repair is complete remove the steering wheel and make sure that the spiral cable is aligned properly. Refer to the necessary service procedures in this Chapter.*

1. Disconnect the negative battery cable. Remove the steering column cover.

2. Disconnect universal joint from the gear housing. Place matchmarks before removing set bolts.

3. Raise and safely support the vehicle.

4. Remove both front wheels.

5. Place a drain pan below the power steering rack assembly. Clean the area around the line fittings on the rack.

6. Remove the cotter pins and nuts from both tie rod joints. Separate the joints from the knuckle using a tie rod joint separator.

7. Support the transaxle with a jack.

8. Remove the rear bolts holding the engine crossmember to the bolt.

9. Remove the nut and bolt holding the rear engine mount to the mount bracket.

10. Label and disconnect the fluid pressure and return lines at the steering rack.

11. Remove the bolts and nuts holding the rack brackets to the body. It will be necessary to slightly raise and lower the rear of the transaxle to gain access to the bolts.

12. Remove the steering rack through the access hole.

To install:

13. Place the steering rack in position through the access hole and install the retaining brackets to the body. Tighten the nuts and bolts EVENLY to 43 ft. lbs.

14. Connect the fluid lines (always start the threads by hand before using a tool) to the steering rack.

15. Install the nut and bolt holding the rear engine mount to the mount bracket.

16. Reinstall the engine crossmember bolts and tighten.

17. Remove the jack from the transaxle.

18. Connect the tie rod ends to the knuckles. Tighten the nuts to 36 ft. lbs. and install NEW cotter pins. Wrap the prongs of the cotter pin firmly around the flats of the nut.

19. Install the wheels and lower the vehicle to the ground.

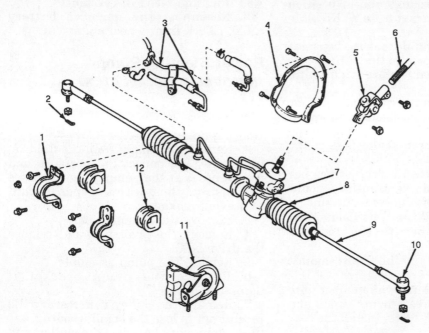

1. Mounting bracket
2. Cotter pin
3. Pressure and return
   lines
4. Column hole cover
5. Universal joint (yoke)
6. Intermediate shaft
7. Steering gear housing
8. Boot
9. Tie rod
10. Tie rod end
11. Engine mount
12. Grommet

84348036

Power steering gear/rack and pinion-2WD models

20. Align matchmarks and connect universal joint to the steering gear housing. Tighten the upper and lower set bolts to 26 ft. lbs.

21. Install the steering column cover. Add fluid and bleed the system.

22. Reconnect the negative battery cable. Check front wheel alignment.

4WD Models

1. Disconnect the negative battery cable. Remove the steering column cover.

2. Disconnect universal joint from the gear housing. Place matchmarks before removing set bolts.

3. Raise and safely support the vehicle.

4. Remove both front wheels and engine undercovers.

5. Install an engine support and tension it to support the engine without raising it.

CAUTION: *The engine hoist is now in place and under tension. Use care when repositioning the vehicle and make necessary adjustments to the engine support.*

6. Disconnect and (position out of the way) front exhaust pipe. Matchmark and remove the propeller shaft assembly. Disconnect the front stabilizer bar.

7. Remove the bolts holding the center crossmember to the radiator support. Remove the covers from the front and center mount bolts.

8. Remove the front mount bolts, then the center mount bolts and then the rear mount bolts.

9. Remove the bolts holding the center crossmember to the main crossmember.

10. Use a floor jack and a wide piece of wood to support the main crossmember.

11. Remove the bolts holding the main crossmember to the body.

12. Remove the bolts holding the lower control arm brackets to the body.

13. Slowly lower the main crossmember while holding onto the center crossmember.

14. Remove the cotter pins from both tie rod ball joints and remove the nuts.

15. Using a tie rod separator, remove both tie rod joints from the knuckles.

16. Label and disconnect the fluid pressure and return lines from the rack.

17. Remove the nuts and bolts attaching the steering rack to the body.

18. Remove the steering rack.

To install:

19. Place the steering rack in position and tighten the bracket bolts EVENLY to 43 ft. lbs.

20. Connect the fluid lines to the steering rack. Make certain the fittings are correctly threaded before tightening them.

21. Attach the tie rods to the knuckles. Tighten the nuts to 36 ft. lbs. and install NEW cotter pins. Wrap the prongs of the cotter pin firmly around the flats of the nut.

22. Position the center crossmember over the center and rear transaxle mount studs; start nuts on the center mount.

23. Loosely install the bolts holding the center crossmember to the radiator support.

24. Loosely install the front mount bolts.

25. Raise the main crossmember into position over the rear mount studs and align all underbody bolts. Install the rear mount nuts loosely.

26. Install the main crossmember to underbody bolts loosely.

27. Install the lower control arm bracket bolts loosely.

28. Loosely install the bolts holding the center crossmember to the main crossmember.

29. The crossmembers, bolts and brackets should now all be in place and held loosely by their nuts and bolts. If any repositioning is necessary, do so now.

30. Tighten the components below in the order listed to the correct torque specification:

- Main crossmember to underbody bolts: 152 ft. lbs.
- Lower control arm bolts: 105 ft. lbs.
- Center crossmember to radiator support bolts: 45 ft. lbs.
- Front, center and rear mount bolts: 45 ft. lbs.

31. Install the covers on the front and center mount bolts. Install the propeller (align matchmarks) shaft assembly. Reconnect front exhaust pipe. Connect the front stabilizer bar.

32. Install the front wheels and engine undercovers.

33. Lower the vehicle to the ground. Align matchmarks and connect universal joint to the steering gear housing. Tighten the upper and lower set bolts to 26 ft. lbs.

34. Install the steering column cover. Add fluid and bleed the system.

35. Reconnect the negative battery cable. Check front wheel alignment.

Power Steering Pump

REMOVAL & INSTALLATION

4A-FE And 7A-FE Engines

1. Place a drain pan below the power steering pump.

2. Remove the clamp from the fluid return hose. Disconnect the pressure and return hoses at the pump. Plug the hoses and suspend them with the ends upward to prevent leakage.

3. Remove the adjusting bolt.

4. Remove the pivot bolt and remove the drive belt.

5. Remove the pump assembly.

6. Remove the pump bracket if necessary.

7. Remove the pulley if necessary. Be careful not to lose the small woodruff key (if so equipped) between the pulley and the shaft.

To install:

8. Install the pump pulley and the woodruff key. Tighten the pulley nut to 32 ft. lbs.

9. Install the pump bracket and tighten the bolts to 29 ft. lbs.

10. Place the pump in position and temporarily install the mounting bolts and adjusting bolt.

11. Install the drive belt. Adjust the belt to the proper tension. Tighten all mounting and adjusting bolts.

12. Connect the pressure and return lines to the pump. Tighten the banjo fitting to 40 ft. lbs. Install the clamp on the return hose.

13. Fill the reservoir to the proper level with power steering fluid and bleed the system.

14. After the vehicle has been driven for about an hour, double check the belt adjustment.

4A-GE Engine

1. Place a drain pan below the pump.

2. Remove the air cleaner assembly if necessary.

3. Disconnect the return hose from the pump, then disconnect the pressure hose. Plug the lines immediately to prevent fluid loss and contamination.

4. Remove the splash shield under the engine.

4A-FE ENGINE

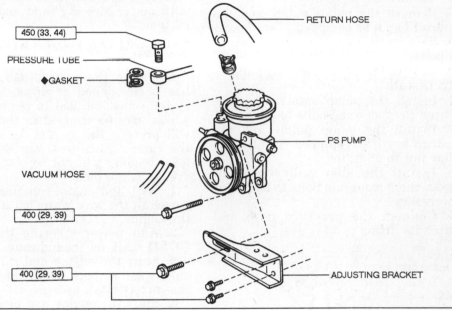

RETURN HOSE

450 (33, 44)

PRESSURE TUBE

◆GASKET

PS PUMP

VACUUM HOSE

400 (29, 39)

400 (29, 39)

ADJUSTING BRACKET

4A-GE ENGINE

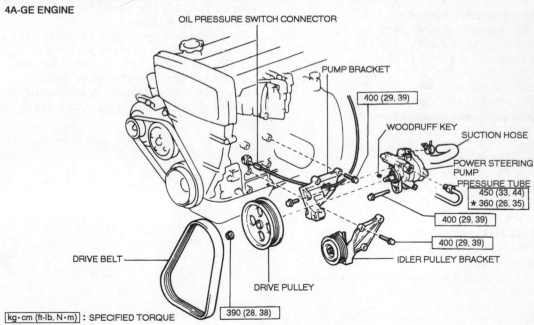

OIL PRESSURE SWITCH CONNECTOR

PUMP BRACKET

400 (29, 39)

WOODRUFF KEY   SUCTION HOSE

POWER STEERING PUMP

PRESSURE TUBE
450 (33, 44)
★ 360 (26, 35)

400 (29, 39)

400 (29, 39)

IDLER PULLEY BRACKET

DRIVE BELT

DRIVE PULLEY

390 (28, 38)

kg·cm (ft-lb, N·m) : SPECIFIED TORQUE

◆ NON-REUSABLE PART

★ FOR USE WITH SST

84348038

Power steering pumps

5. Remove the pulley nut. Push down on the drive belt to prevent the pulley from turning.

6. Loosen the idler pulley nut an loosen the adjusting bolt.

7. Remove the drive belt.

8. Remove the pump pulley and the woodruff key if so equipped.

9. Remove the upper and lower mounting bolts.

10. Remove the power steering pump.

To install:

11. Install the pump onto the engine. Tighten the mounting bolts to 29 ft. lbs.

12. Install the pump pulley and the woodruff key if so equipped. Tighten the pulley nut to 28 ft. lbs.

13. Install the idler pulley bracket; tighten the 3 mounting bolts to 29 ft. lbs. if necessary

14. Connect the pressure hose and tighten its fitting to 33 ft. lbs.

84348039

Idler pulley and adjusting bolt

15. Connect the return hose.

16. Adjust the belt to the proper tension.

17. Install the air cleaner if necessary and install the lower splash shield.

18. Fill the reservoir to the proper level with power steering fluid and bleed the system.

BLEEDING THE POWER STEERING SYSTEM

Any time the power steering system has been opened or disassembled, the system must be bled to remove any air which may be trapped in the lines. Air will prevent the system from providing the correct pressures. The correct fluid level reading will not be obtained if the system is not bled.

1. With the engine running, turn the wheel all the way to the left and shut off the engine.

2. Add power steering fluid to the **COLD** mark on the indicator.

3. Start the engine and run. Stop the engine and recheck the fluid level. Add to the correct mark as needed.

4. Start the engine and bleed the system by turning the wheels fully from left to right 3 or 4 times.

5. Stop the engine and check the fluid level and condition. Fluid with air in it is a light tan color. This air must be eliminated from the system before normal operation can be obtained. Repeat until the correct fluid color and fluid level is obtained.

BRAKE OPERATING SYSTEM

ADJUSTMENT

REAR DRUM BRAKES

Most models are equipped with self-adjusting rear drum brakes. Under normal conditions, adjustment of the rear brake shoes should not be necessary. However, if an initial adjustment is required insert the blade of a brake adjuster tool or a screw driver into the hole in the brake drum and turn the adjuster slowly. The tension is set correctly if the tire and wheel assembly will rotate approximately 3 times when spun with moderate force. Do not over adjust the brake shoes. Before adjusting the rear drum brake shoes, make sure emergency brake is in the OFF position, and all cables are free.

BRAKE PEDAL

Before adjusting the pedal height, measure the distance from the top of the pedal rubber to the asphalt sheet. This distance should be approximately 5.47–5.87 in. in. (139–149 Nm). for vehicles till 1992. On the 1993 model, the distance should be approximately 5.65–6.05 in. in. (144–154 Nm). If the actual mea-

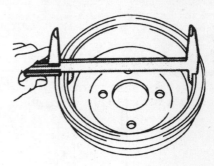

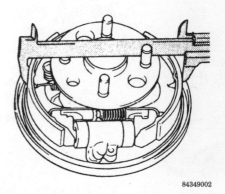

84349002

Measuring the diameters of the drum and shoe assemblies

surement does not agree with the range given, the pedal height and the pedal free-play must be adjusted.

To adjust the pedal height perform the following:

1. If necessary, remove the instrument lower finish panel, air duct and floor mats to gain access to the pedal and pedal linkages.

2. Loosen the stop light switch locknut and loosen the stop light switch until it can be moved freely by hand.

3. Loosen the push rod locknut and adjust the height of the pedal by rotating the push rod as needed. Torque the push rod locknut to 19 ft. lbs. (25 Nm).

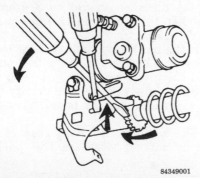

84349001

Backing the rear drum brake adjuster

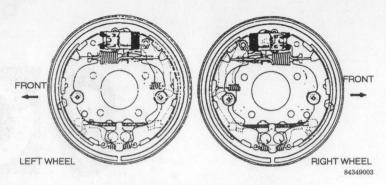

FRONT

FRONT

LEFT WHEEL

RIGHT WHEEL

84349003

Correct brake hardware installation

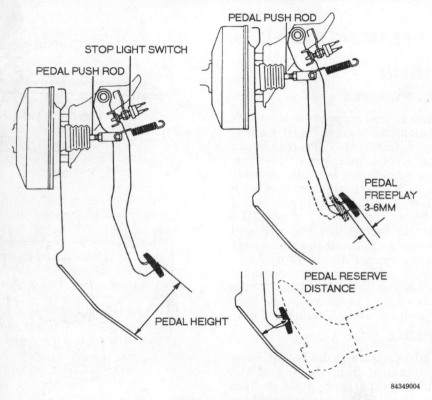

PEDAL PUSH ROD

STOP LIGHT SWITCH

PEDAL PUSH ROD

PEDAL FREEPLAY 3-6MM

PEDAL HEIGHT

PEDAL RESERVE DISTANCE

84349004

Brake pedal checks and adjustments

4. Install the stop light switch until it lightly contacts the pedal stop and tighten the two locknuts.

5. Start the engine.

6. Depress the pedal and have an assistant verify the stop lights illuminate.

7. Stop the engine adjust the pedal free-play.

To check and adjust pedal free-play, perform the following:

8. With the engine off depress the brake pedal several times until all the vacuum is removed from the booster.

9. Push the pedal by hand until resistance can just be felt and measure the distance--refer to the illustration. The free-play distance should be 3–6mm for all models till 1992 and (1–6mm on the 1993 vehicle).

10. If the free-play is not correct, loosen the push rod locknut until the free-play is within the given range.

11. Start the engine and verify that there is free-play in the pedal. Check the pedal height.

12. Check that the pedal reserve distance is correct. Release the parking

brake lever. With the engine running, depress the pedal and measure the pedal reserve distance--refer to the illustration.

13. Measure pedal reserve distance from asphalt sheet at 110 lbs. of force. The pedal reserve distance should be:

    a. 1990–92 models rear drum brake type--more than 2.17 in. (55mm).

    b. 1993 model rear drum brake type--more than 2.76 in. (70mm).

    c. Rear disc brake type--more than 2.36 in. (60mm).

    d. 4WD model--more than 2.56 in. (65mm).

14. If the pedal reserve distance is not correct, troubleshoot the brake system.

15. If all adjustments are satisfactory, install the air duct and lower instrument finish panel.

Brake Light Switch

REMOVAL & INSTALLATION

1. Disconnect the negative battery cable.

2. Remove the instrument lower finish panel and the air duct if required to gain access to the stoplight switch.

3. Disconnect the stoplight switch connector.

4. Remove the switch mounting nut, then slide the switch from the mounting bracket on the pedal.

To install:

5. Install the switch into the mounting bracket and adjust.

6. Connect the switch connector and reconnect the negative battery cable.

7. Depress the brake pedal and verify that the brake lights illuminate.

8. Install the air duct and the lower finish panel, if removed.

Brake Pedal

REMOVAL & INSTALLATION

1. Disconnect the negative battery cable.

2. Remove the instrument lower finish panel and the lower air duct, as required.

3. Remove the brake pedal return spring. Disconnect and remove the brake light switch.

4. Remove clip and clevis pin.

5. Unbolt and remove the brake pedal assembly from the vehicle.

6. The installation is the reverse of the removal procedure. Check and adjust the

brake pedal as required. Assure that the brake lights are fully functional.

Master Cylinder

REMOVAL & INSTALLATION

NOTE: *Before the master cylinder is reinstalled, the brake booster pushrod must be adjusted. This adjustment requires the use of factory special tool SST No. 09737–00010 or its equivalent.*

1. Open the hood and disconnect the level warning switch connector. Disconnect the negative battery cable.

2. Remove the cap from the master cylinder and drain the fluid out with the use a turkey baster or similar syringe. Deposit the fluid into a container.

3. Disconnect the brake tubes from the master cylinder. Drain the fluid from the lines into the container. Plug the lines to prevent fluid from leaking onto and damaging painted surfaces or the entry of moisture into the brake system.

4. Remove the three nuts that attach the master cylinder and 3-way union to the brake booster.

5. Remove the master cylinder from the booster studs. Remove and discard the old gasket.

To install:

6. Clean the brake booster gasket and the master cylinder flange surfaces. Install a new gasket onto the brake booster.

7. Adjust the length of the brake booster push rod as follows: set the special tool on the master cylinder with the gasket and lower the pin of the tool until it lightly contacts the piston. Turn the special tool upside-down and position it onto the booster. Measure the clearance between the booster push rod and the pin head of the tool. There must be zero clearance. To obtain zero clearance, adjust the push rod length until the push rod just contacts the head of the pin.

8. Before installing the master cylinder, make sure that the **UP** mark is in the correct position. Install the master cylinder over the mounting studs and tighten the three nuts to 9 ft. lbs. (13 Nm).

9. Connect the tubes to the master cylinder outlet plugs and torque the union nuts to 11 ft. lbs.

10. Connect the level warning switch connector.

11. Fill the brake fluid reservoir to the proper level with clean brake fluid and

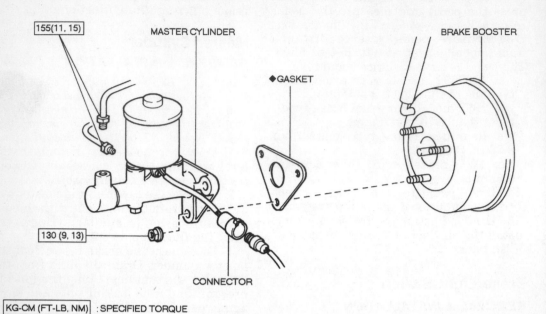

155(11, 15)

MASTER CYLINDER

BRAKE BOOSTER

◆GASKET

130 (9, 13)

CONNECTOR

KG-CM (FT-LB, NM) : SPECIFIED TORQUE

◆ NON-REUSABLE PART

84349005

Master cylinder assembly — removal

SST

GASKET

SST

84349006

Adjusting the length brake booster push rod

bleed the brake system as described in this Section.

12. Check for leaks. Check and/or adjust the brake pedal.

OVERHAUL

Disassembly

1. Remove the master cylinder from the vehicle.

2. Remove the setscrew at the bottom of the reservoir tank and pull the reservoir from the body. Remove the cap and strainer.

3. Remove the two rubber grommets from the housing.

4. Clamp the master cylinder body in a view.

5. Push the pistons all the way in with a tapped screwdriver and remove the piston stopper bolt and gasket.

6. Keep the piston depressed and remove the snapring using snapring pliers.

7. Place a rag on two blocks of wood and **lightly** tap the flange of the body against the blocks until the tip of the piston is visible.

8. Pull the pistons with springs by hand straight out of the bore. If the pis-

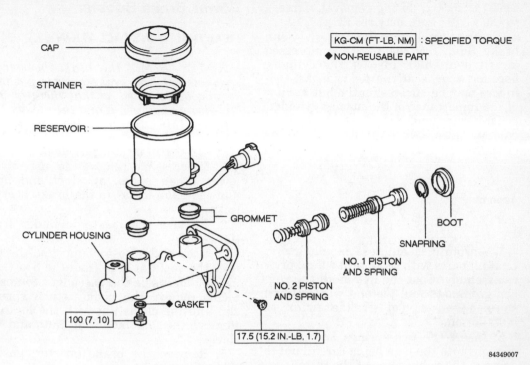

KG-CM (FT-LB, NM) : SPECIFIED TORQUE
◆ NON-REUSABLE PART

CAP

STRAINER

RESERVOIR

GROMMET

CYLINDER HOUSING

BOOT

SNAPRING

NO. 1 PISTON
AND SPRING

NO. 2 PISTON
AND SPRING

GASKET

100 (7, 10)

17.5 (15.2 IN.-LB, 1.7)

84349007

Exploded view of the master cylinder assembly — 1990–92

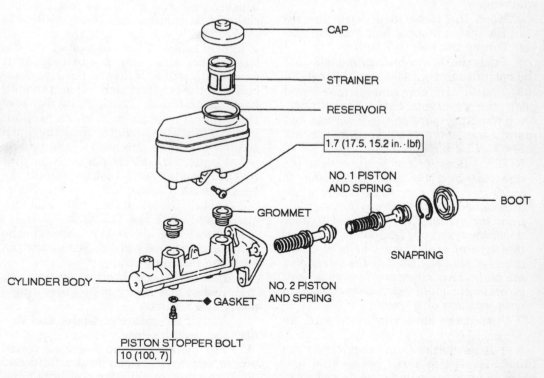

CAP

STRAINER

RESERVOIR

1.7 (17.5, 15.2 in. · lbf)

NO. 1 PISTON
AND SPRING

GROMMET

BOOT

SNAPRING

CYLINDER BODY

NO. 2 PISTON
AND SPRING

GASKET

PISTON STOPPER BOLT
10 (100, 7)

84349008

Exploded view of the master cylinder assembly — 1993

ton(s) is cocked during removal, damage to the piston bore may result.

9. After washing all parts in clean brake fluid, dry them with compressed air (if available). Inspect the cylinder bore for wear, scuff marks, or nicks. Cylinders may be honed slightly, but in view of the importance of the master cylinder, it is recommended that it is replaced rather than overhauled if worn or damaged.

Assembly

1. Absolute cleanliness is important. Coat all parts with clean brake fluid prior to assembly. Coat the lips of all the rubber grommets and pistons with lithium soap based glycol grease prior to installation.

2. Insert the two springs and pistons straight into the bore being careful not to damage the rubber lips of the piston.

3. Depress the pistons all the way in with a screwdriver and install the snapring.

4. Keep the piston depressed and install the piston stopper bolt over the gasket. Torque the bolt to 7 ft. lbs.

5. Push the two rubber grommets into the openings in the master cylinder body.

6. Install the cap and strainer and push the reservoir onto the cylinder. Keep hand pressure on the reservoir and install the set screw. Torque the set screw to 15.2 inch lbs.

NOTE: *Because the seal between the reservoir and the master cylinder is made by rubber grommets, the set screw is designed not to separate the reservoir from the cylinder and will not tighten down the reservoir. Due to the nature of this type of seal, there will be a clearance between the head of the screw and the body. This clearance is normal and no attempt should be made to shim it up with washers or a spacer.*

7. Install the master cylinder onto the vehicle.

8. Fill the brake fluid reservoir to the proper level with clean brake fluid and bleed the master cylinder as described in this Section.

9. Check for leaks. Check and/or adjust the brake pedal as required.

Power Brake Booster

REMOVAL & INSTALLATION

NOTE: *Before the brake booster is reinstalled, the brake booster pushrod must be adjusted so that there is zero clearance between it and the master cylinder. This adjustment requires the use of factory special tool SST No. 09737–00010 or its equivalent.*

1. If necessary, remove the instrument lower finish panel, air duct and floor mats to gain access to the brake booster linkage.

2. Remove the master cylinder from the vehicle.

3. Loosen the hose clamp and disconnect the vacuum hose from the booster.

4. From inside the passenger compartment, remove the pedal return spring, clip and the clevis pin with the locknut. Remove the four mounting nuts and the clevis.

5. Remove the brake booster, gasket and clevis.

To install:

6. Adjust the length of the brake booster push rod as follows: set the special tool on the master cylinder with the gasket and lower the pin of the tool until it lightly contacts the position. Turn the special tool upside-down and position it onto the booster. Measure the clearance between the booster push rod and the pin head of the tool. There must be zero clearance. To obtain zero clearance, adjust the push rod length until the push rod light contacts the head of the pin.

7. Connect the clevis pin with locknut to the booster and install the brake booster with a new gasket.

8. Install the mounting nuts and torque them to 9 ft. lbs. (13 Nm).

9. Insert the clevis pin through the clevis and the brake pedal. Secure the pin with the retaining clip.

10. Install the pedal return spring.

11. Install the instrument lower finish panel and air duct.

12. Install the master cylinder and connect the vacuum hose.

13. Fill the brake fluid reservoir to the proper level with clean brake fluid and bleed the master cylinder and brake system as described in this Section.

14. Check for leaks. Check and/or adjust the brake pedal.

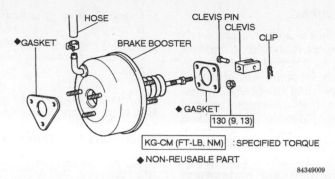

HOSE   CLEVIS PIN   CLEVIS   CLIP

◆GASKET   BRAKE BOOSTER

◆ GASKET

130 (9, 13)

KG-CM (FT-LB, NM) : SPECIFIED TORQUE

◆ NON-REUSABLE PART

84349009

Brake booster — removal

15. Perform a brake booster operational check and air tightness check as detailed below.

OPERATIONAL AND AIR TIGHTNESS CHECKS

NOTE: *If one is available to you, the use of a brake booster tester is recommended to test the operation of the booster. All vacuum leaks must be repaired, before testing the brake booster.*

To perform the operational check, depress the brake pedal several times with the engine off and check that there is no change in the pedal reserve distance. Depress the brake pedal and start the engine. If the pedal goes down a small amount, the booster is functioning normally.

To perform the air tightness check, start the engine and stop it after one or two minutes. Depress the brake pedal slowly several times. If the pedal goes furthest the first time but rises each consecutive time, the booster is air tight. Start the engine again and stop it with the brake pedal depressed. If the pedal reserve travel does not change with the brake pedal held for thirty seconds, the booster is air tight.

Proportioning Valve

A proportioning valve is used to reduce the hydraulic pressure to the rear brakes because of weight transfer during high speed stops. This helps to keep the rear brakes from locking up by improving front to rear brake balance.

REMOVAL & INSTALLATION

1. Disconnect the brake lines from the valve unions.

2. Remove the valve mounting bolt, if used, and remove the valve.

NOTE: *If the proportioning valve is defective, it must be replaced as an assembly; it cannot be rebuilt.*

3. Installation is the reverse of removal. Bleed the brake system after it is completed.

Brake Hoses

REMOVAL & INSTALLATION

1. Remove the brake line clip.

2. Using a back-up wrench to hold the hose, loosen the connector nut with the proper size flare nut wrench and disconnect the hose from the fitting.

3. Drain the hose into a plastic container. If equipped with gaskets on either side of the hose connections, discard old gaskets and replace with new.

4. Visually inspect the brake hose for signs of cracking, damage and swelling. Inspect the fitting threads for damage. Minor thread damage may be repaired with a jeweler's file. Make replacements as required. If a repair is questionable, replace the part.

5. Visually inspect the brake tubes for damage, cracks, indentations or corrosion. Inspect the threads for damage. Make replacements as required.

To install:

6. Connect the brake hose to the brake tube fitting by hand making sure new gaskets are in place. Slowly tighten the fitting and loosen it several times to ensure the correct mating of the threads.

7. Using the flare nut and back-up wrenches, tighten the fitting and secure the hose with the clip.

8. Fill the master cylinder and bleed the brake system and the master cylinder.

BRAKE PIPE FLARING

Flaring steel lines is a skill that needs to be practiced before it should be done on a line to be used on a vehicle. It is essential that the flare be done uniformly to prevent any leaks when the brake system is under pressure. It is also recommended that the flare be a "double flare" (rolled twice). With the supply of parts available today, a preflared steel brake line should be available to fit your needs. Due to the high pressures in the brake system and the serious injuries that could occur if the brake system (flare in a brake line) should fail, it is strongly advised that preflared lines are installed when repairing the braking system. If a line were to leak brake fluid due to an defective flare, and the leak was to go undetected, brake failure would result

Bleeding the Brake System

NOTE: *If any maintenance or repairs were performed on the brake system, or if air is suspected in the system, the system must be bled. If the master cylinder has been replaced, overhauled or if the fluid reservoir was run dry, start the bleeding procedure with the master cylinder. Otherwise (and after bleeding the master cylinder), start with the wheel cylinder which is farthest from the master cylinder (longest hydraulic line).*
CAUTION: *Brake fluid will remove the paint from any surface that it comes in contact with. If brake fluid spills on a painted surface, wash it off immediately.*

MASTER CYLINDER

1. Check the fluid level in the master cylinder reservoir and add fluid as required to bring to the proper level.
2. Loosen the two brake tubes from the master cylinder.
3. Have an assistant depress the brake pedal and hold it in the down position.
4. While the pedal is depressed, tighten the fluid lines and then release the brake pedal.
5. Repeat the procedure three or four times.
6. Bleed the brake system, if needed.

BRAKE SYSTEM

NOTE: *Start the brake system bleeding procedure on the wheel cylinder that is the furthest away from the master cyl-*inder. *To bleed the brakes you will need a supply of clean brake fluid, a long piece of clear vinyl tubing and a small container that is half full of clean brake fluid.*
1. Clean all the dirt and grease from the bleeder plugs and remove the protective caps. Connect one end of a clear vinyl tube to the fitting.
2. Insert the other end of the tube into a jar which is half filled with clean brake fluid.
3. Have an assistant slowly depress the brake pedal while you open the bleeder plug $1/3$–$1/2$ of a turn. Fluid should run out of the tube. When the pedal is at its full range of travel, close the bleeder plug.
4. Have your assistant slowly pump the brake pedal. Repeat Step 3 until there are no more air bubbles in the fluid.
5. Repeat Steps 1 to 4 for each bleeder plug. Add brake fluid to the master cylinder reservoir as necessary, so that it does not completely drain during bleeding.

FRONT DISC BRAKES

CAUTION: *Brake shoes contain asbestos, which has been determined to be a cancer causing agent. Never clean the brake surfaces with compressed air! Avoid inhaling any dust from any brake surfaces. When cleaning brake surfaces, use a commercially available brake cleaning fluid.*

Brake Pads

REMOVAL & INSTALLATION

1. Raise and support the vehicle safely.
2. Remove the wheels.
3. Siphon a sufficient quantity of brake fluid from the master cylinder reservoir to prevent any brake fluid from overflowing the master cylinder when removing or installing new pads. This is necessary as the piston must be forced into the caliper bore to provide sufficient clearance when installing the new pads.
4. Grasp the caliper from behind and carefully pull it to seat the piston in its bolt.
5. Loosen and remove the 2 caliper mounting pins (bolts) and then remove

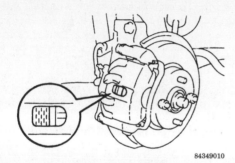

Inspect the front disc brake pads

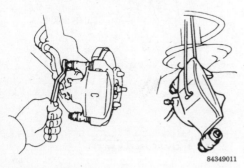

Remove the 2 mounting bolts and use a wire to suspend the caliper from the suspension

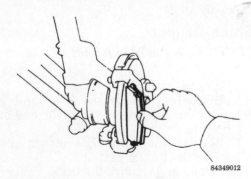

Removing the front brake pad

the caliper assembly. Position it aside. Do not disconnect the brake line.

6. Slide out the old brake pads along with any anti-squeal shims, springs, pad wear indicators and pad support plates. Make sure to note the position of all assorted pad hardware.

To install:

7. Check the brake disc (rotor) for thickness and run-out. Inspect the caliper and piston assembly for breaks, cracks, fluid seepage or other damage. Overhaul or replace as necessary.

8. Install the 4 pad support plates into the torque plate.

9. Install the pad wear indicators onto the pads. Be sure the arrow on the indicator plate is pointing in the direction of rotation.

10. Install the anti-squeal shims on the outside of each pad. Do not allow oil or grease to get on the rubbing face of the pads, then install the pad assemblies into the torque plate. Install 2 anti-squeal springs.

11. Position the caliper back down over the pads. If it won't fit, use a C-clamp or a special tool and carefully force the piston into its bore.

12. Install and tighten the caliper mounting bolts to 18 ft. lbs. (25 Nm) on 1990–92 vehicles and 25 ft. lbs (34 Nm) on the 1993 vehicle.

13. Install the wheels and lower the vehicle. Check the brake fluid level. Before moving the vehicle, make sure to pump the brake pedal a few times to seat the brake pads against the rotors.

INSPECTION

If you hear a squealing noise coming from the front brakes while driving, check the brake lining thickness and pad

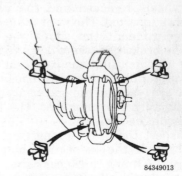

Install 4 new pad support plates

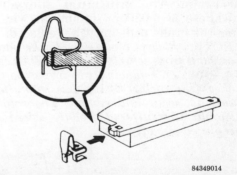

Install a pad wear indicator on the inside pad

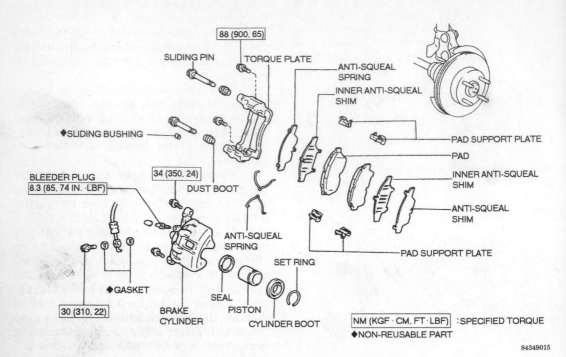

Exploded view of the front disc brake assembly

wear indicator by looking into the inspection hole on the brake cylinder with the front wheels removed and the vehicle properly supported. The wear indicator is designed to emit the squealing noise when the brake pad wears down to about 2.5mm at which time the pad wear plate and the rotor disc rub against each other. If there are traces of the pad wear indicator contacting the rotor disc, the brake pads should be replaced.

To inspect the brake lining thickness, look through the inspection hole and measure the lining thickness using a machinists rule. Also looks for signs of uneven wear. Standard thickness is 10–12mm. The **minimum** allowable thickness is 0.039 in. (1mm) at which time the brake pads must be replaced.

NOTE: *Always replace the brake pads on both front wheels as a set. When inspecting or replacing the brake pads, check the surface of the disc rotors for scoring, wear and runout. The rotors should be resurfaced if badly scored or replaced if badly worn.*

Brake Caliper

REMOVAL & INSTALLATION

1. Raise and support the vehicle safely.
2. Remove the front wheels.
3. Disconnect the brake hose and 2 gaskets from the caliper. Plug the end of the hose to prevent loss of fluid.
4. Remove the bolts that attach the caliper to the torque plate.
5. Lift up and remove the brake caliper assembly.
6. Installation is the reverse of the removal procedure. Always use NEW gaskets for the brake hose. Grease the brake caliper slides and bolts with Lithium grease or equivalent. Install and tighten the caliper mounting bolts to 18 ft. lbs. (25 Nm) on 1990–92 vehicles and 25 ft. lbs (34 Nm) on the 1993 vehicle. Fill and bleed the system. Before moving the vehicle, make sure to pump the brake pedal a few times to seat the pads against the rotors.

OVERHAUL

1. Remove the caliper from the vehicle.
2. Withdraw the two slide bushings from their respective bores.
3. Remove the dust boots.

4. Gently pry the cylinder boot set ring from the boot and remove the boot.

5. Place a folded towel between the piston and housing. Apply compressed air to the brake line union fitting to force the piston out of its bore. Be careful, the piston may come out forcefully.

CAUTION: *Do not attempt to catch the piston with your fingers. Let the towel do this for you.*

6. Pry the piston seal from the bore with a machinists scribe.

7. Check the piston and cylinder bore for wear and/or corrosion. Replace components if excess wear or corrosion is present.

8. To assemble, coat all necessary parts and seal surfaces with lithium soap base glycol grease.

9. Install the piston seal into the bore and install the piston.

10. Install the boot and set ring in the cylinder.

11. Install dust boots and cylinder sliding bushings to the brake cylinder.

12. Install the brake pads into the cylinder and install the cylinder onto the torque plate. Tighten the caliper mounting bolts to 18 ft. lbs. (25 Nm) on 1990–92 vehicles and 25 ft. lbs (34 Nm) on the 1993 vehicle.

13. Fill the master cylinder reservoir and bleed the brake system.

14. Pump the brake pedal a few times, and check the brake system for leaks.

Brake Disc (Rotor)

REMOVAL & INSTALLATION

1. Loosen the front wheel lugs slightly, then raise and safely support the front of the vehicle. Remove the front wheel(s) and temporarily attach the rotor disc with two of the wheel lug nuts.

2. Remove and position aside the brake caliper. Unbolt and remove the torque plate from the steering knuckle.

3. Remove the two wheel nuts and pull the brake disc from the axle hub.

To install:

4. Position the new rotor disc onto the axle hub and reinstall the two wheel nuts temporarily.

5. Install the torque plate onto the steering knuckle. Torque the plate bolts to 65 ft. lbs. (88 Nm). Install the brake caliper assembly-refer to the necessary service procedure.

6. Remove the wheel lug nuts and install the front wheels. Secure the wheel lugs. Before moving the vehicle, make sure to pump the brake pedal a few times to seat the brake pads against the rotors.

INSPECTION

NOTE: *The brake disc rotors should be refinished on a brake lathe, when replacing the front brake pads for the brake pads to wear properly.*

Examine the brake disc. If it is worn, warped or scored, it must be replaced. Check the thickness of the brake disc against the specifications given in the Brake Specifications Chart. If it is below specifications, replace it. Use a micrometer to measure the thickness.

The disc run-out should be measured before the disc is removed and again, after the disc is installed. Use a dial indicator mounted on a magnet type stand to determine runout. Position the dial so the stylus is 0.039 in. (10mm) from the outer edge of the rotor disc. Check the run-out specification of brake disc against the specifications given in the Brake Specifications Chart. If run-out exceeds the specification, replace the brake disc.

NOTE: *Be sure that the front hub bearing play is with specifications. If it is not, an inaccurate run-out reading may be obtained.*

REAR DRUM BRAKES

CAUTION: *Brake shoes contain asbestos, which has been determined to be a cancer causing agent. Never clean the brake surfaces with compressed air! Avoid inhaling any dust from any brake surface. When cleaning brake surfaces, use a commercially available brake cleaning fluid.*

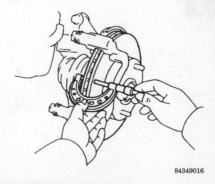

84349016

Measure rotor disc thickness

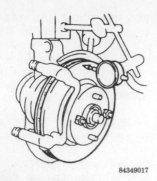

84349017

Measure rotor disc runout

Brake Drums

REMOVAL & INSTALLATION

1. Loosen the rear wheel lug nuts slightly. Release the parking brake.

2. Block the front wheels, raise the rear of the vehicle, and safely support it with jackstands.

3. Remove the wheel lug nuts and the wheel.

4. Tap the brake drum lightly with a rubber mallet to free the drum if resistance is felt. Sometimes brake drums are stubborn. If the drum is difficult to remove, perform the following: Insert the end of a bent wire (a coat hanger will do nicely) through the hole in the brake drum and hold the automatic adjusting lever away from the adjuster. Reduce the brake shoe adjustment by turning the adjuster bolt with a brake tool. The drum should now be loose enough to remove without much effort.

To install:

5. Clean the drum and inspect it as detailed in this section.

6. If the adjuster was loosened to remove the brake drum, turn the adjuster

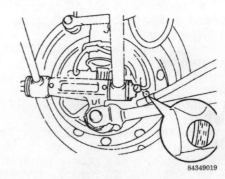

84349019

Inspect the rear brake shoes

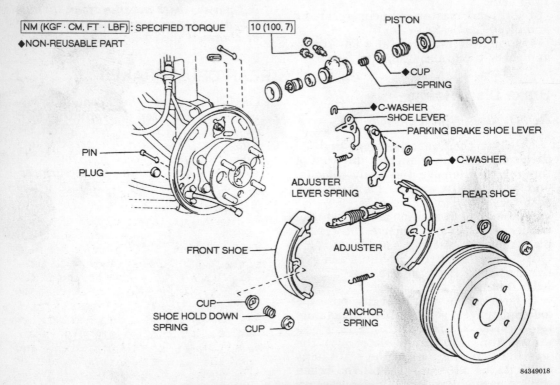

NM (KGF·CM, FT·LBF): SPECIFIED TORQUE   10 (100, 7)

◆NON-REUSABLE PART

PISTON
BOOT
◆CUP
SPRING
◆C-WASHER
SHOE LEVER
PARKING BRAKE SHOE LEVER
◆C-WASHER
REAR SHOE
PIN
PLUG
ADJUSTER LEVER SPRING
ADJUSTER
FRONT SHOE
CUP
SHOE HOLD DOWN SPRING
CUP
ANCHOR SPRING

84349018

Exploded view of the rear brake shoes

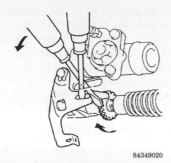

Hold the automatic adjusting lever away from the adjuster to remove the brake drum if necessary

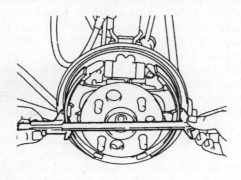

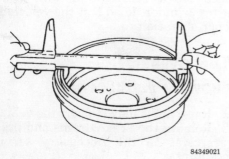

84349021

Check clearance between the rear brake shoes and brake drum

bolt to adjust the length to the shortest possible amount.

7. Hold the brake drum so that the hole on the drum is aligned with the large hole on the axle carrier and install the drum.

8. Pull the parking lever all the way up until a clicking sound can no longer be heard. Check the clearance between brake shoes and brake drum if necessary.

9. Install the rear wheels, tighten the wheel lug nuts and lower the vehicle.

10. Retighten the wheel lug nuts and pump the brake pedal a few times before moving the vehicle.

INSPECTION

1. Remove the inspection hole plug from the backing plate, and with the aide of a flashlight, check the lining thickness. The minimum brake lining thickness is 0.039 in. (1.0mm). If the brake lining does not meet the minimum specification, replace the brake shoes as a set.

2. Remove the brake drum and clean it thoroughly.

3. Inspect the drum for scoring, cracks, grooves and out-of-roundness. Replace or refinish the brake drum, as required. Light scoring may be removed by dressing the drum with fine grit emery cloth. Heavy scoring will require the use of a brake drum lathe to turn or refinish the brake drum.

4. Using inside calipers or equivalent, measure the inside diameter of the brake drum. The standard inside diameter is 7.874 in. (200mm). The maximum inside diameter is 7.913 in. (201mm). If the brake drum exceeds the maximum diameter, replace it.

Brake Shoes

INSPECTION

1. Inspect all brake parts and springs for rust, wear and damage.

2. Measure the brake lining thickness. The minimum allowable thickness is 0.039 in. (1.0mm). If the lining does not meet the minimum specification, replace it.

NOTE: *If one of the brake shoes needs to be replaced, replace all the rear shoes in order to maintain even braking.*

3. Measure inside diameter of the drum as detailed in this section.

4. Place the shoe into the brake drum and check that the lining is in proper contact with the drum's surface. If the contact is improper, repair the lining with a brake shoe grinder or replace the shoe.

5. To measure the clearance between brake shoe and parking brake lever, temporarily install the parking brake and automatic adjusting levers onto the rear shoe, using a new C-washer. With a feeler gauge, measure the clearance between the shoe and the lever. The clearance should be within 0.0138 in. (0-0.35mm). If the clearance is not as specified, use a shim to adjust it. When the clearance is correct, stake the C-washer with pliers.

REMOVAL & INSTALLATION

NOTE: *The brake drums should be refinished on a brake lathe, when replacing the rear brake shoes for the brake shoes to wear properly.*

1. Raise and support the vehicle safely. Remove the wheels.

2. Perform the brake drum removal procedure as previously detailed. Do one set of shoes at a time. Note the position and direction of each component part so that they may be reinstalled in the correct order.

NOTE: *Do not depress the brake pedal once the brake drum has been removed.*

3. Carefully unhook the return spring from the leading (front) brake shoe. Grasp the hold-down spring pin with pliers and turn it until its in line with the slot in the hold-down spring. Remove the hold-down spring and the pin. Pull out the brake shoe and unhook the anchor spring from the lower edge.

4. Remove the hold-down spring from the trailing (rear) shoe. Pull the shoe out with the adjuster strut, automatic adjuster assembly and springs attached and disconnect the parking brake cable. Unhook the return spring and then remove the adjusting strut. Remove the anchor spring.

5. Remove the adjusting strut. Unhook the adjusting lever spring from the rear shoe and then remove the automatic adjuster assembly by popping out the C-clip.

To install:

6. Inspect the shoes for signs of unusual wear or scoring.

7. Check the wheel cylinder for any sign of fluid seepage or frozen pistons.

8. Clean and inspect the brake backing plate and all other components. Check that the brake drum inner diameter is within specified limits. Lubricate the backing plate bosses and the anchor plate.

9. Mount the automatic adjuster assembly onto a new rear brake shoe. Make sure the C-clip fits properly. Connect the adjusting strut/return spring and then install the adjusting spring.

10. Connect the parking brake cable to the rear shoe and then position the shoe so the lower end rides in the anchor plate and the upper end is against the boot in the wheel cylinder. Install the pin and the hold-down spring. Rotate the pin so the crimped edge is held by the retainer.

11. Install the anchor spring between the front and rear shoes and then stretch the spring enough so the front shoe will fit as the rear did in Step 10. Install the hold-down spring and pin. Connect the return spring/adjusting strut between the 2 shoes and connect it so it rides freely.

12. Check that the automatic adjuster is operating properly; the adjusting bolt should turn when the parking brake lever (in the brake assembly) is moved. Adjust the strut as short as possible and then install the brake drum. Set and release the parking brake fully several times.

13. Check clearance between brake shoes and drum if necessary by measuring the brake drum inside diameter and diameter of the brake shoes. Check that the difference between the diameters is the correct rear brake shoe clearance. The rear brake shoe clearance specification is 0.024 in. (0.6mm) for all vehicles.

14. Install the wheel and lower the vehicle. Bleed brake system if necessary. Check the level of brake fluid in the master cylinder. Road test the vehicle for proper operation.

Wheel Cylinder

REMOVAL & INSTALLATION

1. Raise and safely support the vehicle.

2. Remove the brake drums and brake shoes-refer to the necessary service procedures.

3. Working from behind the backing plate, disconnect the hydraulic line from the wheel cylinder, use a line wrench or equivalent.

4. Remove the bolts retaining the wheel cylinder and withdraw the cylinder.

To install:

5. Attach the wheel cylinder to the backing plate. Torque the bolts to 7 ft. lbs.

6. Connect the hydraulic line to the wheel cylinder and tighten it.

7. Install the brake shoes and drums. Make all the necessary adjustments.

8. Fill the master cylinder to the proper level with clean brake fluid bleed the brake system. Check the brake system for leaks.

REAR DISC BRAKES

CAUTION: *Brake shoes contain asbestos, which has been determined to be a cancer causing agent. Never clean the brake surfaces with compressed air! Avoid inhaling any dust from any brake surface. When cleaning brake surfaces, use a commercially available brake cleaning fluid.*

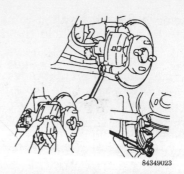

Correct method of raising the rear caliper for access to the brake pads

Brake Pads

REMOVAL & INSTALLATION

1. Raise and safely support the rear of the vehicle on jackstands. Block the front wheels.
2. Siphon a sufficient quantity of brake fluid from the master cylinder reservoir to prevent the brake fluid from overflowing the master cylinder when removing or installing the brake pads. This is necessary as the piston must be forced into the cylinder bore to provide sufficient clearance to install the new brake pads.

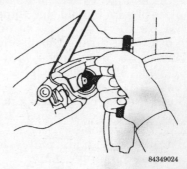

Using a special tool to retract the rear caliper piston

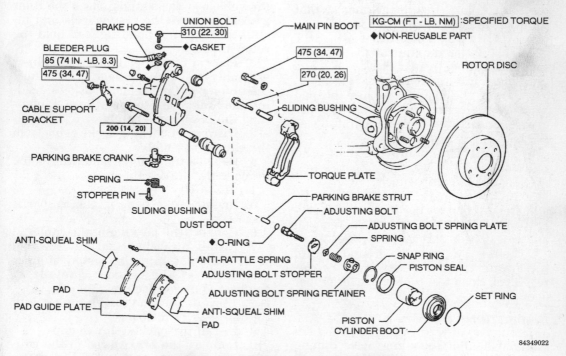

Exploded view of the rear disc brake assembly

3. Remove the wheel, then reinstall 2 lug nuts finger tight to hold the disc in place.

NOTE: *Disassemble brakes one wheel at a time. This will prevent parts confusion and also prevent the opposite caliper piston from popping out during pad installation.*

4. Remove the mounting (lower) bolt from the torque plate. Do not remove the caliper from the main (upper) pin. Do not disconnect the brake hose.

5. Lift the caliper from the bottom so that it hinges upward on the upper pin. Use a piece of wire to hold the caliper up. Do not allow the brake hose to become twisted or kinked during this operation.

6. Remove the brake pads with their shims, springs and support plates.

To install:

7. Check the rotor thickness and run-out. Refer to the Specifications Chart at the end of this section.

8. Install pad support plates to the lower sides of the torque plate.

9. Install anti-rattle springs to the upper side of the torque plate.

10. Install a new anti-squeal shim to the back of each pad and install the pads on the torque plate. Install the pads so that the wear indicator is at the top side.

11. Using a special tool SST 09719–14020 or its equivalent to slowly turn the caliper piston clockwise while pressing it into the bore until it locks.

12. Lower the caliper so that the pad protrusion fits into the piston stopper groove. Insert the cylinder carefully so the boot is not wedged.

13. Install the mounting bolt and tighten it to 14 ft. lbs.

14. Install the rear wheels.

15. Adjust the parking brake automatic adjuster by depressing brake pedal several times. Refer to rear caliper removal and installation service procedures.

16. Lower the car to the ground and fill the master cylinder reservoir to the correct level. Road test the vehicle for proper operation.

INSPECTION

If you hear a squealing noise coming from the rear brakes while driving, check the brake lining thickness and pad wear indicator by looking into the inspection hole on the brake cylinder with the rear wheels removed and the vehicle properly supported. The wear indicator is designed to emit the squealing noise when the brake pad wears down to 2.5mm at which time the brake pad wear plate and the rotor disc rub against each other. If there are traces of the pad wear indicator contacting the rotor disc, the brake pads should be replaced.

To inspect the brake lining thickness, look through the inspection hole and measure the lining thickness using a machinists rule. Also looks for signs of uneven wear. Standard thickness is 10mm. The **minimum** allowable thickness is 0.039 in. (1.0mm), at which time the brake pads must be replaced.

NOTE: *Always replace the brake pads on both rear wheels as a set. The brake disc rotors should be refinished on a brake lathe, when replacing the rear brake pads for the brake pads to wear properly.*

Brake Caliper

REMOVAL & INSTALLATION

1. Raise and safely support the rear of the vehicle on jackstands. Block the front wheels. Remove the rear wheels and install two lug nuts hand tight to hold the rotor in place.

2. Place a container under the caliper assembly to catch spillage. Disconnect the union bolt (and remove gaskets) holding the brake hose to the caliper. Plug or tape the hose immediately.

3. Disconnect parking brake cable from the caliper assembly.

4. Remove the caliper mounting bolts. Remove the brake caliper.

To install:

5. Install brake pads in the caliper if necessary.

6. Connect the parking brake cable.

7. Install the caliper so that the pad protrusion fits into the piston stopper groove. Insert the cylinder carefully so the boot is not wedged.

8. Install the mounting bolts and tighten it to 14 ft. lbs.

9. Install the parking brake clip.

10. Connect the brake hose to the caliper, install new gaskets. Torque the union bolt to 22 ft. lbs.

11. Install the rear wheels.

12. Fill the brake reservoir with brake fluid and bleed brake system.

13. Adjust the parking brake lever travel as follows:

 a. Pull the parking brake lever a few times.

 b. Release the parking brake lever.

 c. Depress the brake pedal several times and adjust the rear brakes automatically.

 d. Check that the parking brake crank touches the stopper pin.

 e. Pull the parking brake lever all the way up and count the number of clicks. The correct specification for parking brake lever travel is at 44.1 lbs. of pull 5–8 clicks. If necessary adjust the parking brake lever travel at the parking brake lever assembly.

OVERHAUL

NOTE: *The use of the correct special tools or their equivalent is REQUIRED for this procedure.*

1. Remove the slide bushings and dust boots.

2. Remove the set ring and dust boot from the caliper piston.

3. Remove the caliper piston (turn piston counterclockwise and remove) from the bolt.

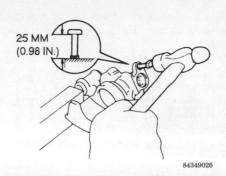

Install stopper pin — rear brake caliper

4. Remove the seal from the inside of the caliper bolt.

5. Install a special tool SST 09756-00010 or its equivalent onto the adjusting bolt and lightly tighten it with a 14mm socket. Do not overtighten the tool; damage to the spring may result.

WARNING: *Always use this tool during disassembly. The spring may fly out, causing personal injury and/or damage to the caliper bore.*

6. Remove the snapring from the caliper bore.

7. Carefully remove the adjusting bolt and disassemble it.

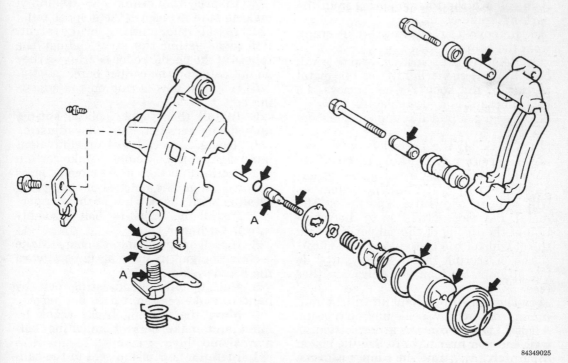

Exploded view of the rear brake caliper

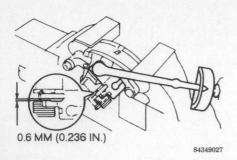

0.6 MM (0.236 IN.)

84349027

Install cable support bracket — rear brake caliper

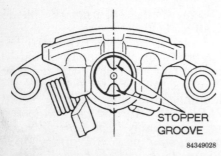

STOPPER
GROOVE

84349028

**Align the center of the piston stopper groove
with the positioning protrusion of the cylinder —
rear brake caliper**

8. Remove the parking brake strut.

9. Remove the cable support bracket, then remove the torsion spring from the parking brake crank.

10. Remove the parking brake crank from the caliper.

11. Remove the parking brake crank boot by tapping it lightly on the metal portion of the boot. Do not remove the boot unless it is to be replaced.

12. Use a pin punch to tap out the stopper pin.

13. Check all the parts for wear, scoring, deterioration, cracking or other abnormal conditions. Corrosion — generally caused by water in the system — will appear as white deposits on the metal. Pay close attention to the condition of the inside of the caliper bore and the outside of the piston. Any sign of corrosion or scoring requires new parts; do not attempt to clean or resurface either face.

14. The caliper overhaul kit will, at minimum, contain new seals and dust boots. A good kit will contain a new piston as well, but you may have to buy the piston separately. Any time the caliper is disas-

sembled, a new piston is highly recommended in addition to the new seals.

15. Clean all the components to be reused with an aerosol brake solvent and dry them thoroughly. Take any steps necessary to eliminate moisture or water vapor from the parts.

16. Coat all the caliper components with fresh brake fluid from a new can.

NOTE: *Some repair kits come with special assembly lubricant for the piston and seal. Use this lubricant according to directions with the kit.*

17. Install the stopper pin into the caliper until the pin extends 25mm.

18. Install the parking brake crank boot. Use a 24mm socket to tap the boot to the caliper.

19. Install the parking brake crank onto the caliper. Make certain the crank boot is securely matched to the groove of the crank seal.

20. Install the cable support bracket. Press the surface of the bracket flush against the wall of the caliper and tighten the bolt to 34 ft. lbs.

21. Check that the clearance between the parking brake crank and the cable support is 6mm.

22. Install the torsion spring.

23. Inspect the crank sub-assembly, making sure it touches the stopper pin.

24. Install the parking brake strut. Before adjusting the strut, adjust the rollers of the needle roller bearing so they do not catch on the caliper bore.

25. Install a new O-ring on the adjusting bolt.

26. Install the stopper, plate, spring, and spring retainer onto the adjusting bolt. Using a special tool or equivalent hand tighten the assembly. Make certain the inscribed portion of the stopper faces upward. Align the notches of the spring retainer with the notches of the stopper.

27. Install the adjusting bolt assembly into the cylinder.

28. Install snapring into the bore. Make certain the gap in the ring faces toward the bleeder side.

29. Pull up on the adjusting bolt by hand to make certain it does not move.

30. Move the parking brake crank by hand and make certain adjusting bolt moves smoothly.

31. Install a new piston seal in the caliper bore.

32. Install the piston into the caliper bore. Using a special tool or its

equivalent, slowly screw the piston clockwise until it will not descend any further.

33. Align the center of the piston stopper groove with the positioning marks of the caliper bore.

34. Install the piston dust boot and its set ring.

35. Install a new boot on the main (upper) caliper pin. Use a 21mm socket to press in the new boot.

36. Install the slide bushings and boots onto the caliper.

Brake Disc (Rotor)

REMOVAL & INSTALLATION

1. Loosen the rear wheel lugs slightly, then raise and safely support the rear of the vehicle. Remove the rear wheel(s) and temporarily attach the rotor disc with two of the wheel lug nuts.

2. Remove and position aside the brake caliper. Unbolt and remove the torque plate from the axle carrier.

3. Remove the two wheel nuts and pull the brake disc from the axle hub.

To install:

4. Position the new rotor disc onto the axle hub and reinstall the two wheel nuts temporarily.

5. Install the torque plate onto the axle carrier. Torque the plate bolts to 34 ft. lbs. Install the brake caliper assembly-refer to the necessary service procedure.

6. Remove the wheel lug nuts and install the rear wheels. Secure the wheel lugs. Before moving the vehicle, make sure to pump the brake pedal a few times to seat the brake pads against the rotors.

NOTE: *The brake disc rotors should be refinished on a brake lathe, when replacing the rear brake pads for the brake pads to wear properly.*

INSPECTION

Run-out

1. Mount a dial indicator with a magnetic or universal base on the strut or shock assembly so that the tip of the indicator contacts the rotor about ½ in. from the outer edge.

2. Zero the dial indicator. Turn the rotor one complete revolution and observe the total indicated run-out.

3. If the run-out exceeds 0.0039 in. (0.10mm), clean the wheel hub and rotor mating surfaces and remeasure. If the run-out still exceeds maximum, remove the rotor and remount it so that the wheel studs now run through different holes. If this re-indexing does not provide correct run-out measurements, the rotor should be considered warped beyond use and either resurfaced or replaced.

Thickness

The thickness of the rotor partially determines its ability to withstand heat and provide adequate stopping force. Every rotor has a minimum thickness established by the manufacturer. This minimum measurement must not be exceeded. A rotor which is too thin may crack under braking; if this occurs the wheel can lock instantly, resulting in sudden loss of control.

If any part of the rotor measures below minimum thickness, the disc must be replaced. Additionally, a rotor which needs to be resurfaced may not allow sufficient cutting before reaching minimum. Since the allowable wear from new to minimum is about 1mm, it is wise to replace the rotor rather than resurface it.

Thickness and thickness variation can be measured with a micrometer capable of reading to one ten-thousandth inch. All measurements must be made at the same distance in from the edge of the rotor. Measure at four equally spaced points around the disc and record the measurements. Compare each measurement to the minimum thickness specifications in the chart at the end of this section.

Condition

A new rotor will have a smooth, even surface which rapidly changes during use. It is not uncommon for a rotor to develop very fine concentric scoring (like the grooves on a record) due to dust and grit being trapped by the brake pad. This slight irregularity is normal, but as the grooves deepen, wear and noise increase and stopping may be affected. As a general rule, any groove deep enough to snag a fingernail during inspection is cause for action or replacement.

Any sign of blue spots, discoloration, heavy rusting or outright gouges require replacement of the rotor. If you are checking the disc on the car (such as during pad replacement or tire rotation) remember to turn the disc and check both the inner and outer faces completely. If anything looks questionable or requires consideration, choose the safer option and replace the rotor. The brakes are a critical system and must be maintained at 100% reliability.

Any time a rotor is replaced, the pads should also be replaced so that the surfaces mate properly. Since brake pads should be replaced in axle sets (both front or rear wheels), consider replacing both rotors instead of just one. The restored feel and accurate stopping make the extra investment worthwhile.

PARKING BRAKE

Cables

REMOVAL & INSTALLATION

NOTE: *This procedure is general service procedure (no factory service procedure are given). Modify the service steps as required.*

1. Elevate and safely support the car. If only the rear wheels are elevated, block the front wheels. Release the parking brake after the car is supported.
2. Remove the rear wheel(s).
3. If equipped with drum brakes, remove the brake drum and remove the brake shoes.
4. If equipped with disc brakes, remove the clip from the parking brake cable and remove the cable from the caliper assembly.
5. If equipped with drum brakes, remove the parking brake retaining bolts at the backing plate.
6. Remove any exhaust heat shields which interfere with the removal of the cable.
7. Remove the 2 cable clamps.
8. Disconnect the cable retainer.
9. Remove the cable from the equalizer (yoke).
To install:
10. Fit the end of the new cable into the equalizer and make certain it is properly seated.

11. Install the cable retainer, and, working along the length of the cable, install the clamps.
   NOTE: *Make certain the cable is properly routed and does not contain any sharp bends or kinks.*
12. Feed the cable through the backing plate and install the retaining bolts.
13. If equipped with disc brakes, connect the cable to the arm and install the clip.
14. If equipped with drum brakes, reinstall the shoes. The cable will be connected to the shoes during the installation process.
15. Reinstall the wheel(s) and lower the car to the ground. Adjust the parking brake.

ADJUSTMENT

Pull the parking brake lever all the way up and count the number of clicks. The correct range is 4–7 clicks rear drum brake type and 5–8 clicks rear disc brake type for full application. A system which is too tight or too loose requires adjustment.
   NOTE: *Before adjusting the parking brake cable, make certain that the rear brake shoe or rear brake pad clearance is correct. Refer to the necessary service procedures.*
1. Remove the center console box.

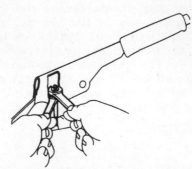

84349029

Parking brake adjustment
2. At the rear of the handbrake lever, loosen the locknut on the brake cable.
3. Turn the adjusting nut until the parking brake travel is correct.
4. Tighten the locknut.
5. Reinstall the console.

CHILTON'S
AUTO BODY REPAIR TIPS

Tools and Materials • Step-by-Step Illustrated Procedures
How To Repair Dents, Scratches and Rust Holes
Spray Painting and Refinishing Tips

With a little practice, basic body repair procedures can be mastered by any do-it-yourself mechanic. The step-by-step repairs shown here can be applied to almost any type of auto body repair.

TOOLS & MATERIALS

You may already have basic tools, such as hammers and electric drills. Other tools unique to body repair — body hammers, grinding attachments, sanding blocks, dent puller, half-round plastic file and plastic spreaders — are relatively inexpensive and can be obtained wherever auto parts or auto body repair parts are sold. Portable air compressors and paint spray guns can be purchased or rented.

Auto Body Repair Kits

The best and most often used products are available to the do-it-yourselfer in kit form, from major manufacturers of auto body repair products. The same manufacturers also merchandise the individual products for use by pros.

Kits are available to make a wide variety of repairs, including holes, dents and scratches and fiberglass, and offer the advantage of buying the materials you'll need for the job. There is little waste or chance of materials going bad from not being used. Many kits may also contain basic body-working tools such as body files, sanding blocks and spreaders. Check the contents of the kit before buying your tools.

BODY REPAIR TIPS

Safety

Many of the products associated with auto body repair and refinishing contain toxic chemicals. Read all labels before opening containers and store them in a safe place and manner.
• Wear eye protection (safety goggles) when using power tools or when performing any operation that involves the removal of any type of material.
• Wear lung protection (disposable mask or respirator) when grinding, sanding or painting.

Sanding

1 Sand off paint before using a dent puller. When using a non-adhesive sanding disc, cover the back of the disc with an overlapping layer or two of masking tape and trim the edges. The disc will last considerably longer.

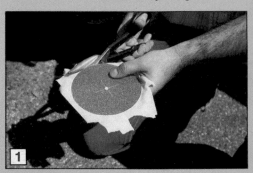

2 Use the circular motion of the sanding disc to grind *into* the edge of the repair. Grinding or sanding away from the jagged edge will only tear the sandpaper.

3 Use the palm of your hand flat on the panel to detect high and low spots. Do not use your fingertips. Slide your hand slowly back and forth.

WORKING WITH BODY FILLER

Mixing The Filler

Cleanliness and proper mixing and application are extremely important. Use a clean piece of plastic or glass or a disposable artist's palette to mix body filler.

1 Allow plenty of time and follow directions. No useful purpose will be served by adding more hardener to make it cure (set-up) faster. Less hardener means more curing time, but the mixture dries harder; more hardener means less curing time but a softer mixture.

2 Both the hardener and the filler should be thoroughly kneaded or stirred before mixing. Hardener should be a solid paste and dispense like thin toothpaste. Body filler should be smooth, and free of lumps or thick spots.

Getting the proper amount of hardener in the filler is the trickiest part of preparing the filler. Use the same amount of hardener in cold or warm weather. For contour filler (thick coats), a bead of hardener twice the diameter of the filler is about right. There's about a 15% margin on either side, but, if in doubt use less hardener.

3 Mix the body filler and hardener by wiping across the mixing surface, picking the mixture up and wiping it again. Colder weather requires longer mixing times. Do not mix in a circular motion; this will trap air bubbles which will become holes in the cured filler.

Applying The Filler

1 For best results, filler should not be applied over ¼" thick.

Apply the filler in several coats. Build it up to above the level of the repair surface so that it can be sanded or grated down.

The first coat of filler must be pressed on with a firm wiping motion.

Apply the filler in one direction only. Working the filler back and forth will either pull it off the metal or trap air bubbles.

REPAIRING DENTS

Before you start, take a few minutes to study the damaged area. Try to visualize the shape of the panel before it was damaged. If the damage is on the left fender, look at the right fender and use it as a guide. If there is access to the panel from behind, you can reshape it with a body hammer. If not, you'll have to use a dent puller. Go slowly and work the metal a little at a time. Get the panel as straight as possible before applying filler.

1 This dent is typical of one that can be pulled out or hammered out from behind. Remove the headlight cover, headlight assembly and turn signal housing.

2 Drill a series of holes ½ the size of the end of the dent puller along the stress line. Make some trial pulls and assess the results. If necessary, drill more holes and try again. Do not hurry.

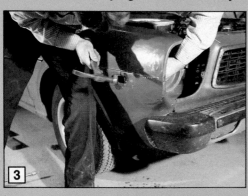

3 If possible, use a body hammer and block to shape the metal back to its original contours. Get the metal back as close to its original shape as possible. Don't depend on body filler to fill dents.

4 Using an 80-grit grinding disc on an electric drill, grind the paint from the surrounding area down to bare metal. Use a new grinding pad to prevent heat buildup that will warp metal.

5 The area should look like this when you're finished grinding. Knock the drill holes in and tape over small openings to keep plastic filler out.

6 Mix the body filler (see Body Repair Tips). Spread the body filler evenly over the entire area (see Body Repair Tips). Be sure to cover the area completely.

7 Let the body filler dry until the surface can just be scratched with your fingernail. Knock the high spots from the body filler with a body file ("Cheesegrater"). Check frequently with the palm of your hand for high and low spots.

8 Check to be sure that trim pieces that will be installed later will fit exactly. Sand the area with 40-grit paper.

9 If you wind up with low spots, you may have to apply another layer of filler.

10 Knock the high spots off with 40-grit paper. When you are satisfied with the contours of the repair, apply a thin coat of filler to cover pin holes and scratches.

11 Block sand the area with 40-grit paper to a smooth finish. Pay particular attention to body lines and ridges that must be well-defined.

12 Sand the area with 400 paper and then finish with a scuff pad. The finished repair is ready for priming and painting (see Painting Tips).

Materials and photos courtesy of Ritt Jones Auto Body, Prospect Park, PA.

REPAIRING RUST HOLES

There are many ways to repair rust holes. The fiberglass cloth kit shown here is one of the most cost efficient for the owner because it provides a strong repair that resists cracking and moisture and is relatively easy to use. It can be used on large and small holes (with or without backing) and can be applied over contoured areas. Remember, however, that short of replacing an entire panel, no repair is a guarantee that the rust will not return.

1 Remove any trim that will be in the way. Clean away all loose debris. Cut away all the rusted metal. But be sure to leave enough metal to retain the contour or body shape.

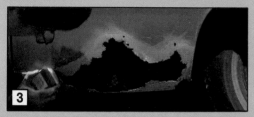

2 Grind away all traces of rust with a 24-grit grinding disc. Be sure to grind back 3-4 inches from the edge of the hole down to bare metal and be sure all traces of paint, primer and rust are removed.

3 Block sand the area with 80 or 100 grit sandpaper to get a clear, shiny surface and feathered paint edge. Tap the edges of the hole inward with a ball peen hammer.

4 If you are going to use release film, cut a piece about 2-3″ larger than the area you have sanded. Place the film over the repair and mark the sanded area on the film. Avoid any unnecessary wrinkling of the film.

5 Cut 2 pieces of fiberglass matte to match the shape of the repair. One piece should be about 1″ smaller than the sanded area and the second piece should be 1″ smaller than the first. Mix enough filler and hardener to saturate the fiberglass material (see Body Repair Tips).

6 Lay the release sheet on a flat surface and spread an even layer of filler, large enough to cover the repair. Lay the smaller piece of fiberglass cloth in the center of the sheet and spread another layer of filler over the fiberglass cloth. Repeat the operation for the larger piece of cloth.

7 Place the repair material over the repair area, with the release film facing outward. Use a spreader and work from the center outward to smooth the material, following the body contours. Be sure to remove all air bubbles.

8 Wait until the repair has dried tack-free and peel off the release sheet. The ideal working temperature is 60°-90° F. Cooler or warmer temperatures or high humidity may require additional curing time. Wait longer, if in doubt.

9

9 Sand and feather-edge the entire area. The initial sanding can be done with a sanding disc on an electric drill if care is used. Finish the sanding with a block sander. Low spots can be filled with body filler; this may require several applications.

10

10 When the filler can just be scratched with a fingernail, knock the high spots down with a body file and smooth the entlre area with 80-grit. Feather the filled areas into the surrounding areas.

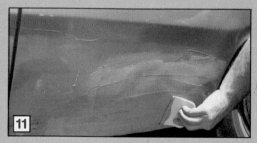

11

11 When the area is sanded smooth, mix some topcoat and hardener and apply it directly with a spreader. This will give a smooth finish and prevent the glass matte from showing through the paint.

12

12 Block sand the topcoat smooth with finishing sandpaper (200 grit), and 400 grit. The repair is ready for masking, priming and painting (see Painting Tips).

Materials and photos courtesy Marson Corporation, Chelsea, Massachusetts

PAINTING TIPS

Preparation

1 SANDING — Use a 400 or 600 grit wet or dry sandpaper. Wet-sand the area with a 1/4 sheet of sandpaper soaked in clean water. Keep the paper wet while sanding. Sand the area until the repaired area tapers into the original finish.

2 CLEANING — Wash the area to be painted thoroughly with water and a clean rag. Rinse it thoroughly and wipe the surface dry until you're sure it's completely free of dirt, dust, fingerprints, wax, detergent or other foreign matter.

3 MASKING — Protect any areas you don't want to overspray by covering them with masking tape and newspaper. Be careful not get fingerprints on the area to be painted.

4 PRIMING — All exposed metal should be primed before painting. Primer protects the metal and provides an excellent surface for paint adhesion. When the primer is dry, wet-sand the area again with 600 grit wet-sandpaper. Clean the area again after sanding.

4

Painting Techniques

P aint applied from either a spray gun or a spray can (for small areas) will provide good results. Experiment on an old piece of metal to get the right combination before you begin painting.

SPRAYING VISCOSITY (SPRAY GUN ONLY) — Paint should be thinned to spraying viscosity according to the directions on the can. Use only the recommended thinner or reducer and the same amount of reduction regardless of temperature.

AIR PRESSURE (SPRAY GUN ONLY) — This is extremely important. Be sure you are using the proper recommended pressure.

TEMPERATURE — The surface to be painted should be approximately the same temperature as the surrounding air. Applying warm paint to a cold surface, or vice versa, will completely upset the paint characteristics.

THICKNESS — Spray with smooth strokes. In general, the thicker the coat of paint, the longer the drying time. Apply several thin coats about 30 seconds apart. The paint should remain wet long enough to flow out and no longer; heavier coats will only produce sags or wrinkles. Spray a light (fog) coat, followed by heavier color coats.

DISTANCE — The ideal spraying distance is 8"-12" from the gun or can to the surface. Shorter distances will produce ripples, while greater distances will result in orange peel, dry film and poor color match and loss of material due to overspray.

OVERLAPPING — The gun or can should be kept at right angles to the surface at all times. Work to a wet edge at an even speed, using a 50% overlap and direct the center of the spray at the lower or nearest edge of the previous stroke.

RUBBING OUT (BLENDING) FRESH PAINT — Let the paint dry thoroughly. Runs or imperfections can be sanded out, primed and repainted.

Don't be in too big a hurry to remove the masking. This only produces paint ridges. When the finish has dried for at least a week, apply a small amount of fine grade rubbing compound with a clean, wet cloth. Use lots of water and blend the new paint with the surrounding area.

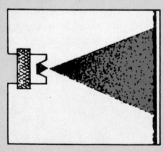

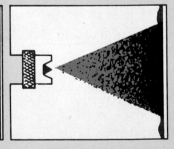

WRONG

CORRECT

WRONG

Thin coat. Stroke too fast, not enough overlap, gun too far away.

Medium coat. Proper distance, good stroke, proper overlap.

Heavy coat. Stroke too slow, too much overlap, gun too close.

10

EXTERIOR

Doors

REMOVAL & INSTALLATION

1. Disconnect the negative battery terminal.

2. If equipped with power door locks, windows or any other power option located on the door, remove the inner door panel and disconnect the electrical component.

3. Remove the wire harness retainers and extract the harness from the door.

4. Disconnect the door check rod. To prevent the rod from falling inside the door, install the retainer into the hole in the end of the check rod.

5. Matchmark the position of both the upper and lower door hinge to aid in installation. While supporting the door, remove the door-to-hinge bolts and lift the door from the vehicle.

To install:

6. Position the door on the vehicle and loosely install the hinge bolts.

7. Align each hinge to the matchmarks and secure the bolts.

8. Install and connect the electrical wire harness and secure to the door (if removed).

9. Connect the door check rod and reinstall the interior door trim panel(if removed).

10. Close the door slowly and check for proper alignment. Adjust the door as required and reconnect the negative battery cable.

ADJUSTMENT

To adjust the door in forward, rearward and vertical directions, perform the following adjustment:

1. Loosen the body side hinge bolts or nuts.

2. Adjust the door to the desired position.

3. Secure the body side hinge bolts or nuts and check the door for proper alignment.

To adjust the door in left, right and vertical directions, perform the following adjustments:

4. Loosen the door side hinge bolts slightly.

5. Adjust the door to the desired position.

6. Secure the door side hinge bolts and check the door for proper alignment.

To adjust the door lock striker, perform the following procedure:

7. Check that the door fit and the door lock linkages are adjusted properly.

8. Slightly loosen the striker mounting screws and tap striker with a hammer until the desired position is obtained.

9. Tighten the striker mounting screws.

Hood

REMOVAL & INSTALLATION

1. Open the hood completely.

2. Protect the cowl panel and hood from scratches during this operation. Apply protection tape or cover body surfaces before starting work.

3. Scribe a mark showing the location of each hinge on the hood to aid in alignment during installation.

4. Prop the hood in the upright position.

5. Have an assistant help hold the hood while you remove the hood-to-hinge bolts. Use care not to damage hood or vehicle during hood removal.

6. Lift the hood off of the vehicle.

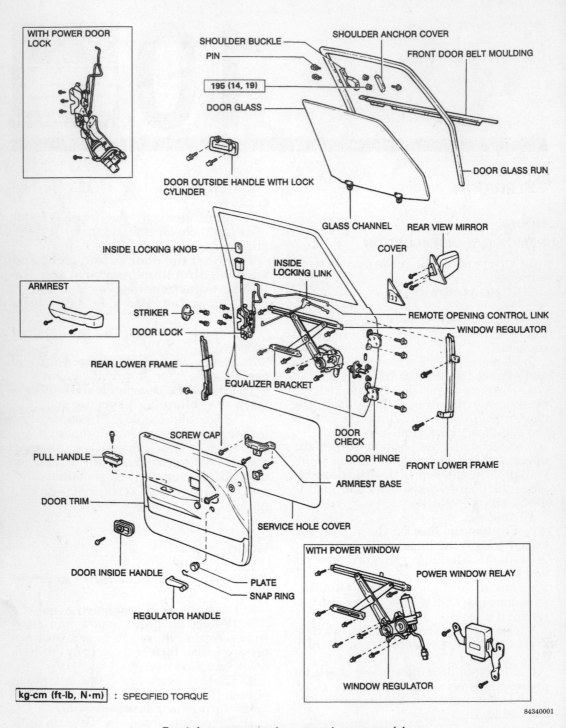

WITH POWER DOOR LOCK

SHOULDER BUCKLE

PIN

SHOULDER ANCHOR COVER

FRONT DOOR BELT MOULDING

195 (14, 19)

DOOR GLASS

DOOR GLASS RUN

DOOR OUTSIDE HANDLE WITH LOCK CYLINDER

GLASS CHANNEL

REAR VIEW MIRROR

INSIDE LOCKING KNOB

COVER

INSIDE LOCKING LINK

ARMREST

STRIKER

REMOTE OPENING CONTROL LINK

WINDOW REGULATOR

DOOR LOCK

REAR LOWER FRAME

EQUALIZER BRACKET

DOOR CHECK

DOOR HINGE

FRONT LOWER FRAME

SCREW CAP

PULL HANDLE

DOOR TRIM

ARMREST BASE

SERVICE HOLE COVER

DOOR INSIDE HANDLE

PLATE

SNAP RING

REGULATOR HANDLE

WITH POWER WINDOW

POWER WINDOW RELAY

WINDOW REGULATOR

kg-cm (ft-lb, N·m) : SPECIFIED TORQUE

84340001

Front door components — except coupe models

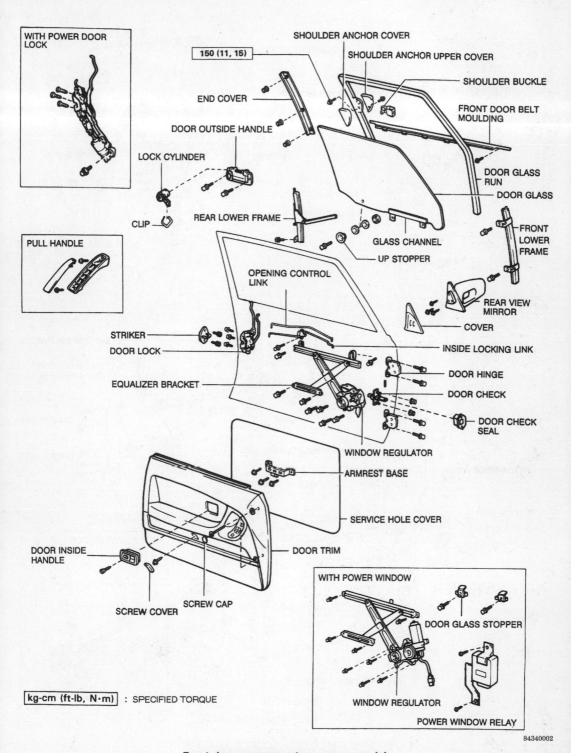

WITH POWER DOOR LOCK

PULL HANDLE

SHOULDER ANCHOR COVER

150 (11, 15)

SHOULDER ANCHOR UPPER COVER

SHOULDER BUCKLE

END COVER

FRONT DOOR BELT MOULDING

DOOR OUTSIDE HANDLE

LOCK CYLINDER

DOOR GLASS RUN

DOOR GLASS

CLIP

REAR LOWER FRAME

GLASS CHANNEL

UP STOPPER

FRONT LOWER FRAME

OPENING CONTROL LINK

REAR VIEW MIRROR

COVER

STRIKER

DOOR LOCK

INSIDE LOCKING LINK

DOOR HINGE

EQUALIZER BRACKET

DOOR CHECK

DOOR CHECK SEAL

WINDOW REGULATOR

ARMREST BASE

SERVICE HOLE COVER

DOOR INSIDE HANDLE

DOOR TRIM

SCREW COVER

SCREW CAP

WITH POWER WINDOW

DOOR GLASS STOPPER

WINDOW REGULATOR

POWER WINDOW RELAY

kg-cm (ft-lb, N·m) : SPECIFIED TORQUE

84340002

Front door components — coupe models

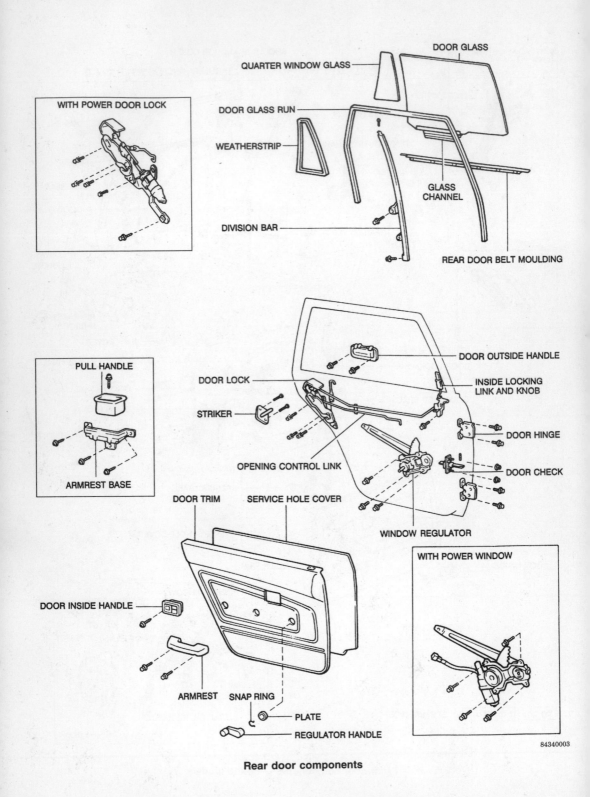

WITH POWER DOOR LOCK

QUARTER WINDOW GLASS

DOOR GLASS

DOOR GLASS RUN

WEATHERSTRIP

GLASS CHANNEL

DIVISION BAR

REAR DOOR BELT MOULDING

PULL HANDLE

ARMREST BASE

DOOR LOCK

STRIKER

OPENING CONTROL LINK

DOOR OUTSIDE HANDLE

INSIDE LOCKING LINK AND KNOB

DOOR HINGE

DOOR CHECK

WINDOW REGULATOR

DOOR TRIM

SERVICE HOLE COVER

WITH POWER WINDOW

DOOR INSIDE HANDLE

ARMREST   SNAP RING

PLATE

REGULATOR HANDLE

84340003

Rear door components

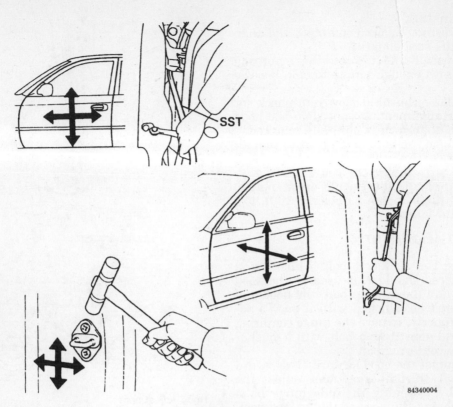

84340004

Front door adjustment

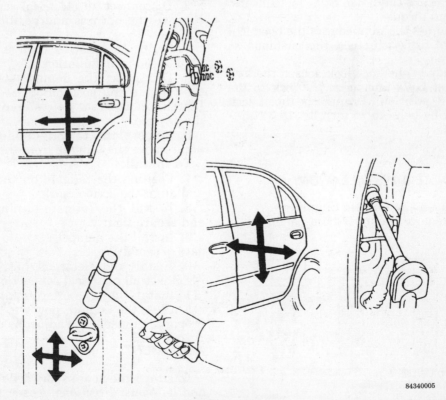

84340005

Rear door adjustment

To install:

7. Position he hood on hinges and align with the scribe marks.

8. Install and tighten the mounting bolts with enough torque to hold hood in place.

9. Close the hood slowly to check for proper alignment. Do not slam the hood closed, alignment is normally required.

10. Open the hood and adjust so that all clearances are the same and the hood panel is flush with the body.

11. After all adjustments are complete, torque hinge mounting bolts to 10 ft. lbs. (14 Nm) torque.

HOOD ALIGNMENT

Since the centering bolt, which has a chamfered shoulder, is used as the hood hinge and the lock set bolt, the hood and lock can't be adjusted with it on. To adjust properly, remove the hinge centering bolt and substitute a bolt with a washer for the centering bolt.

To adjust the hood forward or rearward and left or right directions, adjust the hood by loosening the side hinge bolts and moving the hood to the desired position. Secure the hinge bolts to 10 ft. lbs. (14 Nm) torque.

To adjust the front edge of the hood in a vertical direction, turn the cushions as required.

To adjust the hood lock, loosen the lock retainer bolts and move the lock to the desired position. Torque the hood lock mounting bolts to 74 inch lbs. (8.3 Nm).

Tailgate

REMOVAL & INSTALLATION

1. Open the tailgate completely.
2. Remove the inner trim panel.

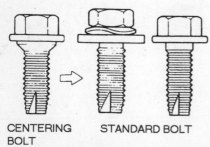

CENTERING BOLT   STANDARD BOLT

84340006

Hood adjustment bolts

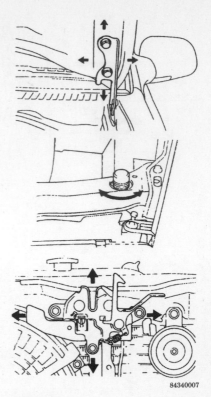

84340007

Hood adjustment

3. Disconnect all electrical connectors. Remove the harness and position out of the way.

4. Scribe the hinge location on the tailgate to aid in installation.

5. Disconnect the damper stays from the tailgate and position out of the way. Disconnect the rear defroster connector, if equipped.

6. Remove the tailgate-to-hinge bolts and remove the tailgate from the vehicle.

To install:

7. Position the tailgate on the vehicle and align the scribe marks.

8. Install the tailgate-to-hinge bolts and secure tightly.

9. Install the damper stays to the tailgate assembly.

10. Install the electrical harness and reconnect all electrical connections.

11. Install the interior trim panel.

12. Close the tailgate slowly to check for proper alignment, and adjust as required.

ALIGNMENT

To adjust the door in forward/rearward and left/right directions, loosen the body side hinge bolts and position the tailgate as required.

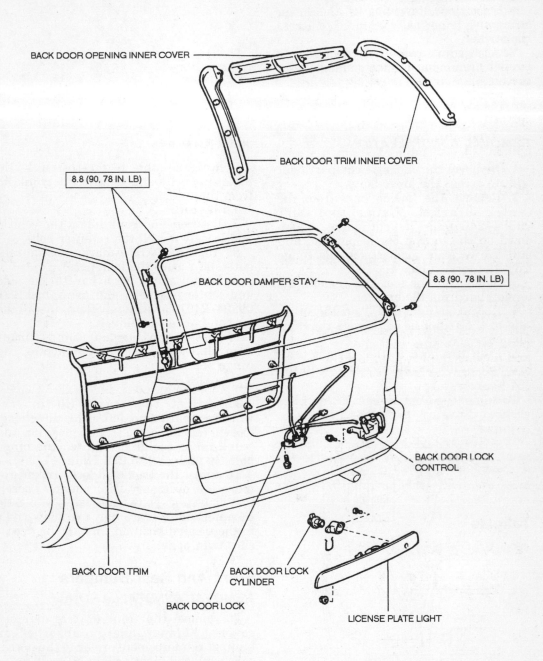

BACK DOOR OPENING INNER COVER

BACK DOOR TRIM INNER COVER

8.8 (90, 78 IN. LB)

BACK DOOR DAMPER STAY

8.8 (90, 78 IN. LB)

BACK DOOR LOCK CONTROL

BACK DOOR TRIM

BACK DOOR LOCK CYLINDER

BACK DOOR LOCK

LICENSE PLATE LIGHT

Nm (kg.cm, ft.lb) : SPECIFIED TORQUE

84340008

Tailgate components

To adjust the tailgate lock striker, loosen the mounting bolts and using a plastic hammer, tap the striker to the desired position. Removing of the lower trim panel is normally required to access the striker.

Vertical adjustment of the door edge is made by removing or adding shims under the hinges.

Sedan Trunk Lid

REMOVAL & INSTALLATION

1. Remove the luggage compartment trim to access the hinge bolts.
2. Remove the torsion bars from the center bracket. Using tool SST 09804–24010 or its equivalent, push down on the torsion bar at one end and pull the luggage compartment lid hinge from the torsion bar.
3. Slowly lift the tool and remove the torsion bar from the bracket.
4. Repeat steps 2 and 3 on the other side of the trunk lid to remove that torsion bar.
5. Prop the hood in the upright position and scribe the hinge locations in the trunk.

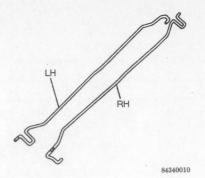

Install torsion bars

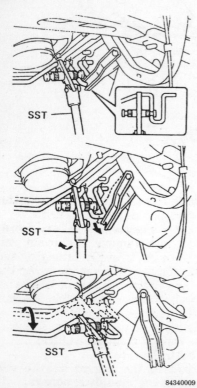

SST

SST

SST

84340009

Removing torsion bars

6. Remove the hinge-to-trunk lid mounting bolts and remove the trunk lid from the vehicle.
To install:
7. Position the trunk lid on the vehicle and loosely install the retainer bolts.
8. Align the scribe marks on the tailgate and secure the fasteners.
9. Install the torsion bar to the side and center brackets, and using tool SST 09804–24010 or its equivalent, install the torsion bar to the hinges.
10. Install the luggage compartment trim that was removed to access the hinge bolts.

ALIGNMENT

To adjust the trunk lid in forward/rearward and left/right directions, loosen the hinge bolts and position the trunk lid as required. Tighten the hinge bolts to 48 inch lbs. (5.4 Nm).

To adjust the trunk lid lock striker, remove the necessary trim panels. Loosen the mounting bolts and using a plastic hammer and a brass bar, tap the striker to the desired position. Install the necessary trim panels.

Front And Rear Bumpers

REMOVAL & INSTALLATION

To remove the front or rear bumper covers, bumper energy absorber or bumper reinforcement--refer to the necessary exploded views. Align all body parts after installation.

Grille

REMOVAL & INSTALLATION

The grille can be removed without removing any other parts. The grille is held on by a number of fasteners. Raise the hood and look for screws placed vertically

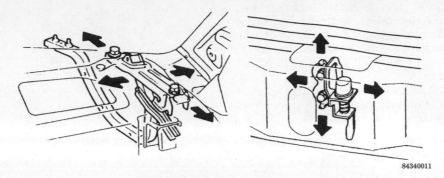

84340011

Luggage compartment adjustment

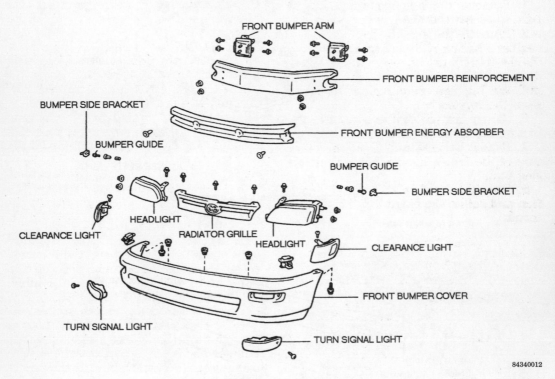

84340012

Front bumper components

in front of the metalwork. Remove the retainer screws and lift the grille from the vehicle.

On installation, make sure that all the retainers are installed in their original locations.

Outside Mirrors

REMOVAL & INSTALLATION

Manual and Power Type

1. Disconnect the negative battery cable.

2. On manual mirrors, remove the set screw and the adjustment knob.

3. Using a screwdriver, pry loose the retainer and remove the inner mirror cover. In order to avoid damaging the interior surfaces of the vehicle, wrap the tip of the screwdriver with tape before using.

4. If the mirror is electric, disconnect the wire harness.

5. Remove the mounting screws and lift the mirror from the vehicle.

To install:

6. Position the mirror on the vehicle and install the mounting screws.

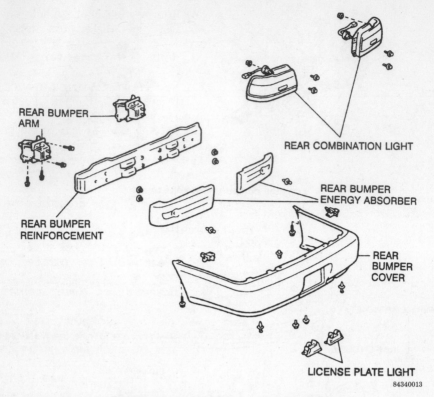

REAR BUMPER ARM

REAR BUMPER REINFORCEMENT

REAR COMBINATION LIGHT

REAR BUMPER ENERGY ABSORBER

REAR BUMPER COVER

LICENSE PLATE LIGHT

84340013

Rear bumper components — except wagon

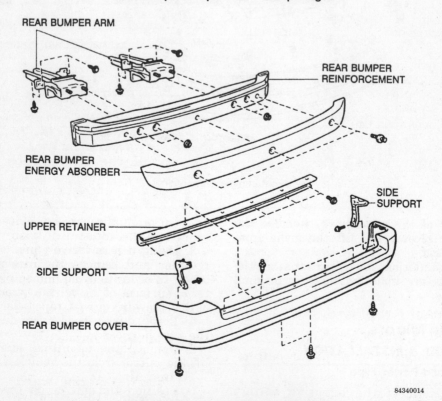

REAR BUMPER ARM

REAR BUMPER REINFORCEMENT

REAR BUMPER ENERGY ABSORBER

UPPER RETAINER

SIDE SUPPORT

SIDE SUPPORT

REAR BUMPER COVER

84340014

Rear bumper components — wagon

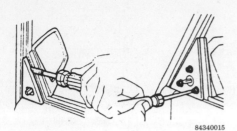

84340015

Removal of the outside mirror

7. If the mirror is electric, reconnect the wire harness.

8. Install the inner cover and retainer.

9. On manual mirrors, install the knob and set screw.

10. Connect the negative battery cable.

11. Cycle the mirror several times to make sure that it works properly.

Antenna

REPLACEMENT

1. Disconnect the negative battery cable.

2. Remove the antenna panel covers, as required.

3. Remove the antenna mounting screws.

4. Disconnect the electrical lead(s) and remove antenna from the vehicle.

5. The installation is the reverse of the removal procedure.

INTERIOR

Disarming the Air Bag System

On models with an airbag, wait at least 90 seconds from the time that the ignition switch is turned to the LOCK position and the battery is disconnected before performing any further work.

Instrument Panel and Pad

REMOVAL & INSTALLATION

1. Disconnect the negative battery cable.

2. Remove the steering wheel-disarm air bag system if so equipped.

3. Remove the right and left front pillar garnish trim.

4. Remove the floor console bin.

5. Remove the engine hood release lever.

6. Remove the lower finish No. 1 trim panel.

7. Remove the steering column cover.

8. Remove the center cluster finish panel.

9. Remove the cluster finish panel.

10. Remove the radio.

11. Remove the stereo opening cover or center differential control switch if so equipped.

12. Remove the combination meter assembly.

13. Remove the lower finish No. 2 panel with glove compartment door.

14. Remove the heater control assembly.

15. Remove the lower center finish panel.

NOTE: *The defroster nozzle has a boss on the reverse side for clamping onto the clip on the body side. When removing, pull upward at an angle.*

16. Remove the No. 1 and No. 2 side defroster nozzles.

17. Remove the safety pad assembly from the vehicle.

To install:

18. Install the safety pad assembly in the vehicle.

19. Install the No. 1 and No. 2 side defroster nozzles.

20. Install the lower center finish panel.

21. Install the heater control assembly.

22. Install the lower finish No. 2 panel with glove compartment door.

23. Install the combination meter assembly.

24. Install the stereo opening cover or center differential control switch if so equipped.

25. Install radio.

26. Install cluster finish panel.

27. Install center cluster finish panel.

28. Install steering column covers.

29. Install No. 1 lower finish panel.

30. Reconnect the engine hood release lever.

31. Install floor console box.

32. Install the right and left front pillar garnish trim.

33. Install the steering wheel.

34. Reconnect the negative battery cable. Check operation of all necessary components.

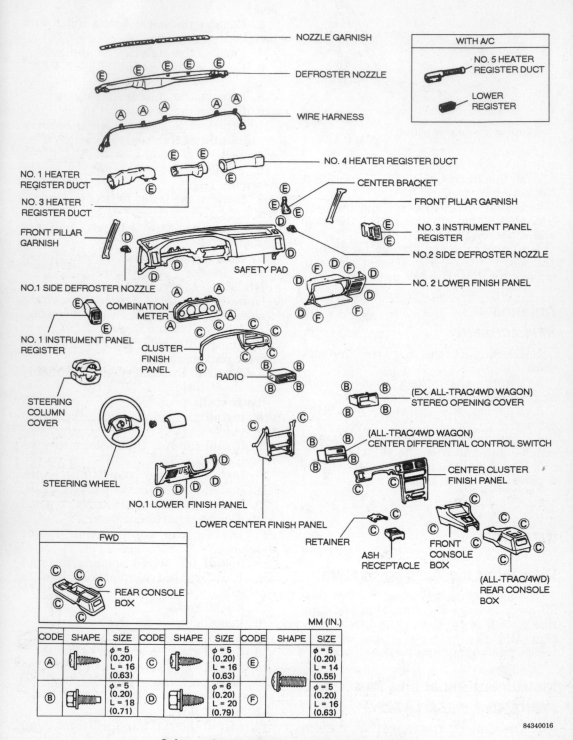

Safety pad components — except coupe models

WITH A/C
NO. 5 HEATER REGISTER DUCT
LOWER REGISTER

CODE	SHAPE	SIZE	CODE	SHAPE	SIZE	CODE	SHAPE	SIZE
Ⓐ		φ = 5 (0.20) L = 16 (0.63)	Ⓒ		φ = 5 (0.20) L = 16 (0.63)	Ⓔ		φ = 5 (0.20) L = 14 (0.55)
Ⓑ		φ = 5 (0.20) L = 18 (0.71)	Ⓓ		φ = 6 (0.20) L = 20 (0.79)	Ⓕ		φ = 5 (0.20) L = 16 (0.63)

MM (IN.)

84340016

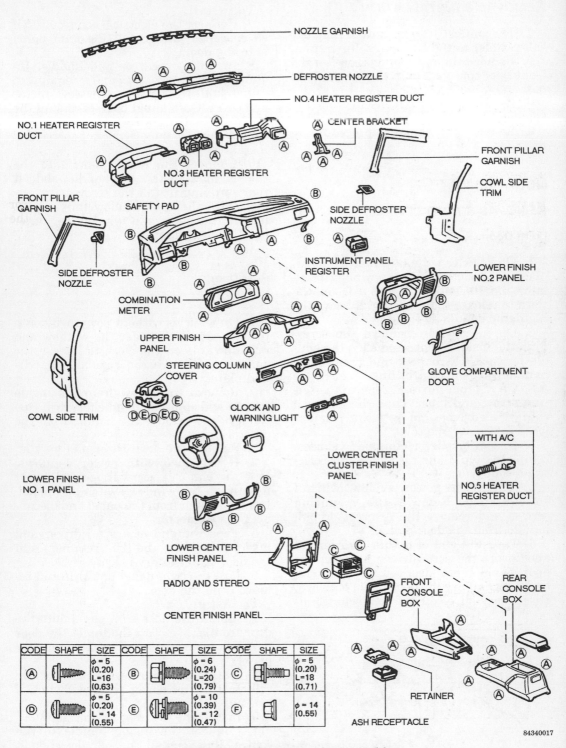

NOZZLE GARNISH

DEFROSTER NOZZLE

NO.4 HEATER REGISTER DUCT

CENTER BRACKET

NO.1 HEATER REGISTER DUCT

FRONT PILLAR GARNISH

COWL SIDE TRIM

NO.3 HEATER REGISTER DUCT

FRONT PILLAR GARNISH

SAFETY PAD

SIDE DEFROSTER NOZZLE

SIDE DEFROSTER NOZZLE

INSTRUMENT PANEL REGISTER

LOWER FINISH NO.2 PANEL

COMBINATION METER

UPPER FINISH PANEL

STEERING COLUMN COVER

CLOCK AND WARNING LIGHT

GLOVE COMPARTMENT DOOR

COWL SIDE TRIM

LOWER CENTER CLUSTER FINISH PANEL

WITH A/C

NO.5 HEATER REGISTER DUCT

LOWER FINISH NO. 1 PANEL

LOWER CENTER FINISH PANEL

RADIO AND STEREO

CENTER FINISH PANEL

FRONT CONSOLE BOX

REAR CONSOLE BOX

RETAINER

ASH RECEPTACLE

CODE	SHAPE	SIZE	CODE	SHAPE	SIZE	CODE	SHAPE	SIZE
Ⓐ		$\phi = 5$ (0.20) L=16 (0.63)	Ⓑ		$\phi = 6$ (0.24) L=20 (0.79)	Ⓒ		$\phi = 5$ (0.20) L=18 (0.71)
Ⓓ		$\phi = 5$ (0.20) L = 14 (0.55)	Ⓔ		$\phi = 10$ (0.39) L = 12 (0.47)	Ⓕ		$\phi = 14$ (0.55)

84340017

Safety pad components — coupe models

Center Console

REMOVAL & INSTALLATION

1. Disconnect the negative battery cable. Refer to the necessary illustration.
2. Remove the mounting screws in the front floor console and in the rear console box.
3. Remove the floor console from the vehicle.
4. Reverse the removal procedure to install.

Door Panels

REMOVAL & INSTALLATION

Front Door

1. On vehicles without power windows, place a soft cloth under the window regulator handle and pull upwards on the cloth to release the snapring. Remove the regulator handle and plate.
2. On all models, remove the screw from the inside handle and slide the handle forward. Disconnect and remove the handle from the control link.
3. On manual mirrors, remove the setting screw and knob. Tape the end of a thin screwdriver and pry the retainer loose to remove the cover.
4. On power mirror equipped vehicles, complete Step 3 and disconnect the electrical connector.
5. Remove the power window switch if so equipped. Remove the mounting screws and remove the armrest or pull handle from the door panel.
6. Tape the end of a thin screwdriver and insert the screwdriver between the door panel (near door panel retainers) and door and pry the door panel outward. Disconnect all electrical connector(s) af-

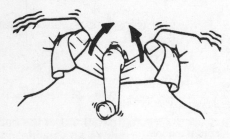

84340018

Removing the door regulator handle with a soft cloth

ter the panel is free and remove the panel from the vehicle.

To install:

7. Connect the electrical connector(s) if so equipped and install the trim panel onto the door.
8. Install armrest or pull handle. Install power window switch if so equipped.
9. Install the outside rear view mirror and cover. On manual mirrors, install the knob and setting screw. On power mirrors, reconnect the electric connector and install the mirror.
10. Connect the inside handle to the control link. Install the handle, slide it rearward and install the screw.
11. With the door window fully closed, install the plate and window regulator handle with snapring.

Rear Door

1. On vehicles without power windows, place a soft cloth under the window and pull upwards on the cloth to release the snapring. Remove the regulator handle and plate.
2. Remove the screw from the inside handle and slide the handle forward. Disconnect and remove the handle from the control link.
3. Remove the armrest or pull handle.
4. If equipped with power windows, tape the end of a screwdriver and insert it between the window switch and panel. Pry the switch from the panel and disconnect the connector.
5. Tape the end of a screwdriver and insert it between the trim retainers and the door panel to pry it loose.
6. Pull the trim panel upwards and remove from the door.

To install:

7. Install the door trim panel onto the door from above. Tap the top of the door panel to insure it is fully seated on door panel.
8. Install all trim retainers and secure.
9. Install the power window switch if so equipped.
10. Install the armrest or pull handle.
11. Connect the inside handle to the control link. Install the handle, slide it rearward and install the screw.
12. With the door window fully closed, install the plate and window regulator handle with snapring.

Interior Trim Panel

REMOVAL & INSTALLATION

The interior trim panels are generally retained by screws, push type or spring loaded fasteners. To remove the spring type fasteners, apply light hand pressure to separate the trim. To remove the push type fasteners, insert a clip remover tool or the blade of a screwdriver that has been taped between the trim panel and the fastener to be removed, and pry the retainer upward.

Door Locks

REMOVAL & INSTALLATION

Front or Rear Doors

1. Disconnect the negative battery cable.
2. Remove the door panel and watershield. Remove the service hole cover.
3. Disconnect the door outside opening linkage. Remove the two mounting bolts and remove the door handle if in need of replacement.
4. Disconnect the lock cylinder control linkage.
5. Remove the lock knob and the child protector lock lever knob.
6. Remove the lock assembly retaining screws and remove the door lock. If equipped with power locks, disconnect the electrical connector.
7. To remove the lock cylinder, remove the lock cylinder retaining clip and pull the cylinder from the door.
   To install:
8. Coat all the door lock sliding surfaces with multi-purpose grease.
9. Install the outside handle with the two retaining bolts, if removed.
10. Install the door lock solenoid linkage to the door lock.
11. Connect the link to the outside handle.
12. Install the lock knob and the child protector lock lever knob.
13. Install the door opening control link.
14. Install the door lock cylinder control linkage.
15. Install the door panel and watershield.
16. Reconnect the negative battery cable.

Tailgate Lock

REMOVAL & INSTALLATION

1. Disconnect the negative battery cable.
2. Remove the back door inside garnish trim.
3. Remove the trim panel.
4. Disconnect the links from the door control and door lock cylinder.
5. Remove the bolts and the door lock control with the solenoid.
6. To remove the door lock cylinder, remove the retaining screws and then remove the cylinder.
   To install:
7. Install the door lock cylinder and secure with the retaining screws.
8. Install the bolts and the door lock control with the solenoid.
9. Connect the links to the door control and door lock cylinder.
10. Install the trim panel.
11. Install the back door inner garnish trim.
12. Connect the negative battery cable.

Sedan Trunk Lock

REMOVAL & INSTALLATION

1. Disconnect the negative battery cable.
2. Remove the inside trunk garnish trim.
3. Remove the bolts and the door lock assembly.
4. The installation is the reverse of the removal procedure.

Door Glass and Regulator

REMOVAL & INSTALLATION

Front Door

1. Disconnect the negative battery cable.
2. Remove the front door panel to gain access to the regulator assembly.
3. Remove the service hole cover.
4. Lower the regulator until the door glass is in the fully open position.
5. Remove the two glass channel mount bolts.
6. Pull the glass up and out of the door.
7. Unbolt and remove the inside door panel frame if so equipped.
8. If equipped with power windows, disconnect the electrical connector.

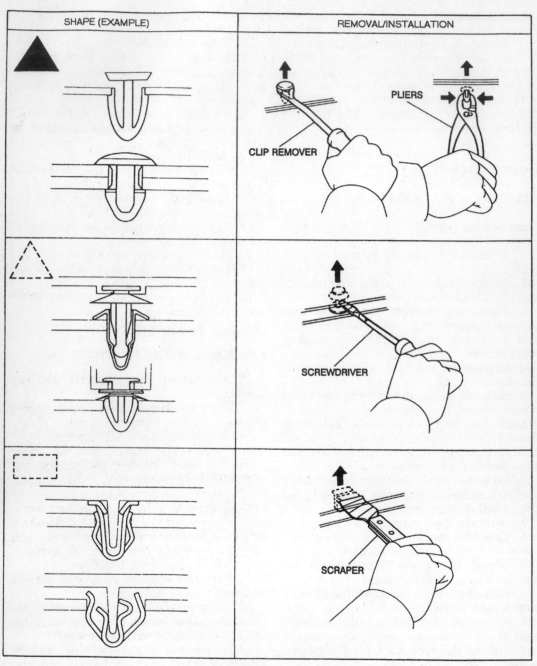

Clips — removal and installation methods

84340019

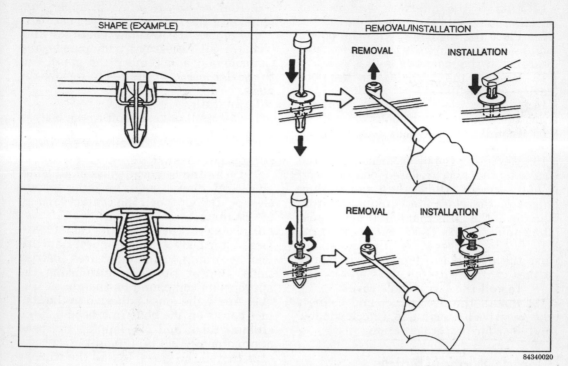

SHAPE (EXAMPLE)	REMOVAL/INSTALLATION

Clips — removal and installation methods

9. Remove the equalizer arm bracket mounting bolts.

10. Remove the window regulator mounting bolts and remove the regulator (with the power window motor attached) through the service hole.

To install:

11. Coat all the window regulator sliding surfaces with multi-purpose grease.

12. Place the regulator (with the power window motor) through the service hole and install the mounting bolts. Connect the power window connector if equipped.

13. Place the door glass into the door cavity.

14. Connect the glass to the regulator with the channel mount bolts.

15. With the equalizer arm, raise the glass to the almost closed position and make sure that the leading and trailing edges of the glass are equidistant from the top of the glass channel. If not, adjust the equalizer arm to achieve an even fit.

16. Install the service hole cover.

17. Install the door panel and reconnect the negative battery cable. Check window and door for proper operation.

Rear Door

1. Disconnect the negative battery cable.

2. Remove the rear door panel to gain access to the regulator assembly.

3. Remove the service hole cover.

4. Remove the clips from the outer edge of the belt molding and remove the rear door belt molding from the vehicle.

5. Remove the door glass run.

6. Remove the division bar by removing the two screws under the weatherstripping, the screw from the panel and pulling the glass run from the division bar. Pull the bar from the door.

7. Remove the glass mounting screws and remove the door glass.

8. To remove the quarter window, remove the glass along with the weatherstrip by pulling assembly forward.

9. To remove the regulator, unbolt from door panel and remove from vehicle. If equipped with power windows, disconnect the electrical connector and remove the regulator with the power window motor attached.

To install:

10. Install the glass down into the door cavity.

11. Install the quarter window and weather-strip into the door frame.

12. Place the regulator (with the power window motor) through the service hole and install the mounting bolts.

13. Position the door glass in the door cavity and regulator.

14. Connect the glass to the regulator with the channel mount bolts.

15. Install the rear door belt molding, division bar and the door glass run.

16. With the equalizer arm, raise the glass to the almost closed position and make sure that the leading and trailing edges of the glass are equidistant from the top of the glass channel. If not, adjust the equalizer arm to achieve an even fit.

17. With the door glass fully closed, adjust the door glass stopper so it lightly makes contact with the glass plate.

18. Install the service hole cover.

19. Install the door panel and connect the negative battery cable. Check window and door for proper operation.

Electric Window Motor

REMOVAL & INSTALLATION

The power window motor, if equipped, is attached to the window regulator. If service is required, remove the window regulator from the inside of the door panel and detach the motor from the regulator. Removal and installation of the window regulator is described in this Chapter.

Windshield Glass

REMOVAL & INSTALLATION

Windshield replacement on cars with bonded windhsields is extremely difficult and requires special tools and adhesives. Therefore, we recommend that it be left to a professional shop.

Quarter Window Glass

REMOVAL & INSTALLATION

1. Remove the rear quarter glass drip molding.

2. Using a scraper with the blade taped to prevent scratching the vehicle, pry off the window moldings.

3. Pull off, by hand, the belt molding.

4. Remove the rear seat back from the vehicle and all necessary interior components for access of quarter window glass.

5. Remove the rear inside upper trim panel and the rear pillar upper garnish.

6. Remove the window glass set nuts (remove all necessary trim panels and components) and remove the glass. Cut the sealer loose as required to remove the glass.

To install:

7. Clean all adhesive off of the body of the vehicle.

8. Clean all contact surfaces with an appropriate cleaner.

9. Clean the removed glass of all adhesive and clean with an appropriate cleaner. Do not touch the contact area after cleaning.

10. Using a brush, coat the contact surface on the body with the appropriate primer according to manufactures instructions. Repeat the procedure using the appropriate compound on the glass.

11. Apply the glass adhesive to the contact points on the body in a bead 0.39 in. (10mm) thick and overlapping the bead approximately 2.0 in. (50mm).

12. Install the glass. Install the window glass set nuts.

13. Install the rear inside upper trim panel and the rear pillar upper garnish and the belt molding.

14. Install the rear seat back to the vehicle. Install all necessary interior components.

15. Install the window moldings.

16. Leak test the window when the sealer is completely dry.

Inside Rear View Mirror

REMOVAL & INSTALLATION

Remove the inner rear view mirror by loosening the set screw on the mirror stem (remove the cover) and lifting mirror off of the base, which is glued onto the windshield. The installation is the reverse of the removal procedure.

Seats

REMOVAL & INSTALLATION

Refer to the necessary illustrations for removal and installation service procedures of the seat for your vehicle. On models where the rear seat cushion lower mounting is retained by clips, pull the front left and right levers forward and pull up the rear seat cushion.

WAGON

N·m (kgf·cm, ft·lbf) : SPECIFIED TORQUE

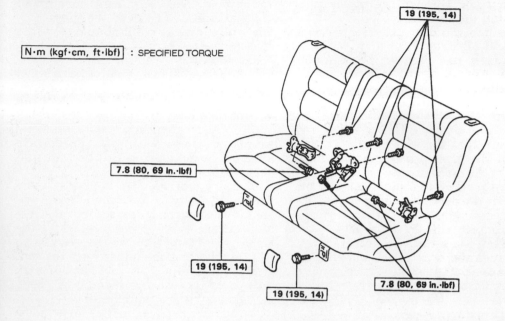

19 (195, 14)

7.8 (80, 69 in.·lbf)

19 (195, 14)

19 (195, 14)

7.8 (80, 69 in.·lbf)

84340027

Rear seat components

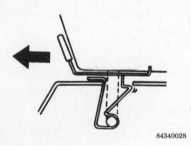

84340028

Removing the rear seat

Seat Belt System

REMOVAL & INSTALLATION

Front Seat

1. Remove the trim cover at the upper shoulder anchor bolt.
2. Remove the anchor bolts.
3. Remove the lower cover on the outer retractor. Unbolt the retractor from the inner floor panel.
4. Remove the retractor portion of the seat belt.

5. To remove the buckle end of the seat belt, remove the cover on the base of the belt and remove the mounting bolt.
6. Installation of the belts is the reverse of the removal procedure. Torque the upper shoulder mounting bolt to 32 ft. lbs. (43 Nm), the lower retractor mounting bolt to 69 inch lbs. (8.0 Nm), and the buckle retainer bolt to 32 ft. lbs. (43 Nm).
7. Do not remove safety belts from any vehicle. Inspection of the seat belts for proper operation is recommended for the safety of the vehicle's occupants and is required in most states by law.

Rear Seat

1. Remove the trim cover at the upper shoulder anchor bolt.
2. Remove the upper shoulder anchor bolt.
3. Unbolt the outer belt anchor from the body panel. Removal of the rear seat is required. Unbolt the lower end of the belt under the retractor from the side panel.
4. Remove the retractor portion of the seat belt.
5. To remove the center belt buckle of the seat belt, remove the seat cushion

and remove the center belt mounting bolt.

6. Installation of the belts is the reverse of the removal procedure. Torque all mounting bolts on the belt to 32 ft. lbs. (43 Nm).

11

General Conversion Table

Multiply By	To Convert	To	
LENGTH			
2.54	Inches	Centimeters	.3937
25.4	Inches	Millimeters	.03937
30.48	Feet	Centimeters	.0328
.304	Feet	Meters	3.28
.914	Yards	Meters	1.094
1.609	Miles	Kilometers	.621
VOLUME			
.473	Pints	Liters	2.11
.946	Quarts	Liters	1.06
3.785	Gallons	Liters	.264
.016	Cubic inches	Liters	61.02
16.39	Cubic inches	Cubic cms.	.061
28.3	Cubic feet	Liters	.0353
MASS (Weight)			
28.35	Ounces	Grams	.035
.4536	Pounds	Kilograms	2.20
—	To obtain	From	Multiply by

Multiply By	To Convert	To	
AREA			
.645	Square inches	Square cms.	.155
.836	Square yds.	Square meters	1.196
FORCE			
4.448	Pounds	Newtons	.225
.138	Ft./lbs.	Kilogram/meters	7.23
1.36	Ft./lbs.	Newton-meters	.737
.112	In./lbs.	Newton-meters	8.844
PRESSURE			
.068	Psi	Atmospheres	14.7
6.89	Psi	Kilopascals	.145
OTHER			
1.104	Horsepower (DIN)	Horsepower (SAE)	.9861
.746	Horsepower (SAE)	Kilowatts (KW)	1.34
1.60	Mph	Km/h	.625
.425	Mpg	Km/1	2.35
—	To obtain	From	Multiply by

Tap Drill Sizes

National Coarse or U.S.S.

Screw & Tap Size	Threads Per Inch	Use Drill Number
No. 5	40	39
No. 6	32	36
No. 8	32	29
No. 10	24	25
No. 12	24	17
1/4	20	8
5/16	18	F
3/8	16	5/16
7/16	14	U
1/2	13	27/64
9/16	12	31/64
5/8	11	17/32
3/4	10	21/32
7/8	9	49/64

National Coarse or U.S.S.

Screw & Tap Size	Threads Per Inch	Use Drill Number
1	8	7/8
1 1/8	7	63/64
1 1/4	7	1 7/64
1 1/2	6	1 11/32

National Fine or S.A.E.

Screw & Tap Size	Threads Per Inch	Use Drill Number
No. 5	44	37
No. 6	40	33
No. 8	36	29
No. 10	32	21

National Fine or S.A.E.

Screw & Tap Size	Threads Per Inch	Use Drill Number
No. 12	28	15
1/4	28	3
5/16	24	1
3/8	24	Q
7/16	20	W
1/2	20	29/64
9/16	18	33/64
5/8	18	37/64
3/4	16	11/16
7/8	14	13/16
1 1/8	12	1 3/64
1 1/4	12	1 11/64
1 1/2	12	1 27/64

Drill Sizes In Decimal Equivalents

Inch	Decimal	Wire	mm
1/64	.0156		.39
	.0157		.4
	.0160	78	
	.0165		.42
	.0173		.44
	.0177		.45
	.0180	77	
	.0181		.46
	.0189		.48
	.0197		.5
	.0200	76	
	.0210	75	
	.0217		.55
	.0225	74	
	.0236		.6
	.0240	73	
	.0250	72	
	.0256		.65
	.0260	71	
	.0276		.7
	.0280	70	
	.0292	69	
	.0295		.75
	.0310	68	
1/32	.0312		.79
	.0315		.8
	.0320	67	
	.0330	66	
	.0335		.85
	.0350	65	
	.0354		.9
	.0360	64	
	.0370	63	
	.0374		.95
	.0380	62	
	.0390	61	
	.0394		1.0
	.0400	60	
	.0410	59	
	.0413		1.05
	.0420	58	
	.0430	57	
	.0433		1.1
	.0453		1.15
	.0465	56	
3/64	.0469		1.19
	.0472		1.2
	.0492		1.25
	.0512		1.3
	.0520	55	
	.0531		1.35
	.0550	54	
	.0551		1.4
	.0571		1.45
	.0591		1.5
	.0595	53	
	.0610		1.55
1/16	.0625		1.59
	.0630		1.6
	.0635	52	
	.0650		1.65
	.0669		1.7
	.0670	51	
	.0689		1.75
	.0700	50	
	.0709		1.8
	.0728		1.85

Inch	Decimal	Wire	mm
	.0730	49	
	.0748		1.9
	.0760	48	
	.0768		1.95
5/64	.0781		1.98
	.0785	47	
	.0787		2.0
	.0807		2.05
	.0810	46	
	.0820	45	
	.0827		2.1
	.0846		2.15
	.0860	44	
	.0866		2.2
	.0886		2.25
	.0890	43	
	.0906		2.3
	.0925	42	
	.0935		2.35
3/32	.0938		2.38
	.0945		2.4
	.0960	41	
	.0965		2.45
	.0980	40	
	.0981		2.5
	.0995	39	
	.1015	38	
	.1024		2.6
	.1040	37	
	.1063		2.7
	.1065	36	
	.1083		2.75
7/64	.1094		2.77
	.1100	35	
	.1102		2.8
	.1110	34	
	.1130	33	
	.1142		2.9
	.1160	32	
	.1181		3.0
	.1200	31	
	.1220		3.1
1/8	.1250		3.17
	.1260		3.2
	.1280		3.25
	.1285	30	
	.1299		3.3
	.1339		3.4
	.1360	29	
	.1378		3.5
	.1405	28	
9/64	.1406		3.57
	.1417		3.6
	.1440	27	
	.1457		3.7
	.1470	26	
	.1476		3.75
	.1495	25	
	.1496		3.8
	.1520	24	
	.1535		3.9
	.1540	23	
5/32	.1562		3.96
	.1570	22	
	.1575		4.0
	.1590	21	
	.1610	20	

Inch	Decimal	Wire & Letter	mm
	.1614		4.1
	.1654		4.2
	.1660	19	
	.1673		4.25
	.1693		4.3
	.1695	18	
11/64	.1719		4.36
	.1730	17	
	.1732		4.4
	.1770	16	
	.1772		4.5
	.1800	15	
	.1811		4.6
	.1820	14	
	.1850	13	
	.1850		4.7
	.1870		4.75
3/16	.1875		4.76
	.1890	12	
	.1890		4.8
	.1910	11	
	.1929		4.9
	.1935	10	
	.1960	9	
	.1969		5.0
	.1990	8	
	.2008		5.1
	.2010	7	
13/64	.2031		5.16
	.2040	6	
	.2047		5.2
	.2055	5	
	.2067		5.25
	.2087		5.3
	.2090	4	
	.2126		5.4
	.2130	3	
	.2165		5.5
7/32	.2188		5.55
	.2205		5.6
	.2210	2	
	.2244		5.7
	.2264		5.75
	.2280	1	
	.2283		5.8
	.2323		5.9
	.2340	A	
15/64	.2344		5.95
	.2362		6.0
	.2380	B	
	.2402		6.1
	.2420	C	
	.2441		6.2
	.2460	D	
	.2461		6.25
	.2480		6.3
1/4	.2500	E	6.35
	.2520		6.
	.2559		6.5
	.2570	F	
	.2598		6.6
	.2610	G	
	.2638		6.7
17/64	.2656		6.74
	.2657		6.75
	.2660	H	
	.2677		6.8

Inch	Decimal	Letter	mm
	.2717		6.9
	.2720	I	
	.2756		7.0
	.2770	J	
	.2795		7.1
	.2810	K	
9/32	.2812		7.14
	.2835		7.2
	.2854		7.25
	.2874		7.3
	.2900	L	
	.2913		7.4
	.2950	M	
	.2953		7.5
19/64	.2969		7.54
	.2992		7.6
	.3020	N	
	.3031		7.7
	.3051		7.75
	.3071		7.8
	.3110		7.9
5/16	.3125		7.93
	.3150		8.0
	.3160	O	
	.3189		8.1
	.3228		8.2
	.3230	P	
	.3248		8.25
	.3268		8.3
21/64	.3281		8.33
	.3307		8.4
	.3320	Q	
	.3346		8.5
	.3386		8.6
	.3390	R	
	.3425		8.7
11/32	.3438		8.73
	.3445		8.75
	.3465		8.8
	.3480	S	
	.3504		8.9
	.3543		9.0
	.3580	T	
	.3583		9.1
23/64	.3594		9.12
	.3622		9.2
	.3642		9.25
	.3661		9.3
	.3680	U	
	.3701		9.4
	.3740		9.5
3/8	.3750		9.52
	.3770	V	
	.3780		9.6
	.3819		9.7
	.3839		9.75
	.3858		9.8
	.3860	W	
	.3898		9.9
25/64	.3906		9.92
	.3937		10.0
	.3970	X	
	.4040	Y	
13/32	.4062		10.31
	.4130	Z	
	.4134		10.5
27/64	.4219		10.71

Inch	Decimal	mm
	.4331	11.0
7/16	.4375	11.11
	.4528	11.5
29/64	.4531	11.51
15/32	.4688	11.90
	.4724	12.0
31/64	.4844	12.30
	.4921	12.5
1/2	.5000	12.70
	.5118	13.0
33/64	.5156	13.09
17/32	.5312	13.49
	.5315	13.5
35/64	.5469	13.89
	.5512	14.0
9/16	.5625	14.28
	.5709	14.5
37/64	.5781	14.68
	.5906	15.0
19/32	.5938	15.08
39/64	.6094	15.47
	.6102	15.5
5/8	.6250	15.87
	.6299	16.0
41/64	.6406	16.27
	.6496	16.5
21/32	.6562	16.66
	.6693	17.0
43/64	.6719	17.06
11/16	.6875	17.46
	.6890	17.5
45/64	.7031	17.85
	.7087	18.0
23/32	.7188	18.25
	.7283	18.5
47/64	.7344	18.65
	.7480	19.0
3/4	.7500	19.05
49/64	.7656	19.44
	.7677	19.5
25/32	.7812	19.84
	.7874	20.0
51/64	.7969	20.24
	.8071	20.5
13/16	.8125	20.63
	.8268	21.0
53/64	.8281	21.03
27/32	.8438	21.43
	.8465	21.5
55/64	.8594	21.82
	.8661	22.0
7/8	.8750	22.22
	.8858	22.5
57/64	.8906	22.62
	.9055	23.0
29/32	.9062	23.01
59/64	.9219	23.41
	.9252	23.5
15/16	.9375	23.81
	.9449	24.0
61/64	.9531	24.2
	.9646	24.5
31/32	.9688	24.6
	.9843	25.0
63/64	.9844	25.0
1	1.0000	25.4

mechdat2

AIR/FUEL RATIO: The ratio of air to gasoline by weight in the fuel mixture drawn into the engine.

AIR INJECTION: One method of reducing harmful exhaust emissions by injecting air into each of the exhaust ports of an engine. The fresh air entering the hot exhaust manifold causes any remaining fuel to be burned before it can exit the tailpipe.

ALTERNATOR: A device used for converting mechanical energy into electrical energy.

AMMETER: An instrument, calibrated in amperes, used to measure the flow of an electrical current in a circuit. Ammeters are always connected in series with the circuit being tested.

AMPERE: The rate of flow of electrical current present when one volt of electrical pressure is applied against one ohm of electrical resistance.

ANALOG COMPUTER: Any microprocessor that uses similar (analogous) electrical signals to make its calculations.

ARMATURE: A laminated, soft iron core wrapped by a wire that converts electrical energy to mechanical energy as in a motor or relay. When rotated in a magnetic field, it changes mechanical energy into electrical energy as in a generator.

ATMOSPHERIC PRESSURE: The pressure on the Earth's surface caused by the weight of the air in the atmosphere. At sea level, this pressure is 14.7 psi at 32{248}F (101 kPa at 0{248}C).

ATOMIZATION: The breaking down of a liquid into a fine mist that can be suspended in air.

AXIAL PLAY: Movement parallel to a shaft or bearing bore.

BACKFIRE: The sudden combustion of gases in the intake or exhaust system that results in a loud explosion.

BACKLASH: The clearance or play between two parts, such as meshed gears.

BACKPRESSURE: Restrictions in the exhaust system that slow the exit of exhaust gases from the combustion chamber.

BAKELITE: A heat resistant, plastic insulator material commonly used in printed circuit boards and transistorized components.

BALL BEARING: A bearing made up of hardened inner and outer races between which hardened steel balls roll.

BALLAST RESISTOR: A resistor in the primary ignition circuit that lowers voltage after the engine is started to reduce wear on ignition components.

BEARING: A friction reducing, supportive device usually located between a stationary part and a moving part.

BIMETAL TEMPERATURE SENSOR: Any sensor or switch made of two dissimilar types of metal that bend when heated or cooled due to the different expansion rates of the alloys. These types of sensors usually function as an on/off switch.

BLOWBY: Combustion gases, composed of water vapor and unburned fuel, that leak past the piston rings into the crankcase during normal engine operation. These gases are removed by the PCV system to prevent the buildup of harmful acids in the crankcase.

BRAKE PAD: A brake shoe and lining assembly used with disc brakes.

BRAKE SHOE: The backing for the brake lining. The term is, however, usually applied to the assembly of the brake backing and lining.

BUSHING: A liner, usually removable, for a bearing; an anti-friction liner used in place of a bearing.

CALIPER: A hydraulically activated device in a disc brake system, which is mounted straddling the brake rotor (disc). The caliper contains at least one piston and two brake pads. Hydraulic pressure on the piston(s) forces the pads against the rotor.

CAMSHAFT: A shaft in the engine on which are the lobes (cams) which operate the valves. The camshaft is driven by the crankshaft, via a belt, chain or gears, at one half the crankshaft speed.

CAPACITOR: A device which stores an electrical charge.

CARBON MONOXIDE (CO): A colorless, odorless gas given off as a normal byproduct of combustion. It is poisonous and extremely dangerous in confined areas, building up slowly to toxic levels without warning if adequate ventilation is not available.

CARBURETOR: A device, usually mounted on the intake manifold of an engine, which mixes the air and fuel in the proper proportion to allow even combustion.

CATALYTIC CONVERTER: A device installed in the exhaust system, like a muffler, that converts harmful byproducts of combustion into carbon dioxide and water vapor by means of a heat-producing chemical reaction.

CENTRIFUGAL ADVANCE: A mechanical method of advancing the spark timing by using flyweights in the distributor that react to centrifugal force generated by the distributor shaft rotation.

CHECK VALVE: Any one-way valve installed to permit the flow of air, fuel or vacuum in one direction only.

CHOKE: A device, usually a moveable valve, placed in the intake path of a carburetor to restrict the flow of air.

CIRCUIT: Any unbroken path through which an electrical current can flow. Also used to describe fuel flow in some instances.

CIRCUIT BREAKER: A switch which protects an electrical circuit from overload by opening the circuit when the current flow exceeds a predetermined level. Some circuit breakers must be reset manually, while most reset automatically

COIL (IGNITION): A transformer in the ignition circuit which steps up the voltage provided to the spark plugs.

COMBINATION MANIFOLD: An assembly which includes both the intake and exhaust manifolds in one casting.

COMBINATION VALVE: A device used in some fuel systems that routes fuel vapors to a charcoal storage canister instead of venting them into the atmosphere. The valve relieves fuel tank pressure and allows fresh air into the tank as the fuel level drops to prevent a vapor lock situation.

COMPRESSION RATIO: The comparison of the total volume of the cylinder and combustion chamber with the piston at BDC and the piston at TDC.

CONDENSER: 1. An electrical device which acts to store an electrical charge, preventing voltage surges.
2. A radiator-like device in the air conditioning system in which refrigerant gas condenses into a liquid, giving off heat.

CONDUCTOR: Any material through which an electrical current can be transmitted easily.

CONTINUITY: Continuous or complete circuit. Can be checked with an ohmmeter.

COUNTERSHAFT: An intermediate shaft which is rotated by a mainshaft and transmits, in turn, that rotation to a working part.

CRANKCASE: The lower part of an engine in which the crankshaft and related parts operate.

CRANKSHAFT: The main driving shaft of an engine which receives reciprocating motion from the pistons and converts it to rotary motion.

CYLINDER: In an engine, the round hole in the engine block in which the piston(s) ride.

CYLINDER BLOCK: The main structural member of an engine in which is found the cylinders, crankshaft and other principal parts.

CYLINDER HEAD: The detachable portion of the engine, fastened, usually, to the top of the cylinder block, containing all or most of the combustion chambers. On overhead valve engines, it contains the valves and their operating parts. On overhead cam engines, it contains the camshaft as well.

DEAD CENTER: The extreme top or bottom of the piston stroke.

DETONATION: An unwanted explosion of the air/fuel mixture in the combustion chamber caused by excess heat and compression, advanced timing, or an overly lean mixture. Also referred to as "'ping".

DIAPHRAGM: A thin, flexible wall separating two cavities, such as in a vacuum advance unit.

DIESELING: A condition in which hot spots in the combustion chamber cause the engine to run on after the key is turned off.

DIFFERENTIAL: A geared assembly which allows the transmission of motion between drive axles, giving one axle the ability to turn faster than the other.

DIODE: An electrical device that will allow current to flow in one direction only.

DISC BRAKE: A hydraulic braking assembly consisting of a brake disc, or rotor, mounted on an axle, and a caliper assembly containing, usually two brake pads which are activated by hydraulic pressure. The pads are forced against the sides of the disc, creating friction which slows the vehicle.

DISTRIBUTOR: A mechanically driven device on an engine which is responsible for electrically firing the spark plug at a predetermined point of the piston stroke.

DOWEL PIN: A pin, inserted in mating holes in two different parts allowing those parts to maintain a fixed relationship.

DRUM BRAKE: A braking system which consists of two brake shoes and one or two wheel cylinders, mounted on a fixed backing plate, and a brake drum, mounted on an axle, which revolves around the assembly.

DWELL: The rate, measured in degrees of shaft rotation, at which an electrical circuit cycles on and off.

ELECTRONIC CONTROL UNIT (ECU): Ignition module, module, amplifier or igniter. See Module for definition.

ELECTRONIC IGNITION: A system in which the timing and firing of the spark plugs is controlled by an electronic control unit, usually called a module. These systems have no points or condenser.

ENDPLAY: The measured amount of axial movement in a shaft.

ENGINE: A device that converts heat into mechanical energy.

EXHAUST MANIFOLD: A set of cast passages or pipes which conduct exhaust gases from the engine.

FEELER GAUGE: A blade, usually metal, of precisely predetermined thickness, used to measure the clearance between two parts.

FIRING ORDER: The order in which combustion occurs in the cylinders of an engine. Also the order in which spark is distributed to the plugs by the distributor.

FLOODING: The presence of too much fuel in the intake manifold and combustion chamber which prevents the air/fuel mixture from firing, thereby causing a no-start situation.

FLYWHEEL: A disc shaped part bolted to the rear end of the crankshaft. Around the outer perimeter is affixed the ring gear. The starter drive engages the ring gear, turning the flywheel, which rotates the crankshaft, imparting the initial starting motion to the engine.

FOOT POUND (ft.lb. or sometimes, ft. lbs.): The amount of energy or work needed to raise an item weighing one pound, a distance of one foot.

FUSE: A protective device in a circuit which prevents circuit overload by breaking the circuit when a specific amperage is present. The device is constructed around a strip or wire of a lower amperage rating than the circuit it is designed to protect. When an amperage higher than that stamped on the fuse is present in the circuit, the strip or wire melts, opening the circuit.

GEAR RATIO: The ratio between the number of teeth on meshing gears.

GENERATOR: A device which converts mechanical energy into electrical energy.

HEAT RANGE: The measure of a spark plug's ability to dissipate heat from its firing end. The higher the heat range, the hotter the plug fires.

HUB: The center part of a wheel or gear.

HYDROCARBON (HC): Any chemical compound made up of hydrogen and carbon. A major pollutant formed by the engine as a byproduct of combustion.

HYDROMETER: An instrument used to measure the specific gravity of a solution.

INCH POUND (in.lb. or sometimes, in. lbs.): One twelfth of a foot pound.

INDUCTION: A means of transferring electrical energy in the form of a magnetic field. Principle used in the ignition coil to increase voltage.

INJECTOR: A device which receives metered fuel under relatively low pressure and is activated to inject the fuel into the engine under relatively high pressure at a predetermined time.

INPUT SHAFT: The shaft to which torque is applied, usually carrying the driving gear or gears.

INTAKE MANIFOLD: A casting of passages or pipes used to conduct air or a fuel/air mixture to the cylinders.

JOURNAL: The bearing surface within which a shaft operates.

KEY: A small block usually fitted in a notch between a shaft and a hub to prevent slippage of the two parts.

MANIFOLD: A casting of passages or set of pipes which connect the cylinders to an inlet or outlet source.

MANIFOLD VACUUM: Low pressure in an engine intake manifold formed just below the throttle plates. Manifold vacuum is highest at idle and drops under acceleration.

MASTER CYLINDER: The primary fluid pressurizing device in a hydraulic system. In automotive use, it is found in brake and hydraulic clutch systems and is pedal activated, either directly or, in a power brake system, through the power booster.

MODULE: Electronic control unit, amplifier or igniter of solid state or integrated design which controls the current flow in the ignition primary circuit based on input from the pick-up coil. When the module opens the primary circuit, the high secondary voltage is induced in the coil.

NEEDLE BEARING: A bearing which consists of a number (usually a large number) of long, thin rollers.

OHM:(Ω) The unit used to measure the resistance of conductor to electrical flow. One ohm is the amount of resistance that limits current flow to one ampere in a circuit with one volt of pressure.

OHMMETER: An instrument used for measuring the resistance, in ohms, in an electrical circuit.

OUTPUT SHAFT: The shaft which transmits torque from a device, such as a transmission.

OVERDRIVE: A gear assembly which produces more shaft revolutions than that transmitted to it.

OVERHEAD CAMSHAFT (OHC): An engine configuration in which the camshaft is mounted on top of the cylinder head and operates the valve either directly or by means of rocker arms.

OVERHEAD VALVE (OHV): An engine configuration in which all of the valves are located in the cylinder head and the camshaft is located in the cylinder block. The camshaft operates the valves via lifters and pushrods.

OXIDES OF NITROGEN (NOx): Chemical compounds of nitrogen produced as a byproduct of combustion. They combine with hydrocarbons to produce smog.

OXYGEN SENSOR: Used with the feedback system to sense the presence of oxygen in the exhaust gas and signal the computer which can reference the voltage signal to an air/fuel ratio.

PINION: The smaller of two meshing gears.

PISTON RING: An open ended ring which fits into a groove on the outer diameter of the piston. Its chief function is to form a seal between the piston and cylinder wall. Most automotive pistons have three rings: two for compression sealing; one for oil sealing.

PRELOAD: A predetermined load placed on a bearing during assembly or by adjustment.

PRIMARY CIRCUIT: Is the low voltage side of the ignition system which consists of the ignition switch, ballast resistor or resistance wire, bypass, coil, electronic control unit and pick-up coil as well as the connecting wires and harnesses.

PRESS FIT: The mating of two parts under pressure, due to the inner diameter of one being smaller than the outer diameter of the other, or vice versa; an interference fit.

RACE: The surface on the inner or outer ring of a bearing on which the balls, needles or rollers move.

REGULATOR: A device which maintains the amperage and/or voltage levels of a circuit at predetermined values.

RELAY: A switch which automatically opens and/or closes a circuit.

RESISTANCE: The opposition to the flow of current through a circuit or electrical device, and is measured in ohms. Resistance is equal to the voltage divided by the amperage.

RESISTOR: A device, usually made of wire, which offers a preset amount of resistance in an electrical circuit.

RING GEAR: The name given to a ring-shaped gear attached to a differential case, or affixed to a flywheel or as part a planetary gear set.

ROLLER BEARING: A bearing made up of hardened inner and outer races between which hardened steel rollers move.

ROTOR: 1. The disc-shaped part of a disc brake assembly, upon which the brake pads bear; also called, brake disc.
2. The device mounted atop the distributor shaft, which passes current to the distributor cap tower contacts.

SECONDARY CIRCUIT: The high voltage side of the ignition system, usually above 20,000 volts. The secondary includes the ignition coil, coil wire, distributor cap and rotor, spark plug wires and spark plugs.

SENDING UNIT: A mechanical, electrical, hydraulic or electromagnetic device which transmits information to a gauge.

SENSOR: Any device designed to measure engine operating conditions or ambient pressures and temperatures. Usually electronic in nature and designed to send a voltage signal to an on-board computer, some sensors may operate as a simple on/off switch or they may provide a variable voltage signal (like a potentiometer) as conditions or measured parameters change.

SHIM: Spacers of precise, predetermined thickness used between parts to establish a proper working relationship.

SLAVE CYLINDER: In automotive use, a device in the hydraulic clutch system which is activated by hydraulic force, disengaging the clutch.

SOLENOID: A coil used to produce a magnetic field, the effect of which is produce work.

SPARK PLUG: A device screwed into the combustion chamber of a spark ignition engine. The basic construction is a conductive core inside of a ceramic insulator, mounted in an outer conductive base. An electrical charge from the spark plug wire travels along the conductive core and jumps a preset air gap to a grounding point or points at the end of the conductive base. The resultant spark ignites the fuel/air mixture in the combustion chamber.

SPLINES: Ridges machined or cast onto the outer diameter of a shaft or inner diameter of a bore to enable parts to mate without rotation.

TACHOMETER: A device used to measure the rotary speed of an engine, shaft, gear, etc., usually in rotations per minute.

THERMOSTAT: A valve, located in the cooling system of an engine, which is closed when cold and opens gradually in response to engine heating, controlling the temperature of the coolant and rate of coolant flow.

TOP DEAD CENTER (TDC): The point at which the piston reaches the top of its travel on the compression stroke.

TORQUE: The twisting force applied to an object.

TORQUE CONVERTER: A turbine used to transmit power from a driving member to a driven member via hydraulic action, providing changes in drive ratio and torque. In automotive use, it links the driveplate at the rear of the engine to the automatic transmission.

TRANSDUCER: A device used to change a force into an electrical signal.

TRANSISTOR: A semi-conductor component which can be actuated by a small voltage to perform an electrical switching function.

TUNE-UP: A regular maintenance function, usually associated with the replacement and adjustment of parts and components in the electrical and fuel systems of a vehicle for the purpose of attaining optimum performance.

TURBOCHARGER: An exhaust driven pump which compresses intake air and forces it into the combustion chambers at higher than atmospheric pressures. The increased air pressure allows more fuel to be burned and results in increased horsepower being produced.

VACUUM ADVANCE: A device which advances the ignition timing in response to increased engine vacuum.

VACUUM GAUGE: An instrument used to measure the presence of vacuum in a chamber.

VALVE: A device which control the pressure, direction of flow or rate of flow of a liquid or gas.

VALVE CLEARANCE: The measured gap between the end of the valve stem and the rocker arm, cam lobe or follower that activates the valve.

VISCOSITY: The rating of a liquid's internal resistance to flow.

VOLTMETER: An instrument used for measuring electrical force in units called volts. Voltmeters are always connected parallel with the circuit being tested.

WHEEL CYLINDER: Found in the automotive drum brake assembly, it is a device, actuated by hydraulic pressure, which, through internal pistons, pushes the brake shoes outward against the drums.

Index

A

AIR CONDITIONER
  A/C Control Assembly, 176
  Compressor, 172
  Condenser, 173
  Cooling Unit (Evaporator), 174
AUTOMATIC TRANSAXLE
  Adjustments, 207
  Back-Up light Switch, 208
  Fluid Pan, 206
  Halfshafts, 209
  Identification, 206
  Neutral Safety Switch, 207
  Transaxle, 208

B

BRAKE OPERATING SYSTEM
  ADJUSTMENT, 249
  Bleeding the Brake System, 256
  Brake Hoses, 255
  Brake Light Switch, 251
  Brake Pedal, 251
  Master Cylinder, 251
  Power Brake Booster, 254
  Proportioning Valve, 255

C

CIRCUIT PROTECTION
  Circuit Breakers, 189
  Fuses And Fusible Links, 188
  Turn Signal and Hazard Flasher, 189
CLUTCH
  Adjustments, 202
  Clutch Master Cylinder, 203
  Clutch Release Cylinder, 204
  Driven Disc and Pressure Plate, 202

D

DISARMING THE AIR BAG SYSTEM, 237
DRIVELINE
  Center Support Bearings, 213
  Propeller Shaft, 209

E

ELECTRONIC FUEL INJECTION SYSTEM
  Air Flow Meter, 156
  Auxiliary Air Valve, 159
  Cold Start Injector, 155
  Description of System, 148
  Electric Fuel Pump, 148
  Fuel Injectors, 152
  Fuel Pressure Regulator, 156
  Idle Air Control Valve, 161
  Relieving Fuel Pressure, 148
  Throttle Body, 157
  Throttle Position Sensor, 161
ELECTRONIC IGNITION
  Adjustments, 43
  Description and Operation, 42
  Diagnosis and Testing, 42
  Parts Replacement, 43
  Service Precautions, 42
EMISSION CONTROLS
  Dash Pot (DP) System, 137
  Exhaust Gas Recirculation (EGR)
  System, 138
  Fuel Evaporative Emission Control System
  (EVAP), 136
  Positive Crankcase Ventilation (PCV)
  System, 135
  Three-Way and Oxidation Catalyst (TWC)
  System, 142
ENGINE ELECTRICAL
  Alternator, 61
  Battery, 62
  Distributor, 58
  Igniter (Ignition Module), 59
  Ignition Coil, 57
  Regulator, 62
  Sending Units and Sensors, 66
  Starter, 64
ENGINE MECHANICAL
  Camshaft and Bearings, 112
  Crankshaft Pulley, 106
  Crankshaft and Main Bearings, 125
  Cylinder Block, 129
  Cylinder Head, 91
  Electric Cooling Fan, 86
  Engine Core Plugs (Freeze Plugs), 124
  Engine Overhaul Tips, 66
  Engine, 74
  Exhaust Manifold, 85
  Flywheel and Ring Gear, 129
  Intake Manifold, 82
  Oil Pan, 102
  Oil Pump, 102
  Pistons and Connecting Rods, 116
  Radiator, 85
  Rear Main Seal, 124
  Thermostat, 82
  Timing Belt Cover, 106
  Timing Belt and Camshaft Sprockets, 108
  Valve Cover (Cam Cover), 81
  Valve Guides, 100
  Valve Lifters, 102
  Valve Seats, 100
  Valve Springs, Valves and Valve Stem
  Seals, 98
  Water Pump, 88
EXHAUST SYSTEM
  Safety Precautions, 130

Special Tools, 130
EXTERIOR
  Antenna, 279
  Doors, 269
  Front And Rear Bumpers, 276
  Grille, 276
  Hood, 269
  Outside Mirrors, 277
  Sedan Trunk Lid, 276
  Tailgate, 274

F

FIRING ORDERS, 42
FLUIDS AND LUBRICANTS
  Automatic Transaxle, 26
  Body Lubrication, 31
  Brake and Clutch Master Cylinders, 30
  Chassis Greasing, 31
  Cooling System, 29
  Engine, 22
  Fluid Disposal, 21
  Manual Transaxle, 25
  Oil and Fuel Recommendations, 21
  Power Steering Pump, 31
  Rear Drive Axle, 28
  Wheel Bearings, 31
FRONT DISC BRAKES
  Brake Caliper, 258
  Brake Disc (Rotor), 259
  Brake Drums, 260
  Brake Pads, 256
  Brake Shoes, 261
  REAR DRUM BRAKES, 259
  Wheel Cylinder, 262
FRONT SUSPENSION
  Front End Alignment, 226
  Front Hub and Bearing, 226
  Lower Ball Joint, 220
  Lower Control Arm, 220
  McPherson Struts, 217
  Stabilizer Bar, 220
  Steering Knuckle, Hub And Bearing, 223
  Upper Ball Joint, 220
  Wheel Lug Studs, 217
  Wheels, 217
FUEL TANK
  Tank, 164

H

HEATER
  Blower Motor Resistor, 172
  Blower Motor, 170
  Blower Speed Control Switch, 172
  Control Assembly, 171
  Control Cables, 171
  Heater Core, 171
  Heater Unit, 170

Heater Water Control Valve, 171
HOW TO USE THIS BOOK, 1

I

IDLE SPEED AND MIXTURE
  ADJUSTMENT
  Parts Replacement, 52
IGNITION TIMING
  Parts Replacement, 49
INSTRUMENTS AND SWITCHES
  Clock, 181
  Headlight Switch, 181
  Instrument Cluster (Combination
  Meter), 180
  Rear Window Wiper/Washer Switch, 181
  Speedometer Cable, 180
  Speedometer, 180
  Windshield Wiper/Washer Switch, 181
INTERIOR
  Center Console, 282
  Disarming the Air Bag System, 279
  Door Glass and Regulator, 283
  Door Locks, 283
  Door Panels, 282
  Electric Window Motor, 286
  Inside Rear View Mirror, 286
  Instrument Panel and Pad, 279
  Interior Trim Panel, 283
  Quarter Window Glass, 286
  Seat Belt System, 287
  Seats, 286
  Sedan Trunk Lock, 283
  Tailgate Lock, 283
  Windshield Glass, 286

J

JACKING, 34

L

LIGHTING
  Dome Light, 187
  Headlights, 182
  High Mounted Stoplight, 187
  License Plate Lights, 187
  Signal and Marker Lights, 184

M

MANUAL TRANSAXLE
  Adjustments, 192
  Back-up Light Switch, 194
  Halfshafts, 196
  SHIFT CABLES, 192
  Transaxle, 194

P

PARKING BRAKE
Cables, 268
PUSHING AND TOWING
Pushing Starting the Vehicle, 33
Towing the Vehicle, 34

R

RADIO
Radio/Tape Player, 176
Speakers, 177
REAR AXLE
Axle Housing, 215
Axle Shaft, Bearing and Seal, 213
Differential Carrier, 214
Pinion Seal, 214
REAR DISC BRAKES
Brake Caliper, 264
Brake Disc (Rotor), 267
Brake Pads, 263
REAR SUSPENSION
Coil Springs, 229
Control Arms, 233
Lateral Control Rod Upper And Lower
Control Arms, 229
Lower Suspension Arm and Strut
Rod, 234
McPherson Struts (2WD Models), 231
Rear Axle Hub, Carrier And Bearing, 234
Rear Stabilizer Bar, 229, 234
Rear Wheel Alignment, 237
Shock Absorbers, 229
Wheel Lug Studs, 228
Wheels, 228
ROUTINE MAINTENANCE
Air Cleaner, 7
Air Conditioning System, 15
Battery, 10
Belts, 13
Evaporative Canister and System, 10
Fuel Filter, 8
Hoses, 15
PCV Valve, 9
Tires and Wheels, 18
Windshield Wipers, 17

S

SERIAL NUMBER IDENTIFICATION
Engine, 7
Transaxle, 7
Vehicle, 7
SERVICING YOUR VEHICLE SAFELY
Don'ts, 6
Dos, 5
SPECIFICATIONS CHARTS
CAMSHAFT SPECIFICATIONS, 71
CAPACITIES, 37
CRANKSHAFT AND CONNECTING
RODS SPECIFICATIONS, 72
ENGINE IDENTIFICATION, 7
GENERAL ENGINE
SPECIFICATIONS, 71
PISTON AND RING ENGINE
SPECIFICATIONS, 73
TORQUE SPECIFICATIONS, 73
TUNE-UP SPECIFICATIONS, 41
VALVE SPECIFICATIONS, 72
WHEEL ALIGNMENT
SPECIFICATIONS, 228
STEERING
Combination Switch, 237
Ignition Switch/Ignition Lock
Cylinder, 239
Manual Steering Gear, 242
Power Steering Gear, 244
Power Steering Pump, 246
Steering Column, 241
Steering Wheel, 237
Tie Rod Ends, 241
SUPPLEMENTAL RESTRAINT SYSTEM
(SRS)
General Information, 168

T

TOOLS AND EQUIPMENT, 2
TRAILER TOWING
Cooling System, 32
General Recommendations, 32
Handling A Trailer, 33
Transaxle, 32
TRAILER WIRING, 187
TRANSFER CASE
Rear Output Shaft Seal, 209
Transfer Case, 209
Transfer Vacuum Actuator, 209
TUNE-UP PROCEDURES
Spark Plug Wires, 41
Spark Plugs, 38

V

VACUUM DIAGRAMS, 143
VALVE LASH
Parts Replacement, 51

W

WINDSHIELD WIPERS
Blade and Arm, 177
Front Wiper Linkage, 177
Windshield Washer Fluid Motor, 180
Windshield Washer Fluid Reservoir, 179
Windshield Wiper Motor, 177